Intermediate C Programming

Intermediate C Programming

Yung-Hsiang Lu

Purdue University
West Lafayette, IN, USA

CRC Press
Taylor & Francis Group
Boca Raton   London   New York

CRC Press is an imprint of the
Taylor & Francis Group, an **informa** business

A CHAPMAN & HALL BOOK

CRC Press
Taylor & Francis Group
6000 Broken Sound Parkway NW, Suite 300
Boca Raton, FL 33487-2742

© 2015 by Taylor & Francis Group, LLC
CRC Press is an imprint of Taylor & Francis Group, an Informa business

Printed on acid-free paper
Version Date: 20150407

International Standard Book Number-13: 978-1-4987-1163-0 (Paperback)

Library of Congress Cataloging-in-Publication Data

Lu, Yung-Hsiang (Computer scientist)
    Intermediate C programming / Yung-Hsiang Lu.
        pages cm
    Includes index.
    ISBN 978-1-4987-1163-0 (alk. paper)
    1. C (Computer program language) I. Title.

QA76.73.C15L83 2015
005.13'3--dc23
                                                                      2015002234

Visit the Taylor & Francis Web site at
http://www.taylorandfrancis.com

and the CRC Press Web site at
http://www.crcpress.com

Contents

List of Figures

List of Tables

Foreword

Imagine you run a research or development group where writing software is the means to examine new physics or new designs. You look for students or employees who have a technical background in that specific physics or science, yet you also look for some software experience. You will typically find that students will have taken a programming class or have tinkered around with some small programs. But in general they have never written software with any serious complexity, they have never worked in a team of people, and they are scared to dive into an existing piece of scientific software.

Well, that is my situation. My research group studies electron flow at the nanometer scale in the very transistors that power your future computer. As a faculty member I have found that most of today's graduated bachelor students in engineering or physical sciences are used to writing small programs in scripting languages and are not even familiar with compiling, practical debugging, or good programming practices.

I believe my situation is not unique but quite common in academia and industry. How can you bring these novices up to speed? How can you give them the day-to-day practical insights fast, that I had to learn through years of slow cut and try experiences?

Most advanced programming books explain complex or larger programs that are correct and beautiful. There is an analogy here between reading a well-written book and composing a new novel yourself. Literature analysis helps the reader to appreciate the content or the context of a novel. While many people can read a correctly formulated algorithm in C, few people would be able to write this code even if they were given the pseudocode (the storyline). This book provides an entry into writing your own real code in C.

I believe that this new book provides an excellent entry way into practical software development practices that will enable my beginning and even advanced students to be more productive in their day-to-day work, by avoiding typical mistakes and by writing cleaner code, since they understand the underlying implications better. This book will also facilitate the collaborations within the group through exemplary coding styles and practices.

This book explains the importance of detecting hidden problems. A common mistake among most students is that they pay attention to only the surface: the outputs of their programs. Their programs may have serious problems beneath the surface. If the programs generate correct outputs in a few cases, the students believe that the programs are correct. This is dangerous in this connected world: A small careless mistake may become a security threat to large complex systems. Creating a secure and reliable system starts from paying attention to details. This book certainly covers many details where careless mistakes may cause serious problems.

I wished I had this book some 20 years ago after I had read through Kernighan and Richie. Back then I began writing a large code basis in C after my coding experience in FORTRAN. Passing by reference, passing by value—simple concepts, but this book plays out these concepts in a pedagogically sound approach. I truly like the hands-on examples that are eye opening.

I recommend this book to anyone who needs to write software beyond the tinkering level. You will learn how to program well. You will learn how to identify and eliminate bugs. You will learn how to write clean code, that cleans up after itself, so it can be called millions of times without crashing your own or someone else's computer. You will learn how to share code with others. All along you will begin to use standard LINUX-based tools such as ddd, valgrind, and others.

Gerhard Klimeck
Reilly Director of the Center for Predictive Materials and Devices (c-PRIMED) and the
NCN (Network for Computational Nanotechnology)
Professor of Electrical and Computer Engineering at Purdue.
Fellow of the Institute of Physics (IOP), the American Physical Society, (APS) and
Institute of Electrical and Electronics Engineers (IEEE).

Preface

Why Is This Book Needed?

There are hundreds of books about programming, many of them about C programming. Why do I write this book? Why should you spend time reading it? How is this book different from any other book? Like many authors, I wanted to write this book because I perceive a need for it. *Because I think the approach in this book is better.*

I divide existing programming books into two types: *introductory* and *advanced.* Introductory books are written for beginners. These books assume readers have no background in programming and explain the basic concepts, sometimes starting with the "Hello World!" program: a program that prints a "Hello World!" message on the computer screen. These books explain language features step-by-step: keywords, data types, control structures, strings, file operations, and so on. These books have a common characteristic: Every program is short, usually one or two pages. This works because a short program can serve to explain one new concept about the programming language. If we think of learning a computer language as learning a natural language like English, Chinese, French, or Korean, these books teach us how to write sentences and short paragraphs.

The second type of book is written for people comfortable with programming. These books describe programs solving real problems. Many books about computer games or graphics belong to this second category. The examples in these books are usually quite long, sometimes thousands of lines of code, and too long to print inside the books. As a result, only sections of the programs are explained in the books, and the source code is either included on a CD or can be downloaded from the Internet. These books do not talk about how to write programs. Instead, they focus mostly on algorithms to solve particular problems and, sometimes, include detailed information on performance. You definitely won't find "Hello World!" examples anywhere in these books. Returning to the natural language analogy, these books teach us how to write short novels, maybe a twenty-page story.

The problem is that it is difficult to jump from writing a paragraph to writing a novel.

A Book for Intermediate-Level Students

There are very few books for intermediate-level students. These students know something about programming already. They are not surprised when they see `if` or `while`. They know how to create functions and call functions. They can write short programs, perhaps dozens of lines of code, but they are not ready to handle thousand-line programs. They make mistakes often but most books talk about how to write correct programs without much help with avoiding common mistakes. The students are unfamiliar with many concepts and tools that can help them write better programs. These students need a stepping stone to take them from being capable of writing short programs to being capable of writing real programs.

Currently, the gap is partially filled by books that cover Data Structures and Algorithms. These books provide programs that *implement* the data structures or algorithms. However, this is not an ideal solution. These books focus on the subjects, Data Structures and Algorithms, but rarely provide information that helps students write correct code. In fact, they usually include the programs without much explanation. They do not explain *programming* concepts—for example, why a function needs a pointer as an argument or the difference between deep and shallow copy. As a result, students have to learn these programming skills by themselves.

To fill this need, I am writing this book for intermediate-level students. This book is ideal as a second book on programming.

An Emphasis on Preventing Mistakes ("Bugs") and Debugging

Most programming books talk about how to *write* programs. However, very few books talk about how to *develop* software. Developing software is not simply typing code. Developing software requires much more knowledge and skill. To bridge this gap, it is useful to learn by studying what is correct *and* what is wrong. Explaining how to write correct programs is insufficient. It is also important to explain common mistakes and compare them with correct programs.

A careless mistake can make a program behave unexpectedly. Worse, the program may be correct in some scenarios and wrong in others. Such bugs are difficult to find as well as to correct. This book explains some common mistakes so that readers understand how to prevent making these mistakes. Debugging is ignored in most books. Few books mention the word "debugger" and sometimes readers simply do not know the existence of such tools. Learning how to use a debugger takes less than thirty minutes and can save many hours. Even fewer books talk about how to use debuggers and the strategies for debugging.

Integration of Programming and Discrete Mathematics

Programming and discrete mathematics are two important subjects in computing. However, most books treat these two topics independently. It is rare to see mathematical equations in programming books. It is rare to see code in books on discrete mathematics. I believe that students can benefit if they can see a closer connection between these two subjects, as is shown in this book.

Why Does This Book Use C?

C was invented in the late 1960s and early 1970s. Many languages were invented after C and some of them were strongly influenced by C. Despite its age, the simplicity of C has ensured that it remains the foundation of computing on almost all modern platforms. Like many operating systems, Linux is written in C. Android is mostly written in Java but has an interface with C, called JNI (Java Native Interface). Most computer languages can communicate with and through C. In fact, this is generally required for a programming language to be useful, since most operating system interfaces use C. When a brand new system is designed, C is often the first (in many cases, the only) programming language supported by the system.

C is a good choice for intermediate-level students because learning C requires knowing many concepts about computers. The web site `langpop.com` compares the popularity of programming languages and C is the most popular language, followed by Java. A report in IEEE Spectrum [1] ranks popular programming languages. This report considers four types of software: mobile, enterprise, embedded, and web. C is the most popular language for embedded systems. When all four types are considered, the top five are:

1. Java (100%)
2. C (99.3%)
3. C++ (95.5%)
4. Python (93.4%)
5. C# (92.4%)

As you can see, three (C, C++, C#) of the top five languages are based on C. Java is influenced by C++.

Who should read this book?

If you are a student in computer science, computer engineering, or electrical engineering, you should definitely read this book. This book covers many concepts essential for understanding how programs work inside computers. If your major is engineering, science, mathematics, or technology, you will very likely need to work with computers and this book will be helpful. If your major is not engineering, science, mathematics, or technology, you may still find many concepts in this book (such as recursion) useful.

[1] Stephen Cass, Nick Diakopoulos, Joshua J. Romero, "Interactive: The Top Programming Languages IEEE Spectrums 2014 Ranking", July 1, 2014, `http://spectrum.ieee.org/static/interactive-the-top-programming-languages`.

Author, Reviewers, and Artist

Author

Yung-Hsiang Lu is an associate professor at the School of Electrical and Computer Engineering in Purdue University, West Lafayette, Indiana, U.S.A. He is an ACM (Association for Computing Machinery) Distinguished Scientist and ACM Distinguished Speaker. In August-December 2011, he was a visiting associate professor at the Department of Computer Science in the National University of Singapore. He received the Ph.D. degree from the Department of Electrical Engineering in Stanford University, California, U.S.A.

Reviewers

Aaron Michaux is a graduate student at the School of Electrical and Computer Engineering in Purdue University, West Lafayette, Indiana, U.S.A. He was awarded a BSc in computer science from the University of Queensland, Australia, and a BA in psychology from Saint Thomas University, New Brunswick, Canada. Aaron worked as a professional programmer for 10 years before heading back to school to work on a Ph.D. His research focuses mainly around computer vision and human visual perception.

Pranav Marla is an undergraduate student at the College of Science in Purdue University, West Lafayette, Indiana, U.S.A. He is pursuing a major in Computer Science, with minors in Computer Engineering, Psychology, and Philosophy. He is hoping to specialize in Machine Learning and Artificial Intelligence.

Artist

The book's cover is painted by Kyong Jo Yoon. Yoon is a Korean artist and often places heroic figures in natural settings. He is an adviser of the Korean Fine Arts Association and his work is on display in the Ann Nathan Gallery in Chicago, Illinois, U.S.A.

Rules in Software Development

Would you be satisfied with a bank's service if the bank lost 0.1% of your money every day due to a software mistake? Would you accept a wrist watch that lost 40 minutes every month? Both of these are cases of "99.9% success" but are nonetheless unacceptable. Computers are now being used in many applications, some of which could affect human safety. If your program works correctly 99.9% of the time, then your program could kill people during the remaining 0.1%. This is totally unacceptable, and such a program is a failure. Thus, *99.9% success is failure.*

If you live in Pasadena, California, and want to go to New York, which route should you take? Perhaps you could go to the Los Angeles Airport and take a flight. New York is at the east side of Pasadena but the airport is at the west side of Pasadena. Why don't you drive (or even walk) east from Pasadena right away? Why do you travel farther than necessary and go west of your destination to the airport? After one hour of travel, you would be close to New York if you drove rather than waiting in lines at an airport. The answer is simple: An airplane is a better tool than a car for long-distance travel. In program development, there are many tools designed for managing larger programs. You need to learn these tools. Yes, learning these tools takes time but you spend much more time when using inappropriate tools, or not using any tool at all. *Spending time learning programming tools can save time in development and debugging.*

Despite decades of effort, computers are still pretty "dumb". Computers cannot guess what is on your mind. If your programs tell a computer to do the wrong thing, then the computers will do the wrong thing. If your program is wrong, it is your fault. *Computers cannot read your mind.* There are many instances in which "small" mistakes in computer programs cause significant financial damages, injuries, or loss of lives. Missing a single semicolon (;) can make a C program unusable. Replacing . by , can also make a C program fail. *Computer programs cannot tolerate "small" mistakes.*

Passing test cases does not guarantee a program is correct. Testing can only tell you that a program is wrong. Testing cannot tell you that a program is correct. Why? Can test cases cover every possible scenario? Covering all scenarios is difficult and, in many cases, impossible. Problems can be hidden inside your programs because it is difficult for test cases to detect idiosyncratic behavior.

Producing correct outputs does not mean a program is correct. Would you consider a plane safe if the plane has taken off and landed without any injuries? If the plane leaks fuel, would you demand the airline fix the plane before boarding? Would you accept the airline's response "Nobody was hurt so this means that plane is safe."? If a driver runs a red light without an accident, does that mean running a red light is safe? A program that produces correct outputs is like a plane that lands without injury. There may be problems beneath the surface. Many tools are available to detect hidden problems in human health, for example X-ray, MRI, and ultrasonic scan. To detect hidden problems in computer programs, we need good tools. We need to fix programs even though they produce correct outputs.

You have to assume that your programs will fail and develop a strategy to detect and correct mistakes. When writing a program, focus on one small part each time. Check it carefully and ensure that it is correct before working on other small parts. For most programs, you need to write additional code for testing these small parts. You will save a lot of time if you write additional testing code, even though the testing code is not included in the final program. Sometimes, the testing code is more than the programs themselves. My own experience suggests 1:3 ratio—for every line in the final program, about three lines of testing code are needed.

No tools can replace a clear mind. Tools can help but nothing can replace deep and thorough understanding of the concepts. If you want to be a good software developer, then you need to fully understand every detail. Do not rely on tools to think for you: They cannot.

Source Code

The sample programs in this book are available at `github.com`. Please use the following command to retrieve the files:

$ git clone 'https://github.com/yunghsianglu/IntermediateCProgramming.git'

here $ is the shell prompt of a Linux terminal.

Part I

Computer Storage: Memory and File

Chapter 1

Program Execution

1.1   Compile

This chapter explains how to write, compile, and execute programs in Linux. We use a Linux terminal and explain the commands you need to type. Why do you learn how to use the terminal? First, the terminal is a flexible and convenient interface for working with a computer. It may take some experience to realize this, but learning how to use the terminal may improve your productivity. Second, many cloud computing or web services offer terminal access. This is a natural method of providing computing resources, especially when working with many computers (like in a data center). A graphical user interface (GUI) is nice when working with one computer. However, when dealing with many computers, GUI can become a distraction. Also, using the terminal helps you understand how UNIX systems work. After becoming familiar with terminal commands, you may understand integrated development environments (IDEs), and what they can do for you. The Eclipse IDE is explained later in this book.

Start a terminal in Linux and type

```
$ cd
$ pwd
$ mkdir cprogram
$ cd cprogram
```

In this book, $ is used as the terminal prompt.

The first command `cd` means "change directory". If no argument is added after `cd`, as in the first command, then it will return to your home directory (also called "folder").

The second command `pwd` means "print the current working directory". It will be something like `/home/yourname/`.

The third command `mkdir` means "make a directory". The command `mkdir cprogram` means "make a directory whose name is cprogram".

You should not create a directory or a file whose name includes spaces. The reason is very simple: The international standard for directory names and file names (called International Standard Organization or ISO 9660) disallows spaces. If a directory's or a file's name has spaces, then some programs may not work.

The last command `cd cprogram` means "change directory to (i.e., enter) cprogram". This is the directory that was just created.

In the terminal, type

```
$ which emacs
```

If nothing appears in the terminal or it says "Command not found", then please install

3

Emacs first. If you do not know how to install software in Linux, please read Section A.5. In the terminal, type

    $ emacs prog1.c &

This command starts Emacs to edit a file called prog1.c. Adding & allows you to use the terminal as well as the Emacs editor at the same time. Without the trailing &, the terminal will force you to wait until Emacs quits. Inside Emacs, type the following code:

```
1  // prog1.c
2  #include <stdio.h>
3  #include <stdlib.h>
4  int main(int argc, char * * argv)
5  {
6    int a = 5;
7    int b = 17;
8    printf("main:␣a␣=␣%d,␣b␣=␣%d,␣argc␣=␣%d\n", a, b, argc);
9    return EXIT_SUCCESS;
10 }
```

Save the file. You can probably guess that this program prints something like

```
main: a = 5, b = 17, argc =
```

This is the first complete program shown in this book and requires some explanation. This program prints something by calling `printf`. This is a function provided by the C language but you need to include `stdio.h` before you can use this function. This is a *header file* for standard input and output functions. In a C program, the starting point is the `main` function. The program returns `EXIT_SUCCESS` after it successfully prints the addresses. As you can guess, if a program can return `EXIT_SUCCESS`, another program can return `EXIT_FAILURE`. Why should a program return either `EXIT_SUCCESS` or `EXIT_FAILURE`? In today's complex computer systems, many programs are called by other computer programs. Thus, it is important that your programs inform the calling programs whether your programs have successfully accomplished what they are designed to do. This information allows the calling programs to decide what actions to take next. `EXIT_SUCCESS` and `EXIT_FAILURE` are symbols defined in `stdlib.h` so it is included at the second line.

In this book, source code is listed with line numbers, starting from 1. Sometimes, the code refers to a previously mentioned example and the line number corrsponds to the value in the earlier example.

The `main` function is the starting point of a C program but this is not always true for a C++ program. If a C++ program has a static object, the object's constructor will be called before the `main` function is called. Since this book is about C programming, it is safe to assume that the `main` function is the starting point of all the programs.

What is `argc`? It is easier to answer this question by running the program. First, we need to explain how to convert this program from a human-readable format to a computer-readable format.

What is typed into Emacs is a "C source file". It is vaguely similar to English and consists of Latin alphabet letters. However, since the computer does not understand this format, the "source file" needs to be converted into a computer-readable format called an *executable*. A *compiler* is the tool needed for this conversion and `gcc` is a popular compiler on Linux. In the terminal, type

    $ gcc prog1.c -o prog

This command means the following:

- Execute the `gcc` command installed in Linux.
- Use `prog1.c` as the input for the `gcc` command.
- Set the output file name to be `prog` (`-o` specifies the name of the output file). The output file is an *executable* file, meaning that the computer can run it.

Do not do this:

$ gcc prog1.c -o prog1.c

This command erases the file `prog1.c`.

The `gcc` compiler has many options. Please read the documentation to learn more. To find the documentation, type "linux gcc" in an Internet search engine and you will see something like the following:

```
GCC(1)                            GNU                            GCC(1)


NAME
       gcc - GNU project C and C++ compiler

SYNOPSIS
       gcc [-c|-S|-E] [-std=standard]
           [-g] [-pg] [-Olevel]
           [-Wwarn...] [-pedantic]
           [-Idir...] [-Ldir...]
           [-Dmacro[=defn]...] [-Umacro]
           [-foption...] [-mmachine-option...]
           [-o outfile] [@file] infile...


       Only the most useful options are listed here; see below for the
       remainder.  g++ accepts mostly the same options as gcc.


DESCRIPTION

       When you invoke GCC, it normally does preprocessing,
       compilation, assembly and linking.  The "overall options" allow you
       to stop this process at an intermediate stage.  For example, the -c
       option says not to run the linker.  Then the output consists of
       object files output by the assembler.

       Other options are passed on to one stage of processing.  Some
       options control the preprocessor and others the compiler itself.  Yet
       other options control the assembler and linker; most of these are not
       documented here, since you rarely need to use any of them.

       Most of the command line options that you can use with GCC are
       useful for C programs; when an option is only useful with another
       language
```

The document is also called the "man page", where "man" means manual. These manual pages are typically well written but terse. Early computers were very expensive and the designers tried to keep everything as short as possible. We have seen a few Linux commands already:

- `cd`: change directory
- `gcc`: convert a human-readable file to a computer-readable file
- `man`: display a manual page
- `mkdir`: make a new directory

The output of the `gcc` command is an executable. In Linux, it is possible to find some information about a file by using the `file` command. Please type this in the terminal:

$ file prog

The output should be similar to the following, but the specifics will vary depending on the computer the program is compiled on:

```
ELF 64-bit LSB executable, x86-64, version 1 (SYSV), dynamically linked
(uses shared libs), for GNU/Linux 2.6.24,
 BuildID[sha1]=0x65dfd5517523d920d9fbaf4ededa84792a9e9c61, not
stripped
```

The most important thing to pay attention to is the word "executable". This word means that the file "prog" is a program. By convention, executable files in Linux have no extension, unlike ".exe" used in Windows. How do you execute the program? Type this command:

$ ./prog

Here, `prog` is the name of the program; `./` means the current directory. Why is it necessary to add `./` in front of the program? It is necessary because it is possible to have files of the same name in different directories. By adding `./`, the terminal knows that the desired program is in this directory. Some people like to call their programs "test". This is a bad name for your program because "test" is also a built-in command in Linux. If you type

$ test

then the Linux command is run. If you type

$ ./test

then your program in the directory is run.

What exactly is `argc`? It stores the number of arguments given to the program. Let me demonstrate what I mean by running the program a few times.

$ ./prog
   main: a = 5, b = 17, argc = 1

$ ./prog abc
   main: a = 5, b = 17, argc = 2

$ ./prog abc 123
   main: a = 5, b = 17, argc = 3

$ ./prog abc 123 C Programs
   main: a = 5, b = 17, argc = 5

Do you notice the changes in **argc**? When the program is executed without anything else, **argc** is 1. If some words are added after the program, then **argc** becomes larger. The more words (i.e., *arguments*) that are added, the larger **argc** becomes. This illustrates that arguments can be given to programs when they are run. Consecutive arguments are separated by one or more spaces. The terminal tells your program (specifically, the **main** function) the number of arguments. As can be seen in the examples below, adding extra spaces between words makes no difference. One space has the same effect as several spaces.

```
$ ./prog abc 123 C Programs
    main: a = 5, b = 17, argc = 5

$ ./prog abc      123           C Programs
    main: a = 5, b = 17, argc = 5

$ ./prog              abc         123 C Programs
    main: a = 5, b = 17, argc = 5
```

The program itself is always the first argument. Since you must type the program's name to run the program, the value of **argc** is always at least one. What is the value of **argc** when using this **gcc** command?

```
$ gcc prog1.c -o prog
```

The answer is 4.

1. **gcc**
2. **prog1.c**
3. **-o**
4. **prog**

The arguments themselves are strings, and are stored in **argv**. This will be covered when explaining strings in Chapter 6.

1.2   Redirect Output

The **printf** function is probably one of the first things that people learn about writing C programs. The famous "Hello World!" program is often used as an example for beginners. In this computer program, the text is printed to the terminal. In some cases, however, it is useful to *redirect* the information from the program and save it to a file. Here are some scenarios when this may be useful:

- A program prints too much too fast and the computer screen cannot display everything printed.
- You do not want to wait while the program runs, but instead want to see the information later.
- Sometimes it is useful to check whether the program produces the same information when it is run again. If the program produces more than several lines of output, checking the output line-by-line is too much work.
- The program may need to be run on many computers simultaneously. It may be impossible to watch many screens at once.

- You need to write a program that produces correct outputs based on given inputs. This is frequently the case when taking programming courses. The correctness of the program is evaluated by whether your program produces correct outputs. In many cases, the programs are graded by computer programs based on the input-output pairs. In this case, nobody reads the information on a computer screen.

If > and a file name is added after the command, then the output is saved in that file.

$ ./prog abc 123 C Programs > output

Nothing appears on the computer screen because the information is redirected to the file whose name is `output`. You can use a text editor to see the contents of this file. You can also use the Linux command `more` or `less` or `cat` to see the file's content. If you type `more output` in the terminal, this is what appears on the computer screen:

main: a = 5, b = 17, argc = 5

Since the output is saved in a file, you can use the `diff` command to check whether that output is the same as the correct output, assuming you have the correct output saved in another file. The `diff` command requires the names of two files and determines whether these files are the same or not. If they are different, the command shows the line-by-line differences. The `diff` program will compare the files exactly. It is often useful to ignore whitespace and this can be done by adding `-w` after `diff`. Adding `-q` after `diff` shows only whether the files are different or not, without showing the line-by-line differences. Although the `diff` command is useful, sometimes we want to see the differences side-by-side. The `meld` program in Linux does precisely that.

Chapter 2

Stack Memory

2.1   Values and Addresses

In a computer, programs and data must be stored somewhere called *storage*. Without storage, a computer has nothing to compute. Storage can be divided into volatile and non-volatile. Volatile storage requires electricity, and can keep data only when a computer is turned on. Volatile storage is usually called "memory". Non-volatile storage persists when a computer is turned off or rebooted: for example, flash memory or hard disks. Flash memory is also called a *solid-state disk* or *SSD*.

A typical laptop computer today has several GB memory. G means "giga" and is the metric system prefix for 1 billion. B means "byte" and is a sequence of 8 bits. Each bit can store either 0 or 1. If a laptop has 8 GB of memory, the computer can store 64 billion bits in memory. As a reference, the world's population was about 7 billion in 2013.

A computer's memory is organized into *address-value* pairs. These pairs are analogous to street addresses and the families that live there. Consider the following scenario:

- The Jones family lives at One Silicon Street.
- The Smith family lives at Two Silicon Street.
- The Brown family lives at Three Silicon Street.
- The Taylor family lives at Four Silicon Street.
- The Clark family lives at Five Silicon Street.

We can express this information in a table:

Address	Family
One	Jones
Two	Smith
Three	Brown
Four	Taylor
Five	Clark

In a computer's memory, each location stores either a zero or a one—something like the following:

- Zero is stored at the first location.
- Zero is stored at the second location.
- One is stored at the third location.
- Zero is stored at the fourth location.
- One is stored at the fifth location.

We can also express this as a table:

Address	Value
First	Zero
Second	Zero
Third	One
Fourth	Zero
Fifth	One

Programmers usually consider more than one bit at a time. For the time being, let us set aside the *size* of data. Instead, assume that each piece of data occupies one unit of memory. Operating systems guarantee that everything has a unique and positive address. The address is never zero or negative. The symbol NULL is defined as the zero address and indicates an invalid address. It would be impossible to remember the addresses of all of the bits of memory that a computer program manipulates. Early computer science pioneers found an elegant solution: Create *symbols*, such as counter or sum to refer to the relevant bits of memory. If the value stored corresponding to a symbol may change during the program's execution, this symbol is called a *variable*. The symbols have meaning to humans writing computer programs, and compilers (such as gcc) convert these symbols into addresses. The final computer program manipulates the values, and does not see the symbols. Inside a computer's memory, there are only addresses and values. This was a major early innovation in easing the task of writing computer programs. The following figure shows the relationships between symbols and addresses:

source code .c or .h files		executable program
human readable	$\longrightarrow$	computer readable
symbols	compiler	addresses

Consider the following sample code:

```
1  int a = 5;
2  double b = 6.7;
3  char z = 'c';
```

The relationship between symbol, address, and value may look something like this inside a computer's memory:

Symbol	Address	Value
a	100	5
b	131	6.7
z	145	'c'

A programmer has no control over the addresses—that is the job of the operating system (e.g., Linux) and the compiler. Programmers do not need to know the addresses of a, b, or z as long as the following rules are observed:

- Each piece of data has a unique address.
- The address cannot be zero (NULL) or negative.
- The compiler can convert symbols to addresses.

2.2 Stack

Modern computers usually organize volatile memory into three types:

1. stack memory
2. heap memory
3. program memory

The first two store data and the last stores the machine code of computer programs. This chapter focuses on stack memory. Heap memory will be explained in a later chapter. Before talking about stack memory, we must first introduce the concept of a *stack*.

Technical terms in computing are often related to the everyday meanings of the words that they comprise. "Stack" is no exception. Ever heard of a "stack of books"? The easiest way to add a book to a stack of books is to place it on top of the stack. The easiest way to remove will be from the top. Thus, the first book to be removed from the stack will be the last book previously placed on the stack. Computer scientists refer to this arrangement as "last in, first out" (or "first in, last out"). Placing an item is called *push*, and removing an item is called *pop*.

The stack concept is used in everyday life. To wear both socks and shoes, the socks must go on before the shoes—push the socks, push the shoes. Then, to remove both the socks and the shoes, the shoes come off before the socks—pop the shoes, pop the socks. The order is reversed and this is characteristic of "last in, first out".

Stack memory strictly follows *first in, last out*. New data enters the stack memory at the top, and data are always removed from the top. It would be equivalent to add and remove data from the bottom (i.e., it is still first in, last out); however, by convention, we use the top instead of the bottom. The concept is the same. Data are *pushed* onto the top of the stack and, later, *popped* from the top of the stack. Fig. 2.1 illustrates these two operations of stack memory.

2.3 The Call Stack

2.3.1 The Return Location

How do computers use stack memory? Consider the following code snippet:

```
1  void f1(void)
2  // void before f1 means no returned value
3  // void in the parentheses means no argument
4  {
5      // ...
```

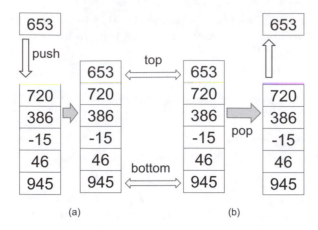

(a)   (b)

FIGURE 2.1: Pushing and popping data on a stack. (a) Originally, the top of the stack stores the number 720. The number 653 is pushed onto the top of the stack. (b) Data are retrieved (popped) from the stack. Pushes and pops can only occur at the top of the stack. Although this figure illustrates the idea with integers, a stack is a general concept and can manage any type of data.

```
6   }
7   void f2(void)
8   {
9       f1();
10      // program continues from here after f1 finishes
11  }
```

The function `f2` calls `f1` at line 10. After `f1` finishes its work, the program continues running `f2` from the line after `f1`. Fig. 2.2 illustrates the flow of the program.

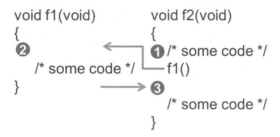

FIGURE 2.2: The flow of the program as indicated by the numbers 1, 2, and 3.

Imagine that a mark is inserted right below the place where `f1` is called, as shown in Fig. 2.3. This mark tells the program where it should continue after `f1` finishes. It is called the "return location", meaning that this is the place where the program should continue after the function `f1` returns (i.e., after `f1` finishes its work).

A function is finished when it executes the **return** statement—anything below this statement is ignored. Consider the following example:

```
1   void f(void)
2   {
3       if (...)
```

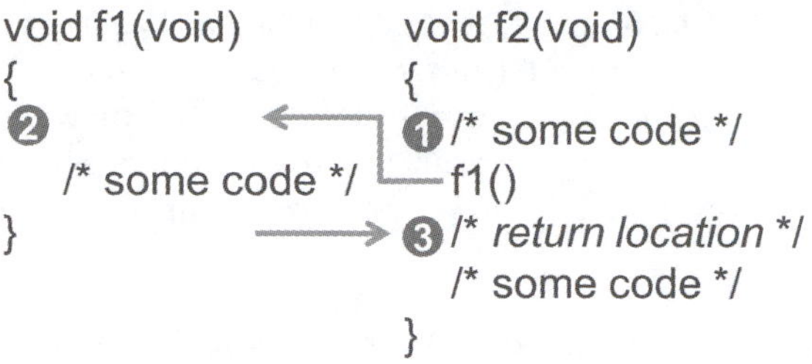

```
void f1(void)            void f2(void)
{                        {
  ❷                        ❶ /* some code */
      /* some code */      └─ f1()
}                        ❸ /* return location */
                           /* some code */
                         }
```

FIGURE 2.3: The return location is the place where the program continues after the function `f1` returns.

```
4      {
5        // ...
6        return;
7        // the program will never reach here
8      }
9    // else not needed
10   // ...
11   return;
12   // the program will never reach here
13   }
```

In this function, if the condition at line 3 is true, then the function will execute the `return` at line 6. In this case, anything at line 7 is ignored and the program continues from the return location. However, if the condition at line 3 is false, then the function will execute the code at line 9. Note that it is not necessary to have an `else` at line 9. When the function reaches line 11, a `return` is executed, and the function stops—line 12 is ignored. Here, "ignored" means that the code is not executed when the program runs. Even though lines 7 and 12 are never executed, if they contain any syntax errors, the source code will not compile. Next, let's consider three functions:

```
void f1(void)
{
  // ...
}

void f2(void)
{
  f1();
  // line after calling f1, return location B
  // ...
}

void f3(void)
{
  f2();
  // line after calling f2, return location A
  // ...
}
```

Function f3 calls f2 at line 15, and f2 calls f1 at line 8. When f1 finishes, the program continues from the line after calling f1 (line 9). When f2 finishes, the program continues from the line after calling f2 (line 16). How does the program know where to continue after a function finishes? When f3 calls f2, the machine-code equivalent to "line number 16" is pushed to the stack memory. Fig. 2.4 shows the flow of function calls when running this program.

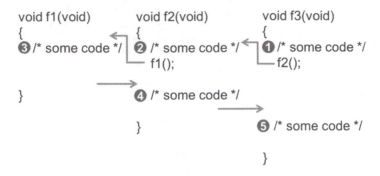

FIGURE 2.4: The flow of the program with the three functions.

Imagine that the line after each function call is marked as a return location (RL), as shown in Fig. 2.5. This book uses line numbers as the return locations. The call stack in this book is a simplified conceptual model and does not reflect any specific processor. Real processors use *program counters* instead of line numbers.

```
void f1(void)          void f2(void)              void f3(void)
{                      {                          {
❸/* some code */|    ❷/* some code */◄━┐      ❶/* some code */
                       └─f1();                     └─f2();
                  ─────►  /* RL B */
}                      ❹/* some code */

                                         ─────►  /* RL A */
       }                                 ❺/* some code */

                                              }
```

FIGURE 2.5: The return locations (RLs) are marked at the lines after calling f2 (RL A) and f1 (RL B).

Why is the *last in, first out* nature of stack memory important? The stack memory stores the *reverse order* of function calls. This is how the program knows that it should continue from RL B instead of RL A after f1 finishes. The program uses the stack memory to remember the return locations. This *stack memory* is also called the *call stack* (or *callstack*), and every C program has one to control the flow of execution of its functions. Almost all computer programming languages employ this scheme.

As our three-function program executes, the *call stack* may appear as follows: When f3 calls f2, the line number after calling f2 (RL A) is pushed to the call stack.

line number (16) after calling f2, i.e., RL A

When f2 calls f1, the line number after calling f1 (RL B) is pushed to the call stack.

| line number (9) after calling f1, i.e., RL B |
| line number (16) after calling f2, i.e., RL A |

When f1 finishes, the line number 9 is popped and the program continues at this line number (9). The call stack now has line number 16.

| line number (16) after calling f2, i.e., RL A |

When f2 finishes, the line number is popped and the program continues at this line number (16). Programmers do not need to worry about marking return locations; the compiler takes care of inserting the appropriate code to do this.

It is instructive to note why the stack must store the return locations. Consider this example:

```
1  void f1(void)
2  {
3      // ...
4  }
5
6  void f2(void)
7  {
8      f1();
9      // RL A
10     // some statements ...
11     f1();
12     // RL B
13     // ...
14  }
```

Function f1 is called in two different locations (line 8 and line 11). When f1 is called the first time at line 8, the program continues from line 9 (RL A) after f1 finishes. When f1 is called the second time at line 11, the program continues from line 12 (RL B) after f1 finishes. A call stack is a simple scheme to manage the fact that, since the same function (f1) can be called from multiple places, something must track the next line of code to execute.

The rules for the call stack can be summarized as follows:

- When a function is called, the line number after this call is pushed onto the call stack. This line number is the "return location" (RL). This is the place from which the program will continue after the called function finishes (i.e., returns).
- If the same function is called from multiple lines, then each call has a corresponding return location (the line after each function call).
- When a function finishes, the program continues from the line number stored at the top of the call stack. The top of the call stack is then popped.

2.3.2 Function Arguments

To understand function arguments, we must elaborate on the rather simplified examples seen so far. To start with, most functions take input arguments and have return values. The Merriam-Webster Dictionary defines an argument as "one of the independent variables upon whose value that of a function depends". For a mathematical function, such as $f(x, y, z)$, the variables x, y, and z are the arguments of the function f. In C programs, functions have a similar syntax. Consider the following example:

```
1  void f1(int a, char b, double c)
2  {
3     // ...
4  }
5
6  void f2(void)
7  {
8     f1(5, 'm',␣3.7);
9  ␣␣//␣RL␣A
10 ␣␣//␣...
11 }
```

The inputs a, b, and c are the arguments for f1. When f1 is called, f2 must provide three arguments and this information is pushed onto the call stack. The call stack stores the arguments and their values above the return location.

Symbol	Value
c	3.7
b	'm'
a	5
Return Location	line 9

Remember that there are no symbols inside of a computer program. Instead, as previously discussed, the computer's memory has only addresses and values. Thus, the table above is extended with another column to show the addresses. Every value has a unique address—the arguments are stored in different physical parts of the computer's circuitry—and this property is guaranteed by the operating system and the hardware. A programmer has no control over the precise addresses used. The addresses can vary widely on different types of computers. This book uses 100, 101, ... for these addresses. By convention, the addresses start from a smaller number at the bottom and increase upward.

Symbol	Address	Value
c	103	3.7
b	102	'm'
a	101	5
Return Location	100	line 9

The return location and the arguments together form a *frame* for the called function f1. A frame occupies a contiguous chunk of memory. The above table can now be extended to show the frame that the symbols, addresses, and values belong to.

Frame	Symbol	Address	Value
	c	103	3.7
	b	102	'm'
f1	a	101	5
	Return Location	100	line 9

What happens when there is another function call? Consider the following example:

```
1  void f1(int t, int u)
2  {
3     // ...
```

```
4  }
5
6  void f2(int a, int b)
7  {
8    f1(a - b, a + b);
9    // RL B
10   // ...
11 }
12
13 void f3(void)
14 {
15   f2(5, -17);
16   // RL A
17   // ...
18 }
```

Function f3 calls f2 so f2's frame is pushed to the call stack. Argument a's value is 5 because that is the value given to a when f3 calls f2 at line 15. Similarly, argument b's value is -17 because that is the value given to b when f3 calls f2 at line 15.

Frame	Symbol	Address	Value
	b	102	-17
f2	a	101	5
	Return Location	100	line 16

Function f2 calls f1 and f1's frame is pushed onto the call stack. Argument t's value is 22 because that is the value of a−b at line 8. Similarly, argument u's value is -12 because that is the value of a + b at line 8.

Frame	Symbol	Address	Value
	u	105	-12
f1	t	104	22
	Return Location	103	line 9
	b	102	-17
f2	a	101	5
	Return Location	100	line 16

Please remember that frames and symbols are for humans only. Computers do not understand frames and symbols. Instead, they only work with addresses and values. Previously, in Section 2.3.1, we listed the rules of the call stack; now we add some more.

- If a function has arguments, then the arguments are stored above the return location.
- The arguments and the return location together form the frame of the called function.
- When a function is called, the line number after this call is pushed onto the call stack. This line number is the "return location" (RL). This is the place from which the program will continue after the called function finishes (i.e., returns).
- If the same function is called from multiple lines, then each call has a corresponding return location (the line after each function call).
- When a function finishes, the program continues from the line number stored at the top of the call stack. The top of the call stack is then popped.

2.3.3   Local Variables

If a function has local variables, then the local variables are stored in the call stack.
Consider the following program:

```
1  void f1 (int k, int m, int p)
2  {
3    int t = k + m;
4    int u = m * p;
5  }
6
7  void f2 (void)
8  {
9    f2 (5, 11, -8);
10   // RL A
11 }
```

The arguments k, m, and p are stored above the return location A. The local variables
t and u are stored on the call stack above the arguments.

Frame	Symbol	Address	Value
	u	105	-88
	t	104	16
f1	p	103	-8
	m	102	11
	k	101	5
	Return Location	100	line 12

Now one more call stack rule must be added.
- If a function has local variables, then the local variables are stored above the arguments.
- If a function has arguments, then the arguments are stored above the return location.
- The arguments and the return location together form the frame of the called function.
- When a function is called, the line number after this call is pushed onto the call stack. This line number is the "return location" (RL). This is the place from which the program will continue after the called function finishes (i.e., returns).
- If the same function is called from multiple lines, then each call has a corresponding return location (the line after each function call).
- When a function finishes, the program continues from the line number stored at the top of the call stack. The top of the call stack is then popped.

Local variables are always stored on the stack, where they reside for the duration of the function call. They exist in contrast to "global variables", which persist between function calls. Global variables are usually specified at the top of a given source file, and any function can read and write to them. While sometimes convenient, global variables can lead to subtle software bugs. In 1973, Wulf et al. wrote an article, "Global Variables Considered Harmful". It explained in some detail why programmers should avoid global variables. The software community generally concurs, and use of global variables has been strongly discouraged since then. Although C allows global variables, well-written software almost always avoids global variables. The main problem is that global variables may be changed anywhere in a program. As the program becomes larger and more complex, it becomes increasingly harder to track the places where these global variables may change. Losing track of the changes can often lead to surprising behavior in the program. For further information, please read Wulf's paper to understand why global variables are problematic. Although global variables are strongly discouraged, global constants are acceptable and commonly used because they cannot change.

2.3.4 Value Address

So far, all our functions' return types have been `void`, i.e., the functions have all returned nothing. Functions can return values. Consider this example:

```
1  int f1(int k, int m)
2  {
3    return (k + m);
4  }
5
6  void f2(void)
7  {
8    int u;
9    u = f1(7, 2);
10   // RL A
11 }
```

The local variable `u` is inside `f2` so it is in `f2`'s frame. The value of `u` is undefined because it has not yet been assigned to anything. Remember that **C does not initialize variables,** so uninitialized variables could store any values (i.e., garbage). The frame for `f2` contains the variable `u` whose value is undefined yet.

Frame	Symbol	Address	Value
f2	u	100	garbage

The address of `u` is stored in the call stack before `f1` is called. This address is called the *value address* because it is the address where the return value of function `f1` will be stored. Thus, when the frame for `f1` is constructed, one more row is added for the value address, and its value is the address of `u`.

Frame	Symbol	Address	Value
	m	104	2
f1	k	103	7
	Value Address	102	100
	Return Location	101	line 10
f2	u	100	garbage

When function `f1` executes, it adds the values of `k` and `m`, producing the value 9. The number 9 is then written to (i.e., replaces) the original garbage value at address 100. After `f1` finishes, and its frame has been popped, the call stack will be as follows:

Frame	Symbol	Address	Value
f2	u	100	9

This rule can be incorporated into the previous rules of the call stack.
- If a function returns a value, the value is written to a local variable in the caller's frame. This variable's address (called the value address) is stored in the call stack.
- If a function has local variables, then the local variables are stored above the arguments.
- If a function has arguments, then the arguments are stored above the return location.

- The arguments and the return location together form the frame of the called function.
- When a function is called, the line number after this call is pushed onto the call stack. This line number is the "return location" (RL). This is the place from which the program will continue after the called function finishes (i.e., returns).
- If the same function is called from multiple lines, then each call has a corresponding return location (the line after each function call).
- When a function finishes, the program continues from the line number stored at the top of the call stack. The top of the call stack is then popped.

Note that the caller (`f2`) is not obliged to store the return value of the callee (`f1`), and line 9 in the example above can be written as:

```
9    f1(7, 2);
```

In this case, function `f1` is called but the returned value is discarded. Since there is no need to store the return value, the value address is not pushed onto the call stack.

The keyword `return` can be used for two different purposes:

- If `void` is in front of the function's name, the function does not return any value. The word `return` stops the function and the program continues from the return location in the caller.
- If the function is not `void`, the word `return` assigns a value to the variable given by the value address in the call stack.

Please remember that if a function executes a `return` statement, anything after the `return` is ignored and will not be executed. Executing a `return` statement stops the function, and its frame is popped from the call stack. The program then continues from the return location.

2.3.5   Arrays

The following example creates an array of five elements. Each element contains one integer, which will be uninitialized.

```
1    int arr[5];
```

Symbol	Address	Value
arr[4]	104	garbage
arr[3]	103	garbage
arr[2]	102	garbage
arr[1]	101	garbage
arr[0]	100	garbage

If an array has five elements, the valid indexes are 0, 1, 2, 3, and 4. The first index is 0, not 1; the last index is 4, not 5. The array is said to be "zero indexed". In general, if an array has n elements, the valid indexes are 0, 1, 2, ..., $n - 1$. **Please remember that n is not a valid index**. This is a common mistake among students.

Programmers have no control over addresses and this is still true for arrays. The addresses of an array's elements are, however, always contiguous. Suppose $i < j < k$ and all of them are valid indexes for an array called `arr`. Then the address of `arr[j]` is between the addresses of `arr[i]` and `arr[k]`. If an array's elements are not initialized (like in the example above), then the values are garbage.

The following example illustrates C's facility to initialize arrays:

```
1    int arr[5] = {-31, 52, 65, 49, -18};
```

Symbol	Address	Value
arr[4]	104	−18
arr[3]	103	49
arr[2]	102	65
arr[1]	101	52
arr[0]	100	−31

It is possible to initialize all the elements to zero in this way:

```
int arr[5] = {0};
```

It is possible to create an array without giving the size:

```
int arr[] = {-31, 52, 65, 49, -18};
```

In this case, the compiler automatically calculates the size as 5.

2.3.6 Retrieving Addresses

It is possible to get a variable's address by adding an & in front of it. This address can be printed with the printf function by using the "%p" format specifier. The following example prints the addresses of both a and c.

```
// address.c
#include <stdio.h>
#include <stdlib.h>
int main(int argc, char * * argv)
{
   int a = 5;
   int c = 17;
   printf("a's address is %p, c's address is %p\n", &a, &c);
   return EXIT_SUCCESS;
}
```

Below is a sample output from this program:

```
a's address is 0x7fff2261aea8, c's address is 0x7fff2261aeac
```

The output will probably be different when the program is run again:

```
a's address is 0x7fffb8dad0b8, c's address is 0x7fffb8dad0bc
```

As you can see, the addresses change. If you execute the same program, you will likely see different addresses.

2.4 Visibility

Every time a function is called, a new frame is pushed to the call stack. **A function can see only its own frame.** Consider these two examples:

```
1  int f1(int k, int m)
2  {
3    return (k + m);
4  }
5
6  void f2(void)
7  {
8    int a = 5;
9    int b = 6;
10   int u;
11   u = f1(a + 3, b - 4);
12   // some additional code
13 }
```

```
1  int f1(int a, int b)
2  {
3    return (a + b);
4  }
5
6  void f2(void)
7  {
8    int a = 5;
9    int b = 6;
10   int u;
11   u = f1(a + 3, b - 4);
12   // some additional code
13 }
```

These two programs are identical. Renaming the arguments of f1 from k and m to a and b has no effect. What about the call stack? This is the call stack when f1 is called in the first example:

Frame	Symbol	Address	Value
	m	106	2
	k	105	8
f1	Value Address	104	102
	Return Location	103	line 14
	u	102	garbage
f2	b	101	6
	a	100	5

The call stack in the second example is the same, except that the arguments in frame f1 have different symbols. Note that the addresses are the same. The second example highlights the fact that the a and b in f1 refer to different address–value pairs than the a and b in f2. This is the call stack:

Frame	Symbol	Address	Value
	b	106	2
	a	105	8
f1	Value Address	104	102
	Return Location	103	line 14
	u	102	garbage
f2	b	101	6
	a	100	5

The a in f1's frame has nothing to do with the a in f2's frame. Renaming a to k makes no difference to the behavior of the program. The same rule applies to b. Remember that computers do not know about symbols. Computers only use addresses and values. Symbols are only useful for any humans that are reading the code, and are discarded when a program is compiled into machine-readable format.

This can be a source of confusion among students. It may seem intuitive that the a in f1's frame and the a in f2's frame are related. In fact, they occupy different locations in the call stack and are unrelated. The following example offers a further explanation:

```
1  int f1(int a, int b)
2  {
3    a = a + 9;
```

```
4     b = b * 2;
5     return (a + b);
6   }
7
8   void f2(void)
9   {
10    int a = 5;
11    int b = 6;
12    int u;
13    u = f1(a + 3, b - 4);
14    // some additional code
15  }
```

The following table shows the call stack when the program has entered `f1` but has not yet executed line 3:

Frame	Symbol	Address	Value
	b	106	2
f1	a	105	8
	Value Address	104	102
	Return Location	103	line 14
	u	102	garbage
f2	b	101	6
	a	100	5

After line 3 has been executed, the call stack will appear as in the table below. Note that function `f1` only modifies the variable `a` that is in its frame, since a function can only see arguments and variables in its own frame.

Frame	Symbol	Address	Value
	b	106	2
f1	a	105	$8 \rightarrow 17$
	Value Address	104	102
	Return Location	103	line 14
	u	102	garbage
f2	b	101	6
	a	100	5

The following table shows the call stack after the program has executed line 4:

Frame	Symbol	Address	Value
	b	106	$2 \rightarrow 4$
f1	a	105	$8 \rightarrow 17$
	Value Address	104	102
	Return Location	103	line 14
	u	102	garbage
f2	b	101	6
	a	100	5

Function `f1` returns `a + b`, which is $17 + 4 = 21$. The value 21 is written to the value at address 102 (i.e., the value address). After `f1` returns, the call stack is as follows:

Frame	Symbol	Address	Value
	u	102	21
f2	b	101	6
	a	100	5

Note that the values of a and b in f2 have not changed.

Even though the same symbol may appear in different frames, the same name cannot be defined twice within the same frame. The following program is invalid because a is used as both an argument and a local variable, in the same function:

```
int f1(int a, int b)
{
  int k = 3;
  int m = -5;
  int a = k + 2; // cannot define 'a' twice
  int b = m - 1;
  return (k + m);
}

void f2(void)
{
  int a = 5;
  int b = 6;
  int u;
  u = f1(a + 3, b - 4);
  // some additional code
}
```

In review, this chapter explains the concept of the call stack, which is used whenever a function is called. The call stack stores the return location, the value address, the arguments, and the local variables for each function.

2.5 Exercises

This book has two types of homework: exercises and programming problems. Exercises are problems that do not require writing programs—they are "paper-and-pencil" problems. Programming problems, obviously, are done on a computer.

Understanding the call stack is one of the most essential skills for programmers. If you want to understand C programs (and many other programming languages), then a solid understanding about the call stack is necessary.

2.5.1 Draw Call Stack I

```
int f1(int k, int m)
{
  int y;
  y = k + m;
  return y;
```

```
 6  }
 7
 8  void f2(void)
 9  {
10      int a = 83;
11      int c = -74;
12      c = f1(a, c);
13      /* RL */
14  }
```

Draw the call stack
- before `f1` is called.
- when the program has finished line 4.
- when the program has finished `f1` and the top frame has been popped.

2.5.2 Draw Call Stack II

```
 1  void f1(int k, int m)
 2  {
 3      int y;
 4      y = k;
 5      k = m;
 6      m = y;
 7  }
 8
 9  void f2(void)
10  {
11      int a = 83;
12      int c = -74;
13      f1(a, c);
14      /* RL */
15  }
```

Draw the call stack
- when the program has entered `f1` and finished line 4. What are the values of `k` and `m`?
- when the program has finished line 6, and before `f1`'s frame is popped. What are the values of `k` and `m`?
- when the program has finished `f1` and `f1`'s frame has been popped. What are the values of `a` and `c`?

2.5.3 Addresses

- How can a programmer control the address of a variable?
- If the same program runs multiple times, will the address of the same variable be the same?
- Are the addresses of an array's elements contiguous or scattered?

2.6   Answers

2.6.1   Draw Call Stack I

- before calling `f1`

Frame	Symbol	Address	Value
f2	c	101	−74
	a	100	83

- finished line 4

Frame	Symbol	Address	Value
f1	y	106	9
	m	105	−74
	k	104	83
	Value Address	103	101
	Return Location	102	line 13
f2	c	101	−74
	a	100	83

- after `f1`'s frame popped

Frame	Symbol	Address	Value
f2	c	101	9
	a	100	83

2.6.2   Draw Call Stack II

- finished line 4

Frame	Symbol	Address	Value
f1	y	105	83
	m	104	−74
	k	103	83
	Return Location	102	line 14
f2	c	101	−74
	a	100	83

- finished line 6

Frame	Symbol	Address	Value
f1	y	105	83
	m	104	83
	k	103	−74
	Return Location	102	line 14
f2	c	101	−74
	a	100	83

The values of `k` and `m` have been swapped.

- `f1`'s frame popped

Frame	Symbol	Address	Value
f2	c	101	−74
	a	100	83

The values of a and c have not changed.

2.6.3 Addresses

- A programmer cannot control the address of a variable.
- If the same program runs multiple times, the address of the same variable will likely be different.
- The addresses of an array's elements are contiguous.

2.7 Examine the Call Stack with DDD

Type the following program into an editor and save it under the name `p1.c`

```c
/* p1.c */
#include <stdio.h>
#include <stdlib.h>
int g1(int a, int b)
{
   int c = (a + b) * b;
   printf("g1:   a = %d, b = %d, c = %d\n", a, b, c);
   return c;
}

int g2(int a, int b)
{
   int c = g1(a + 3, b - 11);
   printf("g2:   a = %d, b = %d, c = %d\n", a, b, c);
   return c - b;
}

int main(int argc, char ** argv)
{
   int a = 5;
   int b = 17;
   int c = g2(a - 1, b * 2);
   printf("main: a = %d, b = %d, c = %d\n", a, b, c);
   return EXIT_SUCCESS;
}
```

Do not worry about fully understanding `argv` in the `main` function yet; this will be discussed later. Create the executable using the following command in a Linux terminal:

$ gcc -g -Wall -Wshadow p1.c -o p1

This uses gcc to convert the source file of the C program (p1.c), into an executable file that the computer can understand. Adding -g enables debugging so that we can examine the call stack. Adding -Wall and -Wshadow enables warning messages. Shadow variables will be explained in Section 4.1. Warning messages are sometimes benign, but they usually indicate deeper problems in the code. It is good practice to always enable warning messages, and to act on gcc's advice. The name of the output file (i.e., the executable file) is specified by -o. In this example, p1 is the output of the gcc command and, thus, is the executable file (i.e., the program). It can be run in the terminal by typing:

```
$ ./p1
```

The output should be the same as the following:

```
g1:   a = 7, b = 23, c = 690
g2:   a = 4, b = 34, c = 690
main: a = 5, b = 17, c = 656
```

To view the call stack, we will need to start the debugger. In this example, we will use DDD (Data Display Debugger). DDD is a graphical user interface for the GDB debugger. Start DDD, go to the menu and click

File - Open Program - select p1 - Open

Here, we have selected the executable program, not the .c file. The debugger will automatically find the .c file based on information that gcc leaves in the executable. This is useful when debugging a program that uses multiple source files.

Set breakpoints at the two functions g1 and g2 with the following commands after the (gdb) prompt in the bottom window:

(gdb) b g1

(gdb) b g2

The command b g1 instructs DDD to set a breakpoint when the function g1 starts. When the program reaches the first line of g1, the program will stop and you will get a chance to check the status of the program. The command b g2 instructs DDD to similarly set a breakpoint when the function g2 starts.

Execute the program by typing the following command at the (gdb) prompt:

(gdb) run

The program will start, and then pause at the breakpoint of function g2. Why does the program stop at g2, not g1? Because main calls g2, so g2 is encountered before g1. If several breakpoints are set, the program will pause at the breakpoints based on the order in which they are executed, not the order in which they are set. In this example, although the breakpoint at g1 is set first, the program executes g2 first. Thus, the program pauses at the breakpoint g2 first.

To continue the program, type the following command:

(gdb) continue

The program will continue executing and then pause at the next breakpoint, located at function g1. The call stack can be viewed by asking for the backtrace. This is done with the following command:

(gdb) bt

This command means "backtrace". What do you see in the debugger?

(gdb) bt

> #0 g1 (a=7, b=23) at p6.c:6
>
> #1 0x0000000000400554 in g2 (a=4, b=34) at p6.c:13
>
> #2 0x00000000004005b2 in main (argc=1, argv=0x7fffffffe4f8) at p1.c:22

The values of a and b are shown in the top frame. The beginning of each line shows the frames (0, 1, and 2) of the call stack, corresponding to the functions g1, g2, and main. You can use the f command to see different frames: for example, type

(gdb) f 1

to go to frame 1, i.e., the frame of function g2. The values of a and b can be displayed again. What are their values? The digits after 0x are likely different on your computer; these are the addresses. In g2's frame, the values of a and b are different from the values in the top frame. Fig. 2.6 to Fig. 2.9 show some screenshots of DDD.

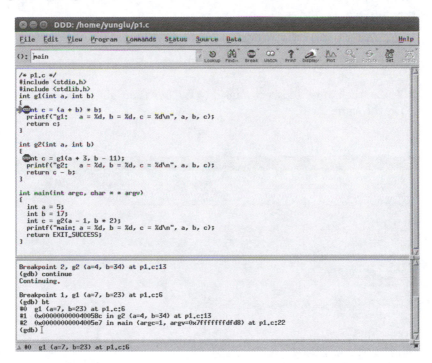

FIGURE 2.6: Enter the commands at the bottom of DDD.

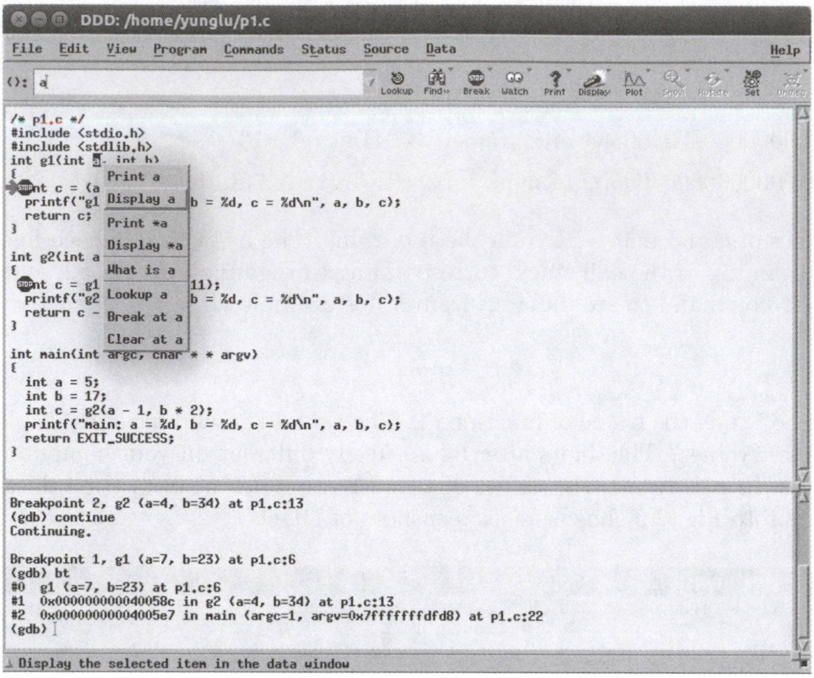

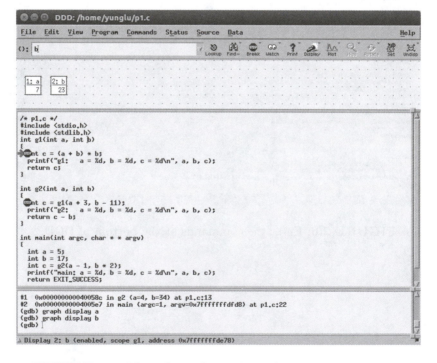

FIGURE 2.7: Use the mouse to select a inside g1. Click the right mouse button and select "Display a". Do the same for b.

FIGURE 2.8: The values of a and b in function g1 are shown.

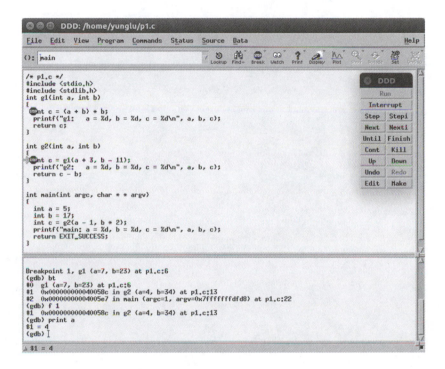

FIGURE 2.9: Use the `f` command to see different frames.

Chapter 3

Prevent, Detect, and Remove Bugs

Some books suggest that software should be well-designed, carefully written, and never debugged. These books do not say anything about debugging. From my experience writing programs, working with students, and talking to people in the software industry, debugging is difficult to avoid completely, even when software is planned and written carefully. In some ways, debugging is like editing an article. It is very difficult to write a good article without any editing. Even though debugging is difficult to avoid completely, it should not be relied upon. Experienced programmers carefully prevent bugs from happening and detect them as early as possible.

Many people learn software development by writing small programs (tens of lines for each program). This is good because learning should progress in stages. The problem is that many people hold onto habits acceptable for small programs when they attempt to write larger programs. Writing a program of 400 lines requires different strategies than writing a program of 40 lines. This book is written for people learning how to write programs that are between 100 and 1,000 "lines of code" (LoC). Although LoC is not a particularly good way of measuring software complexity, it does serve as a very basic yardstick for how complex a program might be. Finding a good way to measure software complexity is beyond the scope of this book. Instead, this book gives some suggestions on how to write correct programs.

3.1 Developing Software $\neq$ Coding

From the experience of writing small programs, some students have the habit of "coding $\rightarrow$ testing $\rightarrow$ debugging". Unfortunately, this is the wrong approach to developing software. Expert programmers use strategies to prevent, detect, and remove software bugs. Coding is **not** developing software. Coding means typing statements in a text editor. Coding is only one small part of developing software.

Before typing a single line of code, you first need to know why you are developing the software. Perhaps you are working on homework assignments for a programming class. In this case, you should ask the purposes of these assignments. In particular, there should be some learning objectives. Without knowing the purposes, it is impossible to understand how to evaluate software. This is increasingly important as software becomes more complex. Complex software has many parts and you need to understand why these parts are needed and how they affect each other. Developing software requires many steps before, during, and after coding. The following gives a few principles for you.

3.1.1   Before coding

- Read the specification and understand the requirements.
- Consider possible inputs and expected outputs.
- Identify valid but unexpected inputs and the correct outputs. For example, when writing a sorting program, what would the program do if the input is already sorted? What would the program do if the same number occurs multiple times? Identifying unexpected inputs is a key concern for developing reliable software.
- Identify invalid inputs and the ways to detect them. Consider the sorting program as an example again. If the specification says valid inputs are positive integers. What would the program do if the input contains floating-point numbers? What would the program do if the input contains negative numbers? What would the program do if the input contains symbols (such as !@#&)? Even when the input is invalid, your program should never crash (for example, producing a segmentation fault). Besides being incorrect, software that crashes is a sign of security risks.
- Think about the solution and sketch down an approach on paper.
- Draw block diagrams showing how information is exchanged among different parts of the program.
- After you have a design, plan the implementation aspect of the program: How many functions should be created? What does each function do? How many files are needed? When you design a function, try to keep these two suggestions in mind: Each function should do only one thing, and should consist of no more than 40 lines of code. This number is not rigid: 45 lines are all right; 120 lines are too long. A general rule is that the entire function should fit in your computer screen using a readable font size.
- If you have a detailed design, you will save time on coding and debugging.

3.1.2   During coding

- This may surprise you: If you want to finish the programs correctly and faster, write more code. Write code that is not needed. Before you put the code for *one* requirement into a larger program, write a small program to test your solution. This is called the *unit test*. If you cannot make one function work, you will definitely be incapable of making anything work after putting many functions together. After you have done some parts of the programs, make sure these parts work before continuing. You need to write additional code to test these parts, since the other parts are not ready yet. A rule of thumb is this: For every line of code you have to write, you should write three additional lines of code. This additional work helps you understand what you must do and helps you test what you have done.
- Always use a text editor that automatically indents programs. Such an editor can help you detect braces at wrong places. Why is indentation important? Because it is easier to visually detect misaligned code. Using the right tools can save you valuable time.
- Read your code line by line before running any test case. If you have not tried this method, you may be surprised at how effective this method can be. Reading code can help you find problems that are difficult to find by testing. One example is:

```
1  if (a > 0);
2  {
3    ... // always runs, not controlled by the if condition
4  }
```

The semicolon ; ends the `if` condition. As a result, the code inside { and } is not controlled by the `if` condition and always runs.

- Run some simple test cases in your head. If you do not understand what your program does, the computer will not be able to do what you want.
- Write code to test whether certain conditions are met, before proceeding. Suppose sorting is part of a program: Check whether the data is sorted before the program does anything else.
- Avoid copying and pasting code; instead, *refactor* the code by creating a function and, thus, avoiding duplication. If you need to make slight changes to the copied code, use the function's argument(s) to handle the differences. This is a tried-and-true principle: Similar code invites mistakes. You will soon lose track of the number of copies and the differences among similar code. It is difficult to maintain the consistency of multiple copies of the code. You will likely find that your program is correct in some situations and wrong in others. Finding and removing this type of bug can be very time-consuming. Your best strategy is to avoid it in the first place. It is better to write a program that is *always* wrong than a program that is *sometimes* right. If it is always wrong, and the problems come from only a single place, you can focus on that place. If the problems do not consistently appear and come from many possible places, it is more difficult to identify and remove the mistakes.
- Use version control. Have you ever had an experience like this: "Some parts of the program worked yesterday. I made some changes and nothing works now. I changed so many places that I don't remember exactly what I have changed."? Version control allows you to see the changes from the previous commit.
- Resolve all compiler warnings. Many studies have shown that warnings are likely to be serious errors, even though they are not syntax errors. Some people ignore warning messages, thinking that they can handle the warnings after they get their programs to work. However, the warning messages frequently indicate the problems preventing their programs from working.

3.1.3   After coding

Read your program after you think you have finished it. Check the common mistakes described below. Do not rely on testing: Testing can tell you that the program does not work; it cannot tell you that the program does work. It is possible that the test cases do not cover all possible scenarios. It is usually difficult to design test cases that cover all possible scenarios. For a complex program, covering all possible scenarios is usually impossible.

3.2   Common Mistakes

Here is a list of some common mistakes I have seen in the programs written by students (sometimes even by myself). Many students assure me that they will never make these mistakes. The reality is that people do make these mistakes, and more often than they think. This section considers only coding mistakes, not design mistakes. Design mistakes require a different book on the subject of designing software.

3.2.1 Uninitialized Variables

One common mistake is uninitialized variables. Some students think all variables are initialized to zero automatically. This is wrong. Uninitialized variables store garbage values. The values may be zero but there is no guarantee. This type of mistake is difficult to discover via testing. Sometimes, the values may happen to be zero, leading you to think that the program is correct. When the values are not zero, the programs have problems. Some students think that initializing variables slows down a program—however, these nanoseconds of delay are negligible. It is better to slow down your program by a few nanoseconds than to spend hours debugging.

3.2.2 Wrong Array Indexes

For an array of n elements, the valid indexes are 0, 1, 2, ..., n − 1 and n is an invalid index. When a program has a wrong index, the program may *seem* to work on some occasions, but may crash on others. You do not want to write a program whose behavior depends on luck.

3.2.3 Wrong Types

You can ride a bicycle. You can write with a pen. You cannot ride a pen. You cannot write with a bicycle. In a program, types specify what can be done. You need to understand and use types correctly. The trend of programming languages is to make types more restrictive and to prevent programmers from making accidental mistakes. Sometimes `gcc` treats suspicious type problems as warnings. You should treat these warnings as serious mistakes.

3.3   Post-Execution and Interactive Debugging

To debug a program, you need a strategy. You need to divide the program into stages and *isolate the problems based on the stages*. Ensure the program is correct in each stage before integrating the stages. For example, consider a program with three stages: (i) reads some integers from a file, (ii) sorts the integers, and (iii) saves the sorted integers to another file. Testing each stage before integration is called *unit testing*. For unit tests, you often need to write additional code as the "drivers" of a stage. For example, to test whether sorting works without getting the data from a file, you need to write code that generates the data (maybe using a random number generator). Debugging can be interactive or post-execution. If a program takes hours, you may not want to debug the program interactively. Instead, you may want the program to print debugging messages (this is called *logging*). The messages help you understand what occurs during the long execution. Another situation is debugging a program that communicates with another program that has timing requirements. For example, you debug a program that communicates with another program through networks. If you debug the program interactively and slow it down too much, the other program may think the network is disconnected and stop communicating with your program. Yet another scenario is that your program interfaces with the physical world (e.g., controlling a robot). The physical world does not wait for your program and it cannot slow down too much. Logging also slows down a program; thus, do not add excessive amounts of logging.

In many other cases, you can slow down your programs and debug the programs interactively—run some parts of the programs, see the intermediate results, change the programs, run them again, continue the process until you are convinced the programs are correct. For interactive debugging, printing debugging messages is usually ineffective and time-wasting. There are several problems with printing debugging messages for interactive debugging:

- Code needs to be inserted for printing debugging messages . This can be a considerable amount of effort. In most cases, the debugging messages must be removed later because debugging messages should appear in neither the final code nor its output.
- If there are too few messages, there is insufficient information to help you determine what is wrong.
- If there are too many messages, some messages may be irrelevant and should be ignored. Getting the right amount of messages, not too few and not too many, can be difficult.
- Worst of all, problems are likely to occur at unexpected places where no debugging messages have been inserted. As a result, more and more debugging messages must be added. This can be time-consuming and frustrating.

Instead of using debugging messages in interactive debugging, gdb (or DDD) is a better tool in most cases. I have shown you some gdb commands. I will describe more commands later in this book.

3.4 Separate Testing Code from Production Code

You should write programs that can detect their own bugs. If you want to check whether an array is sorted, do not print the elements on screen and check by your eyes. Write a function that checks whether an array is sorted. The code is usually not printing debugging messages. Instead, write code that can help you debug without relying on your own eyes.

You should consider writing testing code *before* you write a program. This is a common practice called *test-driven development*. How to write testing code? Many books have been written about software testing. This section gives you one suggestion. Consider the following two examples of testing your code. Suppose `func` is the function you want to test and `test_func` is the code for testing `func`.

```
func(arguments)                      test_func(arguments)
{                                    {
    /* do work to get result */          /* create arguments */
    /* test to check result */           result = func(arguments);
}                                        /* check the result */
                                     }
```

What is the difference between these two approaches? The first (located on the left) calls the testing code *inside* a function of your program. In the second (located on the right), the testing code is *outside* your program and the testing code calls `func`. This difference is important because the first mixes the testing code with the actual code needed for your program (sometimes called "production code"). As a result, it will be difficult for you to remove the testing code. The second approach separates the testing code from the production code, so that you can easily remove the testing code later on. You should take the second approach whenever you test your program.

Chapter 4

Pointers

4.1 Scope

Chapter 2 described several rules. One of those rules was that each function can see only its own frame. This is called *scope*. A new scope is created every time a pair of { and } is used. This could be inside of a function body, for example, an if statement, or a while loop. The following example shows two scopes:

```
1  void f(int a, int b)
2  {
3    /* this is a scope, call it X */
4    int i;
5    for (i = 0; i < a + b; i ++)
6      {
7        /* this is another scope, call it Y */
8        int j;
9      }
10 }
```

In the scope marked X (in the comments), a and b are arguments and i is a local variable. Another scope called Y is created inside of X. Scopes are always nested inside of each other like this. Variables from outer scopes are still accessible, so scope Y can "see" a, b, and i. A local variable j is created inside of scope Y and is accessible only inside scope Y; scope X cannot "see" j.

The following example has three scopes: X, Y, and Z. The arguments a and b in f1 have nothing to do with the arguments of a and b in f2 because they are in different and non-overlapping scopes: f1 is not nested in f2 or vice versa.

The variable j is in the inner scope, and can only be "seen" between the { and } of the for loop.

```
1   void f1(int a, int b)
2   {
3       /* this is a scope, call it X */
4       int i;
5       for (i = 0; i < a + b; i ++)
6         {
7           /* this is another scope, call it Y */
8           int j;
9         }
10  }
11
12  void f2(int a, int b)
13  {
14      /* this is a scope, call it Z */
15      f1(a + b, a - b);
16      /* RL A */
17  }
```

It is legal to create another variable of the same name in an inner scope, like u.

```
1   void f1(int u, int v)
2   {
3       /* this is a scope, call it X */
4       int i;
5       for (i = 0; i < u + v; i ++)
6         {
7           /* this is another scope, call it Y */
8           int j;
9           int u; /* shadow variable */
10        }
11  }
```

In the inner scope Y, we create a new variable called u. Please note that Y already has an argument called u. By adding the type int in front of u, a new variable is created. This function now has two variables both called u in the overlapping scopes (Y is nested inside of X). This makes the u in Y a *shadow variable* of the u in X. These two variables have two different memory addresses. Modifying the u in scope Y does **not** change the u in scope X. Shadow variables are considered bad programming style because they make programs difficult to understand, and can introduce subtle errors. Consider the following example:

```
1   void f1(int u, int v)
2   {
3       /* this is a scope, call it X */
```

```
4    int i;
5    u = 27;
6    for (i = 0; i < u + v; i ++)
7      {
8        /* this is another scope, call it Y */
9        int u; /* shadow variable because of int */
10       u = 5;
11     }
12   /* u is 27 even though it was assigned to 5 two lines
13      earlier */
14 }
```

The value of u is 5 just above the closing brace (line 11) that encloses scope Y. After leaving Y, the value of u is 27 because the outer u was never changed. This can make the program confusing, and confusing programs are error-prone. Fortunately most compilers make it is easy to detect shadow variables. For example, `gcc` compiler warns about shadow variables when you add `-Wshadow` to `gcc`.

4.2   The Swap Function

A function can return only one value. The returned value can be used to modify one thing in the caller. For example,

```
1  int f1(int a, int b)
2  {
3    return (a + b);
4  }
5
6  void f2(void)
7  {
8    int s;
9    s = f1(2, 37);
10   /* RL A */
11 }
```

In the function f2, we see s becomes the sum of 2 and 37. By calling f1 we are able to change one variable in the caller f2. What can we do if we want to change two or more variables in the caller? Suppose we want to write a "swap function",

```
1  void swap(int x, int y)
2  {
3
4    /* do something to swap x and y */
5
6  }
7
8  void f2(void)
9  {
10   int a = 2;
11   int b = 37;
```

```
12    swap(a, b);
13    /* RL A */
14  }
```

Can this swap function work?

```
1  void swap(int x, int y)
2  {
3    int z = x;
4    x = y;
5    y = z;
6  }
```

When the swap function is called, the values of a and b are **copied** to the arguments x and y. The call stack is shown below.

Frame	Symbol	Address	Value
	z	106	-
swap	y	105	37
	x	104	2
	Return Location	103	line 13
f2	b	102	37
	a	101	2

The value of x is stored in a temporary variable z. Then y's value is assigned to x and z's value is assigned to y. After these three steps, x has y's old value and y has x's old value (through z). After finishing line 5 in swap and before the top frame is popped, this is the call stack:

Frame	Symbol	Address	Value
	z	106	2
swap	y	105	2
	x	104	37
	Return Location	103	line 13
f2	b	102	37
	a	101	2

Inside swap, the values of x and y have been swapped. As explained in Chapter 2, when swap finishes, the top frame is popped. After the top frame is popped, the call stack becomes

Frame	Symbol	Address	Value
f2	b	102	37
	a	101	2

The swap function was called and finished, and the values of a and b have **not** changed. This swap function does not work. C programs use "call-by-value" when calling functions That means that values are copied from the caller to the arguments of the called function (i.e., callee). This is the only way to call functions in C. Java and C++ have call-by-value and call-by-reference but C only uses call-by-value.

Does this mean it is impossible to write a swap function?

4.3 Pointers

C solves this problem by creating the concept of *pointers*. A pointer is a variable (or an argument) whose value is a memory address. To create a pointer, add * after the type.

```
1  type * ptr; // ptr is a pointer, meaning its value is a
2     memory address
```

This creates a pointer called `ptr`. Its value is an address. At that address is stored a value of the given type. This may seem abstract so let us see some concrete examples:

```
1  int    * iptr;
2  char   * cptr;
3  double * dptr;
```

name	value	at that address
iptr	an address	an integer
cptr	an address	a character
dptr	an address	a double-precision floating-point number

In each case, the pointer stores a memory address. Chapter 2 said programmers cannot control addresses. How can a program obtain valid addresses? C provides special syntax for precisely that purpose: by adding an & in front of a variable. For example,

```
1  int a = -61;    // a is an integer
2  int * iptr;     // iptr is a pointer
3  iptr = & a;     // iptr's value is a's address
```

Symbol	Address	Value
iptr	101	100
a	100	−61

Section 2.3.6 prints the addresses of two variables a and c. It shows that the addresses change when the same program runs again. By using an ampersand (&) in front of a, iptr's value changes every time the program runs. Please remember that **a programmer can change variables' values but a programmer cannot change variables' addresses**. You may want to ask why this example uses 100 for a's address but the addresses in Section 2.3.6 are much larger values. In order to make the book easier to read, the book uses small addresses instead of the much larger addresses that are common on modern computers.

How are pointers useful? First, just like any other variable type, two pointers can have the same value.

```
1  int a = 632;
2  int c;          /* c's value is garbage now */
3  c = a;          /* c's value is the same as a's value */
4  int * iptr1;    /* iptr1's value is garbage now */
5  int * iptr2;    /* iptr2's value is garbage now */
6  iptr1 = & a;    /* iptr1's value is a's address */
7  iptr2 = iptr1;  /* iptr2 and iptr1 have the same value */
```

After executing the first line, an integer called a has been created and its value is 632. The second line creates another integer variable called c and its value is not defined yet. This is the snapshot of the call stack after finishing line 2.

Symbol	Address	Value
c	101	garbage
a	100	632

The third line makes c's value the same as a's value.

Symbol	Address	Value
c	101	632
a	100	632

The fourth and the fifth lines create two pointers. Their values are currently undefined.

Symbol	Address	Value
iptr2	103	garbage
iptr1	102	garbage
c	101	632
a	100	632

The sixth line assigns a's address to iptr1's value.

Symbol	Address	Value
iptr2	103	garbage
iptr1	102	100
c	101	632
a	100	632

The seventh line assigns iptr1's value, 100, to iptr2's value.

Symbol	Address	Value
iptr2	103	100
iptr1	102	100
c	101	632
a	100	632

The third and the seventh lines are similar: The third line assigns a's value to c's value; the seventh line assigns the value of iptr1 to the value of iptr2.

A second way to use pointers is to retrieve the value stored at their addresses.

```
1  int a = 632;
2  int * iptr;
3  int c;
4  iptr = & a;
5  c = * iptr;
6  /* read iptr's value as an address, go to that address,
7     read the value at that address, assign the value to c */
8  printf("%d", * iptr);
9  * iptr = -84;
```

Shown below is the call stack after the program finishes the fourth line.

Symbol	Address	Value
iptr	102	100
c	101	garbage
a	100	632

The fifth line does the following things:
1. Takes `iptr`'s value as an address. The value is 100.
2. Goes to that address (100).
3. Reads the value at that address and it is 632.
4. Assigns 632 to `c`.

After the fifth line, the call stack becomes:

Symbol	Address	Value
iptr	102	100
c	101	632
a	100	632

This is the rule: If a program has something like the following:

```
= * iptr; // iptr is a pointer
```

the program will
1. take `iptr`'s value as an address.
2. go to that address.
3. read the value at that address.
4. assign the value to the variable at the left.

This rule is applicable if `* iptr` is at the right hand side (RHS) of the assignment sign (=). This is also called *dereferencing* a pointer. The assignment sign = is not strictly necessary, in which case the rule still works without part 4 of the assignment. For example, the eighth line of the code above prints 632.

The emphasis on the "right hand side" is important. When `* iptr` is on the left hand side (LHS), it works in a similar but opposite way. For example, the last line of code above does the following:
1. Takes `iptr`'s value as an address and it is 100.
2. Goes to that address (100).
3. **Modifies** the value at address 100 to -84.

Thus, after the last line, the call stack becomes

Symbol	Address	Value
iptr	102	100
c	101	632
a	100	-84

Many students find pointers confusing at first. This confusion is well justified. The same symbol `*` has different meanings. The symbol also means multiplication when it is between two numeric values (integer, float, double). The following table summarizes the different meanings:

It is time to test your understanding of the different usages of `*`. Draw the call stack for the following code snippet:

Example	Meaning
1. `int * iptr;`	Create a pointer variable. `ptr`'s value is an address. An integer is stored at that address. `*` is after the type (`int` in this case)
2. `iptr = & val`	Assign `val`'s address to `ptr`'s value. This is how to assign a valid address to `ptr`; note that `*` is not used.
3. `= * ptr`	(right hand side of assignment, RHS) Take `ptr`'s value as an address and read the value at that address. `=` is not always necessary, for example, when printing or calling a function.
4. `* ptr =`	(left hand side of assignment, LHS) Take `ptr`'s value as an address and modify the value at that address.
5. `5 * 17`	Multiplication: `5 * 17` is 85. In this case, `*` is between two numbers

TABLE 4.1: Different usages of `*` in C programs. Please notice that `ptr =` and `* ptr =` have different meanings.

```
1  int a = 21;
2  int c = -4;
3  int * ptr;
4  ptr = & a;
5  * ptr = 7;
6  c = * ptr;
7  * ptr = a * c;
```

After executing the first three lines, the call stack is shown below.

Symbol	Address	Value
ptr	102	garbage
c	101	−4
a	100	21

The fourth line assigns `a`'s address to `ptr`'s value.

Symbol	Address	Value
ptr	102	100
c	101	−4
a	100	21

The fifth line has `* ptr` at the left hand side of the assignment sign. This assigns value 7 to the address 100.

Symbol	Address	Value
ptr	102	100
c	101	−4
a	100	21 → 7

The sixth line reads the value at address 100; the value is 7. This value is assigned to `c`. The call stack is shown below.

Symbol	Address	Value
ptr	102	100
c	101	$-4 \to 7$
a	100	7

The seventh line reads the values of a and c; both are 7. The symbol * is used twice. At the right hand side, * means multiplication and the result is 49. Then, 49 is assigned to the value at address 100. This changes a's value to 49.

Symbol	Address	Value
ptr	102	100
c	101	7
a	100	$7 \to 49$

4.4 The Swap Function Revisited

Section 4.2 explains that

```
1  void swap(int x, int y)
2  {
3    int z = x;
4    x = y;
5    y = z;
6  }
```

does not work because the changes to x and y are lost after the swap function finishes (i.e., returns) and the top frame is popped. How do you write a correct swap function? The swap function needs to change the values of a and c. Their addresses reside outside of the function. To do so, swap **must have the addresses** of a and c.

```
1  void swap( /* the addresses of a and c */ )
2  {
3
4
5
6  }
7
8  void f(void)
9  {
10   int a = 83;
11   int c = -74;
12   swap( /* the addresses of a and c */ );
13   /* RL */
14 }
```

Since the function f must provide the addresses of a and c, the swap function's arguments must be pointers that store these addresses.

```
1  void swap(int * k, int * m)
2  {
```

```
3
4
5
6  }
7
8  void f(void)
9  {
10     int a = 83;
11     int c = -74;
12     swap(& a, & c);
13     /* RL */
14  }
```

This is the call stack when starting the `swap` function.

Frame	Symbol	Address	Value
	m	104	101
swap	k	103	100
	Return Location	102	line 13
f	c	101	−74
	a	100	83

The following code implements the `swap` function:

```
1
2  void swap (int * k, int * m)
3  {
4    int s = * k;
5    * k = * m;
6    * m = s;
7  }
8
9  void f(void)
10 {
11   int a = 83;
12   int c = -74;
13   swap (& a, & c);
14 }
```

The third line reads the value at the address of 100 and stores the value in `s`.

Frame	Symbol	Address	Value
	s	105	83
swap	m	104	101
	k	103	100
	Return Location	102	line 13
f	c	101	−74
	a	100	83

The fourth line reads the value stored at address 101; the value is −74. This value is stored at the address 100.

Frame	Symbol	Address	Value
	s	105	83
swap	m	104	101
	k	103	100
	Return Location	102	line 13
f	c	101	−74
	a	100	−74

The fifth line assigns 83 to the value at address 101.

Frame	Symbol	Address	Value
	s	105	83
swap	m	104	101
	k	103	100
	Return Location	102	line 13
f	c	101	83
	a	100	−74

After the `swap` function finishes, the top frame is popped.

Frame	Symbol	Address	Value
f	c	101	83
	a	100	−74

Note that the values of a and c have been changed. Pointers are a central feature of C programming, and they must be handled carefully. The `swap` function should be understood thoroughly, since it is a simple example of using pointers. You should understand how to call swap, how it is implemented, and why it is implemented in the way that it is.

Section 2.4 says a function can see only its own frame. However, the `swap` function modifies the values of a and c even though a and c are in a different frame. Does this mean the rule in Section 2.4 is violated? The answer is no. The `swap` function still cannot access a or c directly. The `swap` function can access a or c **indirectly** because k and m store the addresses of a and c. **Through pointers, a function can access (i.e., read or write) the values of variables in another frame.**

By using pointers, the `swap` function can read or write the values in f's frame. Is it possible for f to use pointers to read or write variables in `swap`'s frame? We can illustrate this question with a simple example. Will the following code change m's value from 0 to 7?

```
1   int * f1(void)
2   {
3     int m = 0;
4     return & m;
5   }
6
7   void f2(void)
8   {
9     int * iptr = f1();
10    /* RL */
11    * iptr = 7;
12  }
```

The answer is no: m exists only inside of f1's frame.
- Before calling f1, m does not exist.
- When running the code in f1, the program executes the statements in f1, not in f2.

- After f1 finishes, the program continues from the return location (line 10). The top frame has been popped and m no longer exists.

Hence, it is impossible for f2 to modify m. In fact, most compilers will warn you that the fourth line is likely a mistake. Using pointers to read or write only works in one direction. If f2 calls f1, f1 can read or write values in f2's frame but f2 cannot read or write values in f1's frame. This rule can be generalized: Through pointers, a function can read or write values stored in the function's frame or the stack frames below it. It is impossible to read or write values in a frame that is above the function's frame.

4.5   Type Errors

Every time I teach pointers, I get questions like this: What happens if the types are mixed up? For example,

```
1    int  a = 5;
2    char * cptr;
3    cptr = & a;
```

The type of a is int and cptr is a pointer to char. What will happen? The simple answer is **don't do it.** Mixing types is asking for trouble. In this case, the program will assume that there is a char variable at the address of a, when clearly there is an int variable there. It makes no sense. The precise value of * cptr will depend on the type of hardware that is running the program. Fortunately, gcc will tell you there is a problem by adding -Wall after calling gcc.

How about this?

```
1    int  a = 5;
2    int * iptr;
3    iptr = a;
4    * iptr = -12;
```

This is also problematic. If we manage to convince the compiler to actually compile it, we will end up assigning 5 to iptr. Although this makes no sense, it will not cause problems per se. The real problem comes when we attempt to use the pointer. When creating pointers, we almost always want to dereference them at some stage. That is, we add * in front of the pointer to read from or to write to the value stored at address stored in the pointer. The third line assigns 5 (a's value, not a's address) to iptr's value. Now adding * in front of iptr will cause the program to try to read from or write to the value at address 5. However, programmers have no control over the specific addresses a program uses. The fourth line intends to write −12 to the value at address 5. This is **not** a's address—a's address is & a—and a problem will ensue. In fact, modern operating systems will stop the program from doing it. Address 5 is almost certainly inaccessible to your program, and attempting to read from or write to the value at this address will cause the operating system to stop the program.

4.6 Arrays and Pointers

What is an array? Consider the following example:

```
int arr[5];
```

This line of code creates an array of 5 elements; each element is an integer. The elements have not been initialized so the values are garbage. The following example shows how to write to the array elements.

```
arr[0] = 6;      // assign 6 to the first element
arr[1] = -11;    // assign -11 to the second element
arr[2] = 9;      // assign 9 to the third element
```

Please remember that an array's indexes **always** start from zero.

Arrays have a special relationship with pointers, and in many cases are indistinguishable from pointers. We can illustrate this by explaining the specific meaning of the third line above. This line does three things:

1. Interprets **arr**'s value as a pointer whose value is the address of the first element of the array.
2. Finds the address of two elements after the address of the first element to get a new address. Here, the value 2 is the index inside [ ] and is called address *offset*.
3. Modifies the value at that address to 9.

How about the following example?

```
int c;         // create an integer variable called c
c = arr[1];    // read the value of the second element
               // and assign it to c
```

The second line does four things:

1. Interprets **arr**'s value as a pointer whose value is the address of the first element
2. Finds the address of one element after that address to get a new address. Here, the value 1 is the address offset.
3. **Reads** the value at that address and it is -11.
4. Writes -11 to c's value.

Note that **arr** can always be interpreted as a pointer whose value is the address of the first element of the array. The first element is **arr[0]**. Thus, the following equality is always true:

```
arr == & arr[0]
```

In Section 2.3.5, we noted that the addresses of array elements are contiguous. If **arr** stores the address of the first element, a compiler can easily calculate the address of any element. The address of **arr[k]** is the address of **arr[0]** plus k × the size of each element. For the time being, let's assume that each element occupies only one unit of memory space. We will examine the size of data in a later chapter.

Since **arr** is the address of the first element, calling a function with **arr** allows the called function to access the array's elements (both reading and writing). We can use a pointer type as the argument for the array. The following example adds the elements in an array:

```
int sumarr(int * intarr, int len)
{
  int ind;
  int sum2 = 0; // remember to initialize to zero
```

```
5    for (ind = 0; ind < len; ind ++)
6      {
7         sum2 += intarr[ind];
8      }
9    return sum2;
10  }
11  void f(void)
12  {
13    int sum = 0;
14    int arr[5];
15    arr[0] = 4;
16    arr[1] = -7;
17    arr[2] = 2;
18    arr[3] = 3;
19    arr[4] = 9;
20    sum = sumarr(arr, 5);
21    /* RL */
22    printf("sum_=_%d\n", sum);
23  }
```

The function f2 creates arr, an array of five elements and sum, an integer. This is the call stack before calling sumarr.

Frame	Symbol	Address	Value
	arr[4]	105	9
	arr[3]	104	3
f	arr[2]	103	2
	arr[1]	102	−7
	arr[0]	101	4
	sum	100	0

Function f calls function sumarr with two arguments: arr and 5. The former is the address of arr[0]. This is the call stack after starting function sumarr before the fifth line.

Frame	Symbol	Address	Value
	sum2	111	0
	ind	110	garbage
sumarr	len	109	5
	intarr	108	101
	value address	107	100
	return location	106	line 21
	arr[4]	105	9
	arr[3]	104	3
f	arr[2]	103	2
	arr[1]	102	−7
	arr[0]	101	4
	sum	100	0

Please pay special attention to the value of intarr at address 108. The value is 101 because the address of the first element, i.e., & arr[0], is 101. In C programs, an array itself does not provide information about the number of elements. As a result, when calling sumarr, another argument is needed for the number of elements. Because intarr has the address of the array's first element, function sumarr can read the array's elements even though the array is stored in a different frame. The `for` loop adds the elements' values and stores the result in sum2. This is the call stack after finishing the `for` loop.

Frame	Symbol	Address	Value
	sum2	111	$0 \rightarrow 11$
	ind	110	5
sumarr	len	109	5
	intarr	108	101
	value address	107	100
	return location	106	line 21
	arr[4]	105	9
	arr[3]	104	3
f	arr[2]	103	2
	arr[1]	102	-7
	arr[0]	101	4
	sum	100	0

The value of sum2 is then written to the value at address 100 (sum's address). This is the call stack after function sumarr has finished.

Frame	Symbol	Address	Value
	arr[4]	105	9
	arr[3]	104	3
f	arr[2]	103	2
	arr[1]	102	-7
	arr[0]	101	4
	sum	100	$0 \rightarrow 11$

Because an array is passed as a pointer to the first element, a function can modify the values of an array in another frame. Consider this example:

```
1  void incrarr(int * intarr, int len)
2  {
3    int ind;
4    for (ind = 0; ind < len; ind ++)
5      {
6        intarr[ind] ++;
7      }
8  }
9  void f(void)
10 {
11   int arr[5];
12   arr[0] = 4;
13   arr[1] = -7;
14   arr[2] = 2;
15   arr[3] = 3;
16   arr[4] = 9;
17   incrarr(arr, 5);
18   /* RL */
19 }
```

This is the call stack after entering `incrarr` before executing the `for` loop.

Frame	Symbol	Address	Value
	ind	110	garbage
	len	107	5
sumarr	intarr	106	100
	return location	105	line 18
	arr[4]	104	9
	arr[3]	103	3
f	arr[2]	102	2
	arr[1]	101	−7
	arr[0]	100	4

What is the difference between the following two statements?

```
1  a ++; // assume a is an integer
2         // same as a = a + 1;
3  intarr[ind] ++; // assume intarr[ind] is an integer
4                   // same as intarr[ind] = intarr[ind] + 1
```

The first line executes the following steps:

1. Reads a's value.
2. Increments the value by one.
3. Writes the incremented value back to a.

The second statement does something similar:

1. Reads `intarr[ind]`'s value.
2. Increments the value by one.
3. Writes the incremented value back to `intarr[ind]`.

Because **intarr** is the address of the array's first element, the function **incrarr** can read and modify the array's elements even though the array is stored in a different frame. This is the call stack after **incrarr** has finished, and its frame has been popped.

Frame	Symbol	Address	Value
	arr[4]	104	10
	arr[3]	103	4
f	arr[2]	102	3
	arr[1]	101	−6
	arr[0]	100	5

4.7 Type Rules

Here are some rules about types:

- If var's type is t, then & var's type is t *.
- If ptr's type is t *, then * ptr's type is t.
- If arr is an array of type t, then each element stores a value of type t. Thus, the type of an element (such as arr[1]) is t. Please notice the presence of an index.
- If arr is an array of type t, then arr's (without any index) type is t * because arr is equivalent to & arr[0].
- An array's name is always a pointer. If arr is an array of type t and t * ptr is a pointer of type t, then ptr = arr is a valid assignment. It is equivalent to ptr = & arr[0], or assigning the address of the first element to ptr.

- Pointers are not necessarily arrays. For example, t * ptr creates a pointer of type t and it is not related to any array. Hence, arr = ptr can be a dangerous assignment because operations like arr[1] may read from (or write to) an invalid address.

4.8   Pointer Arithmetic

Pointers can be used to iterate through (visit) the elements of an array. This is called *pointer arithmetic.* Consider the following example.

```
1   // arithmetic1.c
2   #include <stdio.h>
3   #include <stdlib.h>
4   int main (int argc ,char * * argv)
5   {
6       int    arr1[] = {7, 2, 5, 3, 1, 6, -8, 16, 4};
7       char   arr2[] = {'m', 'q', 'k', 'z', '%', '>'};
8       double arr3[] = {3.14, -2.718, 6.626, 0.529};
9       int len1 = sizeof(arr1) / sizeof(int);
10      int len2 = sizeof(arr2) / sizeof(char);
11      int len3 = sizeof(arr3) / sizeof(double);
12      printf("lengths = %d, %d, %d\n", len1, len2, len3);
13      int    * iptr = arr1;
14      char   * cptr = arr2;
15      double * dptr = arr3;
16      printf("values = %d, %c, %f\n", * iptr, * cptr, * dptr);
17      iptr ++;
18      cptr ++;
19      dptr ++;
20      printf("values = %d, %c, %f\n", * iptr, * cptr, * dptr);
21      iptr ++;
22      cptr ++;
23      dptr ++;
24      printf("values = %d, %c, %f\n", * iptr, * cptr, * dptr);
25      iptr ++;
26      cptr ++;
27      dptr ++;
28      printf("values = %d, %c, %f\n", * iptr, * cptr, * dptr);
29      return EXIT_SUCCESS;
30  }
```

This is the output of this program:

```
lengths = 9, 6, 4
values = 7, m, 3.140000
values = 2, q, -2.718000
values = 5, k, 6.626000
values = 3, z, 0.529000
```

Lines 6 to 8 create three arrays, one of integers, one of characters, and one of double-precision floating point numbers. In a C program, you can create a constant array without giving the size, by putting nothing between [and]. The compiler will automatically calculate the array's size. Lines 9 to 11 calculate the lengths of the three arrays. So far we use the same size for different types (`int`, `char`, `double`) but different types actually take up different amounts of memory, and therefore have different sizes. Thus, these three lines divide the array sizes by the types' sizes in order to get the numbers of the elements. Line 12 prints the lengths. As you can see, the program prints the correct lengths. This method for calculating an array's size is valid only for constant arrays. If an array is created using `malloc`, this method will not work. A later chapter will explain `malloc`.

Lines 13 to 15 assign the addresses of the first element in each array to the pointers. These three lines are equivalent to

```
int    * iptr = & arr1[0];
char   * cptr = & arr2[0];
double * dptr = & arr3[0];
```

Do not mix the pointer types. For example, the following statements are wrong:

```
int * iptr = arr2;
int * iptr = arr1[1];
```

The first is wrong because `arr2` is an array of `char`. The second is wrong because `arr1[1]` is an `int`, and is not an address.

Line 16 prints the values stored at the corresponding addresses. The printed values are the first elements. Lines 17 to 19 are called *pointer arithmetic*. Each pointer is advanced by one. This means specifically, that each pointer now points to the next element of the array. Line 20 prints the values stored at the corresponding addresses. The printed values are the second elements. Lines 21 to 23 make each pointer point to the next element. Line 24 prints the values stored at the corresponding addresses. The printed values are the third elements. Even though different types have different sizes in memory, the compiler will automatically move the pointers to correctly point to the next elements.

The sizes of types are not fixed by the C language, and can vary depending on the computer, operating system, and specific compiler options chosen to compile the code. The following program prints the sizes of various types:

```
// arithmetic2.c
#include <stdio.h>
#include <stdlib.h>
int main (int argc ,char * * argv)
{
  int    arr1[] = {7, 2, 5, 3, 1, 6, -8, 16, 4};
  char   arr2[] = {'m', 'q', 'k', 'z', '%', '>'};
  double arr3[] = {3.14, -2.718, 6.626, 0.529};
  long int addr10 = (long int) (& arr1[0]);
  long int addr11 = (long int) (& arr1[1]);
  long int addr12 = (long int) (& arr1[2]);
  printf("%ld, %ld, %ld\n", addr12, addr11, addr10);
  printf("%ld, %ld\n", addr12 - addr11, addr11 - addr10);
  long int addr20 = (long int) (& arr2[0]);
  long int addr21 = (long int) (& arr2[1]);
  long int addr22 = (long int) (& arr2[2]);
  printf("%ld, %ld, %ld\n", addr22, addr21, addr20);
  printf("%ld, %ld\n", addr22 - addr21, addr21 - addr20);
  long int addr30 = (long int) (& arr3[0]);
  long int addr31 = (long int) (& arr3[1]);
```

```
21    long int addr32 = (long int) (& arr3[2]);
22    printf("%ld,␣%ld,␣%ld\n", addr32, addr31, addr30);
23    printf("%ld,␣%ld\n", addr32 - addr31, addr31 - addr30);
24    return EXIT_SUCCESS;
25 }
```

The output of the program is:

```
140735471859144, 140735471859140, 140735471859136
4, 4
140735471859186, 140735471859185, 140735471859184
1, 1
140735471859120, 140735471859112, 140735471859104
8, 8
```

We have already discussed lines 6 to 8, but what do lines 9 to 11 do? At the right side of the assignment, & arr1[0] gets the address of the first element of arr1. This address is assigned to addr10. Because this code is compiled on a 64-bit computer, the memory addresses use 64 bits, and require the long int type to store the addresses. We need to use some special syntax (called a type cast) to tell the compiler to store the memory address inside an integer. This is why we have (long int) after =. In general, storing memory addresses in integers is a very bad idea, because it can lead to subtle problems when the code is compiled under different circumstances. Using (long int) is telling the compiler "I know this is wrong, but trust me, I want to do it." The purpose of this program is to show you that the sizes of different types can be different.

Lines 10 and 11 get the addresses of the second, and the third elements of the array. Line 12 prints the values of these long integers. In printf, %ld is used to print a longer integer. The value changes if you execute the program again. However, line 13 always prints 4, 4 meaning that the addresses of two adjacent elements differ by 4. This means each integer uses 4 bytes of memory. Line 17 prints some addresses and they change when the program is executed again. Line 18 always prints 1, 1 meaning that the addresses of two adjacent elements differ by 1. Thus, each character needs 1 byte of memory. Line 23 always prints 8, 8 meaning that the addresses of two adjacent elements differ by 8. Thus, each double needs 8 bytes of memory.

The next example combines these two programs.

```
1  // arithmetic3.c
2  #include <stdio.h>
3  #include <stdlib.h>
4  int main (int argc ,char * * argv)
5  {
6      int     arr1[] = {7, 2, 5, 3, 1, 6, -8, 16, 4};
7      char    arr2[] = {'m', 'q', 'k', 'z', '%', '>'};
8      double arr3[] = {3.14, -2.718, 6.626, 0.529};
9      int     * iptr = & arr1[3];
10     printf("%d\n", * iptr);
11     long int addr13 = (long int) iptr;
12     iptr --;
13     printf("%d\n", * iptr);
14     long int addr12 = (long int) iptr;
15     printf("addr13␣-␣addr12␣=␣%ld\n", addr13 - addr12);
16     printf("===================================\n");
```

```
17
18     char    * cptr = & arr2[1];
19     printf("%c\n", * cptr);
20     long int addr21 = (long int) cptr;
21     cptr ++;
22     printf("%c\n", * cptr);
23     long int addr22 = (long int) cptr;
24     printf("addr22_-_addr21_=_%ld\n", addr22 - addr21);
25     printf("===================================\n");
26
27     double * dptr = & arr3[2];
28     printf("%f\n", * dptr);
29     long int addr32 = (long int) dptr;
30     dptr --;
31     printf("%f\n", * dptr);
32     long int addr31 = (long int) dptr;
33     printf("addr32_-_addr31_=_%ld\n", addr32 - addr31);
34     return EXIT_SUCCESS;
35  }
```

This is the output of the program:

```
3
5
addr13 - addr12 = 4
=======================================
q
k
addr22 - addr21 = 1
=======================================
6.626000
-2.718000
addr32 - addr31 = 8
```

Line 9 assigns the address of `arr1[3]` to `iptr` and line 10 prints the value stored at that address. As you can see in this example, `iptr` does not have to start from the first element of the array. Line 11 stores `iptr`'s value in `addr13`. Please remember that `iptr`'s value is an address. Line 12 decrements `iptr`'s value and line 13 prints the value at address. The value is 5, the same as `arr1[2]`. Line 14 stores `iptr`'s value in `addr12`. Line 15 shows the differences of the two addresses stored in `addr13` and `addr12` and the difference is 4, not 1.

What does this mean? Even though line 12 decrements `iptr` by one, the compiler actually decreases `iptr`'s value by 4 *because the size of an integer is 4*. In other words, the specific change in `iptr`'s value depends on the size of the type being pointed to. The outputs for the other two arrays further illustrate this point. Line 24 prints 1 and line 33 prints 8 because of the sizes of the types being pointed to. This explains why mixing types can be problematic. For example,

```
1     int * iptr = arr2; // arr2 is a char array
2     int * iptr = arr3; // arr3 is a double array
```

Programs have odd behavior when the types are mixed like this.

4.9 Exercises

4.9.1 Swap Function 1

Does this program have any syntax problems because of wrong types (such as assigning an integer to a pointer's value)? Will this function actually swap the values of u and t? What is the program's output? Please draw the call stack and explain.

```
1  // swap1.c
2  #include <stdio.h>
3  #include <stdlib.h>
4  void swap1 (int a , int b)
5  {
6    int k = a;
7    a = b;
8    b = k;
9  }
10 int main (int argc ,char * * argv)
11 {
12   int u;
13   int t;
14   u = 17;
15   t = -96;
16   printf ("before swap1: u = %d , t = %d\n" , u , t);
17   swap1 (u , t);
18   printf ("after  swap1: u = %d , t = %d\n" , u , t);
19   return EXIT_SUCCESS;
20 }
```

4.9.2 Swap Function 2

How about this program?

```
1  // swap2.c
2  #include <stdio.h>
3  #include <stdlib.h>
4  void swap2 (int * a , int * b)
5  {
6    int * k = a;
7    a = b;
8    b = k;
9  }
10
11 int main (int argc ,char * * argv)
12 {
13   int u;
14   int t;
15   u = 17;
16   t = -96;
17   printf ("before swap2: u = %d , t = %d\n" , u , t);
```

```
18   swap2 (& u , & t);
19   printf ("after␣␣swap2:␣u␣=␣%d␣,␣t␣=␣%d␣\n" , u , t);
20   return EXIT_SUCCESS;
21   }
```

4.9.3   Swap Function 3

How about this program?

```
1   // swap3.c
2   #include <stdio.h>
3   #include <stdlib.h>
4
5   void swap3 (int * a, int * b)
6   {
7     int k = * a;
8     a = b;
9     * b = k;
10  }
11
12
13  int main (int argc ,char * * argv)
14  {
15    int u;
16    int t;
17    u = 17;
18    t = -96;
19    printf ("before␣swap3:␣u␣=␣%d␣,␣t␣=␣%d␣\n" , u , t);
20    swap3 (& u , & t);
21    printf ("after␣␣swap3:␣u␣=␣%d␣,␣t␣=␣%d␣\n" , u , t);
22    return EXIT_SUCCESS;
23  }
```

4.9.4   Swap Function 4

How about this program?

```
1   // swap4.c
2   #include <stdio.h>
3   #include <stdlib.h>
4
5   void swap4 (int * a, int * b)
6   {
7     int k = * a;
8     * a = * b;
9     * b = * k;
10  }
11
12
13  int main (int argc ,char * * argv)
14  {
```

```
15    int  u;
16    int  t;
17    u = 17;
18    t = -96;
19    printf  ("before␣swap4:␣␣u␣=␣%d␣,␣t␣=␣%d␣\n"  , u , t);
20    swap4 (& u  , & t);
21    printf  ("after␣␣swap4:␣␣u␣=␣%d␣,␣t␣=␣%d␣\n"  , u , t);
22    return EXIT_SUCCESS;
23  }
```

4.9.5   Swap Function 5

How about this program?

```
1  // swap5.c
2  #include <stdio.h>
3  #include <stdlib.h>
4
5  void swap5 (int * a,  int * b)
6  {
7    int k = a;
8    a = b;
9    b = k;
10  }
11
12  int main (int argc  ,char * * argv)
13  {
14    int u;
15    int t;
16    u = 17;
17    t = -96;
18    printf  ("before␣swap5:␣␣u␣=␣%d␣,␣t␣=␣%d␣\n"  , u , t);
19    swap5 (& u  , * t);
20    printf  ("after␣␣swap5:␣␣u␣=␣%d␣,␣t␣=␣%d␣\n"  , u , t);
21    return EXIT_SUCCESS;
22  }
```

4.9.6   15,552 Variations

There are many variations of the **swap** function. To be specific, there are 15,552 variations and only one of them is correct. Some variations have syntax errors (wrong types) and some of them do not swap the values in the **main** function. Let me explain why there are so many variations. First, this is the correct **swap** function and the correct way to call it:

```
1  void swap (int * k, int * m)
2  {
3    int s;
4    s = * k;
5    * k = * m;
6    * m = s;
7  }
```

```
8
9    void f(void)
10   {
11      int a = 83;
12      int c = -74;
13      swap (& a, & c);
14   }
```

How do we get 15,552 variations? In the first line, there are two options for k:
  1. int k
  2. int * k
int & k is illegal so it is not considered.

Similarly, there are two options for m and two options for s. So far, there are 8 variations of the function up to the third line. Next, consider the number of options for s = k at the fourth line; there are six options:
  1. s = * k;
  2. s = & k;
  3. s = k;
  4. * s = * k;
  5. * s = & k;
  6. * s = k;
& s = is illegal so it is not considered.

Similarly, there are also six options for k = m and another six options for m = s. So far there are $8 \times 6 \times 6 \times 6 = 1,728$ variations for swap function.

From the main function, calling swap has three options for using a in the thirteenth line:
  1. a
  2. & a
  3. * a

Similarly, there are another three options in using c. Thus, in total, there are $1,728 \times 3 \times 3 = 15,552$ variations.

Among all these variations, if the swap function is called without using addresses, the changes are lost when the swap function finishes. In other words, regardless what happens inside swap, calling swap in this way,

```
1    swap (a, c);
```

is always wrong.

4.10   Answers

4.10.1   Swap Function 1

There are no syntax errors or warnings but this function does not swap u and k. This is the output of the program:

```
before swap1: u = 17 , t = -96
after  swap1: u = 17 , t = -96
```

4.10.2 Swap Function 2

There are no syntax errors or warnings but this function does not swap u and k. This is the call stack after finishing line 7, before `swap2` finishes. The values of a and b are swapped but the values of u and t remain unchanged.

Frame	Symbol	Address	Value
	k	105	100
	b	104	100
swap	a	103	101
	Return Location	102	line 18
	t	101	−96
main	u	100	17

This is the output of the program:

```
before swap1: u = 17 , t = -96
after  swap1: u = 17 , t = -96
```

4.10.3 Swap Function 3

There are no syntax errors or warnings. The problem is the seventh line. This line assigns b's value to a's value. This is the call stack after finishing the seventh line:

Frame	Symbol	Address	Value
	k	105	17
	b	104	101
swap	a	103	101
	Return Location	102	line 18
	t	101	−96
main	u	100	17

This is the output of the program. Both u and t are 17, and the value −96 has been discarded.

```
before swap3: u = 17 , t = -96
after  swap3: u = 17 , t = 17
```

4.10.4 Swap Function 4

The eighth line has a problem: k is an integer and adding * in front of k is invalid. This program will not compile.

4.10.5 Swap Function 5

The sixth line has a problem: k is an integer but a is a pointer. It is invalid to assign a pointer's value to an integer. The eighteenth line also has a problem: t is an integer and adding * in front of t is invalid.

Chapter 5

Writing and Testing Programs

This chapter uses programming problems to illustrate how to use pointers and how to test programs for correctness.

5.1 Distinct Array Elements

This program has a function with two arguments: an array of integers and the number of array elements. The function returns 1 if the array elements are distinct, and the function returns 0 if two or more elements store the same value.

```
1  int areDistinct(int * arr, int len)
2  // arr stores the address of the first element
3  // len is the number of elements
4  // If len is zero, the function returns 1.
```

The main purpose of this problem is to teach important concepts and tools for writing larger programs. This problem also teaches how to take advantage of the `make` command to compile and test programs more efficiently. This problem teaches the following important concepts:

- function declarations and definitions
- compiling and linking
- the `make` command in Linux

5.1.1   main **Function**

Consider the main function of this program:

```
1  // main.c
2  #include <stdio.h>
3  #include <stdlib.h>
4  #include <string.h>
5  int areDistinct(int * arr, int len);
6  int main(int argc, char * * argv)
7  {
8     if (argc != 2)
9       {
10         return EXIT_FAILURE;
11      }
12     FILE * fptr = fopen(argv[1], "r");
13     if (fptr == NULL)
14       {
15         return EXIT_FAILURE;
16      }
17     int length = 0;
18     int value;
19     while (fscanf(fptr, "%d", & value) == 1)
20       {
21         length ++;
22      }
23     fseek (fptr, 0, SEEK_SET);
24     int * arr = malloc(length * sizeof(int));
25     length = 0;
26     while (fscanf(fptr, "%d", & (arr[length])) == 1)
27       {
28         length ++;
29      }
30     fclose (fptr);
31     int dist = areDistinct(arr, length);
32     printf("The elements are");
33     if (dist == 0)
34       {
35         printf(" not");
36      }
37     printf(" distinct.\n");
38     free (arr);
39     return EXIT_SUCCESS;
40  }
```

The main function has two input arguments: an integer (int) called argc and a pointer to pointers of characters (char * *) called argv. Do not worry about the second argument for now. The names of the arguments are argc and argv. In theory you could change these names; however, this is inadvisable because everyone uses argc and argv. Changing their names would not improve the program in any way. The prefix arg means arguments. Section 1.1 explains that the value of argc means the count of arguments that are passed to the program. We will explain argv in a later chapter after explaining strings.

The condition at line 8 is used to ensure that the program has two arguments. If two arguments are not supplied to the program, then it will not proceed to line 12. The first argument is always the name of the program. By requiring two arguments, one additional argument can specify the name of a file that contains data that we want to process. If the program does not have exactly two arguments, the program stops by returning `EXIT_FAILURE`. This symbol is defined in `stdlib.h`. When the `main` function returns, this program terminates. `EXIT_FAILURE` means that the program failed to accomplish what the program is supposed to do. For now, we can ignore the program between lines 12 and line 30 and also line 38. This part of the program is about reading data from a file, and will be explained in detail in a later chapter.

Line 31 calls the `areDistinct` function. Dependent on the result of line 31, this program prints either "The elements are distinct." or "The elements are not distinct." Finally, the program returns `EXIT_SUCCESS` because it successfully determined whether or not the values are distinct.

The fifth line *declares* the `areDistinct` function so that `main` knows about it. This declaration says that the `areDistinct` function returns an integer and takes two arguments. The first argument is a pointer to integer, and the second argument is an integer. Without this declaration, the `gcc` compiler would not know anything about `areDistinct`. If the fifth line is removed, then `gcc` will give the following warning message

```
warning: implicit declaration of function 'areDistinct'
```

To summarize the `main` function:

- The program checks the value of `argc` to determine whether or not an additional input argument is given.
- If the program cannot accomplish what it is supposed to do, the `main` function returns `EXIT_FAILURE`.
- The `main` function must include `stdlib.h` because that is where `EXIT_FAILURE` and `EXIT_SUCCESS` are defined.
- The program terminates when the `main` function uses `return`.
- The `main` function returns `EXIT_SUCCESS` after it accomplishes its work.

5.1.2 `areDistinct` Function

The fifth line in `main.c` declares the `areDistinct` function; however, the function has not been *defined* yet. A function's definition *implements* the function. Some people also call a function's definition the function's *body*. A function's definition must have a pair of { and } enclosing the body. In contrast, a function's declaration replaces the body (i.e., everything between { and }) by a semicolon.

```
1  /* declaration */
2  int areDistinct(int * arr, int len);
3
4  /* definition */
5  int areDistinct(int * arr, int len)
6  {
7      // some code
8  }
```

Below is the code listing for the definition of the `areDistinct` function. It goes through the elements in the input array one by one, and checks whether any element after this current one has the same value. Checking the elements before the current element is unnecessary, because they have already been checked in earlier iterations. If two elements have the same value, the function returns 0. If no match is found after going through all of the array elements, then this function returns 1. If `len` is zero, the function does not enter the for-loop at the sixth line, goes directly to line 18, and then returns 1.

```
1   // aredistinct.c
2   int areDistinct(int * arr, int len)
3   {
4     int ind1;
5     int ind2;
6     for (ind1 = 0; ind1 < len; ind1 ++)
7       {
8         for (ind2 = ind1 + 1; ind2 < len; ind2 ++)
9           {
10            if (arr[ind1] == arr[ind2])
11              {
12                // found two elements with the same value
13                return 0;
14              }
15          }
16       }
17     // have not found two elements of the same value
18     return 1;
19  }
```

5.1.3 Compiling and Linking

The functions `main` and `areDistinct` are in two different files. Large programming projects use multiple files—perhaps dozens or hundreds, or even thousands. There are many reasons for using so many files when writing large programs. For example,

- Large programming projects require teams of people, and it is easier for individuals to work on individual files.
- A large program is developed in many phases, and files are added in each phase.
- In good software design, each file should implement a set of closely related features.
- If two features are sufficiently different, then they should reside in two different files. This approach makes it easy to manage and navigate large amounts of code.

Attempting to write a large program in a single file would be equivalent to putting everything into a single drawer: It is messy and creates problems every time someone wants to find, add, or remove anything in the drawer. Section 1.1 explained how to use `gcc` to convert a source file into an executable file. It can also be used to convert two or more source files into one executable. This is the command in a Linux Terminal:

$ gcc aredistinct.c main.c -o prog

This command creates an executable file called `prog`. Section 2.7 suggests that `gcc` should always be run with `-Wall -Wshadow`. Furthermore, if you want to run gdb or ddd, then you must also add `-g` after `gcc`. The new command is

$ gcc -g -Wall -Wshadow aredistinct.c main.c -o prog

As more and more files are added, this command becomes too long to type. Running `gcc` may take a rather long time because every source (`.c`) file is recompiled every time.

This seems acceptable for two files, but becomes a serious problem for larger projects. Recompiling every file can take minutes, or even hours.

Fortunately it is possible to *compile* individual files separately. When a source file is compiled, an intermediate file is created. This intermediate file is called an *object* file and it has the `.o` extension. Once an object file has been created for the corresponding source file, gcc has a special procedure, called *linking*, for creating an executable file. The following shows the commands.

```
$ gcc -g -Wall -Wshadow -c aredistinct.c
$ gcc -g -Wall -Wshadow -c main.c
$ gcc -g -Wall -Wshadow ardistinct.o main.o -o prog
```

The first `gcc` command compiles `aredistinct.c` and creates the object file whose name is `aredistinct.o`. Adding `-c` after `gcc` tells `gcc` to create an object file. The object file has the same name as the source file, except the extension is changed from `.c` to `.o`. Similarly, the second command compiles `main.c` and creates `main.o`. The third command takes the two object files and creates the executable file. This command *links* the two files because the input files are object files and uses `-o` for the name of the executable output file. Please notice that the last command has no `-c`.

To see how this saves time, note that `aredistinct.o` only needs to be updated if `aredistinct.c` is changed. Similarly, `main.o` only needs to be updated if `main.c` changes. If either of the object files change, then the link command (the third command above) needs to be rerun to generate the updated executable. Avoiding the unnecessary compilation saves time. This is called *separate compilation*. Even if the advantages of separate compilation are compelling, typing the three commands is even more awkward and tedious than typing one command. It certainly is inefficient to type

```
$ gcc -g -Wall -Wshadow -c main.c
$ gcc -g -Wall -Wshadow ardistinct.o main.o -o prog
```

whenever `main.c` is modified. These commands are too long to type over and over again. Moreover, it is necessary to keep track of which files have been changed and need recompilation. Fortunately, special build tools have been developed to take care of these issues. The `make` program in Linux is one popular tool for this purpose.

5.1.4 `make`

The `make` program in Linux takes a special input file whose name is `Makefile`. The main purpose of the `Makefile` is to decide which files need to be recompiled. The decisions are based on the modification time of the object files and the relevant `.c` files. The object file `aredistinct.o` depends on `aredistinct.c`. If `aredistinct.c` has a newer modification date (or time) than `aredistinct.o`, then `make` recompiles `aredistinct.c`. This is expressed below in the `Makefile`.

```
1  aredistinct.o: aredistinct.c
2      gcc -g -Wall -Wshadow -c aredistinct.c
```

The first line uses `:` to indicate dependence—`aredistinct.o` depends on `aredistinct.c`. If `aredistinct.o` does not exist or `aredistinct.c` is newer than `aredistinct.o`, then the command in the next line will be executed. This command uses `gcc` to recompile `aredistinct.c` and to generate `aredistinct.o`. A **Tab key** is needed before `gcc` at the second line. In `make` Tab cannot be replaced by spaces.

Note that `Makefile` is the name of a file that `make` looks for when it runs. You can tell `make` to use any file by adding `-f name`:

$ make -f name

In this case, the `make` program uses `name` as the input, instead of `Makefile`. Most people just use `Makefile` because it is the default, and everyone understands what the file is for. The following `Makefile` includes the dependence of `main.o` and `main.c`.

```
1  aredistinct.o: aredistinct.c
2      gcc -g -Wall -Wshadow -c aredistinct.c
3
4  main.o: main.c
5      gcc -g -Wall -Wshadow -c main.c
6
7  # This is a comment
```

If a line is blank (e.g., line 3), it is discarded by the `make` command. In `Makefile`, anything after # is treated as a comment and ignored. You can use symbols in `Makefile`. Symbols are usually uppercase letters. After creating a symbol, it can be expressed by using $() to enclose the symbol. The following `Makefile` replaces `gcc -g -Wall -Wshadow` using two symbols `GCC` and `CFLAGS`.

```
1  GCC = gcc
2  CFLAGS = -g -Wall -Wshadow
3
4  aredistinct.o: aredistinct.c
5      $(GCC) $(CFLAGS) -c aredistinct.c  # another comment
6
7  main.o: main.c
8      $(GCC) $(CFLAGS) -c main.c
```

Why are symbols useful? A general principle in software design is to use symbols to express some common things. If changes are needed later, these modifications can be made in only one place. For example, the `Makefile` could be modified to use another compiler, and only the first line needs to be updated. There is another common reason for updating a `Makefile`. When a program has been completed and is ready for customers. In this case, we want to replace `-g` with `-O`. Please notice that the letter is the uppercase `O` for optimization, not zero. The former adds debugging information to the program. The latter optimizes the program and makes it faster. Replacing `-g` by `-O` can make a program noticeably faster. We only need to update the `CFLAGS` symbol. By using a single symbol, we ensure that the change is consistent throughout the entire `Makefile`.

```
1  GCC = gcc
2  CFLAGS = -O -Wall -Wshadow # replace -g by -O
3
4  # This is a comment
5  aredistinct.o: aredistinct.c
6      $(GCC) $(CFLAGS) -c aredistinct.c  # another comment
7
8  main.o: main.c
9      $(GCC) $(CFLAGS) -c main.c
```

The `Makefile` still needs the command to link the two object files together. This is placed below the symbols in the `Makefile`.

```
1  GCC = gcc
2  CFLAGS = -g -Wall -Wshadow
```

```
3
4  prog: aredistinct.o main.o
5          $(GCC) $(CFLAGS) aredistinct.o main.o -o prog # no -c
6
7  aredistinct.o: aredistinct.c
8          $(GCC) $(CFLAGS) -c aredistinct.c
9
10 main.o: main.c
11         $(GCC) $(CFLAGS) -c main.c
```

The fourth line says the executable `prog` depends on both `aredistinct.o` and `main.o`. If either object file is newer than `prog`, then the executable needs to be rebuilt by linking the two object files. Line 7 determines whether `aredistinct.o` needs to be regenerated. Line 10 determines whether `main.o` needs to be regenerated.

In a Linux Terminal, type

$ make

The output is

```
gcc -g -Wall -Wshadow  -c aredistinct.c
gcc -g -Wall -Wshadow  -c main.c
gcc -g -Wall -Wshadow  aredistinct.o main.o -o prog
```

If you type make in the Terminal again, the output is

```
make: 'prog' is up to date.
```

If you change `main.c` (add a comment somewhere) and type `make`, the output is

```
gcc -g -Wall -Wshadow  -c main.c
gcc -g -Wall -Wshadow  aredistinct.o main.o -o prog
```

As you can see, `main.o` is regenerated but `aredistinct.o` is not regenerated.

We have now solved both problems described above in building programs: (1) we have replaced the long awkward commands with `make` and (2) `make` automatically uses dependencies to determine which files need to be recompiled, thus reducing the amount of time required to build large projects. There are three dependence rules in this `Makefile`: `prog`, `aredistinct.o`, and `main.o`. When `make` is typed, we tell the `make` program to check the first rule, i.e., the rule at the top of the `Makefile`. If we put the `prog` dependence and the corresponding action (lines 4 and 5) lower in `Makefile`, we need to explicitly tell `make` to check the `prog` rule first, as follows:

$ make prog

5.2 Test Using `Makefile`

A `Makefile` can be used for many more purposes. One common usage is to test programs. Before explaining how to test programs, please note the following important rules on testing programs:

- It is possible to test a program and demonstrate that the program is incorrect.
- It is almost impossible to test a program and demonstrate that the program is correct.
- If a test fails (assuming the test is valid), then we know that the program is wrong.
- If a program passes a test, what do we know about the program? Not much.

This may seem puzzling. If a program passes many tests, then the program must be correct, right? In a way, this is like the theory of "black swans". If we observe a thousand white swans, we do not know whether black swans exist or not. Similarly, passing a thousand tests does not tell us whether a program is correct. In contrast, if we see one black swan, we know it exists. If a program fails one test, the program has a problem.

The truth is that testing is extremely hard (and important). Passing many tests gives you some confidence, but no guarantee. A non-trivial program can have many possible test cases. It is impossible to test so many cases. Even though testing is imperfect, testing is still useful in developing programs. The following explains how to develop a strategy for testing.

5.2.1   Generating Test Cases

To test a program, we need test cases. To test `areDistinct`, we need different test cases:
- `len` is zero or not.
- `arr` either contains distinct elements or not.

At least three test cases are needed:
1. an empty file making `len` zero
2. a file with distinct numbers
3. a file with duplicate numbers

Creating the first test case is easy: Make an empty file. The `touch` command in Linux can create an empty file. The second and the third test cases can be created by hand. Alternatively, test cases can be developed using an on-line random number generator, saving the results to a file. In this case, how do we know whether the numbers are distinct? The `sort` and `uniq` commands in Linux can be used for this. The first command orders the numbers and the second command tells whether the sorted numbers are unique or not. If we add `-d` after `uniq`, the command displays which numbers duplicate. We chain the two commands together using a *pipe*. The pipe takes the output of the `sort` command, and makes it the input to the `uniq` command. In a Linux Terminal:

```
$ sort filename | uniq -d
```

`filename` is the name of the file that stores the random numbers. If the numbers in this file are distinct, nothing appears. If some numbers duplicate, then the duplicate numbers are shown on the screen.

5.2.2   Redirecting Output

Section 1.2 explained how to *redirect* a program's output. Instead of printing "The elements are distinct." or "The elements are not distinct." on the computer screen, the output can be saved to a file. The following command redirects the output to the file whose name is `outputs/output0`:

```
$ ./prog inputs/input0 > outputs/output0
```

Please check that the directory `outputs` exists before running this command. If it does not exist, then use this command to create the directory:

```
$ mkdir outputs
```

5.2.3 Use `diff` to Compare Output

Next, we use the `diff` command to compare the expected output with the output of the program. Section 1.2 mentions this command and now you know how to use it.

$ diff expected/expected0 outputs/output0

If these two files are identical, then nothing appears on the computer screen. This means that the program generates the correct output for this test case. If these two files are different, then the difference is shown on the screen. We can add `-w` after `diff` to ignore differences caused only by spaces.

5.2.4 Adding Tests to `Makefile`

As explained earlier, `make` can reduce the amount of typing, but it is really much more than that. With `make` we can create jobs with dependent jobs, and only the required jobs are rerun when files are edited. We can use the scheme to add a testing job into our `Makefile`.

```
1  test0: prog
2      ./prog inputs/input0 > outputs/output0
3      diff expected/expected0 outputs/output0
```

This is another dependence rule. If this dependence rule is not the first rule in the `Makefile`, we need to type:

$ make test0

This dependence follows the same rule mentioned earlier even though `test0` is not a file. Because `test0` is not a file, its time can never be later than the time of `prog`. As a result, the following two commands (`./prog` and `diff`) will always be executed. Before executing these two commands, `make` checks the dependence of `prog` because it is at the right side of the colon. The `make` program finds this rule in the `Makefile`,

```
1  prog: aredistinct.o main.o
```

and `make` compares the time of these three files. If `prog` is older, then the executable file `prog` will be regenerated. Before regenerating the executable file, `make` finds another two rules in the `Makefile`:

```
1  aredistinct.o : aredistinct.c
2  main.o : main.c
```

Each object file will be regenerated if it is older than the corresponding `.c` file. Because of these dependences, when you type:

$ make test0

the executable file `prog` will be regenerated if either `.c` file has changed since the last time `make` was invoked. More rules can be added to the `Makefile` for running different cases:

```
1  test1: prog
2      ./prog inputs/input1 > outputs/output1
3      diff expected/expected1 outputs/output1
4
5  test2: prog
6      ./prog inputs/input2 > outputs/output2
```

```
7          diff expected/expected2 outputs/output2
8
9    test3: prog
10         ./prog inputs/input3 > outputs/output3
11         diff expected/expected3 outputs/output3
12
13   test4: prog
14         ./prog inputs/input4 > outputs/output4
15         diff expected/expected4 outputs/output4
```

To test each case, type

> $ make test1
> $ make test2
> $ make test3
> $ make test4

Another rule can be used to test all test cases at once:

```
1    testall: test0 test1 test2 test3 test4
```

Finally, developers usually add a special rule that deletes computer-generated files:

```
1    clean:
2          /bin/rm -f *.o prog outputs/*
```

When we type

> $ make clean

all of the object files (*.o), the executable prog, and the output files outputs/* are deleted. This is the full Makefile after adding all of these rules:

```
1    GCC = gcc
2    CFLAGS = -g -Wall -Wshadow
3
4    prog: aredistinct.o main.o
5          $(GCC) $(CFLAGS) aredistinct.o main.o -o prog # no -c
6
7    aredistinct.o: aredistinct.c
8          $(GCC) $(CFLAGS) -c aredistinct.c
9
10   main.o: main.c
11         $(GCC) $(CFLAGS) -c main.c
12
13   testall: test0 test1 test2 test3 test4
14
15   test0: prog
16         ./prog inputs/input0 > outputs/output0
17         diff expected/expected0 outputs/output0
18
19   test1: prog
20         ./prog inputs/input1 > outputs/output1
21         diff expected/expected1 outputs/output1
22
23   test2: prog
```

```
24          ./prog inputs/input2 > outputs/output2
25          diff expected/expected2 outputs/output2
26
27 test3: prog
28          ./prog inputs/input3 > outputs/output3
29          diff expected/expected3 outputs/output3
30
31 test4: prog
32          ./prog inputs/input4 > outputs/output4
33          diff expected/expected4 outputs/output4
34
35 clean:
36          /bin/rm -f *.o prog outputs/*
```

5.3   Invalid Memory Access

In Section 2.3.5, I said "if an array has n elements, the valid indexes are 0, 1, 2, ..., n−1." What happens if we use an invalid index? The simple answer is **the program's behavior is undefined**. That means anything could happen, and it will not be predictable. If the index is incorrect, the program will access a memory address that does not belong to the array. Remember that as a programmer, you have no control over which memory addresses your program can use. We do not know what is stored at an address outside the range of the array. Consider this program:

```c
1  /*
2   * wrongindex.c
3   */
4  #include <stdio.h>
5  #include <stdlib.h>
6  #include <string.h>
7  int main(int argc, char * * argv)
8  {
9      int x = -2;
10     int arr[] = {0, 1, 2, 3, 4};
11     int y = 15;
12     printf("&x        = %p, &y        = %p\n", & x, & y);
13     printf("& arr[0] = %p, & arr[4] = %p\n", & arr[0],
14             & arr[4]);
15     printf("x = %d, y = %d\n", x, y);
16     arr[-1] = 7;
17     arr[5]  = -23;
18     printf("x = %d, y = %d\n", x, y);
19     arr[6]  = 108;
20     printf("x = %d, y = %d\n", x, y);
21     arr[7]  = -353;
22     printf("x = %d, y = %d\n", x, y);
23     return EXIT_SUCCESS;
24 }
```

An array is created at line 10 and it has 5 elements. The valid indexes are 0, 1, 2, 3, and 4. Lines 12 and 13 print the addresses of x, y, and the array. Lines 16, 17, 19, and 21 use incorrect indexes. If we compile, link, and execute this program, we may find that the values of x or y are changed because we are using incorrect indexes. This is not guaranteed, and the results will depend on the specific compiler. This is the output when I run this program:

```
& x       = 0x7fffcabf4e68, & y      = 0x7fffcabf4e6c
& arr[0] = 0x7fffcabf4e50, & arr[4] = 0x7fffcabf4e60
x = -2, y = 15
x = -2, y = 15
x = 108, y = 15
x = 108, y = -353
```

As we can see, x has changed because of this assignment:

```
19      arr[6]   = 108;
```

Similarly, y is changed because of this assignment:

```
21      arr[7]   = -353;
```

In this example, the `gcc` compiler has reordered the local variables in the call stack. The addresses of x and y are larger than the addresses of the array elements. Thus, x and y are changed when the indexes are 6 and 7 respectively. The program uses addresses that are given to it by the operating system. If we run the above program again, we will likely see different addresses for x and y. It is possible that neither x nor y, but something else, is changed due to using the invalid indexes.

The real problem is that the program's behavior is undefined. What does this mean more precisely? The effects of wrong indexes may change when the program runs on different machines. Sometimes, it seems nothing is wrong, even though there is a pernicious error in the code. Sometimes, the values of x or y may be changed. Sometimes, the program stops with the message "Segmentation fault (core dumped)." This means that the program intends to read from or write to a memory address that does not belong to the program. Modern computers usually run many programs at once. Each program is given part of the memory. If one program tries to read from or write to a wrong address, the operating system may stop the program. This protects the other programs running on the same computer.

Be careful about the word "may" here. The operating system does not keep track of every memory address. Instead, the operating system uses "pages" as a unit. The size of a page of memory varies on the operating system; 4KB is common. If the wrong address is within a page given to a program, then the operating system will not stop the program. That means that a program may modify a variable within a valid page unintentionally without causing a segmentation fault. In this example, x and y are changed. It is called a segmentation fault, and not a page fault, because some processors organize memory by variable sized "segments". Page and segment may be used together: A segment may contain multiple pages. In fact, "page fault" is already used in the context of virtual memory. Thus, the name "segmentation fault" remains. If the wrong address is outside the program's segments, then the operating system will stop the program. Try replacing

```
21      arr[7]   = -353;
```

by

```
21      arr[7000]   = -353;
```

compile, link, and run the program again. We will very likely see "Segmentation fault (core dumped)". The index 7000 is too large and probably outside the page given by the operating system.

5.4   Using `valgrind` to Check Memory Access Errors

In Linux, a program called `valgrind` can help detect problems of accessing invalid addresses. Please check whether `valgrind` has been installed on your computer. To use `valgrind`, add

$ valgrind –tool=memcheck –verbose

before the command running the program. For example,

$ gcc -g -Wall -Wshadow wrongindex.c -o wrongindex
$ valgrind –tool=memcheck –verbose ./wrongindex

The first line uses `gcc` to create the executable file called `wrongindex`. To execute this program, type `./wrongindex`. The second line adds `valgrind --tool=memcheck --verbose` in front of `./wrongindex`. This will cause the program to be run *within* `valgrind`, which in turn carefully checks every memory access to make sure that it is valid. The output will include the following message:

```
Invalid write of size 4
at 0x4005D5: main (wrongindex.c:20)
```

This message says that something is wrong at the 20th line of the program. Sometimes `valgrind` prints a lot to the computer screen. It is useful to direct `valgrind`'s output to a log file, like so:

$ valgrind –tool=memcheck –verbose –log-file=valgrindlog ./wrongindex

Typing this long command repeatedly is too much work, and the command can be put in the `Makefile`. This is the new `Makefile` for the program that determines whether an array has distinct elements:

```
1  GCC = gcc
2  CFLAGS = -g -Wall -Wshadow
3  VALGRIND = valgrind --tool=memcheck --verbose --log-file
4
5
6  prog: aredistinct.o main.o
7          $(GCC) $(CFLAGS) aredistinct.o main.o -o prog # no -c
8
9  aredistinct.o: aredistinct.c
10          $(GCC) $(CFLAGS) -c aredistinct.c
11
12  main.o: main.c
13          $(GCC) $(CFLAGS) -c main.c
14
```

```
15   testall: test0 test1 test2 test3 test4
16
17   test0: prog
18           ./prog inputs/input0 > outputs/output0
19           diff expected/expected0 outputs/output0
20           $(VALGRIND)=log0 ./prog inputs/input0 > /dev/null
21
22   test1: prog
23           ./prog inputs/input1 > outputs/output1
24           diff expected/expected1 outputs/output1
25           $(VALGRIND)=log1 ./prog inputs/input0 > /dev/null
26
27   test2: prog
28           ./prog inputs/input2 > outputs/output2
29           diff expected/expected2 outputs/output2
30           $(VALGRIND)=log2 ./prog inputs/input0 > /dev/null
31
32   test3: prog
33           ./prog inputs/input3 > outputs/output3
34           diff expected/expected3 outputs/output3
35           $(VALGRIND)=log3 ./prog inputs/input0 > /dev/null
36
37   test4: prog
38           ./prog inputs/input4 > outputs/output4
39           diff expected/expected4 outputs/output4
40           $(VALGRIND)=log4 ./prog inputs/input0 > /dev/null
41
42   clean:
43           /bin/rm -f *.o prog outputs/* log*
```

The third line creates a symbol for the `valgrind` command. What is `/dev/null` in the 20th line? Running `prog` will produce the output "The elements are distinct." or "The elements are not distinct." This output has already been stored in `outputs/output0` in line 18. Thus, in line 20, the output is discarded. In Linux, `/dev/null` is a special file that simply discards everything put into this special file. It is the "black hole" in Linux. Line 20 says "ignore any output produced by running `prog`". After making these changes we can type

$ make testall

and a lot of commands will run. The outputs of `valgrind` are stored in the log files. We can use the `grep` command to check whether any error has been detected by `valgrind`:

$ grep ERROR *log*

If the result is

`ERROR SUMMARY: 0 errors from 0 contexts`

`valgrind` has not detected any problems.

Even though `valgrind` is helpful identifying which lines cause problems, `valgrind` is not perfect. Sometimes, a program has problems and `valgrind` fails to detect them. This happens because `valgrind` itself has limitations. The limitations may occur when running certain system calls to talk directly to hardware. Please read the `valgrind` document for more information on its limitations. For example, *On x86 and amd64, there is no support for 3DNow! instructions. ... Valgrind's signal simulation is not as robust as it could be.* ... Please understand that `valgrind` is another tool that can help, but not replace, good software developers. In many cases, `valgrind` can detect memory problems. When `valgrind` says that a program has no invalid memory accesses, it is still possible that the program has problems not tested by the specific test cases. It is also possible that `valgrind` misses an error because of its limitations. How can you prevent memory access errors? When you write programs, be careful how the indexes are calculated. It is important to read your code before testing it, because testing can only determine if a program is wrong.

Some programming languages, such as Java, check the index every time an array element is read or written. If a wrong index is detected, an *exception* is thrown. This guarantees that every invalid index is detected. However, checking indexes slows down the program. C's design principle is to do only what a program says and nothing more. This is a trade-off in the designs of programming languages.

5.5   Test Coverage

Ideally, tests should check every line in the program. If some lines are not checked, it is possible these lines contain mistakes. Checking every line means that every `if` statement (and other conditions) is entered in some test cases. If a line is never tested, it is possible that tests overlook the possible scenarios. It is also possible that the program has a defect in its logic. Consider this example:

```
1    if ((x < 0) && (x > 400))
2    {
3        vx = -vx;
4    }
```

This is part of a computer game of a bouncing ball in a court whose width is 400. The intent of this code is to change the horizontal velocity `vx` when the ball hits the left wall as `x < 0` or hits the right wall as `x > 400`. What is wrong with this code? The intention is

```
1    if ((x < 0) || (x > 400))
2    {
3        vx = -vx;
4    }
```

However, the mistake is using `&&` (and) instead of `||` (or). Since it is impossible for `x` to be smaller than zero and at the same time greater than 400,

```
3        vx = -vx;
```

is never executed.

A programmer needs to read code carefully and detect these types of errors. There are tools that can help find these types of problems, and one such tool examines test coverage. It determines whether a particular line of code has been executed *for a particular test input.* Here is an example:

```
1    /*
2      coverage.c
```

```
3      purpose: a condition that can never be true
4    */
5    #include <stdio.h>
6    #include <stdlib.h>
7    int main(int argc, char * argv[])
8    {
9        int x;
10       int vx = 10;
11       for (x = -100; x < 1000; x ++)
12         {
13           if ((x < 0) && (x > 400))
14             {
15               vx = -vx;
16               printf("change␣direction\n");
17             }
18         }
19       return EXIT_SUCCESS;
20   }
```

The tool gcov finds that the two lines

```
15           vx = -vx;
16           printf("change␣direction\n");
```

are never executed. This tool works in collaboration with gcc, and additional arguments are required when running gcc:

$ gcc -g -Wall -Wshadow -fprofile-arcs -ftest-coverage coverage.c -o cov

The executable file is called cov. Next, run the ./cov program:

$ ./cov

Two output files are generated: coverage.gcda and coverage.gcno. We can now run the gcov command.

$ gcov coverage.c

The output is

```
File 'coverage.c'
Lines executed:71.43% of 7
coverage.c:creating 'coverage.c.gcov'
```

Another new file called coverage.c.gcov is generated. Here is the content of this file:

```
1           -:    0:Source:coverage.c
2           -:    0:Graph:coverage.gcno
3           -:    0:Data:coverage.gcda
4           -:    0:Runs:1
5           -:    0:Programs:1
6           -:    1:/*
7           -:    2:  file: coverage.c
8           -:    3:  purpose: a condition that can never be true
9           -:    4:*/
```

```
      -:      5:#include <stdio.h>
      -:      6:#include <stdlib.h>
      1:      7:int main(int argc, char * argv[])
      -:      8:{
      -:      9:   int x;
      1:     10:   int vx = 10;
   1101:     11:   for (x = -100; x < 1000; x ++)
      -:     12:     {
   1100:     13:       if ((x < 0) && (x > 400))
      -:     14:         {
  #####:     15:           vx = -vx;
  #####:     16:           printf("change direction\n");
      -:     17:         }
      -:     18:     }
      1:     19:   return EXIT_SUCCESS;
      -:     20:}
```

Lines 15 and 16 are marked by **#####** because these two lines are never executed. This tool can be used with complex programs to determine whether particular lines are never executed. If typing these commands is too much work, then it is possible to write the Makefile such that everything is handled by `make` every time the program is modified.

```
# Makefile for gcov
GCC = gcc -g -Wall -Wshadow -fprofile-arcs -ftest-coverage
cov: coverage.c
        $(GCC) coverage.c -o cov
        ./cov
        gcov coverage.c
        grep "#" coverage.c.gcov
clean:
        rm -f *.gcov *.gcno cov
```

If we type `make`, this is the output:

```
gcc -g -Wall -Wshadow -fprofile-arcs -ftest-coverage coverage.c -o cov
./cov
gcov coverage.c
File 'coverage.c'
Lines executed:71.43% of 7
coverage.c:creating 'coverage.c.gcov'
grep "#" coverage.c.gcov
      -:      5:#include <stdio.h>
      -:      6:#include <stdlib.h>
  #####:     15:   vx = -vx;
  #####:     16:   printf("change direction\n");
```

This `Makefile` also has an option called `clean`. Typing `make clean` deletes the file generated by `gcov`. If `gcov` reports that some lines are never executed, then the problem may come from the program, as shown in this case. Sometimes, the problem comes from the test inputs. Designing good test inputs is not trivial and some books discuss in detail how to design test inputs. Here are some suggestions.

Suppose you are writing a program searching whether a value is an element of a sorted array. You should design test inputs to cover the following scenarios:

- The value to search is an element of the array, somewhere in the middle of the array.
- The value is not an element of the array but between some elements in the array.
- The value is the same as the first element.
- The value is the same as the last element.
- The value is smaller than all elements.
- The value is larger than all elements.
- The array has only one element and the value is the same as this only element.
- The array is empty and the value is irrelevant.

Why is it necessary to test these different cases? Depending on the search algorithm and how the algorithm is implemented, one test case may fail to detect any problem. Creating good test inputs is not trivial. A different approach is called *formal verification* by proving a program is correct regardless of inputs. This is an advanced topic and will not be discussed here.

It is important to understand the limitation of test coverage. Low coverage means that the test inputs need improvement. However, high coverage is not necessarily better. A good test input is one that can detect problems in your programs. A simple program like the following can get 100% coverage:

```
1  #include <stdio.h>
2  #include <stdlib.h>
3  int main(int argc, char * argv[])
4  {
5    return EXIT_SUCCESS;
6  }
```

This program does not do anything. Pursuing high coverage should not be a goal in itself. The goal should be detecting and fixing problems.

It is necessary to further explain the limitations of testing. Some students believe that their programs are correct if the programs pass all test cases given by their professors. This is wrong for a very simple reason: It is difficult, almost impossible, to test all possible scenarios. Every `if` condition in a program creates two possible scenarios. Studies show that an `if` condition appears approximately every 10 to 15 lines of code (excluding comments). If your program has 15,000 lines, there are approximately 1,000 `if` conditions and 2^{1000} possible scenarios. How large is this number? The fastest computer in the world can perform about 50×10^{15} (2^{55}) operations per second. Testing 2^{1000} scenarios would simply be impossible.

5.6   Limit Core Size

In some cases, invalid memory accesses will cause a "core dumped" message. The core file is an old way to debug programs. Even though some people still use "core" to debug their programs, this book does not teach how to do that. A core file can occupy a lot of space on your disk. Use the following command to find whether a core file exists.

```
$ cd
$ find . -name "core"
```

The first command returns to your home directory. The second command finds any core file. Core files can be deleted by using the following command:

```
$ rm `find . -name "core"`
```

The command **rm** means remove. The earlier command **find . -name "core"** is now enclosed by single back-quotes. This is the quote mark ' sharing the key with ∼. This is not the single quote ' sharing the same key with the double quote ". The system settings can be modified to eliminate cores. If you use the C shell, you can type

$ limit coredumpsize 0

Limiting the core size prevents the generation of a core file. This does not prevent programs from making invalid memory accesses and having segmentation faults. We still have to correct our programs and remove invalid memory accesses.

5.7 Programs with Infinite Loops

If a program has an infinite loop (i.e., a loop that will never end) and the program prints something inside of the loop, then redirecting output to a file will create an infinitely large file. Here is an example of an infinite loop:

```
1  #define MAX_VALUE 100
2  int count = 0;
3  while (count < MAX_VALUE)
4  {
5      printf("some information\n");
6  }
```

This **while** loop will not end because **count** is zero and never changes. The program will print forever. When this occurs, use **Ctrl-c** to stop the program. This means pressing the **Ctrl** key (usually at the left lower corner of keyboard) and the **c** key at the same time. If you suspect that your program generates exceptionally large files, you can find the existence of these large files by using the following command in the Terminal:

$ cd
$ du -s * | sort -n

The first command returns to the home directory. The second line has two commands: **du -s *** displays the space occupied by each directory. The output is then sorted by treating the values as numbers (not strings). When sorting by numbers 10 comes after 9. When sorting by strings, 10 comes before 9. The vertical bar is called a *pipe* in Linux. It takes the output from the first program and makes it the input to the second program. By piping the directory sizes into **sort** we can easily see which directories occupy a lot of space. We can the enter these directories and run the **du** command again to quickly find large files.

Chapter 6

Strings

Strings can be created by putting characters between double quotations. For example,

- "Hello"
- "The C language"
- "write 2 programs"
- "symbols $%# can be part of a string"

A string can include alphabet characters, digits, spaces, and symbols. The examples above are string constants, which means that their data cannot be edited. In most cases, however, *string variables* are preferable to store strings whose values may change. For example, a program may ask a user to enter a name. The program cannot know the user's name in advance, and thus cannot be compiled with the name. From the program's point of view, the name is a string variable that gets initialized when it receives the name from the keyboard input.

6.1   Array of Characters

Because strings are commonly used, many newer languages, such as C++ and Java, have in-built string types. C, however, does not have a specific data type for strings. Instead, C uses *arrays of characters* for strings. Every string is an array of characters but an array of characters is not necessarily a string. To be a string, one element in the array must be the special character '\0'. This character terminates the string, and is called the *null terminator*. If an array has characters after the null terminator, those characters are not part of the string. Below are four arrays of characters but only **arr3** and **arr4** are strings because only those two arrays contain '\0'.

```
1  char arr1[] = {'T', 'h', 'i', 's', '␣', 'n', 'v', 't'};
2  char arr2[] = {'T', 'h', 'i', 's', '␣', 's', 't', 'r', 'O'};
3  char arr3[] = {'2', 'n', 'd', '␣', 's', 't', '\0', 'M'};
4  char arr4[] = {'C', '␣', 'P', '␣', '@', '-', '\0', '1', '8'};
```

The string in **arr3** is "2nd st". The character 'M' is an array element but it is not part of the string. Similarly, for **arr4**, the string is "C P @-". The trailing characters '1' and '8' are elements of the array but they are not part of the string. We do not need to put any number between [and] because **gcc** calculates the size for each array.

What is the difference between single quotation marks and double quotation marks? Single quotations enclose a single letter, such as 'M' and '@', and represent a character type. Double quotations enclose a string and the null terminator, '\0', is automatically added to the end of the string. Thus, the string stored in **arr3** is "2nd st" (no '\0') but it actually contains the element '\0'. Note that "W" is different from 'W'. The former uses double quotes and means a string, ending with a null terminator even though it is not shown. Hence, "W" actually means two characters. In contrast, 'W' is a character without a null terminator.

To explain this in another way, when storing a string of n characters, the array needs space for $n + 1$ characters. The additional character is used to store the terminating '\0'. For example, to store the string "Hello" (5 characters), we need to create an array of 6 elements:

```
char arr[6];            /* create an array with 6 characters */
arr[0] = 'H';
arr[1] = 'e';
arr[2] = 'l';
arr[3] = 'l';
arr[4] = 'o';
arr[5] = '\0';          /* remember to add '\0' */
```

Forgetting the null terminator '\0' is a common mistake. The null terminator is important because it indicates the end (and thus length) of the string. In the earlier examples, **arr3** and **arr4** were two arrays; **arr3** had 8 elements and **arr4** had 10 elements. However, if they are treated as strings, the length of each is only 6. The null terminator is **not** counted at part of the length. C provides a function **strlen** for calculating the length of strings. Before calling **strlen**, the program needs to include the file **string.h** because **strlen** and many string-related functions are declared in **string.h**.

```
// strlen.c
#include <stdio.h>
#include <stdlib.h>
#include <string.h>
int main(int argc, char * * argv)
{
  char str1[] = {'T','h','i','s',' ','n','v','t'};
  char str2[] = {'T','h','i','s',' ','s','t','r','0'};
  char str3[] = {'2','n','d',' ','s','t','\0','M'};
  char str4[] = {'C',' ','P',' ','@','-','\0','1','8','k'};
  char str5[6];
  int len3;
  int len4;
  int len5;
  str5[0] = 'H';
  str5[1] = 'e';
  str5[2] = 'l';
  str5[3] = 'l';
  str5[4] = 'o';
  str5[5] = '\0';
  len3 = strlen(str3);
```

```
22    len4 = strlen(str4);
23    len5 = strlen(str5);
24    printf("len3␣=␣%d,len4␣=␣%d,len5␣=␣%d\n",len3,len4,len5);
25    return EXIT_SUCCESS;
26  }
```

The output for this program is

```
len3 = 6, len4 = 6, len5 = 5
```

Why is '\0' so important? The string functions use it to determine the end of strings. The manual of **strlen** says the function, "*calculates the length of the string s, excluding the terminating null byte ('\0')*." In other words, '\0' is not counted. Although it is a simple function, the implementation of **strlen** is instructive. This is one way of implementing **strlen**:

```
1  int strlen(char *str)
2  {
3    int length = 0;
4    while ((* str) != '\0')
5      {
6        length++;
7        str ++;
8      }
9    return(length);
10 }
```

Section 4.6 explains that when calling a function, the argument **str** stores the address of the first array element. The sixth line increments an integer. The seventh line uses pointer arithmetic, as explained in Section 4.8. Consider **str5** and **len5** only; this is the call stack before calling **strlen**:

Frame	Symbol	Address	Value
	len5	106	garbage
	str5[5]	105	'\0'
	str5[4]	104	'o'
main	str5[3]	103	'l'
	str5[2]	102	'l'
	str5[1]	101	'e'
	str5[0]	100	'H'

Calling **strlen** pushes a new frame onto the call stack with the return location, the value address, the argument **str**, and the local variable **length**:

Frame	Symbol	Address	Value
	length	110	0
strlen	str	109	100
	value address	108	106
	return location	107	line 23
	len5	106	garbage
	str5[5]	105	'\0'
	str5[4]	104	'o'
main	str5[3]	103	'l'
	str5[2]	102	'l'
	str5[1]	101	'e'
	str5[0]	100	'H'

The argument `str` stores the address of the first array element and that address is 100. The fourth line of `strlen` reads the value stored at the address and it is the character 'H'. Since this is not a '\0', both `length` and `str` increment.

Frame	Symbol	Address	Value
	length	110	1
strlen	str	109	101
	value address	108	106
	return location	107	line 23
	len5	106	garbage
	str5[5]	105	'\0'
	str5[4]	104	'o'
main	str5[3]	103	'l'
	str5[2]	102	'l'
	str5[1]	101	'e'
	str5[0]	100	'H'

The value of `str` is the address of the second element and it is 101. The fourth line * `str` reads the value at address 101 and the value is 'e'. Since this is not '\0', both `length` and `str` increment again. Both `length` and `str` increment until `str` becomes 105, and the condition at the fourth line is false. The function returns 5, without counting '\0'.

Frame	Symbol	Address	Value
	len5	106	garbage $\rightarrow$ 5
	str5[5]	105	'\0'
	str5[4]	104	'o'
main	str5[3]	103	'l'
	str5[2]	102	'l'
	str5[1]	101	'e'
	str5[0]	100	'H'

The `strlen` function ignores everything after '\0', and thus the string lengths of `len3` and `len4` are 6 even though they have 8 and 10 elements.

6.2 String Functions in C

In addition to `strlen`, C provides many functions for processing strings. Each of these functions assumes that a string has '\0' as one of the elements. Below we introduce a few of these functions.

6.2.1 Copy: `strcpy`

This function copies a string into a pre-allocated memory region. This function takes two arguments: The first is the destination and the second is the source. Here is an example:

```
1  char src[] = {'H', 'e', 'l', 'l', 'o', '\0'};
2  char dest[6]; // must be 6 or larger
3  strcpy(dest, src);
```

There are five characters in "Hello" but one element is needed for the null terminator, '\0'. Thus, the destination's size needs to be six or larger. The `strcpy` function does **not** check whether the destination has enough space. You must ensure that there is enough space at the destination. The manual for `strcpy` says: "*The strcpy() function copies the string pointed to by src, including the terminating null byte ('\0'), to the buffer pointed to by dest. The strings may not overlap, and the destination string dest must be large enough to receive the copy.*"

Moreover, the manual says: "*If the destination string of a strcpy() is not large enough, then anything might happen. Overflowing fixed-length string buffers is a favorite cracker technique for taking complete control of the machine. Any time a program reads or copies data into a buffer, the program first needs to check that there's enough space. This may be unnecessary if you can show that overflow is impossible, but be careful: Programs can get changed over time, in ways that may make the impossible possible.*"

What does this mean? When writing a program that uses `strcpy`, the programmer must ensure that the destination has enough space. If sufficient space is not made available, then the program has a serious and unpredictable flaw. Consider a situation where a program reads data from the keyboard. For example, it asks a user to enter the name. To handle this situation correctly, the program must be careful about an extremely long input. If sufficient memory is not allocated and `strcpy` is called, then the program has a serious security flaw, vulnerable to "buffer overflow attacks".

Why does C not check the memory of the destination? To improve speed. Checking would slow down programs. When C was designed in the late 1960s, computers were expensive and slow. To make C programs fast, programmers had to take the responsibility of ensuring that the destination has enough space.

6.2.2 Compare: `strcmp`

This function can be used to compare two strings. It takes two arguments:

```
1  strcmp(str1, str2);
```

The function returns a negative integer, a zero, or a positive integer depending on whether `str1` is less than, equal to, or greater than `str2`. The order of two strings is defined in the same way as the order of words in a dictionary—also known as lexicographical order. For example, "about" is smaller than "forever" because the letter a is before the letter f in a dictionary. "Education" is after "Change".

How are uppercase and lowercase letters compared? How does the function define the order if one or both of the strings contain digits or symbols? The order is determined by the ASCII (American Standard Code for Information Interchange) values. ASCII assigns an integer value to each character. For example, the value for 'A' is 65 and the value of 'a' is 97. ASCII also assigns a value to each symbol or digit. The value for '#' is 35 and for digit '7' it is 55. The last statement may sound strange. Why does the value of digit '7' have a value of 55? The simple answer is that character values are treated differently from integer values. This can be shown using the following example:

```c
1  /*
2   * charint.c
3   * how C treats integer and character differently
4   */
5  #include <stdio.h>
6  #include <stdlib.h>
7  int main(int argc, char * * argv)
8  {
9      int v = 55;
```

```
10    printf("%d\n", v);
11    printf("%c\n", v);
12    return EXIT_SUCCESS;
13 }
```

The output of this program is:

```
55
7
```

Why do the two lines print different values, even though both use v? The first `printf` treats v as an integer by using %d. Hence, the printed value is 55. The second `printf` treats v as a character by using %c. Since 55 is the ASCII value of character '7', 7 is printed on screen. Note that in this case, using %c in `printf` causes the number 55 to be interpreted as a character. C has different types, including `char` for characters and `int` for integers. A `char` is an integer of a smaller range and can store one ASCII character. The character '7' has the value of 55. Even though they are both integers, the interpretations (%c or %d) are different.

6.2.3   Finding Substrings: strstr

If string `str1` is part of another string `str2`, we say `str1` is a *substring* of `str2`. For example, "str" is a substring of "structure" and "ure" is also a substring of "structure". "W" is a substring of "Welcome" but "sea" is not a substring of "sightseeing".

If we want to determine whether one string is part of another string, we can use the `strstr` function. This function takes two arguments: `haystack` and `needle`. The function attempts to locate `needle` within `haystack`. If `needle` is a substring of `haystack`, `strstr(haystack, needle)` returns the address where the `needle` starts within `haystack`. This address must not be NULL. If `needle` is not a substring of `haystack`, `strstr(haystack, needle)` returns NULL. Please notice the order of the two arguments: The first is the longer one. Here are two examples:

```
1 char haystack[] = {'H', 'e', 'l', 'l', 'o', '\0'};
2 char * chptr; // a pointer
3 chptr = strstr(haystack, "llo");
4     // chptr's value is the address of haystack[2]
5 chptr = strstr(haystack, "XY");
6     // chptr's value is NULL
```

In the first call of `strstr`, "llo" is part of "Hello" and the "llo" starts at the third element (index is 2). Thus, `strstr` returns & `haystack[2]`. In the second call of `strstr`, "XY" is not part of "Hello" and `chptr`'s value is NULL. The ending character '\0' in haystack is not considered when finding the needle.

6.2.4   Finding Characters: strchr

specific character. It returns the address of the first occurrence of the character within the string. If this string does not contain the character, then `strchr` returns NULL. Here are some examples:

```
1 char str[] = {'H', 'e', 'l', 'l', 'o', '\0'};
2 char * chptr; // a pointer
3 chptr = strchr(str, 'H'); // chptr's value is str[0]'s address
```

```
4   chptr = strchr(str, 'e'); // chptr's value is str[1]'s address
5   chptr = strchr(str, 'l'); // chptr's value is str[2]'s address
6   chptr = strchr(str, 'o'); // chptr's value is str[4]'s address
7   chptr = strchr(str, 't'); // chptr's value is NULL
```

6.3 Understanding `argv`

The first example of Section 1.1 says that every C program starts at the special `main` function

```
1   int main(int argc, char * * argv)
```

Adding spaces between *, or in front of `argv` makes no difference. The following two function prototypes are exactly the same:

```
1   int main(int argc, char * * argv)
2   int main(int argc, char ** argv)
```

What is `argv`? As explained in the previous chapter and summarized in Table 4.1, adding an asterisk after a type makes the type into a pointer. What does it mean if there are two asterisks?

C has no special type for strings. C uses arrays of characters for strings, and the data in those arrays must have the special property of being terminated by a null character: `'\0'`. As explained in the previous chapter, an array is a pointer. If you imagine that C had a type for strings called `string`, this type would need to be equivalent to `char *` in real C programs. If `string` were a type, then what would be the type for an array of strings? That would be `string *`. Since `string` is actually `char *`, the type of `string *` is `char * *`.

The second argument of `main`, `argv`, is an array of strings. The first string in this array is `argv[0]` and the type of `argv[0]` is `char *`. The first letter of the first string is `argv[0][0]`. The type of `argv[0][0]` is `char`. Please review Section 4.7 for the type rules.

How is this laid out in memory? If `argv` is an array of strings, where is the memory holding the actual characters? When calling the `main` function, the arguments are provided by the operating system, more precisely, by the shell program in the Terminal. Since `main` is also a function, the arguments are stored on the call stack, as any other function.

Frame	Symbol	Address	Value
main	argv	101	?
	argc	100	?

This is how to execute a program called `prog` with some arguments:

$ ./prog some arguments

When running this program, "some" and "arguments" are called the *command-line arguments*. We have been using command-line arguments for some time. For example, in Section 1.1:

$ gcc prog1.c -o prog

Here `gcc` is a program; `prog1.c -o prog` are the arguments. There are four arguments, including the `gcc` command itself. The program itself is always the first argument.

Let me go back to this command:

$ ./prog some arguments

There are three arguments so `argc` is 3, including `./prog` itself. The value of `argv` is the address of the first element, i.e., `& argv[0]`. Where is `argv[0]` stored? Before the `main` function is called, the C runtime places it somewhere on the call stack. As usual, we do not need to know where it is stored. We just need to know how to get the information: by using `argv[0]` to get the first string.

The table below shows the call stack. The value of `argv` is the address of `argv[0]`. As with all arrays, the addresses of `argv[0]`, `argv[1]`, and `argv[2]` are contiguous. For the sake of explanation, we will use "-" for the values of `argv[0]`, `argv[1]`, and `argv[2]` for the time being.

Frame	Symbol	Address	Value
	argv[2]	104	-
	argv[1]	103	-
main	argv[0]	102	-
	argv	101	102
	argc	100	3

Since `argv[0]`, `argv[1]`, and `argv[2]` are strings, each of them is also a pointer storing the starting address of the first letter in each of those strings. The value of `argv[0]` is the address of `argv[0][0]`. To make it clearer a horizontal line separates the strings. Everything still belongs to the same frame.

Frame	Symbol	Address	Value
	argv[0][6]	111	'\0'
	argv[0][5]	110	g
	argv[0][4]	109	o
	argv[0][3]	108	r
	argv[0][2]	107	p
	argv[0][1]	106	/
	argv[0][0]	105	.
main	argv[2]	104	-
	argv[1]	103	-
	argv[0]	102	105
	argv	101	102
	argc	100	3

In this example, the address of `argv[0][0]` is right above the address of `argv[2]`. However, it does not necessarily have to be this way. As previously mentioned, the value of `argv[0]` is the address of `argv[0][0]`. Similarly, the value of `argv[1]` is the address of `argv[1][0]`. The lower part of the call stack is skipped since it is the same as shown earlier.

Frame	Symbol	Address	Value
	argv[1][4]	116	'\0'
	argv[1][3]	115	e
	argv[1][2]	114	m
	argv[1][1]	113	o
	argv[1][0]	112	s
main	argv[0][6]	111	'\0'
	argv[0][5]	110	g
	argv[0][4]	109	o
	argv[0][3]	108	r
	argv[0][2]	107	p
	argv[0][1]	106	/
	argv[0][0]	105	.

Finally, here is the full frame on the call stack, showing all the arguments:

Frame	Symbol	Address	Value
	argv[2][3]	126	'\0'
	argv[2][2]	125	s
	argv[2][2]	124	t
	argv[2][2]	123	n
	argv[2][2]	122	e
	argv[2][2]	121	m
	argv[2][1]	120	u
	argv[2][0]	119	g
	argv[1][4]	118	r
main	argv[1][3]	117	a
	argv[1][4]	116	'\0'
	argv[1][3]	115	e
	argv[1][2]	114	m
	argv[1][1]	113	o
	argv[1][0]	112	s
	argv[0][6]	111	'\0'
	argv[0][5]	110	g
	argv[0][4]	109	o
	argv[0][3]	108	r
	argv[0][2]	107	p
	argv[0][1]	106	/
	argv[0][0]	105	.
	argv[2]	104	117
	argv[1]	103	112
	argv[0]	102	105
	argv	101	102
	argc	100	3

6.4 Counting Substrings

Sometimes, we want to search a string and count the occurrences of a substring. For example, "ice" is a substring of "nice" and it occurs only once. In the string, "This is his history book", the substring "is" occurs 4 times: "This is his history book". The following program combines what we have learned about `strstr` and `argv` to count the occurrences of a substring.

```
1   /*
2    * countsubstr.c
3    * count the occurrence of a substring
4    * argv[1] is the longer string
5    * argv[2] is the shorter string
6    * argv[1] may contain space if the string enclosed by " "
7    */
8
9   #include <stdio.h>
10  #include <stdlib.h>
11  #include <string.h>
12  int main(int argc, char * argv[])
13  {
14     int count = 0;
15     char * ptr;
16     if (argc < 3)
17       {
18         printf("Please enter two strings.\n");
19         return EXIT_FAILURE;
20       }
21     printf("argv[1] = %s, strlen = %d\n", argv[1],
22             (int) strlen(argv[1]));
23     printf("argv[2] = %s, strlen = %d\n", argv[2],
24             (int) strlen(argv[2]));
25     ptr = argv[1];
26     do
27       {
28         ptr = strstr(ptr, argv[2]);
29         if (ptr != NULL)
30           {
31             printf("%s\n", ptr);
32             count ++;
33             ptr ++;
34           }
35       } while (ptr != NULL);
36     if (count == 0)
37       {
38         printf("argv[2] is not a substring of argv[1].\n");
39       }
40     else
41       {
42         printf("argv[2] occurs %d times in argv[1].\n", count);
43       }
44     return EXIT_SUCCESS;
45  }
```

This program is compiled and executed as follows:

```
$ gcc -g -Wall -Wshadow countstr.c -o countstr
$ ./countstr "This is his history book." is
```

The output of the program is:

```
argv[1] = This is his history book., strlen = 25
argv[2] = is, strlen = 2
is is his history book.
is his history book.
is history book.
istory book.
argv[2] occurs 4 times in argv[1].
```

Earlier we noted that spaces separate the command line arguments. If we enclose a sentence in double quotation marks, the whole sentence is treated as a single argument, as shown in this example. Lines 21 prints `argv[1]` and it is the whole sentence. Without the quotation marks, "This" is `argv[1]` and "is" becomes `argv[2]`, etc. We must use two quotation marks; otherwise, the Terminal says:

```
Unmatched "
```

Below is the call stack for this example. It has been formatted to fit onto one page. We have skipped the column for the frame because only one function is displayed. Line 25 assigns the value of `argv[1]` to `ptr`. This value is the address of `argv[1][0]`, namely 116.

Symbol	Address	Value	Symbol	Address	Value
argv[1][6]	122	s	count	146	0
argv[1][5]	121	i	ptr	145	116
argv[1][4]	120		argv[2][2]	144	'\0'
argv[1][3]	119	s	argv[2][1]	143	s
argv[1][2]	118	i	argv[2][0]	142	i
argv[1][1]	117	h	argv[1][25]	141	'\0'
argv[1][0]	116	T	argv[1][24]	140	.
argv[0][10]	115	'\0'	argv[1][23]	139	k
argv[0][9]	114	r	argv[1][22]	138	o
argv[0][8]	113	t	argv[1][21]	137	o
argv[0][7]	112	s	argv[1][20]	136	b
argv[0][6]	111	t	argv[1][19]	135	
argv[0][5]	110	n	argv[1][18]	134	y
argv[0][4]	109	u	argv[1][17]	133	r
argv[0][3]	108	o	argv[1][16]	132	o
argv[0][2]	107	c	argv[1][15]	131	t
argv[0][1]	106	/	argv[1][14]	130	s
argv[0][0]	105	.	argv[1][13]	129	i
argv[2]	104	142	argv[1][12]	128	h
argv[1]	103	116	argv[1][11]	127	
argv[0]	102	105	argv[1][10]	126	s
argv	101	102	argv[1][9]	125	i
argc	100	3	argv[1][8]	124	h
			argv[1][7]	123	

Line 28 finds "is" in "This is his history book." The first occurrence of "is" is at address 118. This line changes `ptr`'s value to 118. Since it is not NULL, `counter` increments. Line 31 prints the string starting at the address where "is" is found. Recall that strings are terminated by a null byte, and thus the entire string is printed starting from address 118. Line 33 increments `ptr` to 119. This allows us to continue to search for "is" in the rest of the `argv[1]`. Without this increment, `strstr` will search "is" from the address of 118, i.e., "is is his history book.", and the first occurrence will be 118 again. The program would enter an infinite loop if line 33 were removed. Instead, line 33 makes the program continue searching from the address 119, i.e., "s is his history book." The next occurrence of "is" is at address 121. As `ptr` increments, it gradually moves toward the end of `argv[1]`. This is evident from the output of line 31. After finding four occurrences, `strstr` cannot find "is" any more and returns `NULL`. Note that `count` was incremented once every time `strstr` returned a result other than `NULL`. Thus `count` now contains the number of times that "is" was found in `argv[1]`.

C provides many more functions for processing strings. You can find a list of the C's string processing functions by typing into the Terminal:

```
$ man string
```

`man` stands for "manual". The manual displays a list of functions related to processing strings, for example `strcat`.

Chapter 7

Programming Problems and Debugging

7.1 Implementing String Functions

This problem asks you to implement several string functions. Even though these functions are already available in the C standard library, it is instructive to learn how these functions are implemented. You will create your own versions of these functions, without using the ones from the C library.

7.1.1 The C Library

Many functions are defined in the standard C library. These functions are commonly used so they are provided in the C language. Programmers do not have to write these functions. The C library can significantly reduce the amount of work each programmer needs to do. Examples of these functions include `printf`, `strlen`, and `strcpy`. During linking, `gcc` adds the library functions from `libc.so`. This file is stored at `/usr/lib`.

Why is C designed in this way? What are the advantages of using library functions?

- Improving *portability*. In computing, portability means running the same program across different operating systems, such as Linux, Windows, and MacOS. Library functions handle low-level activities related to hardware, such as reading files from a disk or sending packets through a network interface. It is better to implement the hardware-specific details in libraries so that the same program can run on different computers, as long as the program uses the correct libraries. Usually the source needs to be recompiled using the compiler on the new machine.
- Reusing other programs. Some people take efforts creating functions useful to themselves and other people. Good programmers take advantage of well-written libraries. Libraries can be used to add new features that do not exist in the programming language. One example is the *OpenCV* library for image processing and computer vision.

The original C language does not support image processing or any specific computer vision functionality. OpenCV provides these features as an extension to the language. If a library is not from the original C language, you need to tell `gcc` to link to the library. For example, if a program uses mathematical functions declared in `math.h`, `-lm` needs to be added when linking the object files into an executable program.

- Enhancing performance. Libraries are usually well optimized so that programs can have better performance.

7.1.2 Header File

So far we have seen something like:

```
1  #include <stdio.h>
2  #include <stdlib.h>
3  #include <string.h>
```

These lines have been placed at the top of the file, before the `main` function. The header files from the C language are stored in the directory `/usr/include`. What are they, and why are they necessary? They are part of the *header files* of the standard C library. These header files declare useful functions, and must be included before the functions are used. For example:

- If a C file uses the `printf` function, the file needs to include `stdio.h`. This is the header file for standard input and output functions for reading and writing to the Terminal and files.

- If a C file uses `EXIT_SUCCESS`, then the file needs to include `stdlib.h` because the symbol `EXIT_SUCCESS` is defined in that header file.

- If a C file calls mathematical functions, such as `sin` or `log`, then the file needs to include `math.h`.

Header files have a `.h` extension. A header may be used for the following purposes:
- Define symbolic constants, for example:

```
1      #define MATH_PI 3.14159
2      #define MAX_LENGTH 50
```

- Declare functions, for example:

```
1      int areDistinct(int * arr, int len);
```

Header files must **not** contain function implementations (definition).
- Define programmer-created data types. We will explore this feature further in Chapter 16.
- Include other header files, for example

```
1      #include <stdio.h>
```

It is very important that header files do **not** contain any function definitions. That means that all functions listed in a header file must end in a ; character. If there is a block of code (statements between { and }), then you will likely run into problems while linking code. The implementations of functions should be kept in `.c` files (or libraries), and not in header files. Header files are *included*; `.c` files are *compiled* and *linked*. Never include `.c` files. Programmers generally write `.h` and `.c` files in pairs: The `.c` file contains the implementation, and the `.h` file contains only the function declarations. The first two lines and the very last line of a header file are usually something like:

```
1  #ifndef FILENAME_H
2  #define FILENAME_H
3  // The rest of the header file
4  #endif // do not add FILENAME_H
```

The `#ifdef` is matched with an `#endif` that appears at the very end of the file.

It is important to replace `FILENAME_H` with the actual name of the file. `FILENAME_H` is a symbol and can only contain alphanumeric characters and the underscore. Thus programmers generally replace the "." that appears before a file extension with "_" in the symbol. As a matter of style, symbols are always typed in upper case. The purpose of `#ifndef` ... `#define` ... `#endif` is to prevent *multiple inclusion*. Sometimes, the same header file is included multiple times, for example included by two different header files, and both of them are included by the same `.c` file. Without this three lines at the very top and the very bottom, `gcc` will report an error when the same header file is included multiple times. Some other languages have no such problems; for example, in Java, the same package can be imported multiple times.

When a header file is included, if this header file is from the standard C library, or some library that is installed on the system, then < and > are used to enclose the file name, for example:

```
1  #include <stdio.h>
2  #include <stdilib.h>
3  #include <math.h>
```

When a programmer-defined header file is included, the file name is enclosed by double quotations, such as:

```
1  #include "myheader.h"
```

7.1.3 `mystring.h`

This programming problem has a header file called `mystring.h` and it declares several string functions:

```
1  // mystring.h
2  #ifndef MYSTRING_H
3  #define MYSTRING_H
4  // Count the number of characters in a string.
5  // Example: my_strlen("foo") should be 3.
6  int my_strlen(const char * str);
7  // ------------------------------------------------------
8  // Count the number of occurrences of a particular
9  // character c in a string.
10 // Example: my_countchar("foo", 'o') should be 2.
11 //
12 int my_countchar(const char * str, char c);
13 // ------------------------------------------------------
14 // Convert a string to uppercase.  Only alphabetical
15 // characters should be converted; numbers and symbols
16 // should not be affected. Hint: toupper(c) is a macro
17 // that is the uppercase version of a character c.
18 // Example: char * str = "foobar";
19 // my_strupper(foobar) is "FOOBAR".
```

```
20  void my_strupper(char * str);
21  // ------------------------------------------------------
22  // Return the pointer to the first occurrence of the character
23  // If the character is not in the string, return NULL.
24  // Example: char * str = "foobar";
25  // my_strchr(foobar, 'b') is the address of str[3]
26  char * my_strchr(const char * str, char ch);
27  #endif /* MYSTRING_H */
```

Notice that my_strlen and my_countchar have const for the arguments but my_strupper does not. By adding const in front of an argument, this header file says the input argument is a constant and cannot be changed inside of the function. This is important when an argument is a pointer. A pointer's value is a memory address. Through the pointer, it is possible to change the value at that memory address. Adding const prevents a function from making such a change. If the function unintentionally changes the value at that memory address, gcc will detect that. This is a good strategy in writing programs: asking gcc to detect unintended changes. The function my_strupper has no const because the input string will be changed: The lowercase letters are changed to the uppercase letters.

7.1.4 Creating Inputs and Correct Outputs

Before writing a program, we should first develop a strategy for testing. To do this we need test inputs and the correct outputs for those inputs. For this program, we use the beginning of Albert Einstein's Nobel speech as the test input:

```
1   If we consider that part of the theory of relativity which may
2   nowadays in a sense be regarded as bona fide scientific knowledge, we
3   note two aspects which have a major bearing on this theory. The whole
4   development of the theory turns on the question of whether there are
5   physically preferred states of motion in Nature (physical relativity
6   problem). Also, concepts and distinctions are only admissible to the
7   extent that observable facts can be assigned to them without
8   ambiguity (stipulation that concepts and distinctions should have
9   meaning). This postulate, pertaining to epistemology, proves to be of
10  fundamental importance.
11
12  These two aspects become clear when applied to a special case, e.g.
13  to classical mechanics. Firstly we see that at any point filled with
14  matter there exists a preferred state of motion, namely that of the
15  substance at the point considered. Our problem starts however with
16  the question whether physically preferred states of motion exist in
17  reference to extensive regions. From the viewpoint of classical
18  mechanics the answer is in the affirmative; the physically preferred
19  states of motion from the viewpoint of mechanics are those of the
20  inertial frames.
21
22  This assertion, in common with the basis of the whole of mechanics as
23  it generally used to be described before the relativity theory, far
24  from meets the above "stipulation␣of␣meaning". Motion can only be
25  conceived as the relative motion of bodies. In mechanics, motion
26  relative to the system of coordinates is implied when merely motion
27  is referred to. Nevertheless this interpretation does not comply with
28  the "stipulation␣of␣meaning" if the coordinate system is considered
29  as something purely imaginary. If we turn our attention to
```

```
30  experimental physics we see that there the coordinate system is
31  invariably represented by a "practically rigid" body. Furthermore it
32  is assumed that such rigid bodies can be positioned in rest relative
33  to one another
```

The `main` function takes three arguments:

1. `argv[0]` is always the name of the program.
2. `argv[1]` is a command. It can be one of the three options: "strlen", "countchar", or "strupper".
3. `argv[2]` is the name of the input file.
4. `argv[3]` is the name of the output file.

The `main` function calls one of the three functions declared in `mystring.h`. This program takes the input file and calls the three functions in the following ways:

- When `argv[1]` is "strlen", we write the length of each line to the output file. For example, if a line is "development of the theory turns on the question of whether there are", then the output is 69. Each line contains an invisible new line character '\n' at the end. This character is the reason why the line ends.

- When `argv[1]` is "countchar", then the program takes the first character of each line and counts the occurrence of this character in that line. If a line is "nowadays in a sense be regarded as bona fide scientific knowledge, we", the output is 6 because the character 'n' occurs 6 times in this line.

- When `argv[1]` is "strupper", the program converts the lowercase characters in the input file to uppercase. For example, if a line is "These two aspects become clear when applied to a special case, e.g. to", then the output is "THESE TWO ASPECTS BECOME CLEAR WHEN APPLIED TO A SPECIAL CASE, E.G. TO".

This `main` function contains some functions that have not been explained yet. Below we will describe the lines to pay attention to.

```c
1   // main.c
2   #include "mystring.h"
3   #include <stdio.h>
4   #include <stdlib.h>
5   #include <string.h>
6   #define LINE_SIZE 1000 // a line has at most 999 characters
7   int main(int argc, char *argv[])
8   {
9       if (argc != 4)
10          {
11              printf("usage: %s command input output\n", argv[0]);
12              return EXIT_FAILURE;
13          }
14
15      FILE *infptr = fopen(argv[2], "r");
16      if (infptr == NULL)
17          {
18              printf("unable to open file %s!\n", argv[2]);
19              return EXIT_FAILURE;
20          }
21      FILE *outfptr = fopen(argv[3], "w");
22      if (outfptr == NULL)
23          {
24              printf("unable to open file %s!\n", argv[3]);
```

```
25          fclose(infptr);
26          return EXIT_FAILURE;
27       }
28
29     int num_lines = 0;
30     char buffer[LINE_SIZE];
31     // count the number of lines in the file
32     while (fgets(buffer, LINE_SIZE, infptr) != NULL)
33       {
34          num_lines++;
35       }
36
37     fseek(infptr, 0, SEEK_SET);
38     // return to the beginning of the file
39     char **lines = malloc(sizeof(char *) * num_lines);
40     int i;
41     for (i = 0; i < num_lines; i++)
42       {
43          if (feof(infptr))
44            {
45               printf("not enough num_lines in file!\n");
46               fclose(infptr);
47               fclose(outfptr);
48               return EXIT_FAILURE;
49            }
50          lines[i] = malloc(sizeof(char) * LINE_SIZE);
51          fgets(lines[i], LINE_SIZE, infptr);
52       }
53     fclose(infptr);
54
55     int total_length = 0;
56     for (i = 0; i < num_lines; i++)
57       {
58          total_length += my_strlen(lines[i]);
59       }
60     // count the length of each line
61     if (strcmp(argv[1], "strlen") == 0)
62       {
63          for (i = 0; i < num_lines; i++)
64            {
65               fprintf(outfptr, "length: %d\n",
66                       my_strlen(lines[i]));
67            }
68       }
69     /* for each line, count the occurrence of the first
70        letter in the line */
71     if (strcmp(argv[1], "countchar") == 0)
72       {
73          for (i = 0; i < num_lines; i++)
74            {
75               fprintf(outfptr, "count(%c): %d\n", lines[i][0],
```

```
76              my_countchar ( lines [i] ,  lines [i][0]));
77          }
78      }
79   if  (strcmp(argv[1] ,  "strupper") == 0)
80      {
81          for  (i = 0;  i < num_lines;  i++) {
82              my_strupper(lines[i]);
83              fprintf(outfptr ,  "%s",  lines[i]);
84          }
85      }
86
87   for  (i = 0;  i < num_lines;  i++)
88      {
89          free(lines[i]);
90      }
91   free(lines);
92   fclose(outfptr);
93   return EXIT_SUCCESS;
94 }
```

The `if` condition at line 9 checks whether or not the program has three arguments in addition to the program's name. For now, we do not need to worry about the code between lines 15 and 59. These lines read the input file line by line. We will return to this subject later. Line 61 checks the command in `argv[1]`. If the command is "strlen", then this program calls `my_strlen` for each line and prints the length to the output file. In similar fashion, line 71 checks whether `argv[1]` is "countchar". Line 76 calls `my_countchar` by using each line as the string and the first character of the line as the character. Line 82 converts the characters in each line to uppercase.

When running the program with this command

$ ./mystring strlen input output_strlen

the output is stored in the file called `output_strlen`. The first four lines of the file are

```
1  length:  63
2  length:  70
3  length:  70
4  length:  69
```

The original article has a blank line at the eleventh line. A blank line means that it only has the new line character '\n'. Thus, this line actually has one character. Similarly, line 21 also has one character. When running the program with this command

$ ./mystring strlen input output_countchar

the output is stored in the file called `output_countchar`. The first four lines of the file are

```
1  count(I):  1
2  count(n):  6
3  count(n):  3
4  count(d):  1
```

This is the final command

$ ./mystring strlen input output_strupper

and the first four lines of the correct output are

```
1  IF WE CONSIDER THAT PART OF THE THEORY OF RELATIVITY WHICH MAY
2  NOWADAYS IN A SENSE BE REGARDED AS BONA FIDE SCIENTIFIC KNOWLEDGE, WE
3  NOTE TWO ASPECTS WHICH HAVE A MAJOR BEARING ON THIS THEORY. THE WHOLE
4  DEVELOPMENT OF THE THEORY TURNS ON THE QUESTION OF WHETHER THERE ARE
```

7.1.5 Makefile

The Makefile should look familiar:

```
1  GCC = gcc
2  CFLAGS = -g -Wall -Wshadow
3  OBJS = mystring.o main.o
4  HDRS = mystring.h
5  VAL = valgrind --tool=memcheck --leak-check=full
6  VAL += --verbose --log-file=
7
8  mystring: $(OBJS) $(HDRS)
9          $(GCC) $(CFLAGS) $(OBJS) -o $@
10
11 .c.o:
12          $(GCC) $(CFLAGS) -c $*.c
13
14 clean:
15          rm -f mystring $(OBJS) out_* log*
16
17 testall: test0 test1 test2
18
19 test0: mystring
20          $(VAL)log0 ./mystring strlen input out_len
21          diff -q out_len expected_strlen
22
23 test1: mystring
24          $(VAL)log1 ./mystring countchar input output_countchar
25          diff -q output_countchar expected_countchar
26
27 test2: mystring
28          $(VAL)log2 ./mystring strupper input out_upper
29          diff -q out_upper expected_strupper
```

This Makefile introduces several new concepts:
- Line 6 appends more options to the symbol VAL. This approach makes it easy to add a symbol with many options.
- The symbol $@ is used on line 9. It means the symbol before the : at line 8. In this case, the $@ means mystring. Using $@ is a convenient way to manage rules.
- Lines 11 and 12 mean "If an object file is needed, compile the corresponding .c file." It determines the object files on an as-needed basis. In this case, mystring depends on OBJS and it depends on mystring.o and main.o. To invoke the mystring rule, make will ensure that both mystring.o and main.o are up to date. If they need updating, then the rule on lines 11 and 12 is invoked in order to generate the object files from the corresponding .c file. Lines 11 and 12 are equivalent to the following:

```
    mystring.o: mystring.c
        $(GCC) $(CFLAGS) -c mystring.c

    main.o: main.c
        $(GCC) $(CFLAGS) -c main.c
```

If a program requires many object files, lines 11 and 12 can shorten Makefile significantly.

7.1.6 mystring.c

The following is a reference solution for mystring.c:

```c
1   // mystring.c
2   #include "mystring.h"
3   #include <ctype.h>
4   int my_strlen(const char * str)
5   {
6      int len = 0;
7      while (str[len] != '\0')
8         {
9            len++;
10        }
11     return len;
12  }
13
14  int my_countchar(const char * str, char ch)
15  {
16     int count = 0;
17     while (* str != '\0')
18        {
19           if (* str == ch)
20              {
21                 count++;
22              }
23           str ++;
24        }
25     return count;
26  }
27
28  void my_strupper(char * str)
29  {
30     while (* str != '\0')
31        {
32           * str = toupper(* str);
33           str++;
34        }
35  }
36
37  char * my_strchr(const char * str, char ch)
38  {
39     int ind = 0;
```

```
40    while (str[ind] != '\0')
41      {
42        if (str[ind] == ch)
43          {
44            return (& str[ind]);
45          }
46        ind ++;
47      }
48    // if the program reaches here, ch is not in str
49    return NULL;
50  }
```

The argument `str` stores the address of the first element of the input string. Since a string is an array of characters, we treat `str` as an array, as shown at line 7. We can also treat `str` as a pointer, as shown at lines 17, 19, 23, 30, 32, and 33. As you can see, lines 7, 17, and 30 use the null terminator character, `'\0'`, to determine the end of the input strings. Lines 17, 19, and 30 read the value at the address stored in `str`. This is the third usage of `*` described in Table 4.1. Both lines *read* the value at that address. Line 23 increments `str` so that it points to the next character in the array. Line 32 both reads from and writes to the address. At the right side of `=`, it reads the value. At the left side of `=`, it writes the value.

Test your understanding of the program by answering this question: What happens if lines 22 and 23 are exchanged (moving `str ++;` into the `if` condition right under `count ++;`)? Is function `my_countchar` still correct? Why?

7.1.7 Using `const`

The arguments of `my_countchar` say that `str` is a constant. However, line 23 modifies `str`. The seeming contradiction happens because `const` can be applied in two different ways, with different meanings. The following example illustrates with two pointers `chptr1` and `chptr2`:

```
1   // const.c
2   #include <stdio.h>
3   #include <stdlib.h>
4   #include <string.h>
5   int main(int argc, char *argv[])
6   {
7     char str1[20];
8     char str2[20];
9     strcpy(str1, "First");
10    strcpy(str2, "Second");
11    const char * chptr1 = & str1[0]; // const before char
12    char * const chptr2 = & str1[0]; // const after  char
13    // * chptr1 = 'C';      // not allowed
14    * chptr2 = 'C';         // OK
15    chptr1 = & str2[0];     // OK
16    // chptr2 = & str2[0];  // not allowed
17    return EXIT_SUCCESS;
18  }
```

Both `chptr1` and `chptr2` are pointers and their values store the address of the first element of `str`. The following shows the call stack. For simplicity, we do not show `argc` and `argv`.

Symbol	Address	Value
chptr2	114	100
chptr1	113	100
str1[6]	112	'\0'
str1[5]	111	d
str1[4]	110	n
str1[3]	109	o
str2[2]	108	c
str2[1]	107	e
str2[0]	106	S
str1[5]	105	'\0'
str1[4]	104	t
str1[3]	103	s
str1[2]	102	r
str1[1]	101	i
str1[0]	100	F

Lines 11 and 12 make `chptr1` and `chptr2` store the address of `str1[0]`. By putting `const` in front of `char *` at line 11, we do not want to change the value at the memory that is pointed by `chptr1`. Line 13 is not allowed because this line attempts to change the value at address 100, i.e., `& str1[0]`, through `chptr1`. Please note the word **through**. It is still possible to change str1[0] as long as the change is not through `chptr1`. Line 15 does not prevent us from changing `chptr1` itself because `chptr1` is not a constant. Hence, we can change the value of `chptr1` at line 15.

Symbol	Address	Value
chptr1	113	100 → 106 by line 15

In contrast, line 12 says `chptr2` is a constant and so it cannot be changed in line 16. However, it is possible to change the value of `str1[0]` through `chptr2` at line 14.

Symbol	Address	Value
chptr2	114	100 (cannot be changed)
chptr1	113	100 → 106 by line 15
str1[0]	100	F → C by line 14

In `my_countchar`, `str` itself is not a constant (similar to `chptr1`) so changing `str` itself at line 23 is allowed. In fact, `const` can be used twice for the same pointer. In this example, `chptr3` stores the address of `& str1[0]`. Changing the value of `chptr3` (line 17) and changing the value at the address (line 18) are disallowed.

```c
// const2.c
#include <stdio.h>
#include <stdlib.h>
int main(int argc, char *argv[])
{
    char str1[20];
    char str2[20];
    strcpy(str1, "First");
    strcpy(str2, "Second");
    const char * chptr1 = & str1[0];
    char * const chptr2 = & str1[0];
    const char * const chptr3 = & str1[0];
    // * chptr1 = 'C';      // not allowed
```

```
14    * chptr2 = 'C';          // OK
15    chptr1 = & str2[0];      // OK
16    // chptr2 = & str2[0];   // not allowed
17    // chptr3 = & str2[0];   // not allowed
18    // * chptr3 = 'C';       // not allowed
19    return EXIT_SUCCESS;
20  }
```

7.2   Debugging

To write good programs, we must abandon the habit of "coding-testing-debugging". Testing does not magically reveal what is wrong with a program and how to fix it. Instead, we must have a plan before writing code. This includes having a testing and debugging strategy. After writing *each* line of code, read it carefully. This saves time. It will help you find simple mistakes, but reading code will also help reveal more subtle problems.

A common problem among learners is forgetting to initialize variables. C does not initialize variables. It is your responsibility. This can lead to apparently inexplicable bugs and worse code that seems to work but then mysteriously fails. It is hard to find these types of bugs by "testing" and "debugging" because the program behavior can be unexpected, or *sometimes* appear correct. In this case, there is no substitute to reading the code, and asking yourself if every variable has been initialized.

Another common mistake is putting ; in the wrong place. In the code listing for `mystring.c`, if an ; is placed at the end of line 7, 17, or 30 then the program is incorrect because the block of code between { and } is no longer related to the `while` or `if` conditions. Putting ; at the end of line 7, 17, or 30 makes the program enter infinite loops. This problem can be difficult to find by testing alone because the program does not stop and the output will probably be incomplete. Putting ; at the end of line 19 increments the `count` regardless of whether `* str` and `ch` match. These problems are easy to find by reading code line by line carefully. Unfortunately, `gcc` cannot offer much help because the program is syntactically correct.

7.2.1   Find Infinite Loops

Even if you are very careful, it is difficult to avoid all mistakes. Thus it is useful to know how to use a debugger such as `gdb`. It allows us to execute code line by line, and inspect the values in the variables. It is important to appreciate that `gdb` is not a substitute to reading your code, and reasoning about it logically. Nonetheless, `gdb` augments our ability to diagnose and fix problems in code, for example, in finding infinite loops.

Infinite loops are typically indicated by a program that should stop quickly but does not. Running the program again and again, of course, will not be helpful. Inserting "debugging messages" into the code may be more helpful, but it also takes a lot of time. We need to know where the actual problem is. Possible but difficult. If we know the problem, we will fix it without inserting debugging messages. After finding and fixing the problem, the debugging messages usually have to be removed. There is a better way: The `gdb` debugger can make this easy.

Assume that we are running the code for `mystring.c` and a ; has accidentally been inserted at the end of line 7. The program enters an infinite loop and does not stop.

```
$ ./mystring strlen input output_strlen
```

What is the fastest way to diagnose this problem? Start `gdb` in a Linux Terminal.

```
$ gdb mystring
```

Please remember that `gdb` takes the executable file as the input, and not a `.c` file. Inside `gdb`, type

```
(gdb) r strlen input output_strlen
```

The first letter `r` means "run" the program. It replaces `./mystring` in the command line. Add the normal command-line arguments after `r`. The program now starts and enters the aforementioned infinite loop. Press `Ctrl-c` to interrupt the normal execution of the program and `gdb` will display something like:

```
Program received signal SIGINT, Interrupt.
0x0000000000400884 in my_strlen (str=0x603590 "If we consider that
part of the theory of relativity which may\n") at mystring.c:7
```

This means that the program has stopped at line 7 of the file `mystring.c`. The message tells us where the infinite loop is. At the `(gdb)` prompt, type `list` to show the code:

```
4   int my_strlen(const char * str)
5   {
6     int len = 0;
7     while (str[len] != '\0');
8       {
9         len++;
```

As explained earlier, infinite loops may occur in many places (lines 7, 17, and 30). Using `gdb` to identify an infinite loop is easy and takes only a few seconds. Moreover, we do not need to modify any line before using `gdb`.

7.2.2 Find Invalid Memory Accesses

An "invalid memory access", or "segmentation fault", is a common error that stops a program. It occurs when a program attempts to access memory outside the allowed regions. A program that has invalid memory accesses may create security vulnerability. We can introduce a memory error into line 17 of `mystring.c`. That line should be:

```
17   while (* str != '\0')
```

Suppose we accidentally write it as:

```
17   while (* str != '0') // without \
```

What is the difference between `'\0'` and `'0'`? The former is a null-terminator, a special invisible character indicating the end of a string. The latter is a normal character like `'a'`, but happens to be the character zero: `'0'`. Do not mix them. When running the program

```
$ ./mystring countchar input output_countchar
```

we get

```
Segmentation fault (core dumped)
```

Segmentation fault means the program tries to access (read or write) memory at an invalid address. The operating system reacts by stopping the program. It is similar to attempting to enter someone else's house. If you do not own the house, entering the house is illegal. We can determine where segmentation fault occurs by using either `gdb` or `valgrind`. If we run the program using `gdb`, we will see something like:

```
Program received signal SIGSEGV, Segmentation fault.
0x00000000004008cd in my_countchar (str=0x624000 $<$Address 0x624000
out of bounds$>$, ch=73 'I') at mystring.c:17
```

Type the `bt` (backtrace) command at the `gdb` prompt, to see the call stack.

```
#0  0x00000000004008cd in my_countchar (str=0x624000
$<$Address 0x624000 out of bounds$>$, ch=73 'I') at mystring.c:17
#1  0x0000000000400cc9 in main (argc=4, argv=0x7fffffffe418) at main.c:74
```

The call stack shows two frames. The top frame is frame 0 and the next is frame 1. In gdb, you can see a specific frame. Type

(gdb) f 1

after the (gdb) prompt to enter frame 1. Type `list` to show the code around line 74 in `main.c`. Type `print i` to print the value of `i`. This is the line number of the input file. Its value is 0 meaning that the `my_countchar` is processing the first line of input.

The first line of the input is "If we consider that part of the theory of relativity which may\n" gdb can tell us that if we type the command `print lines[i]`:

(gdb) print lines[i]

    $3 = 0x603590 "If we consider that part of the theory of relativity which may\n"

The starting address of this string is 0x603590. Something is wrong inside `my_countchar` but at this stage, it is unclear precisely what is wrong. Let's go back to the frame of `my_countchar` by typing `f 0`:

(gdb) f 0

    #0 0x00000000004008cd in my_countchar (str=0x624000

    <Address 0x624000 out of bounds>, ch=73 'I') at mystring.c:17

The segmentation fault occurs at line 17 and this line reads the value at the address stored in `str`. Print the value of `str` in `gdb`:

(gdb) print str

    $4 = 0x624000 <Address 0x624000 out of bounds>

Compare the value of `str` (0x624000) and the starting address of the string in `main` (0x603590). The difference is quite large but the string is not very long, only 63 characters. This means that `str` kept increasing far beyond the end of the string.

You may ask, "Why does the segmentation fault occur when `str` is so large? Doesn't the program start accessing invalid addresses after `str` is larger than 0x603590 + 63?" It is correct that the program starts accessing invalid addresses after `str` is larger than 0x603590 + 63. However, Linux stops the program only when it reads memory that it is not *authorized* to use. Since the memory is given in chunks, as explained in Section 5.3, the segmentation fault occurs when the program accesses a memory address beyond the currently authorized segment. A program may access all the addresses inside the segments given to the program, and the operating system will not stop it. This does not mean that the program is correct. We need to correct the program as soon as possible.

7.2.3 Detect Invalid Memory Accesses

Another way to detect invalid memory accesses is using `valgrind`. The log file from `valgrind` can be quite long. You should go to the very last line. In this example, the line says:

```
ERROR SUMMARY: 59745 errors from 4 contexts (suppressed: 2 from 2)
```

Do not be too concerned about the number of errors detected. Fixing one error will Often fix many of the other detected errors. This is because a single error can be hit many times as a program executes. Go to the very top of the log file and start looking for anything related to the source files, i.e., `mystring.c`, `mystring.h`, and `main.c`. The first detected problem related to `mystring.c` is:

```
==4238== Conditional jump or move depends on uninitialised value(s)
==4238==    at 0x4008D2: my_countchar (mystring2.c:17)
==4238==    by 0x400CC8: main (main.c:74)
```

Another detected problem is:

```
==4238== Conditional jump or move depends on uninitialised value(s)
==4238==    at 0x4008BE: my_countchar (mystring2.c:19)
==4238==    by 0x400CC8: main (main.c:74)
```

This is related to the problem at line 17. If we fix line 17, the problem at line 19 disappears. Some students think that accessing invalid memory is harmless as long as the programs do not have segmentation faults. This is wrong. Allowing invalid addresses is one of the most common security problems in software. It can allow a malicious program to "hijack" another program. If a program accesses invalid addresses, the program's behavior is not defined. That means it may work a hundred or a thousand times, and then mysteriously fail. The same program may fail when using a different compiler, or run on a different computer.

Please remember that testing can demonstrate that something is wrong; however, testing cannot demonstrate that everything is right. As we see, Linux stops the program when `str` is already very far away from valid addresses. Thus, we cannot rely on testing exclusively. Instead, we need to use many methods to prevent and detect mistakes.

"Which one should I use, `gdb` or `valgrind`?", you may ask. The answer is both. These two tools serve different purposes. Choosing `gdb` vs. `valgrind` is like choosing a hammer vs. a screw driver. Use the right tool for the job: `gdb` is interactive, and allows a programmer to see the program's execution line by line. In contrast, `valgrind` runs the program until it stops (or crashes). In general it is a good idea to use `valgrind` first to detect whether there are any memory problems and then use `gdb` to pinpoint the problem. You should always use `valgrind` to check whether your programs have invalid memory accesses. The command is:

```
$ valgrind –leak-check=full –tool=memcheck –verbose
```

What is the difference between `gcc` and `valgrind`? Doesn't `gcc` also check whether a program has problems? The `gcc` compiler checks the source code: i.e., it finds syntax errors. This is a very rudimentary form of error checking. It is like a spell-checker in a document editor. An article without any spelling error does not mean that the article makes any sense. In similar fashion, `gcc` does not check what happens when the program runs. It is impossible for `gcc` to check what the program does when it is running.

In contrast, `valgrind` is a run-time checker. The program must be run for `valgrind` to check anything. This implies the following: If the program does not execute the parts of code that have problems, then `valgrind` will not detect any problems. This is not a limitation in `valgrind`, but more an indication of what type of tool it is. This is a limitation in how you write test cases. You need to think how your program may fail and then test the potential problems. Good tests can make `valgrind` invaluable. Note that this is another reason why passing test cases does not guarantee that the program is correct. If the test cases do not test the problematic parts, then the problems are undetected.

How could it be possible that some parts of the program are not executed? This is because most programs have many `if` conditions. It is extremely difficult—practically impossible—to design test cases that can check every combination of these conditions. For each `if` condition, the condition can be true or false. Hence, there are two possibilities. If there are n `if` conditions and they are independent, there are 2^n possibilities. As a point of reference, in one weekly homework for my class at Purdue University, the sample solution has 25 `if` conditions, about $2^{25} = 34$ million possibilities. Can you create 34 million test cases? Obviously a brute-force approach is impossible, but the task is significantly eased by examining the logic of the program. Even though there are 25 `if` conditions in the sample solution mentioned, there are not 34 million paths through the code because some conditions are related. Careful reasoning is required to make this type of analysis. It is certainly possible that some problems are not detected when this homework assignment is graded.

Chapter 8

Heap Memory

Chapter 2 describes one type of memory: stack memory (also called the call stack). Stack memory follows a simple rule: first in, last out. The call stack is automatically managed by the code generated by the compiler. Every time a function is called, a new frame is pushed. Every time a function ends, the frame is popped. Programmers have no direct control over this process. One consequence is that a function may read from or write to memory addresses in lower frames; however, a function can never "look upward" into memory above its frame. This is because whenever a function is actively executing, there are not valid memory addresses "above" it.

This is natural and convenient for a lot of programming tasks; however, sometimes programmers need more control over memory. They want to be able to *allocate* memory when necessary and *release* memory when the allocated memory is no longer needed. For this purpose, computers have another type of memory: *heap memory*.

Computers also have the third type of memory where the compiled code resides. In general, this memory cannot be modified. Programs can access only stack memory and heap memory. Thus, the rest of this book does not explain the memory where programs are stored.

8.1   Creating Array with `malloc`

If a called function can access the frame of the calling (lower) function through pointers, would this be sufficient? No. At the bottom of the call stack is the frame of the `main` function. Can a program store all of its data in the `main` function, since this data can be accessed by all the other functions? This would make the `main` function rather complex for even a simple program. We would need to consider every possible way the data could be read or written and the `main` would have to manage space for all of the data. Even if we are willing to do this analysis and write this `main` function, we still have problems. Most programs take some form of input. For example, we may need to read an image file from a disk. At the time the code is being written, we cannot know precisely what input will be given to the program. In particular, we do not know the size of the input. We cannot write a program that can handle the inputs whose size is greater than our expectation. This is a severe limitation. We could create an array in `main` and make its size greater than all possible input size. This is very inefficient. What we need is a way to allocate memory as needed while the program is running.

Before talking about how to use heap memory, let's review how to create a fixed-size array. The following example creates an array of six integers and assigns the first three elements to 11, −29, and 74.

```
int arr1 [6];
arr1 [0] = 11;
arr1 [1] = -29;
arr1 [2] = 74;
```

This array is stored inside a frame in the call stack. The values of the other three elements (`arr[3]`, `arr[4]`, and `arr[5]`) are still garbage. To create a fixed-size array, the array's size must be specified in the source code. This is problematic because the size may be unknown at the time the code is written. For example,

```
int num;
printf ("Please␣enter␣a␣number:␣");
scanf ("%d", & num);
```

Note that the number is given *after* the program starts running. We can use this number to create an integer array with `num` elements. The program uses `malloc` to create the array:

```
int * arr2;
arr2 = malloc(num * sizeof(int)); // no * inside sizeof
```

Notice * in front of `arr2`. The value of `num` is entered by a user. To create an array of integers, an integer pointer is needed. This allocation must use `sizeof(int)` because the size of an integer can be different on different machines. If `sizeof(int)` is 4 (typical among computers), then the program allocates `num` * 4 bytes of memory. If `sizeof(int)` is 2 (common in some types of micro controller), then the program allocates `num` * 2 bytes of memory. The type of the pointer must match what is in `sizeof(...)`. The following example has mistakes.

```
int * arr3;
arr3 = malloc(length * sizeof(char)); /* WRONG */
/* types do not match, one is int, the other is char */
int * arr4;
arr4 = malloc(length * sizeof(double)); /* WRONG */
/* types do not match, one is int, the other is double */
```

The program will behave strangely when types do not match. Programs should check whether `malloc` succeeds. If it fails, then it is `NULL`. Programs should handle this problem before doing anything else. Why would `malloc` fail? This happens when the system cannot provide the requested memory. Perhaps the request is unreasonably large. C uses `NULL` to indicate an invalid value for a memory address.

```
int * arr5;
arr5 = malloc(length * sizeof(int));
if (arr5 == NULL)
{
    // malloc has failed, handle the problem here.
}
```

If a program allocates memory successfully, then the program can assign values to the elements in the same way as an array:

```
3   arr2[0] = 11;
4   arr2[1] = -29;
5   arr2[2] = 74;
```

When using `malloc` to allocate an array, the memory addresses of the elements are contiguous. When the memory is no longer needed, the program **must** release (also called free) the memory by calling:

```
6   free(arr2);
```

It is impossible to release only one part of the memory. All the memory allocated in a given call to `malloc` must be freed at once. One common mistake is assuming that `arr2`'s value becomes NULL. This is wrong. The value of `arr2` is still a memory address but that address is no longer valid. It is a good habit to type `free` right after typing `malloc` so that it is not forgotten. After typing malloc and free next to each other, insert code between them:

```
1   int * an_array = malloc(some_size * sizeof(int));
2   /* insert code here to use the array */
3   free(an_array);
```

To use `malloc`, it is necessary to specify the number of elements in the array. When using `free`, you cannot specify the number of elements. The `malloc` and `free` function work together, and `free` knows how much memory should be freed. If a program calls `malloc` without calling `free`, then the program has a *memory leak*. Memory leaks are serious problems because a program has a limited amount of memory that can be allocated by calling `malloc`. The limit depends on the hardware and also the operating systems. Later in this chapter, we will explain how to use `valgrind` to detect memory leaks.

8.2   The Stack and the Heap

When a program declares a pointer, the pointer exists somewhere in the call stack. For example,

```
1   int * arr2;
```

Symbol	Address	Value
arr2	200	?

The address is arbitrarily chosen to be 200. If you prefer, you can choose 400, 5000, or whatever number. Even though the pointer is on the stack, we can create an array on the heap. Remember that the pointer's address and value are independent. This example allocates memory for an array of 6 integers. This is how to create the array on the heap:

```
2   arr2 = malloc(6 * sizeof(int));
```

Section 4.8 mentioned that different types have different sizes. That is the reason why `malloc` is used in conjunction with `sizeof`. From now on, let us assume that each integer requires 4 bytes and the addresses of two adjacent array elements is different by 4. Calling `malloc` returns a valid heap address to a piece of memory large enough to store 6 integers, and `arr2`'s value stores that address. Heap memory is pretty far away from the stack memory. In this example, we use 10000 for the heap address. The memory is uninitialized, so we use "?" for each integer's value.

Symbol	Address	Value		Address	Value
arr2	200	10000		10020	?
				10016	?
				10012	?
				10008	?
				10004	?
				10000	?

(a) Stack Memory	(b) Heap Memory

The following assignment changes the first element of the array:

```
3   arr2[0] = 11;
```

This causes the heap memory at 10000 to change:

Symbol	Address	Value		Address	Value
arr2	200	10000		10020	?
				10016	?
				10012	?
				10008	?
				10004	?
				10000	11

(a) Stack Memory	(b) Heap Memory

```
4   arr2[2] = 74;
```

This changes the heap memory at 10008:

Symbol	Address	Value		Address	Value
arr2	200	10000		10020	?
				10016	?
				10012	?
				10008	74
				10004	?
				10000	11

(a) Stack Memory	(b) Heap Memory

How does this work? What happens when the program executes this line?

```
4   arr2[2] = 74;
```

This is what this statement does precisely:

1. Takes `arr2`'s value as an address. In this example the value is 10000.
2. The index is 2, so `sizeof(int)` $\times$ 2 = 4 $\times$ 2 = 8 is added to 10000 and the new address is 10008.
3. Since this is at the left of the assignment, the value at the address of 10008 is changed to 74.

The following example creates an array whose length is determined by `argc`. The program converts the command line arguments—the elements of `argv`—into integers. This is necessary because each element of `argv` is a string. Then, the program adds up the integers' values and prints the sum.

```
1  // malloc.c
2  // create an array whose size is specified at run time.
3  // The array's elements are the command line arguments.
4  // The program adds the elements and prints the sum.
5  #include <stdio.h>
6  #include <stdlib.h>
7  int main(int argc, char * argv[])
8  {
9     int * arr2;
10    int iter;
11    int sum = 0;
12    if (argc < 2)
13       {
14          printf("Need to provide some integers.\n");
15          return EXIT_FAILURE;
16       }
17    arr2 = malloc(argc * sizeof(int));
18    if (arr2 == NULL)
19       {
20          printf("malloc fails.\n");
21          return EXIT_FAILURE;
22       }
23    /* iter starts at 1 because argv[0] is the program's name */
24    for (iter = 1; iter < argc; iter ++)
25       {
26          arr2[iter] = (int) strtol(argv[iter], NULL, 10);
27       }
28    printf("The sum of ");
29    for (iter = 1; iter < argc; iter ++)
30       {
31          printf("%d ", arr2[iter]);
32          sum += arr2[iter];
33       }
34    printf("is %d.\n", sum);
35
36    free (arr2);
37    return EXIT_SUCCESS;
38 }
```

The program uses `strtol` to convert the strings into integers. Some books suggest using `atoi` but `strtol` is preferred for two reasons: (i) `strtol` is more general because it is not limited to decimal bases. For example, `strtol` can be used to convert binary numbers, or hexadecimal (base 16) numbers. (ii) More important, `strtol` allows the calling program to check whether the conversion fails. The conversion fails when the string contains no number. In contrast, `atoi` provides no information about whether the conversion fails. Use `gcc` to convert the program into an executable file called malloc:

$ gcc -Wall -Wshadow malloc.c -o malloc

The following shows two examples running this program. If an argument is not an integer ("hello" and "C" in the second example), then the value of that argument is zero.

$ ./malloc 5 8 −11 4 3 27

The sum of 5 8 −11 4 3 27 is 36.

$ ./malloc 7 9 hello 1 6 C 2 4 8

The sum of 7 9 0 1 6 0 2 4 8 is 37.

Here is a review of the relationships between arrays and pointers:

- An array always means a pointer. The name of the array is the address of the first element.
- An index ([and]) removes one asterisk from the pointer type. If arr's type is int *, then arr[3] is int.
- A pointer is **not** necessarily an array. For example,

```
int * ptr;
int a = 5;
ptr = & a;
```

In this case, ptr is a pointer but there is no array. A pointer stores a memory address.

8.3 Functions that Return a Heap Address

A function may return the address of heap memory. For example,

```
int * f1(int n)
{
  int * ptr;
  ptr = malloc (n * sizeof(int));
  return ptr;
}
void f2(void)
{
  int * arr;
  arr = f1(6);
  /* return location */
  arr[4] = 7;
  free (arr);
}
```

Let's consider the call stack just before f1 returns ptr:

Symbol	Address	Value	Address	Value
ptr	103	10000	10020	?
value address	102	100	10016	?
return location	101	line 11	10012	?
arr	100	?	10008	?
			10004	?
			10000	?

(a) Stack Memory	(b) Heap Memory

After f1 returns, this is what is in the call stack and heap memory:

Symbol	Address	Value	Address	Value
arr	100	10000	10020	?
			10016	?
			10012	?
			10008	?
			10004	?
			10000	?
(a) Stack Memory			(b) Heap Memory	

The allocated heap memory is still available because the program has not called `free` yet. The stack variable `ptr`, declared on line 3, is destroyed when `f1` returns, because `ptr` is on the stack. However, the allocated heap memory is available until it is freed. This is a fundamental difference between stack and heap memory. Heap memory is more flexible. The statement,

```
arr[4] = 872;
```

changes an element in the array. Now the stack and heap memory look as follows:

Symbol	Address	Value	Address	Value
arr	100	10000	10020	?
			10016	872
			10012	?
			10008	?
			10004	?
			10000	?
(a) Stack Memory			(b) Heap Memory	

Before `f2` finishes, it must call `free`. Otherwise, the program leaks memory. The purpose of this example is to show that memory allocated by `malloc` can be passed between functions. Please be aware that this example does not follow the principle mentioned in Section 8.1. In this example, `malloc` and `free` are called in two different functions. This is sometimes necessary, but also error-prone. It is easy to forget calling `free` in `f2` because `f2` does not call `malloc`. We have used 10000 as the memory address returned by `malloc`. In a real computer, the address can change every time the program runs and the address will likely be a very large number.

8.4 Two-Dimensional Arrays in C

We have seen two-dimensional arrays already. In Section 6.3, `argv` is an array of strings. Each string is an array of characters. Thus, `argv` is a two-dimensional array. The strings may have different sizes. The characters in each string are stored contiguously, and the string pointers are stored contiguously. A C program may create a fixed-size two-dimensional array in the following way:

```
int arr2d[8][3];
    // an array with 8 rows and 3 columns
arr2d[0][2] = 4;
    // assign 4 to the third column of the first row
```

```
5   arr2d[3][1] = 6;
6       // assign 6 to the second column of the fourth row
```

In this example, the first dimension has eight rows and the indexes are between zero and seven (inclusively). The second dimension has three columns; the indexes are between zero and two. A two-dimensional array is like a matrix.

It is a little more complicated creating a two-dimensional array whose size is known only at run time by calling **malloc**. We first create a one-dimensional array of integer pointers (int *) and then each pointer is used to create an integer array. Fig. 8.1 illustrates this concept. The first step creates an array of integer pointers. In the second step, each pointer stores the address of the first element in a one-dimensional integer array. The addresses of &arr2d[0] and &arr2d[1] are adjacent. However, the values of arr2d[0] (corresponding to &arr2d[0][0]) and arr2d[1] (corresponding to &arr2d[1][0]) are likely far apart.

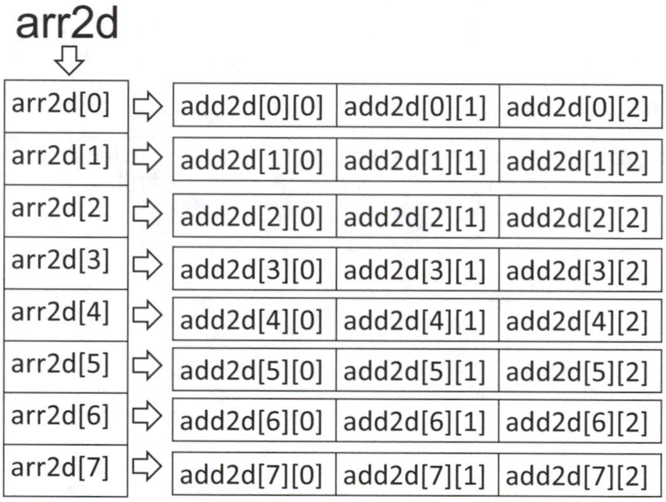

FIGURE 8.1: A two-dimensional array has an array of pointers as the first dimension. Each element points to an array.

An array's name stores the address of the first element. Therefore, the type of a one-dimensional array of integers is an integer pointer. If we want to create an array using malloc, we need to use int *.

```
1   int arr[6]; /* an array of fixed size, 6 elements */
2   int * arr2; /* an integer pointer */
3   arr2 = malloc(9 * sizeof(int)); /* 9 elements */
4   arr2[4] = 19; /* arr2[4] is an integer */
5   free(arr2);
```

Imagine a new type called one_d_array. A two-dimensional array would be an array of one_d_array. To create this two-dimensional array, malloc is used:

```
1   one_d_array * arr2d;
2   arr2d = malloc(numrow * sizeof(one_d_array));
```

The one-dimensional array is itself a pointer to integer; thus, one_d_array should be replaced by int *. Consequently, the type of arr2d is int * *. That means that the arr2d is pointing to int *, and indeed, the first element of arr2d has type int *.

```
1  int * * arr2d;
2  arr2d = malloc(numrow * sizeof(int *));
```

This only allocates enough space for the pointers: `arr2d[i]` is a pointer to an integer. There is no space for the integers yet. It is necessary to allocate the memory for the integers separately:

```
3  for (row = 0; row < NUMROW; row ++)
4    {
5       arr2d[row] = malloc(NUMCOLUMN * sizeof (int));
6    }
```

These arrays must be freed later in the program.

```
7  for (row = 0; row < NUMROW; row ++)
8    {
9       free(arr2d[row]);
10   }
11 free(arr2d); // must be after free(arr2d[row])
```

If we freed `arr2d` before freeing the individual rows, then attempting to free the rows would be an error. Thus, `malloc` and `free` are **always** in the reverse order: `malloc` must be followed by `free`, and the memory must not be accessed after a call to `free`.

This is the code implementing this concept.

```
1  /* twodarray.c
2     purpose: show how to create a two-dimensional array
3     The size of the array is 8 rows x 3 columns
4  */
5  #include <stdio.h>
6  #include <stdlib.h>
7  #define NUMROW 8
8  #define NUMCOLUMN 3
9  int main(int argc, char * argv[])
10 {
11   int * * arr2d;
12   int row;
13   /* step 1: create an array of integer pointers */
14   arr2d = malloc(NUMROW * sizeof (int *));
15   for (row = 0; row < NUMROW; row ++)
16     {
17        /* step 2: for each row (i.e., integer pointer),
18            create an integer array */
19        arr2d[row] = malloc(NUMCOLUMN * sizeof (int));
20     }
21   /* now, the two-dimensional array can be used */
22   arr2d[4][1] = 6;
23   arr2d[6][0] = 19;
24   /* the first index can be 0 to 7 (inclusive) */
25   /* the second index can be 0 to 2 (inclusive) */
26
27   /* memory must be released in the reverse order */
28   for (row = 0; row < NUMROW; row ++)
29     {
```

```
30        /* release the memory for each row first */
31          free (arr2d[row]);
32        }
33      /* now release the array of integer pointers */
34      free (arr2);
35      return EXIT_SUCCESS;
36    }
```

After creating the two-dimensional array, it can be used in the same way as a fixed-size array. Before the program ends, the allocated memory must be released. Memory must be released in the *reverse order* that it was allocated. Please be careful about the types used in creating arrays.

8.5   Pointers and Arguments

A function argument can be a pointer that stores the address in either stack memory or heap memory. The following example passes an array allocated on the heap memory to a function:

```
1   // argument.c
2   // pass the address of heap memory as a function argument
3
4   #include <stdio.h>
5   #include <stdlib.h>
6   int sum(int * array, int length)
7   {
8      int iter;
9      int answer = 0;
10     for (iter = 0; iter < length; iter ++)
11       {
12          answer += array[iter];
13       }
14     return answer;
15   }
16   int main(int argc, char * argv[])
17   {
18      int * arr;
19      int iter;
20      int length = 12;
21      int total;
22      arr = malloc(length * sizeof(int));
23      if (arr == NULL)
24        {
25           printf("malloc␣fails.\n");
26           return EXIT_FAILURE;
27        }
28      for (iter = 0; iter < length; iter ++)
29        {
30           arr[iter] = iter;
```

```
31        }
32      total = sum(arr, length);
33      printf("Total␣is␣%d.\n", total);
34      free (arr);
35      return EXIT_SUCCESS;
36   }
```

In this example, `arr` is passed to function `sum` as an argument. The `sum` function itself does not need to know whether the value in `array` is an address in stack memory or heap memory. The function only needs to know that `array` contains a valid address somewhere in memory. The address is copied when it is passed as the argument `array` in the function called `sum`. The call stack and the heap memory look like the following inside the `sum` function, just before the `for` block starts:

Frame	Symbol	Address	Value		Address	Value
	answer	211	0		10044	11
	iter	210	-		10040	10
	length	209	12		10036	9
sum	array	208	10000		10032	8
	value address	207	205		10028	7
	return location	206	line 33		10024	6
	total	205	?		10020	5
	length	204	12		10016	4
	iter	203	13		10012	3
main	arr	202	10000		10008	2
	argv	201	-		10004	1
	argc	200	-		10000	0
(a) Stack Memory					(b) Heap Memory	

Inside `sum`, `array[0]` refers to the value stored at 10000 and it is 0. Similarly, `array[7]` refers to the value stored at 10028 (10000 + 7 × `sizeof(int)`) and it is 7.

In the following example, the function `multi2` doubles the array elements:

```
1    // double.c
2    #include <stdio.h>
3    #include <stdlib.h>
4    void multi2(int * array, int length)
5    {
6      int iter;
7      for (iter = 0; iter < length; iter ++)
8        {
9          array[iter] *= 2;
10       }
11   }
12   int main(int argc, char * argv[])
13   {
14     int * arr;
15     int iter;
16     int length = 12;
17     arr = malloc(length * sizeof(int));
18     if (arr == NULL)
19       {
```

```
20          printf ("malloc␣fails.\n");
21          return EXIT_FAILURE;
22        }
23    for (iter = 0; iter < length; iter ++)
24        {
25          arr [iter] = iter;
26        }
27
28    printf ("Original␣array:␣");
29    for (iter = 0; iter < length; iter ++)
30        {
31          printf ("%2d␣", arr [iter]);
32        }
33    printf ("\n");
34
35    multi2 (arr, length);
36
37    printf ("New␣array:␣␣␣␣␣␣");
38    for (iter = 0; iter < length; iter ++)
39        {
40          printf ("%2d␣", arr [iter]);
41        }
42    printf ("\n");
43
44    free (arr);
45    return EXIT_SUCCESS;
46 }
```

The output of this program is shown below:

```
Original array:  0  1  2  3  4  5  6  7  8  9 10 11
New array:       0  2  4  6  8 10 12 14 16 18 20 22
```

Remember **free** must be called before the program ends, otherwise, the program has a memory leak. Also, to make the program easier to understand and easier to debug, the program should call **malloc** and **free** in the same function. If a program calls **malloc** and **free** in different functions, then it becomes much harder to track whether:

1. memory allocated by calling **malloc** is released by calling **free** later or,
2. memory released by calling **free** has been allocated by calling **malloc** earlier.

Chapter 9

Programming Problems Using Heap Memory

9.1   Sorting an Array

This problem asks you to write a program that reads integers from a file, sorts the numbers, and writes the sorted numbers out to another file.

9.1.1   Generating Test Input and Expected Output

The previous chapter explained why testing does not guarantee that a program is correct: There are too many possible cases. Nevertheless, testing still plays a central role in software development, because testing helps detect problems. Before writing a program, or even a single function, software developers should always think about how to test it. Often this involves creating test inputs by hand, based on an understanding of where the weakness in the function or program may be. This can be a lot of work, however, and it is often useful to write small programs to generate test case input.

To test sorting, first write a program that generates random integers. To make this program more flexible, it has one command-line argument: `argv[1]` tells the program how many numbers should be generated. The program uses a *random number generator*. In C, the function `rand` returns a number between 0 and the largest integer. These numbers are "random" because it is difficult to predict which number will appear next. If we call `rand` multiple times, it will return an unpredictable sequence of numbers. You can increase the "randomness" by giving a *seed*. The seed is used to initialize the random number generator. If we give the same seed in two different runs of the program, then the program generates the same sequence of numbers. This can be useful for testing and debugging. If the seed changes, the sequence also changes. The function `srand` sets the seed. Linux has a function `time`. This function returns the number of seconds since 00:00:00 January 1st 1970. If `srand` is called with `time` as an argument, then the seed changes every second. This is good enough for many applications that require sequences of random numbers. This is not, however, truly random since the seed is predictable. Generating truly random numbers is beyond the scope of this book. This is the program for generating test inputs:

```
1   // testgen.c
2   #include <stdio.h>
3   #include <stdlib.h>
4   #include <time.h>
5   #include <string.h>
6   #define RANGE        10000
7   int main(int argc, char * * argv)
8   {
9     if (argc < 2)
10       {
11         printf("need a positive integer\n");
12         return EXIT_FAILURE;
13       }
14     int num = strtol(argv[1], NULL, 10);
15     if (num <= 0)
16       {
17         printf("need a positive integer\n");
18         return EXIT_FAILURE;
19       }
20     srand(time(NULL)); // set the seed
21     int count;
22     for (count = 0; count < num; count ++)
23       {
24         printf("%d\n", rand() % RANGE);
25       }
26     return EXIT_SUCCESS;
27   }
```

This problem requires the output to be sorted. If the generator produces a sequence of random numbers, how can we get the correctly sorted result without first knowing that the final program is correct? This is a circular problem: We do not have the program correctly written yet so we do not have the sorted numbers. Without sorted numbers, we cannot check whether the program is correct. Fortunately, we can use the sort program in Linux. The sort program treats the values as strings; "9" is greater than "10" because the character '9' is greater than the character '1'. Adding -n after sort treats the values as numbers, and 9 is smaller than 10. Below is the Makefile—it calls the sort program in Linux.

```
1   GCC = gcc
2   CFLAGS = -g -Wall -Wshadow
3
4   testgen: testgen.c
5           $(GCC) testgen.c -o testgen
6
7   inputgen: testgen
8           ./testgen 6    > input6
9           ./testgen 20   > input20
10          ./testgen 50   > input50
11          ./testgen 100  > input100
12          sort -n input6   > expected6
13          sort -n input20  > expected20
```

```
14          sort -n input50  > expected50
15          sort -n input100 > expected100
16
17 clean:
18          /bin/rm testgen input* expected*
```

Now if we type:

   $ make inputgen

eight files will be generated: Four are called `input` and the other four are called `expected`. The input files have numbers in some random order. The numbers in the expected files are sorted.

9.1.2 Redirecting Input

Section 1.2 describes how to use redirection for program outputs. This program uses redirection for inputs. When a program calls `scanf`, the program waits for the user to enter data from the keyboard. If we execute the program by adding < and a file name, the program reads data from the file instead of from the keyboard. Below is the `main` function for reading the input file. The purpose is to test whether the function can read from a file.

```c
1 /*
2  * main.c
3  */
4 #include <stdio.h>
5 #include <stdlib.h>
6 #include <string.h>
7 #include "mysort.h"
8 int main(int argc, char * * argv)
9 {
10   if (argc != 2)
11     {
12       return EXIT_FAILURE;
13     }
14   int number = strtol(argv[1], NULL, 10);
15   int ind;
16   for (ind = 0; ind < number; ind ++)
17     {
18       int val;
19       scanf("%d", & val);
20       printf("%d\n", val);
21     }
22   return EXIT_SUCCESS;
23 }
```

Below is the `Makefile`. Please pay special attention to the part for `testinput`.

```
1 GCC = gcc
2 CFLAGS = -g -Wall -Wshadow
3 OBJS = mysort.o main.o
4 HDRS = mysort.h
5
```

```
 6   mysort: $(OBJS) $(HDRS)
 7           $(GCC) $(CFLAGS) $(OBJS) -o $@
 8
 9   .c.o:
10           $(GCC) $(CFLAGS) -c $*.c
11
12   testinput: mysort
13           ./mysort 6    < input6    > temp6
14           diff temp6      input6
15           ./mysort 20   < input20   > temp20
16           diff temp20     input20
17           ./mysort 50   < input50   > temp50
18           diff temp50     input50
19           ./mysort 100  < input100 > temp100
20           diff temp100    input100
21
22   testgen: testgen.c
23           $(GCC) testgen.c -o testgen
24
25   inputgen: testgen
26           ./testgen 6    > input6
27           ./testgen 20   > input20
28           ./testgen 50   > input50
29           ./testgen 100 > input100
30           sort -n input6    > expected6
31           sort -n input20   > expected20
32           sort -n input50   > expected50
33           sort -n input100 > expected100
34
35   clean:
36           /bin/rm testgen input* expected* temp*
```

If we type:

   $ make testinput

it ensures that "mysort" has been compiled, and then runs the program in such a way that the program reads input from an input file, instead of from the keyboard.

   $ ./mysort 6 < input6 > temp6

The argument `argv[1]` is the number of integers. The actual values are stored in the input file. In a later chapter we will explain how to get the number of integers from the file itself without using `argv[1]`. With `< input6`, the input comes from the file called `input6`, and not from the keyboard. With `> temp6`, the output is stored in the file called `temp6`, and not printed to the computer screen. Using files like this helps us repeat the same tests easily. The next line,

   $ diff temp6 input6

checks whether the program reads the input values correctly. If the program is incorrect, the values in `temp6` and `input6` are different. It is important to ensure the input values are correct before sorting the values. If the program cannot read the input values correctly, the program should be corrected before attempting to sort the values.

9.1.3 Sorting Integers

The header file declares the sort function:

```
1  // mysort
2  #ifndef MYSORT_H
3  #define MYSORT_H
4  void mysort(int * arr, int len);
5  #endif
```

Many sorting algorithms have been developed. In this example, we use *selection sort*. It selects the smallest value among the array elements and then puts it at the beginning of the array. Then, it selects the second smallest value and puts it as the second element of the array. This process continues until reaching the end of the array. Here is an implementation of the selection sort algorithm:

```
1   /*
2    * mysort.c
3    */
4   #include <stdio.h>
5   static void swap(int * a, int * b)
6   {
7     int t = * a;
8     * a = * b;
9     * b = t;
10  }
11
12  void mysort(int * arr, int len)
13  {
14    /* in each iteration, find the smallest value and
15       put it at the beginning of the array */
16    int ind1;
17    int ind2;
18    for (ind1 = 0; ind1 < len; ind1 ++)
19      {
20        int minind = ind1;
21        for (ind2 = ind1 + 1; ind2 < len; ind2 ++)
22          {
23            if (arr[minind] > arr[ind2])
24              {
25                minind = ind2; // index of the smallest value
26              }
27          }
28        if (minind != ind1)
29          {
30            // move the smallest value to the correct location
31            swap(& arr[ind1], & arr[minind]);
32          }
33      }
34  }
```

In mysort, ind1 is the counter for each iteration. When ind1 is zero, the smallest element is moved to the beginning of the array. When ind1 is one, the second smallest element is moved to the second element of the array. The value ind1 separates the array into two parts: the part before `ind1` has been sorted and the part after `ind1` has not been sorted. To sort the second part, we select the smallest inside this part and move it to the beginning of the second part. Then, `ind1` increases, effectively shrinking the second part.

Line 20 initializes `minind` to `ind1`. This stores the index of the smallest element seen so far in the second part of the array. Then, lines 21 to 27 find the index of the smallest element in the second part of the array. Lines 28 to 32 move the smallest value to the correct place in the array. This is achieved by swapping the smallest value from its current location to the correct location. The number of comparisons (line 23) depends on the number of elements and is independent of the actual values of the elements.

This program uses the same `swap` function described in Section 4.4. The `swap` function is marked *static*. A static function can be called by functions in the same file only. A static function is invisible outside this file.

Consider the following example: The input values are 1694, 8137, 609, 7118, 5614, and 8848. The smallest value is the third element (index is 2). The first iteration of `ind1` swaps the first (index is 0) and the third elements and now the array's elements are 609, 8137, 1694, 7118, 5614, and 8848. The following table shows the array's elements in each iteration, just before calling `swap`:

ind1	minind	Sorted	Unsorted
0	2		1694 8137 **609** 7118 5614 8848
1	2	609	8137 **1694** 7118 5614 8848
2	4	609 1694	8137 7118 **5614** 8848
3	3	609 1694 5614	7118 8137 8848
4	4	609 1694 5614 7118	8137 8848
5	5	609 1694 5614 7118 8137	8848

This is the sorted array: 609 1694 5614 7118 8137 8848. The `main` function has a few places that require explanation:

- This `main` function stores the data in an array. The size of the array is given by `argv[1]`.
- Before using `argv[1]`, the program must check that `argc` is 2. If `argc` is 1, then `argv[1]` does not exist (`argv[0]` does) and attempting to access `argv[1]` will crash the program.
- The program uses `strtol` to convert `argv[1]` from a string to an integer.
- The `main` function must call `malloc` to allocate heap memory for the array before reading data from the file.
- The `main` function must call `free` to release the heap memory of the array before the program ends.

```
1  /*
2   * main.c
3   */
4  #include <stdio.h>
5  #include <stdlib.h>
6  #include <string.h>
7  #include "mysort.h"
8  int main(int argc, char * * argv)
9  {
10    if (argc != 2)
11      {
12        return EXIT_FAILURE;
13      }
14    int number = strtol(argv[1], NULL, 10);
```

```
15    int * arr;
16    arr = malloc(sizeof(int) * number);
17    if (arr == NULL)
18      {
19        return EXIT_FAILURE;
20      }
21    int ind;
22    for (ind = 0; ind < number; ind ++)
23      {
24        scanf("%d", & arr[ind]);
25      }
26    mysort(arr, number);
27    for (ind = 0; ind < number; ind ++)
28      {
29        printf("%d\n", arr[ind]);
30      }
31    free (arr);
32    return EXIT_SUCCESS;
33  }
```

The `Makefile` has a section for testing. It runs the program for the four test cases and compares the outputs with the expected results.

```
1   GCC = gcc
2   CFLAGS = -g -Wall -Wshadow
3   OBJS = mysort.o main.o
4   HDRS = mysort.h
5
6   mysort: $(OBJS) $(HDRS)
7           $(GCC) $(CFLAGS) $(OBJS) -o $@
8
9   .c.o:
10          $(GCC) $(CFLAGS) -c $*.c
11
12  test: mysort
13          ./mysort 6   < input6   > output6
14          diff output6    expected6
15          ./mysort 20  < input20  > output20
16          diff output20   expected20
17          ./mysort 50  < input50  > output50
18          diff output50   expected50
19          ./mysort 100 < input100 > output100
20          diff output100  expected100
21
22  testgen: testgen.c
23          $(GCC) testgen.c -o testgen
24
25  inputgen: testgen
26          ./testgen 6   > input6
27          ./testgen 20  > input20
28          ./testgen 50  > input50
29          ./testgen 100 > input100
```

```
30              sort -n input6   > expected6
31              sort -n input20  > expected20
32              sort -n input50  > expected50
33              sort -n input100 > expected100
34
35   clean:
36              /bin/rm -f temp* testgen input*
37              /bin/rm -f expected* *.o output* mysort
```

As we can see, `Makefile` can substantially simplify testing, because it saves a lot of time typing these commands over and over again.

9.1.4   Using `valgrind` to Detect Memory Leaks

Many people stop when their programs produce correct outputs; however this is problematic. Producing correct outputs is only one part of software development. We also need to check hidden errors. Section 5.4 explained how to use `valgrind` to check invalid memory accesses that may result in security flaws and unpredictable behavior. We can also use `valgrind` to detect memory leaks. This is the new `Makefile` checking memory leaks:

```
1   GCC = gcc
2   CFLAGS = -g -Wall -Wshadow
3   VALGRIND = valgrind --tool=memcheck --leak-check=full
4   VALGRIND += --verbose --log-file=
5   OBJS = mysort.o main.o
6   HDRS = mysort.h
7
8   mysort: $(OBJS) $(HDRS)
9              $(GCC) $(CFLAGS) $(OBJS) -o $@
10
11  .c.o:
12             $(GCC) $(CFLAGS) -c $*.c
13
14  test: mysort
15             $(VALGRIND)log6 ./mysort 6   < input6   > output6
16             diff output6    expected6
17             $(VALGRIND)log20 ./mysort 20  < input20  > output20
18             diff output20   expected20
19             $(VALGRIND)log50 ./mysort 50  < input50  > output50
20             diff output50   expected50
21             $(VALGRIND)log100 ./mysort 100 < input100 > output100
22             diff output100  expected100
23
24  testgen: testgen.c
25             $(GCC) testgen.c -o testgen
26
27  inputgen: testgen
28             ./testgen 6   > input6
29             ./testgen 20  > input20
30             ./testgen 50  > input50
31             ./testgen 100 > input100
32             sort -n input6   > expected6
```

```
33          sort -n input20  > expected20
34          sort -n input50  > expected50
35          sort -n input100 > expected100
36
37 clean:
38          /bin/rm -f temp* testgen input* expected*
39          /bin/rm -f *.o output* mysort log*
```

If we remove

```
31 free(arr);
```

near the end of **main**, then the program will leak memory. The log files generated by **valgrind** will show something like:

```
ERROR SUMMARY: 1 errors from 1 contexts (suppressed: 2 from 2)
```

at the bottom. If we look backwards in the log file, we will something similar to:

```
==4645== 24 bytes in 1 blocks are definitely lost in loss record 1 of 1
==4645==    by 0x40070F: main (main.c:16)
==4645==
==4645== LEAK SUMMARY:
==4645==    definitely lost: 24 bytes in 1 blocks
```

The program leaks 24 bytes of memory, and the memory was allocated at line 16 in **main.c**. Why does the program leak 24 bytes? The program allocates space for 6 integers by calling **malloc**. Each integer occupies 4 bytes so the program leaks 24 bytes. (i.e., sizeof(int) × 4 = 24.) If we put the **free** statement back, **valgrind** reports

```
All heap blocks were freed -- no leaks are possible
```

We should always check **valgrind**'s reports when writing programs. Remember that if **valgrind** reports problems then the program has problems. If **valgrind** reports no problems, then the program may still have problems but **valgrind** failed to detect them.

9.2   Sort Using qsort

The previous problem asks you to write a program that sorted an array of integers. The program uses *selection sort*. Even though the algorithm is easy to understand and to implement, it is inefficient when used with large arrays. The inefficiency occurs because the algorithm does not use the *transitivity* of integers. What is transitivity? Consider three integers x, y, and z. If x > y and y > z, then x > z. C provides a function called **qsort** and it uses the *quick sort* algorithm. It is a much faster general-purpose sorting algorithm than selection sort because it uses transitivity to dramatically reduce the number of comparisons between elements.

9.2.1   qsort

First, let's examine the manual for **qsort**:

NAME
        qsort - sorts an array

SYNOPSIS
        #include <stdlib.h>

        void qsort(void *base, size_t nmemb, size_t Size,
                   int(*compar)(const void *, const void *));

DESCRIPTION

        The qsort() function sorts an array with nmemb elements of size
  Size. The base argument points to the start of the array.

        The contents of the array are sorted in ascending order
  according to a comparison function pointed to by compar, which is
  called with two arguments that point to the objects being compared.

        The comparison function must return an integer less than, equal
  to, or greater than zero if the first argument is considered to be
  respectively less than, equal to, or greater than the second. If two
  members compare as equal, their order in the sorted array is
  undefined.

RETURN VALUE
        The qsort() function returns no value.

It is important to become comfortable with the manual pages for C functions. They may appear terse at first, but they are well written. Their target audience is the people who have some familiarity with C. The manual says qsort requires four arguments:

1. base: the address of the first element of the array. This should be & arr[0].
2. the number of elements (members) in the array.
3. the size of each element in bytes. If it is an integer array, this argument should be sizeof(int). Some students write 4 and this is wrong. The size of an integer is not necessarily 4. Your program will fail if the size is not 4.
4. a comparison function.

What is void *? Why is void * the type of base? It means that the memory address can point to any type. This is important for a general-purpose function. Thus we can use qsort to sort any type of array. It can be int *, or char *, or double *, as long as it is an address of a valid array. The type being pointed to is specified indirectly by the third argument. The third argument informs qsort of the size of each array element. Among the four arguments, the last one requires a new concept: passing a function as an argument to another function.

1. int(*compar)(const void *, const void *) means that this argument is the name of a function. How do I know it is a function? Because of the parenthesis after (*compar).
2. int before (* compar) means that the passed function must return an integer. Why is there an asterisk? Because the name of a function is a pointer to the function. Section 2.3 said that whenever a function is called, the return location is pushed onto the call stack. What does this mean? Each line of a program has a location (i.e., an address). This address is neither in the call stack, nor in the heap. The address

is in another part of memory that stores the compiled program's instructions. The instructions must have addresses because they are stored in memory. Every line of a program is stored at a memory location. Thus, it is possible to use an address to specify a particular line of a program. By convention, C uses the name of a function as the address of the first line of a function. This is the reason a function can be expressed by a pointer: The function name is the address of the first line of that function.

3. The passed function takes two input arguments. Each argument stores an address. Again, `void *` means that the address can be of any type. Section 7.1.7 explains the meaning of `const`. This function cannot change the value stored at the address because `const` is in front of the type (even though the type is `void`).

Putting all these factors together, the comparison function must have the following type:

```
1  int comparefunc(const void * a, const void * b)
```

9.2.2 The Comparison Function

What is the comparison function? Why is it necessary to provide a comparison function as an argument to `qsort`? The goal of `qsort` is to sort arrays of any type. This means that `qsort` needs to know how to compare two elements in an array without knowing the type. This is not possible automatically because different types have different sizes. Moreover, when we talk about programmer-defined structures later in this book, one structure may contain multiple attributes. It is impossible for `qsort` to know how to compare programmer-defined structures. To make it possible, programmers have to tell `qsort` how to compare the elements. The comparison function can decide ascending or descending order. The comparison function must have the following structure:

```
1   // comparefunc.c
2   int comparefunc(const void * arg1, const void * arg2)
3   {
4     // convert void * to a known type (int, char, double ...)
5     const type * ptr1 = (const type *) arg1;
6     const type * ptr2 = (const type *) arg2;
7     // get the value from the address
8     const type val1 = * ptr1;
9     const type val2 = * ptr2;
10    // compare the value
11    if (val1 < val2)
12      { return -1; }
13    if (val1 == val2)
14      { return 0; }
15    return 1;
16  }
```

The comparison function has three steps:

1. The arguments `arg1` and `arg2` point to two distinct elements in the array. If we are sorting an array of integers, then the array elements are of type `int`. The pointers to those elements must be `int *`. In lines 5 and 6 we convert `arg1` and `arg2` to the correct type. This is called *type casting*. The `qsort` function knows the size of each array element because the third argument provides that information.

2. After type casting, `ptr1` and `ptr2` have the same value (point to the same addresses) as `arg1` and `arg2` respectively. The comparison function can now access the data at those memory locations because the function has changed the pointers to the known

type. It is meaningless comparing addresses. Instead, lines 8 and 9 retrieve the values stored at those addresses.

3. Lines 11 to 15 return a negative, zero, or positive value based on whether val1 is less than, equal to, or greater than val2. This comparison function will cause the array elements to be sorted in ascending order. If we want the elements to be sorted in the descending order, then we can change lines 11 to 15 so that the function returns positive, zero, or negative if val1 is less than, equal to, or greater than val2.

The following shows a program that uses qsort to sort an array of integers:

```
1  // compareint.c
2  int comparefunc(const void * arg1, const void * arg2)
3  {
4    const int * ptr1 = (const int *) arg1;
5    const int * ptr2 = (const int *) arg2;
6    int val1 = * ptr1;
7    int val2 = * ptr2;
8    if (val1 < val2)  { return -1; }
9    if (val1 == val2) { return 0; }
10   return 1;
11 }
```

Here is the main function:

```
1  /*
2   * mainqsort.c
3   */
4  #include <time.h>
5  #include <stdio.h>
6  #include <stdlib.h>
7  #include <string.h>
8  #define RANGE 10000
9  int comparefunc(const void * arg1, const void * arg2);
10
11 void printArray(int * arr, int size)
12 {
13   int ind;
14   for (ind = 0; ind < size; ind ++)
15     {
16       printf("%d␣", arr[ind]);
17     }
18   printf("\n");
19 }
20
21 int main(int argc, char * * argv)
22 {
23   if (argc != 2)
24     {
25       return EXIT_FAILURE;
26     }
27   int size = strtol(argv[1], NULL, 10);
28   if (size <= 0)
29     {
30       return EXIT_FAILURE;
```

```
31      }
32   int * arr;
33   arr = malloc(sizeof(int) * size);
34   if (arr == NULL)
35      {
36         return EXIT_FAILURE;
37      }
38   int ind;
39   srand(time(NULL)); // set the seed
40   for (ind = 0; ind < size; ind ++)
41      {
42         arr[ind] = rand() % RANGE;
43      }
44   printArray(arr, size);
45   qsort(& arr[0], size, sizeof(int), comparefunc);
46   printArray(arr, size);
47   free (arr);
48   return EXIT_SUCCESS;
49 }
```

9.2.3 Execution Examples

The following shows two examples of running the program for two arrays, each with eight integers:

```
1  5045 3603 7935 2430 1019 3445 6339 9545
2  comparefunc: 5045 3603
3  comparefunc: 7935 2430
4  comparefunc: 3603 2430
5  comparefunc: 3603 7935
6  comparefunc: 5045 7935
7  comparefunc: 1019 3445
8  comparefunc: 6339 9545
9  comparefunc: 1019 6339
10 comparefunc: 3445 6339
11 comparefunc: 2430 1019
12 comparefunc: 2430 3445
13 comparefunc: 3603 3445
14 comparefunc: 3603 6339
15 comparefunc: 5045 6339
16 comparefunc: 7935 6339
17 comparefunc: 7935 9545
18 1019 2430 3445 3603 5045 6339 7935 9545

1  7529 6434 2810 3835 7986 8812 127 713
2  comparefunc: 7529 6434
3  comparefunc: 2810 3835
4  comparefunc: 6434 2810
5  comparefunc: 6434 3835
6  comparefunc: 7986 8812
7  comparefunc: 127 713
```

```
 8  comparefunc: 7986 127
 9  comparefunc: 7986 713
10  comparefunc: 2810 127
11  comparefunc: 2810 713
12  comparefunc: 2810 7986
13  comparefunc: 3835 7986
14  comparefunc: 6434 7986
15  comparefunc: 7529 7986
16  127 713 2810 3835 6434 7529 7986 8812
```

Both runs have eight integers. Before calling **qsort**, the numbers at line 1 are not sorted. After calling **qsort**, the numbers are sorted (in the output above at lines 18 and 16 respectively). These outputs have been generated with the **printf** function on line 9 of **comparefunc** uncommented. By printing one line per comparison made, the outputs tell us some information about using qsort:

- The comparison function **comparefunc** is called 16 times in the first example and 14 times in the second example. For the selection sort, the number of comparisons is always the same for arrays of the same size.
- Some pairs of numbers are not compared. In the first example, 1019 and 7935 are not compared. In the second example, 127 is not compared with 7529. As mentioned earlier, qsort uses transitivity to reduce the number of comparisons.
- When **comparefunc** is called the first time in either example, the first two array elements (5045 and 3603, 7529 and 6434) are compared. When **comparefunc** is called the second time in either example, the next two array elements (7935 and 2403, 2810 and 3835) are compared. However, when **comparefunc** is called the third time, different pairs are compared. In the first run, the fourth is the smallest among the first four elements. In the second run, the third is the smallest among the first four elements. This is a property of **qsort**: The relative order of the elements affects which pairs are compared.

9.2.4   Sorting Strings

The next example uses **qsort** to sort strings. Consider a program called **sortstr** printing the command-line arguments in the ascending order. If we execute this program with the following arguments:

$ ./sortstr there are several arguments in the command line

the output is

```
./sortstr
are
arguments
command
in
line
several
the
there
```

Below is the **main** function. The function calls **qsort** using **argv** as the argument.
1. The first argument of **qsort** is the address of the first element of the array of strings, i.e., **& argv[0]**.

2. The second argument is the number of strings in the array and it is `argc`.

3. The third argument is the size of each element. Since each element is a string, the type is `char *` and the size is `sizeof(char *)`. Remember that an array of strings is an array of pointers.

4. The last argument is the comparison function.

```
1  // mainqsortstr.c
2  #include <stdio.h>
3  #include <stdlib.h>
4  #include <string.h>
5  int cmpstringp(const void *arg1, const void *arg2);
6  int main(int argc, char * *argv)
7  {
8     int ar;
9     if (argc < 2)
10       {
11          fprintf(stderr, "Usage:␣%s␣<string>...\n", argv[0]);
12          return EXIT_FAILURE;
13       }
14    qsort(&argv[0], argc, sizeof(char *), cmpstringp);
15    for (ar = 0; ar < argc; ar++)
16       {
17          printf("%s\n", argv[ar]);
18       }
19    return EXIT_SUCCESS;
20  }
```

The comparison function is similar to the one for an array of integers but the types are different: `arg1` and `arg2` are the addresses of strings. Thus, their types are `char * *`. Imagine that C has a type called `string` and `arg1` and `arg2` store the addresses of strings. Thus, `arg1` and `arg2` are of type `string *`. Since `string` is actually `char *` in C, `arg1` and `arg2` are of type `char * *`. After casting the types of `arg1` and `arg2`, the program then needs to get the strings from the addresses by adding `*` to retrieve the values stored at the addresses. Finally, the program uses `strcmp` to compare the two strings.

```
1  // comparestr.c
2  #include <string.h>
3  int cmpstringp(const void *arg1, const void *arg2)
4  {
5     // ptr1 and ptr2 are string *
6     // string is char *, thus ptr1 and ptr2 are char * *
7     const char * const * ptr1 = (const char * *) arg1;
8     const char * const * ptr2 = (const char * *) arg2;
9     const char * str1 = * ptr1; // type: string
10    const char * str2 = * ptr2;
11    return strcmp(str1, str2);
12  }
```

Quick sort is faster than selection sort because quick sort uses transitivity. How much faster is it? Fig. 9.1 compares the execution times for sorting arrays of different sizes. When the number of elements increases, the execution time increases for both quick sort and selection sort. However, the execution time for selection sort increases much faster, i.e., the ratio increases. The ratio actually increases to infinity as the size of the array increases. This means that no matter how fast a computer is, if an array is sufficiently large then selection sort will behave poorly when compared to quick sort. Selection sort can be faster for small arrays. This is because the logic of selection sort is simpler. What counts as "small" or "large" may be empirically determined for a given computer.

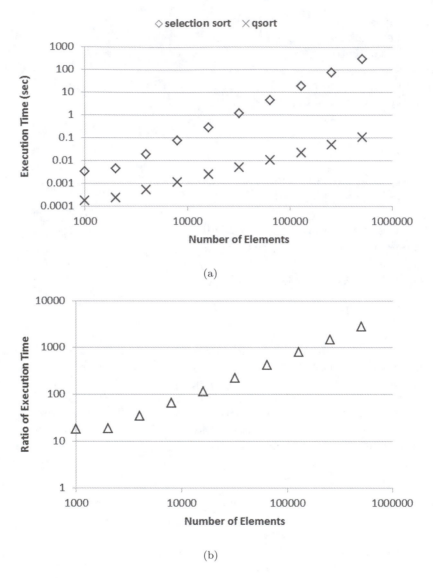

(a)

(b)

FIGURE 9.1: (a) Execution time for selection sort and quick sort. (b) The ratio of the execution time. Please note that both axes use a logarithmic scale.

To summarize, selection sort is an algorithm that selects the smallest value among the remaining unsorted array elements in each iteration. C has a built-in function called `qsort` and it can sort arrays of different types. It knows how to sort elements because programmers tell `qsort` the size of each element and provide functions that compares the elements.

Chapter 10

Reading and Writing Files

We have already taken advantage of redirection to use files as inputs and outputs. This chapter explains how to use C functions to read from or to write to files without using redirection.

10.1   Passing a File Name via `argv`

A program has many ways to obtain input data, for example:

- Using `scanf` to get data from a user through the keyboard.
- Using `scanf` and redirection to get data from a file.
- Using `argc` and `argv` to get data from the command line.
- Using file operations to get data stored on a disk.

For the last option, the program must first obtain the file's name. The file's name is itself a piece of data. The example below uses `argv[1]` as a file's name. The program must check whether `argc` is at least two to decide whether `argv[1]` can be used without generating a memory error.

```
1   /*
2    * checkargc.c
3    */
4   #include <stdio.h>
5   #include <stdlib.h>
6   int main(int argc, char * argv[])
7   {
8      if (argc < 2)
9        {
10          printf("Need to provide the file's name.\n");
11          return EXIT_FAILURE;
12        }
13      printf("The name of the file is %s.\n", argv[1]);
14      return EXIT_SUCCESS;
15   }
```

Running the program without passing the file's name on the command line will cause an error message to be printed and the program returns `EXIT_FAILURE`. Use `gcc` to compile and link the program:

    $ gcc -Wall -Wshadow file1.c -o file1

The program exits if running without any arguments:

    $ ./file1
    Need to provide the file's name.

When the `main` function returns, the program terminates. By returning `EXIT_FAILURE`, this program informs the terminal that this program ends abnormally. If the file's name is given, then the program prints the file's name:

    $ ./file1 xyz
    The name of the file is xyz.

10.2   Reading from Files

10.2.1   Reading Characters: `fgetc`

After getting the file's name, we need to *open* the file for reading. This is accomplished by calling the `fopen` function. The function requires two arguments. The first is the name of the file, and the second specifies the "mode". The mode determines how the file is opened—for reading or for writing. They are two different ways of opening the same file. In this example, we want to read the file, and this mode is specified by "r" in the second argument.

Calling `fopen` does not always open a file successfully. There are many reasons that can make `fopen` fail. For example, the file may not exist, or the user running the program may not have the permission to open the file. When `fopen` fails, it returns `NULL`. It is important to check whether `fopen` returns `NULL` before attempting to read from or write to a file. After opening a file, `fgetc` can be used to read the characters one by one.

```c
1   // countchar.c
2   #include <stdio.h>
3   #include <stdlib.h>
4   int main(int argc, char * argv[])
5   {
6     FILE * fptr;
7     int ch;
8     int counter = 0;
9     if (argc < 2)
10      {
11        printf("Need to provide the file's name.\n");
12        return EXIT_FAILURE;
13      }
14    fptr = fopen(argv[1], "r");
15    if (fptr == NULL)
16      {
```

```
17        printf("fopen␣fail.\n");
18        return EXIT_FAILURE;
19      }
20    printf("The␣name␣of␣the␣file␣is␣%s.\n", argv[1]);
21    do
22      {
23        ch = fgetc(fptr);
24        if (ch != EOF)
25          {
26            counter ++;
27          }
28      } while (ch != EOF);
29    fclose(fptr);
30    printf("The␣file␣has␣%d␣characters.\n", counter);
31    return EXIT_SUCCESS;
32  }
```

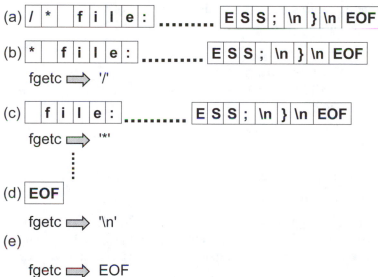

FIGURE 10.1: A file is a stream. This example uses the program source code as the input file. (a) After calling `fopen`, the stream starts from the very first character of the file and ends with `EOF`. `EOF` is a special character that does not actually exist in the file, but signifies that there is no data left in the stream. (b),(c) Each time `fgetc` is called, one character is taken out of the stream. (d) After calling `fgetc` enough times, all the characters in the file are retrieved. We have not yet attempted to read past the end of the file. (e) Finally, the end of file character `EOF` is returned because there are no more characters in the file.

How does `fgetc` work? After calling `fopen`, `fptr` points to a *stream* of characters, as illustrated in Fig. 10.1. This stream starts at the beginning of the file. Every time `fgetc` is called, one character is taken out from the stream. If the program keeps calling `fgetc`, eventually all characters are taken and the special character `EOF` is returned.

This program counts the number of characters. A character may be a Latin character ('a' to 'z' or 'A' to 'Z'), a digit ('0' to '9'), a punctuation mark (such as ',' and ';'), space, or an invisible character. At the end of each line, a new line character ('\n') is also counted.

When the program attempts to read beyond the end of the file, `fgetc` returns EOF. This character is called *end of file* and its symbol EOF is defined in `stdio.h`. If we search EOF using Linux' `grep` command:

    $ grep EOF /usr/include/stdio.h

we should find

    # define EOF (-1)

Its value is −1. The manual for `fgetc` says, "*fgetc() reads the next character from stream and returns it as an unsigned char cast to an int, or EOF on end of file or error.*"

What does this mean? This function reads one character from a file. This character is treated as an unsigned character because ASCII (American Standard Code for Information Interchange) has only positive values. Unsigned characters can have values between 0 and 255 inclusive. The function then casts the character to an integer. Why is this necessary? Because EOF is negative and is not an unsigned character. Thus `fgetc` returns −1, or 0 to 255 inclusive. This guarantees that EOF can be distinguished from the valid characters that are actually in the file. Another way to detect the end of file is by calling the function `feof`. This function returns a non-zero value if the end of file has been reached. Thus we can replace line 21 by:

```
21   while (! feof(fptr))
```

and remove `while ( ch != EOF );` at line 28.

This program reports the number of characters in the file. Suppose that the source for this program is in the file `file2.c` and we compile and execute it like so:

    $ gcc -Wall -Wshadow file2.c -o file2

    $ ./file2 file2.c

    The name of the file is file2.c.

    The file has 656 characters.

Linux has a program called `wc` and it reports the numbers of lines, words, and characters in a file. The program reports that the `file2.c` has 32 lines, 96 words, and 656 characters. The `wc` program considers a word to be a non-zero-length sequence of characters delimited by space.

    $ wc file2.c

    32 96 656 file2.c

Operating systems usually restrict the number files that a program can open at once to ensure that one program does not use too many resources. Thus programs should call `fclose` when a previously opened file is no longer needed. Just as with `malloc` and `free`, it is a good habit to type `fclose` right after typing `fopen` and then insert appropriate code between them. This can prevent forgetting to call `fclose`. In fact, `fopen` will allocate memory in the program. Thus, if a program does not call `fclose`, then the program has memory leak. Some students write this:

```
15   if (fptr == NULL)
16   {
17     printf("fopen fail.\n");
18     fclose(fptr);
19   }
```

This is wrong. If `fptr` is `NULL`, then `fopen` fails to open the file. If the file is not open, then it cannot be closed. The documentation of `fclose` clearly says:

```
The behaviour of fclose() is undefined if the stream parameter is an
illegal pointer, or is a descriptor already passed to a previous
invocation of fclose().
```

Thus, `fclose(NULL)` is bad, since it results in unpredictable behavior. Also, note that it is an error to close the same file pointer twice.

What is stored at the heap memory pointed by `fptr`? The following uses `gdb` to show the contents at the memory address pointed by `fptr`.

```
(gdb) print * fptr
$2 = {_flags = -72539000, _IO_read_ptr = 0x0, _IO_read_end = 0x0,
 _IO_read_base = 0x0, _IO_write_base = 0x0, _IO_write_ptr = 0x0,
 _IO_write_end = 0x0, _IO_buf_base = 0x0, _IO_buf_end = 0x0,
 _IO_save_base = 0x0, _IO_backup_base = 0x0, _IO_save_end = 0x0,
 _markers = 0x0, _chain = 0x7ffff7dd4180, _fileno = 3, _flags2 = 0,
 _old_offset = 0, _cur_column = 0, _vtable_offset = 0 '\000',
 _shortbuf = "", _lock = 0x6020f0, _offset = -1, __pad1 = 0x0, __pad2
 = 0x602100, __pad3 = 0x0, __pad4 = 0x0, __pad5 = 0, _mode = 0,
 _unused2 = '\000' <repeats 19 times>}
```

As we can see, the data that the `FILE *` points to is complicated. Fortunately, we do not need to know the details since they are purely internal to the C library, and should not be modified or examined directly.

10.2.2   Reading Integers: `fscanf(... %d...)`

In addition to `fgetc`, C provides many functions for reading data from a file. One of them is `fscanf`. It is very similar to `scanf`, except that it requires one more argument. The first argument is a `FILE` pointer. The following program adds the numbers in a file.

```
1  // fscanf.c
2  #include <stdio.h>
3  #include <stdlib.h>
4  int main(int argc, char * argv[])
5  {
6    FILE * fptr;
7    int val;
8    int sum = 0;
9    if (argc < 2)
10      {
11        printf("Need to provide the file's name.\n");
12        return EXIT_FAILURE;
13      }
14    fptr = fopen(argv[1], "r");
15    if (fptr == NULL)
16      {
17        printf("fopen fail.\n");
18        return EXIT_FAILURE;
19      }
```

```
20    printf("The␣name␣of␣the␣file␣is␣%s.\n", argv[1]);
21    while (fscanf(fptr, "%d", & val) == 1)
22      {
23        printf("%d␣", val);
24        sum += val;
25      }
26    fclose(fptr);
27    printf("\nThe␣sum␣is␣%d.\n", sum);
28    return EXIT_SUCCESS;
29  }
```

This program keeps reading until no more integers can be read. Each call of `fscanf` function returns the number of value(s) successfully read. We can use `fscanf` to attempt to read multiple values at once. This example reads only one integer at a time. The returned value will be either 1 if a single value is successfully read, or 0 if no value can be successfully read. This means to keep reading as long as `fscanf` can still find another integer in the file. A common mistake is thinking that `fscanf` returns the value read from this file. This is wrong; instead, `fscanf` returns how many values are read from the file. The pattern `"%d"` indicates that we only attempt to read one integer. If only one integer is read, `fscanf` returns 1, regardless of the integer's value. Every time `fscanf` is called, the file stream moves forward and eventually reaches the end of the file.

Suppose we have a file called `intfile` that stores some integers:

```
4 7 8
32
71
6 -2 5 8
```

Below is the output when we run the program with `intfile` as the command-line argument:

```
The name of the file is intfile.
4 7 8 32 71 6 -2 5 8
The sum is 139.
```

Compared with `fgetc`, `fscanf` has several advantages:
- When using `%d`, `fscanf` skips characters (such as space and new line `'\n'`) that are not digits.
- If two integers are separated by characters that are not digits, `fscanf` separates the two integers automatically.
- When `fgetc` reads the first character, it is not the integer 4, but instead the character '4' because it is treated as a character. A character can be converted to an integer using the ASCII table. Type

      $ man ascii

  into the terminal to see an ASCII table, and note that the character '4' has the decimal value 52.
- If a number is greater than 9, the number has two or more digits. Using `fgetc`, only one digit is read at a time. If the number is 123, then we need to call `fgetc` three times in order to get the three digits. Moreover, we need to change the three characters '1', '2', and '3' (ASCII values 49, 50, 51) to the integer value 123 (one hundred and twenty three). This is done by `fscanf` automatically.

Due to the above reasons, if a program reads integers from a file, `fscanf` is a better choice than `fgetc`.

10.3   Writing to Files

We can use `fprintf` to write information to a file. It is very similar to `printf`; the difference is that `fprintf` writes information to a file and `printf` writes information to the computer screen. The following example shows how to write a program that reads integers from two input files, adds the values, and stores the sum (another integer) into the output file, one integer per line. This program takes three command-line arguments:

- `argv[1]`: Name of the first input file.
- `argv[2]`: Name of the second input file.
- `argv[3]`: Name of the output file.

Each input file contains some integers. It is possible that several integers are in the same line separated by space. It is also possible that the two files contain different numbers of integers. If this happens, after running out of the integers from the shorter file, the program copies the remaining integers from the longer input file to the output file. The program does not know how many integers are stored in either file. The program ignores space in each line and it also ignores empty lines. For simplicity, the program does not not consider overflow or underflow of integers.

These are the two sample input files:

```
1   6255  7077
2   6965
3   3474        300
4   4334  5386
5   7380        6610
6   1581
7
8   9955
9   8813  237
10
11  7484  3502
```

```
1   4864  4784
2   8816        8113
3   3895  8677
4   7026
5
6   1937      1282
7   8638
8
9   9561  2391  5681  8452
10  498  9070  4930  8775
11  670  521  3582
12
13  8644
```

The output file should be:

```
1   11119
2   11861
3   15781
4   11587
5   4195
6   13011
7   12412
8   9317
9   7892
10  10219
11  19516
12  11204
13  5918
14  15936
15  4000
```

```
16  9070
17  4930
18  8775
19  670
20  521
21  3582
22  8644
```

The following program solves this problem:

```
1   // addint.c
2   #include <stdio.h>
3   #include <stdlib.h>
4   int main(int argc, char * argv[])
5   {
6     if (argc < 4) // need two inputs and one output
7       {
8         return EXIT_FAILURE;
9       }
10    FILE * fin1;
11    FILE * fin2;
12    // open the two input files
13    fin1 = fopen(argv[1], "r");
14    if (fin1 == NULL) // fail to open
15      {
16        return EXIT_FAILURE;
17      }
18    fin2 = fopen(argv[2], "r");
19    if (fin2 == NULL)
20      {
21        fclose (fin1); // need to close opened file
22        return EXIT_FAILURE;
23      }
24    // open the output file
25    FILE * fout;
26    fout = fopen(argv[3], "w");
27    if (fout == NULL)
28      {
29        fclose (fin1);
30        fclose (fin2);
31        return EXIT_FAILURE;
32      }
33
34    int val1;
35    int val2;
36    int in1ok = 1; // can still read input file 1
37    int in2ok = 1; // can still read input file 2
38    // continue as long as one file still has numbers
39    while ((in1ok == 1) || (in2ok == 1))
40      {
41        val1 = 0; // reset the values before reading from files
42        val2 = 0;
```

```
43    if (fscanf(fin1, "%d", & val1) != 1) // do not use == 0
44      {
45        in1ok = 0; // cannot read input file 1 any more
46      }
47    if (fscanf(fin2, "%d", & val2) != 1)
48      {
49        in2ok = 0; // cannot read input file 1 any more
50      }
51    if ((in1ok == 1) || (in2ok == 1))
52      {
53        fprintf(fout, "%d\n", val1 + val2); // save the sum
54      }
55    }
56  /* close the files */
57  fclose (fin1);
58  fclose (fin2);
59  fclose (fout);
60
61  return EXIT_SUCCESS;
62 }
```

Line 6 checks whether enough arguments have been provided. Lines 13 to 32 open the files. If `fopen` fails, then the program returns `EXIT_FAILURE`. Please remember to close all successfully opened files; otherwise, the program leaks memory allocated by `fopen`. At line 21, the program has failed to open the second file, and thus needs to close the first opened file before returning. The condition at line 39 means "continue if one (or both) of the files still has numbers". This handles the situation when the two files have different numbers of integers. The variables `in1ok` and `in2ok` are updated at lines 45 and 49.

Note that when a file reaches its end, `fscanf` returns `EOF`, and not zero. A common mistake at lines 43 and 47 is using `== 0`. Since `EOF` is -1, if we replace `!= 1` by `== 0` at lines 43 and 47 then the program will enter an infinite loop. If the program reads successfully from at least one of the two files, the program writes the sum to the output file. Lines 41 and 42 reset the values to zero. This is necessary because one file may have already reached the end, in which case calling `fscanf` will not update one of `val1` and `val2`. Without resetting the values we get the wrong answer when one file is longer than the other.

This program specifically does not consider overflowing or underflowing of integers. What does this mean? When a program creates an integer variable, the size of the variable is fixed (dependent on the machine). Suppose an integer has 4 bytes, i.e., `sizeof(int)` is 4. One byte is 8 bits and each bit can hold either 0 or 1. Thus, a 4-byte integer can hold 32 bits, namely 2^{32} possible values. The possible values include both positive and negative integers. An integer can hold a value between $2^{31} - 1$ (2147483647) and -2^{31} (-2147483648), totally 2^{32} possible values. If a file contains a number greater than 2147483647 or smaller than -2147483648, `fscanf` will not work. Thus the behavior of the program is unspecified if the input numbers are too large or too small. By stating this, we put the burden on the user to ensure that the numbers are within the range.

10.4   Reading and Writing Strings

Earlier sections showed how to read characters and integers by using `fgetc` and `fscanf`. How can a program read a string, for example, someone's name? There are several solutions. One solution uses `fgetc` reading one character at a time. Another solution uses `fscanf` with `%s`.

```c
// fscanfstr.c
#include <stdio.h>
#include <stdlib.h>
#define MAXSIZE 6
int main(int argc, char * argv[])
{
  FILE * fptr;
  if (argc < 2)
    {
      printf("Need to provide the file's name.\n");
      return EXIT_FAILURE;
    }
  fptr = fopen(argv[1], "r");
  if (fptr == NULL)
    {
      printf("fopen fail.\n");
      return EXIT_FAILURE;
    }
  char buffer[MAXSIZE];
  while (fscanf(fptr, "%5s", buffer) == 1)
    {
      printf("%s\n", buffer);
    }
  fclose(fptr);
  return EXIT_SUCCESS;
}
```

Line 20 reads one word at a time by using `%s` in `fscanf`. The function distinguishes words by looking for spaces and new line characters ('\n'). Adding a number between `%` and `s` tells `fscanf` to limit the number of characters in a word. For example `fscanf(fptr, "%5s", buffer)` limits the length of the word to 5 characters. Please remember a word is a string and it ends with '\0'. Thus, the length of the buffer (line 19) must be at least one larger than the number between `%` and `s` to accommodate '\0'. If we do not put any number between `%` and `s` and a word in the file is long, then the program will use up the memory space in `buffer`, and write past the end. When this occurs, the program's behavior is undefined due to invalid memory accesses. When writing programs, it is important to make sure that the programs cannot have invalid memory accesses regardless of the input data. Even a malicious user should not be able to cause an invalid memory access. If the input is not checked carefully, a malicious user may, for example, enter 20,000 characters for a person's name. This is called the "buffer overflow attack" and is one of the most common security attacks.

In addition to `fgetc` and `fscanf`, `fgets` is another function for reading data from a file. This function takes three arguments:

1. The starting address of an array of characters to store the data.
2. The number of characters to read.
3. A FILE * to read from.

If the second argument is n, the function reads as many as n - 1 characters from the file. The function then adds the ending character, '\0', automatically. The function may read fewer characters if (i) a new line character occurs before reading n - 1 characters or (ii) the file has reached its end. Please note that fgets does not stop when it reads a space. It can read multiple words in the same line even though these words are separated by one or more spaces. For fscanf(...''%s'' ...), the size between % and s is optional. For fgets, the size is a required argument. If fgets succeeds in reading anything from the file, it returns the value of the first argument, i.e., the starting address to store the data. If fgets fails to read anything from the file, it returns NULL.

The following program reads a file line by line and counts the number of lines. We assume that the maximum length of each line is 80 characters, i.e., at least one '\n' occurs within every 80 characters.

```c
// fgets.c
#include <stdio.h>
#include <string.h>
#include <stdlib.h>
#define MAX_LINE_LENGTH 81
// assume that the maximum length of each line is already know
int main(int argc, char * argv[])
{
    FILE * fptr;
    int numLine = 0; // must initialize to zero
    char oneLine[MAX_LINE_LENGTH];
    if (argc < 2)
        // must check argc before using argv[1]
        {
            printf("Need to provide the file's name.\n");
            return EXIT_FAILURE;
        }
    fptr = fopen(argv[1], "r");
    if (fptr == NULL)
        {
            printf("fopen fail.\n");
            // do not call fclose (fptr) here
            return EXIT_FAILURE;
        }
    printf("The name of the file is %s.\n", argv[1]);
    while (fgets(oneLine, MAX_LINE_LENGTH, fptr) != NULL)
        {
            numLine ++;
        }
    fclose(fptr);
    printf("The file has %d lines.\n", numLine);
    return EXIT_SUCCESS;
}
```

When the program cannot read from the file any more, `fgets` returns `NULL`. This means that the end of the file has been reached. The C library has a function called `getline` and it can be used to a line of arbitrary size.

Chapter 11

Programming Problems Using File

11.1 Sorting a File of Integers

This program reads integers from a file, sorts them, and stores the sorted integers into another file. We have already learned how to read integers from a file in Section 10.2.2. Chapter 9 explains how to sort arrays. Here we put these two things together. This is the first few steps of the program:

1. Check whether there are command-line arguments for the input and the output file names.
2. Open the input file.
3. Read integers from the file and count the number of integers in the file.
4. Allocate memory to store the integers.

As illustrated in Fig. 10.1, a file is a stream. Every time something is read from the file, the stream moves forward. After counting the number of integers, the stream has reached its end. To fill the array, it is necessary to read the file from the beginning again. We can do this in several ways. One way is to close the file and open it again. The preferred way is to use `fseek`. It goes to a particular position in a file. This is how to go to the beginning of a file: `fseek(fptr, 0, SEEK_SET)`.

Some people believe that calling `rewind` is the same as `fseek(fptr, 0, SEEK_SET)`. This is not true. The returned value of `fseek` reports whether it succeeds or not, but `rewind` does not report either success or failure.

The remaining steps are:

5. Use `fseek` to go to the beginning of the file.
6. Read the file again and fill the array.
7. Sort the array.
8. Close the input file.
9. Open the output file.
10. Write the sorted array to the output file.
11. Close the output file.
12. Free the memory for the array.

The order of some of these steps may be changed. For example, the program may free the array memory before or after closing the output file (steps 11 and 12). The orders of steps 8 and 9 can also be exchanged. However, the order of some steps cannot be changed. For example, step 9 (opening the output file) must precede step 10 (writing to the output file). This can only be determined by thinking logically about the code. When writing complex programs, it is important to write down the steps before writing the code. This saves a lot of debugging time, and often potential problems can be considered before typing a single line of code.

Below is a sample solution for this program. If we compare the program and the steps listed above, we will find a close correspondence between them. This program uses the built-in qsort function to sort integers.

```c
// sortint.c
#include <stdio.h>
#include <stdlib.h>
int comparefunc(const void * arg1, const void * arg2)
{
  const int * ptr1 = (const int *) arg1; // cast type
  const int * ptr2 = (const int *) arg2;
  const int val1 = * ptr1; // get the value from the address
  const int val2 = * ptr2;
  if (val1 < val2) // compare the value
    { return -1; }
  if (val1 == val2)
    { return 0; }
  return 1;
}
int main(int argc, char * argv[])
{
  // need two file names: input and output
  if (argc < 3)
    {
      return EXIT_FAILURE;
    }
  // open the input file
  FILE * infptr;
  infptr = fopen(argv[1], "r");
  if (infptr == NULL)
    {
      return EXIT_FAILURE;
    }
  // count the number of integers in the file
  int count = 0;
  int val;
  while (fscanf(infptr, "%d", & val) == 1)
    {
      count ++;
    }
  // allocate memory for the array
  int * arr;
  arr = malloc(sizeof(int) * count);
  if (arr == NULL)
    {
      fclose (infptr);
      return EXIT_FAILURE;
    }
  // go to the beginning of the file
```

```
46    fseek(infptr, 0, SEEK_SET);
47    // read the file again and fill the array
48    int ind = 0; // array index
49    while (fscanf(infptr, "%d", & val) == 1)
50       {
51          arr[ind] = val;
52          ind ++;
53       }
54    // sort the array
55    qsort(& arr[0], count, sizeof(int), comparefunc);
56    // close the input file
57    fclose (infptr);
58    // open the output file
59    FILE * outfptr;
60    outfptr = fopen(argv[2], "w");
61    if (outfptr == NULL)
62       {
63          free (arr); // do not forget to release memory
64          return EXIT_FAILURE;
65       }
66    // write the sorted array to the output file
67    for (ind = 0; ind < count; ind ++)
68       {
69          fprintf(outfptr, "%d\n", arr[ind]);
70       }
71    // close outupt file
72    fclose (outfptr);
73    // release the array's memory
74    free (arr);
75    return EXIT_SUCCESS;
76 }
```

11.2 Counting the Occurrences of Characters

The program reads characters from a file and counts their occurrences. The program does not distinguish between uppercase characters and lowercase characters. Only the 26 Latin letters used in English are counted. If a character is not a Latin letter, the character is ignored. The program then saves the occurrences into an output file.

The program has the following steps:

1. Check whether there are command-line arguments for the input and the output files.
2. Create an array of 26 integers. A fixed size array is preferred because the array's size is known in advance. This means that the array can be placed on the stack, and we do not need to call `malloc` and `free`.
3. Open the input file.
4. Read the characters from the file. If the character is a Latin letter, increment the corresponding array element.
5. Close the input file.

6. Open the output file.

7. Write the array's elements to the output file.

8. Close the output file.

These steps are similar to the steps for the previous program, except the parts for counting the characters. Below is a sample implementation of the above steps:

```
// countchar.c
#include <stdio.h>
#include <stdlib.h>
#include <ctype.h>
#define NUM_CHAR 26
int main(int argc, char * argv[])
{
  if (argc < 3) // need input and output
    {
      return EXIT_FAILURE;
    }
  // create an array of 26 integers
  char charcount[NUM_CHAR] = {0}; // initialize to zeros
  // without initialization, the elements are garbage
  // open the input file
  FILE * infptr;
  infptr = fopen(argv[1], "r");
  if (infptr == NULL)
    {
      return EXIT_FAILURE;
    }
  // count the occurrences of the characters
  int onechar;
  do
    {
      onechar = fgetc(infptr);
      if (isupper(onechar))
        {
          charcount[onechar - 'A'] ++;
        }
      if (islower(onechar))
        {
          charcount[onechar - 'a'] ++;
        }
    } while (onechar != EOF);
  // close the input file
  fclose(infptr);
  // open the output file
  FILE * outfptr;
  outfptr = fopen(argv[2], "w");
  if (outfptr == NULL)
    {
      return EXIT_FAILURE;
    }
  // write the array's elements to the file
```

```
46    int ind;
47    for (ind = 0; ind < NUM_CHAR; ind ++)
48      {
49        fprintf(outfptr, "%c:_%d\n", ind + 'A',
50          charcount[ind]);
51      }
52    // close outupt file
53    fclose (outfptr);
54    return EXIT_SUCCESS;
55  }
```

The main difference between this program and the previous program is in lines 24 to 35. Line 27 uses the function `isupper` to determine whether the character is an uppercase letter. This function is declared in `ctype.h` so the program needs to include this header file. Calling `isupper` is equivalent to checking whether `onechar` is between 'A' and 'Z'. The ASCII value for 'A' is 65 and the ASCII value for 'Z' is 90. However, you should not check whether `onechar` is between 65 and 90. There are a few reasons for this suggestion. First, if you accidentally type 89 instead of 90, it is not easy to detect the mistake. It is difficult remembering that 'Z' is 90, not 89. By contrast, if you type 'Y' instead 'Z', it is easier to detect the mistake. This brings us to the main reason for preferring 'A' and 'Z' to 64 and 90: It is clear and easy to read. Clarity is one of the most important qualities of well-written code. Did you notice that I incorrectly wrote 64, not 65? If you missed that mistake, it is likely that you would miss similar mistakes in your programs.

How about converting uppercase letters to lowercase? Many students write

```
1  if ((onechar >= 65) && (onechar <= 90))
2  {
3      onechar += 32;
4  }
```

This is bad. Why? It is difficult to understand the meaning of 65, 90, and 32. What happens if we accidentally type 31 instead of 32? How much time does it take to find such a mistake? It will take longer than you think. It is much better to write:

```
1  if ((onechar >= 'A') && (onechar <= 'Z'))
2  {
3      onechar = (onechar - 'A') + 'a';
4  }
```

Do not overlook the importance of these details. I have seen many students making "small" mistakes like these. They are overly confident that they do not make mistakes. When you write a complex program, the problems from these details can easily take hours to detect and correct. Good programmers know this well, and dramatically improve their efficiency by making things as simple and as clear as possible. It allows programmers to write sophisticated computer programs more easily.

Lines 29 and 33 use the values in the ASCII table to calculate the corresponding index for the array `charcount`. If the character is 'A', then `onechar - 'A'` is 0. If the character is 'B', then `onechar - 'A'` is 1. If the character is 'c', `onechar - 'a'` is 2. Some students write something like:

```
1  if (onechar == 'A')
2      charcount[0] ++;
3  if (onechar == 'B')
4      charcount[1] ++;
```

```
5   if (onechar == 'C')
6       charcount [2] ++;
7   if (onechar == 'D')
8       charcount [2] ++;
9   if (onechar == 'E')
10      charcount [3] ++;
```

Fifty-two conditions are needed. The problem should be obvious: It is easy to make mistakes. If fact, there are mistakes in the code above. Can you detect them easily? There is a general principle in writing good programs: Do not copy-paste code. Write DRY code. DRY stands for "Don't Repeat Yourself". The opposite of DRY code is WET code, which stands for "We Enjoy Typing".

There are many reasons to follow the DRY principle. If you copy-paste code, then you increase the chances of mistakes. This is especially true when the code is modified after it is written. Once we have two (or more) pieces of WET code, testing, debugging and improving the code becomes more difficult. We need to remember to change all places that the code is repeated. If we forget to change some places, then the program will surprise you: In some situations, the program is correct, but in others it fails.

There are many simple and clear solutions that avoid WET code. For example, if the two (or more) pieces of code are identical, then create a function and call it twice. If they are mostly similar but with a few differences, then the function's arguments can handle the differences. Spending some time fixing WET code usually helps tremendously in developing good test cases, since the programmer must think about and ultimately understand the code. That also helps with debugging, since you will be more familiar with how the program should behave as you step through it line by line.

Line 49 is the reverse way of using the ASCII values. If the index is 0, it corresponds to 'A' so the value of 'A' is added. The output of this program will look something like:

```
A: 39
B: 1
C: 41
D: 16
E: 69
F: 38
```

11.3   Counting the Occurrences of a Word

This program takes three arguments:
1. `argv[1]`: The name of the input file.
2. `argv[2]`: The name of the output file.
3. `argv[3]`: A word to be searched for.

This program detects and counts the occurrences of the word in an input file. If a line in the input file includes the word, the program writes that line to the output file. After checking all lines in the input file, the program writes the total count to the output file. We must first think about how words are counted. If the search word is "eye" and a line in the input file contains "eyeye", do you count 1 or 2? Both definitions are acceptable in different circumstances and we need to decide which definition to use. We will explain how to handle the differences. For simplicity, each line in the input file contains at most 80 characters (and thus needs memory for 81 characters). The program does not count a word that spans two or more lines. The program uses **strstr** to search a word within a line.

```c
// countstr.c
#include <stdio.h>
#include <stdlib.h>
#include <string.h>
#define LINE_LENGTH 81
int main(int argc, char * argv[])
{
    if (argc < 4) // input word output
        {
            return EXIT_FAILURE;
        }
    // open the input file
    FILE * infptr;
    infptr = fopen(argv[1], "r");
    if (infptr == NULL)
        {
            return EXIT_FAILURE;
        }
    // open the output file
    FILE * outfptr;
    outfptr = fopen(argv[2], "w");
    if (outfptr == NULL)
        {
            fclose(infptr);
            return EXIT_FAILURE;
        }
    int count = 0;
    char oneline[LINE_LENGTH];
    while (fgets(oneline, LINE_LENGTH, infptr) != NULL)
        {
            if (strstr(oneline, argv[3]) != NULL)
                {
                    fprintf(outfptr, "%s", oneline);
                }
            char * chptr = oneline;
            while (chptr != NULL)
                {
                    chptr = strstr(chptr, argv[3]);
                    if (chptr != NULL)
                        {
                            count ++;
                            // if "eyeye" counts as two "eye"
                            chptr ++;
                            // if "eyeye" counts as one "eye"
                            // chptr += strlen(argv[3]);
                        }
                }
        }
```

```
49    fprintf(outfptr, "%d\n", count);
50    // close the input file
51    fclose (infptr);
52    // close outupt file
53    fclose (outfptr);
54    return EXIT_SUCCESS;
55  }
```

Lines 41 and 45 implement the two definitions. Line 41 increments the address by only one and searches again. Line 45 increments the address by length of the string. So "eyeye" contains only one "eye", because after finding the first "eye", the program continues its search from "ye".

11.4   How to Comment Code

Almost every programming class requires that students comment their code. Additionally, almost every programming book tells readers to comment their code. However, very few classes or books say how to comment code. Writing comments is like writing an article and it is difficult to grade comments. Comments are about communicating with the readers of the code: Style and clarity are important. If comments do not explain code, then they are not useful. It is not yet possible to check comments' usefulness by using computer programs. Grading comments by human eyes (usually by teaching assistants) is labor-intense. As a result, some professors do not consider comments in grading and most students do not take comments seriously. Sometimes students even write comments like "because the professors tell us so." Some students ask me, "Do I need to write comments for *you*?" My answer is, "You need to write comments for *yourself*." If your program is longer than, say, 20 lines, you need to write comments before writing code.

This book frequently lists the steps before writing a program. These steps should be written in the comments of the code. Remember that programs are written to solve problems. The programs *implement* solutions. The solution must be known before the first line of code is typed. Writing a program without a solution first is like laying bricks for a house before knowing how many rooms the house will have. Almost everyone agrees that a house needs to be designed before it is built. Write code after you know the solution. It is good practice to think about the solution, write down the steps, explain your thinking process in comments.

In addition to explaining the steps, comments are needed to explain specifics of how functions work: what is required of the arguments, and what the return result means. Manual pages are good examples of this. Consider the manual page for `fgets`:

```
char *fgets(char *s, int size, FILE *stream);

fgets() reads in at most one less than size characters from
stream and stores them into the buffer pointed to by s.  Reading
stops after an EOF or a newline.  If a newline is read, it is stored
into the buffer.  A terminating null byte ('\0') is stored after the
last character in the buffer.

fgets() return s on success, and NULL on error or when end of
file occurs while no characters have been read.
```

This explains the arguments, the behavior of the function, and the return value. Notice how clear and dense the text is. No word is wasted.

A common mistake is to repeat information that is obvious from the syntax. The following comment is unnecessary:

```
1  /* This function has two arguments. Both are integers.
2     The function returns an integer. */
3  int func(int a, int b);
```

Compare with the informative comment:

```
1  /* The function returns
2      1  if  a > b
3      0  if  a == b
4     -1  if  a < b
5  */
6  int func(int a, int b);
```

Comments should provide some information that is unavailable from the syntax. Comments are important when explaining complex concepts. The example below shows a call stack:

```
/*
   ----------------------------------------
   | Frame    | Symbol | Address | Value |
   ----------------------------------------
   |          |   z    | 103     | 5     |
   |   f2     |   y    | 102     | 8     |
   |          |   x    | 101     | -7    |
   ----------------------------------------
*/
```

We can also use comments to show the flow of a function:

```
/*
   open input file -> count the number of lines -|
                                                 |
   ----------------------------------------------|
   |
   ---> allocate memory -> return to the beginning of the file

*/
```

The following is also good for those who do not like drawing:

```
/*
   1. open input file
   2. count the number of lines
   3. allocate memory
   4. return to the beginning of the file
*/
```

It should be apparent that comments can express important concepts. It takes practice to write comments well. It is often helpful to read others' code to see what comments are useful, and what are merely distractions. This is important for your own code. If you read a program written six months ago, can you understand it easily? If the meaning is not apparent, then the commenting can be improved.

With practice, comments become a good way to further understand your code by testing your ability to explain it. This, in turn, helps catch subtle problems, and also helps you generate good test cases. By guiding the eye of the reader through the code, good comments augment carefully chosen variable names, and clear syntax. Doing this shows that you have thought deeply about the program.

Part II

Recursion

Chapter 12

Recursion

Recursion is an everyday phenomenon that is natural to the human mind. Sometimes recursive computer programs can be challenging to reason about; however, recursion itself is readily understandable. For example, every person has parents, who have parents, who have parents, etc. That is an example of *recursion*. For another example, take two mirrors and make them face each other. A characteristic pattern will appear with images within images within images, etc. We also see recursion in cell-growth, and this manifests in the shapes of living things. For example, a tree's trunk is divided into main branches. Each branch in turn is further divided into smaller branches. Smaller branches are divided into twigs, and eventually we have leaves. This is the third example of recursion. In this case the recursive branching of the trunk into twigs is bounded by the leaves. Recursion is everywhere around us, and is also part of us. It is part of language, the way we think, and how our bodies grow. Recursion is one of nature's ways for solving complex problems.

There are three essential properties of recursion:

1. Recurring patterns. The examples above describe some recurring patterns: a person, the person's parents, their parents ...

2. Changes. Recursion does not merely mean repeating. A person is younger than the parents and they are younger than their parents. In the two mirrors, images become smaller. For a tree, branches become thinner. Each step of a recursive pattern has a characteristic change.

3. A terminating condition (or conditions). The recurring pattern eventually stops. A family tree stops at the youngest member that has no child. The images in the facing mirrors will become smaller and eventually invisible. When a branch eventually becomes leaves, the pattern stops.

Recursion can be a strategy for solving problems using a concept called *divide and conquer*: Divide a complex problem into smaller problems and solve (conquer) the smaller problems. This works when the smaller problems are related to the larger problem. Recursion uses the following steps:

1. Identify the argument (or arguments) of a problem.

2. Express the solution based on the arguments.
3. Determine the simple case(s) when the solutions are "obvious".
4. Derive the relationships between the complex case(s) and the simpler case(s).

Recursion is a topic that often separates beginning programmers from advanced programmers. Many introductory books treat recursion superficially, giving one or two examples without really explaining why recursion can be useful and how to use recursion to solve problems. On the other hand, the books written for advanced programmers assume readers are already comfortable solving problems with recursion. Thus, neither type of book explains recursion in detail. Because of this gap, many people find recursion mysterious. This book gives many examples that explain how to use recursion to solve problems.

12.1   Selecting Balls with Restrictions

12.1.1   Balls of Two Colors

There are unlimited red ($\mathbb{R}$) and blue ($\mathbb{B}$) balls in a bag. A game selects n balls under the restriction that red balls cannot be selected one after another. The order matters: The selections $\mathbb{R}\mathbb{B}$ and $\mathbb{B}\mathbb{R}$ are considered different from each other. The question is how many different ways can the balls be selected? This problem can be solved recursively by applying the four steps above:

1. Identify the argument (or arguments) of the problem.
   For this problem, the number of balls, n, is the argument.
2. Express the solution based on the arguments.
   Let $f(n)$ be the answer: the number of ways to select the n balls under the restriction (two adjacent balls cannot both be red).
3. Determine the simple case(s) when the solutions are "obvious".
   If only one ball is selected, then there are two possibilities: $\mathbb{R}$ or $\mathbb{B}$. Thus, $f(1)$ is 2. If only two balls are selected, there are three possibilities: $\mathbb{R}\mathbb{B}$, $\mathbb{B}\mathbb{R}$, and $\mathbb{B}\mathbb{B}$. Therefore, $f(2)$ is 3.
4. Derive the relationships between the complex case(s) and the simpler case(s).
   If there are n balls ($n > 2$), the first ball can be $\mathbb{R}$ or $\mathbb{B}$ and vice versa. Therefore, there are exactly two choices for the first ball. Fig. 12.1 shows the two different scenarios in the selection of the second ball.
   (a) If the first ball is $\mathbb{B}$, then the remaining $n - 1$ balls must follow the same rule: no red balls are adjacent. There are $f(n - 1)$ possibilities.
   (b) If the first ball is $\mathbb{R}$, then the second ball must be $\mathbb{B}$. A $\mathbb{B}$ ball resets the possibilities since the third ball can be $\mathbb{R}$ or $\mathbb{B}$, without any additional restriction. Therefore the remaining $n - 2$ balls must follow the same rule and there are $f(n - 2)$ possibilities.

Based on this analysis, $f(n)$ is the sum $f(n - 1) + f(n - 2)$.

$$f(n) = \begin{cases} 2 & \text{when } n \text{ is 1} \\ 3 & \text{when } n \text{ is 2} \\ f(n - 1) + f(n - 2) & \text{when } n > 2 \end{cases} \tag{12.1}$$

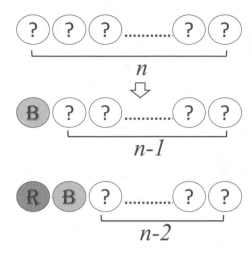

FIGURE 12.1: To decide $f(n)$, consider the possibilities for the first ball. If the first ball is $\mathbb{B}$, the remaining $n-1$ balls have $f(n-1)$ possibilities. If the first ball is $\mathbb{R}$, then the second ball must be $\mathbb{B}$ and the remaining $n-2$ balls have $f(n-2)$ possibilities.

12.1.2 Balls of Three Colors

The question can be extended in many ways. The first extension considers balls of three colors. We still assume that there are unlimited red ($\mathbb{R}$), green ($\mathbb{G}$), and blue ($\mathbb{B}$) balls. We select balls under the restriction that two adjacent balls cannot be both red. Note that the orders matter: $\mathbb{R}\mathbb{B}$ and $\mathbb{B}\mathbb{R}$ are different selections. How many possible sequences can be selected for n balls?

When n is one, there are three possibilities:
1. $\mathbb{R}$
2. $\mathbb{G}$
3. $\mathbb{B}$

When n is two, there are eight possibilities. Please notice that $\mathbb{R}\,\mathbb{R}$ is an invalid option.
1. $\mathbb{R}\ \mathbb{G}$
2. $\mathbb{R}\ \mathbb{B}$
3. $\mathbb{G}\ \mathbb{R}$
4. $\mathbb{G}\ \mathbb{G}$
5. $\mathbb{G}\ \mathbb{B}$
6. $\mathbb{B}\ \mathbb{R}$
7. $\mathbb{B}\ \mathbb{G}$
8. $\mathbb{B}\ \mathbb{B}$

What is the number of possibilities for n balls when $n > 2$? To solve this problem, let $f(n)$ be the answer. We already know that $f(1) = 3$ and $f(2) = 8$.

When $n > 2$, consider the possibilities for the very first ball. Fig. 12.2 shows three scenarios:

1. If the first ball is $\mathbb{G}$, then the second ball can be any of the three colors. There is no further restriction for the remaining $n-1$ balls. Thus, there are $f(n-1)$ possible sequences for the remaining $n-1$ balls.
2. Likewise, if the first ball is $\mathbb{B}$, then the second ball can be any of the three colors. There is no further restriction for the remaining $n-1$ balls. There are $f(n-1)$ possible sequences for the remaining $n-1$ balls.

3. If the first ball is $\mathbb{R}$, then there are two scenarios:
   (a) If the second ball is $\mathbb{G}$, then the third ball can be any of the three colors. There is no further restriction for the remaining $n-2$ balls. Thus, there are $f(n-2)$ possible sequences for the remaining $n-2$ balls.
   (b) If the second ball is $\mathbb{B}$, then the third ball can be any of the three colors. There is no further restriction for the remaining $n-2$ balls. Thus, there are $f(n-2)$ options for the remaining $n-2$ balls.
   (c) Note that the second ball cannot be $\mathbb{R}$, so this possibility is not considered.

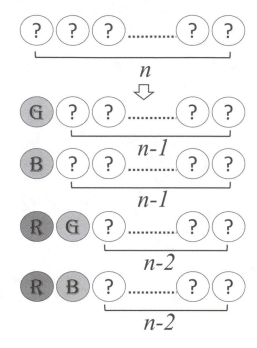

FIGURE 12.2: To decide $f(n)$, consider the possibilities for the first ball. If the first ball is $\mathbb{G}$ or $\mathbb{B}$, the remaining $n-1$ balls have $f(n-1)$ possibilities. If the first ball is $\mathbb{R}$, the second ball must be $\mathbb{G}$ or $\mathbb{B}$ and the remaining $n-2$ balls have $f(n-2)$ possibilities.

Thus, the relationships are:

$$f(n) = \begin{cases} 3 & \text{if } n \text{ is } 1 \\ 8 & \text{if } n \text{ is } 2 \\ f(n-1) + f(n-1) + f(n-2) + f(n-2) = 2f(n-1) + 2f(n-2) & \text{if } n > 2 \end{cases}$$
$$(12.2)$$

12.1.3   A Further Restriction

This question can be extended further with another restriction. Now two adjacent balls cannot both be red or green. Two adjacent balls can both be blue. How many possible sequences can be selected for n balls? When n is one, there still are three possibilities:

1. $\mathbb{R}$
2. $\mathbb{G}$
3. $\mathbb{B}$

When n is two, there are seven possibilities. Please notice that $\mathbb{G}\,\mathbb{G}$ is an invalid option.

1. $\mathbb{R}\,\mathbb{G}$
2. $\mathbb{R}\,\mathbb{B}$
3. $\mathbb{G}\,\mathbb{R}$
4. $\mathbb{G}\,\mathbb{B}$
5. $\mathbb{B}\,\mathbb{R}$
6. $\mathbb{B}\,\mathbb{G}$
7. $\mathbb{B}\,\mathbb{B}$

We use a different approach to solve this problem, by using some additional functions:

- $r(n)$ is the number of possible sequences when selecting n balls and the first ball is $\mathbb{R}$.
- $g(n)$ is the number of possible sequences when selecting n balls and the first ball is $\mathbb{G}$.
- $b(n)$ is the number of possible sequences when selecting n balls and the first ball is $\mathbb{B}$.
- $f(n)$ is the number of possible sequences when selecting n balls and the first ball can be any of the three colors. Thus, $f(n) = r(n) + g(n) + b(n)$.

The following table shows the values of these functions for n equal to 1 or 2:

n	1	2
$r(n)$	1	2
$g(n)$	1	2
$b(n)$	1	3
$f(n)$	3	7

How is $r(n)$ calculated when n is greater than 2? By definition, $r(n)$ means the number of possible sequences of n balls and the first one is $\mathbb{R}$. For the remaining $n-1$ balls, the first ball (the second among the n balls) can be either $\mathbb{G}$ or $\mathbb{B}$. If the first (the second among the n balls) ball is $\mathbb{G}$, there are $g(n-1)$ possibilities. Similarly, when the first ball (the second among the n balls) is $\mathbb{B}$, there are $b(n-1)$ options. Thus, $r(n) = g(n-1) + b(n-1)$. Because the same restrictions apply to both red and green balls, we can use the same reasoning to write $g(n) = r(n-1) + b(n-1)$.

How many possibilities are there when selecting n balls and the first ball is $\mathbb{B}$? When the first is blue then there is no restriction on the second ball in the sequence. The second ball can be red, green, or blue; thus, this is true $b(n) = g(n-1) + b(n-1) + r(n-1)$. This is also $f(n-1)$ because it means selecting $n-1$ balls and the first ball can be $\mathbb{G}$, $\mathbb{B}$, or $\mathbb{R}$. There are $f(n-1)$ possible sequences of length $n-1$ balls so $b(n) = f(n-1)$.

The complete solution is shown below:

$$
\begin{aligned}
r(n) &= g(n-1) + b(n-1) \\
g(n) &= r(n-1) + b(n-1) \\
b(n) &= f(n-1) \\
f(n) &= r(n) + g(n) + b(n)
\end{aligned}
\tag{12.3}
$$

The table below shows the values when n is between 1 and 6:

n	1	2	3	4	5	6
r(n)	1	2	5	12	29	70
g(n)	1	2	5	12	29	70
b(n)	1	3	7	17	41	99
f(n)	3	7	17	41	99	239

12.2   One-Way Streets

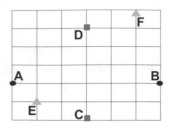

FIGURE 12.3: A city's streets form a grid, and are either east–west bound or north–south bound. A car can move only east or north.

A city has severe traffic congestions during rush hours so the city government considers adopting a rule: During rush hours, cars can move only east or north. All streets run either east–west or north–south, forming a grid, as shown in Fig. 12.3.

Assume we had the location of a car's origin and destination. How many ways can the destination be reached by driving? This example may seem artificial but it is actually a reasonable simplification of the one-way streets in the downtown districts of many cities. These cities generally have one-way streets that run in opposite directions, so that cars can move west and south as well. Nonetheless, the simplification is useful for analyzing traffic patterns.

Fig. 12.3 marks three pairs of origins and destinations: A → B, C → D, and E → F. How many turning options does a driver have going from one origin to their corresponding destination? For the first two pairs A → B and C → D, the driver has only one option: not to turn at all. This is shown in Fig. 12.4 (a) and (b). There are more options for E → F. At E, the driver can go eastbound first or northbound first, as indicated by the two arrows in Fig. 12.4 (c). The question is the number of different paths a driver can make between the origin and the destination.

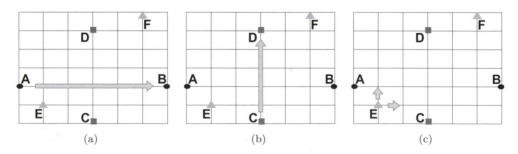

| (a) | (b) | (c) |

FIGURE 12.4: (a) A driver cannot turn anywhere when traversing from A to B. (b) Likewise, a driver cannot turn anywhere when traversing from C to D. (c) There are some turning options when traversing from E to F. At E, the driver can go northbound first or eastbound first, as indicated by the two arrows.

This question can be answered using the four steps for solving the recursive problem:
1. Identify the argument (or arguments) of a problem. Suppose E is at the intersection of $(x1, y1)$ and F is at the intersection of $(x2, y2)$. The distance between them can be expressed as $(\Delta x, \Delta y) = (x2 - x1, y2 - y1)$.

2. Express the solution based on the arguments. Let $f(\Delta x, \Delta y)$ express the number of unique paths.

3. Determine the simple case(s) when the solutions are "obvious". If $\Delta x < 0$, the destination is at the west side of the origin and there is no solution. Similarly, there is no solution if $\Delta y < 0$. If $\Delta x > 0$ and $\Delta y = 0$ (the case A $\rightarrow$ B), then there is precisely one solution. Likewise, if $\Delta x = 0$ and $\Delta y > 0$ (the case C $\rightarrow$ D), there is also precisely one solution. These are the simple cases whose answers can be found easily. A special case occurs when $\Delta x = \Delta y = 0$. This means that the destination is the same as the origin. It can be defined as no solution or one solution depending on what the reader prefers. Our solution considers that there is one solution for $\Delta x = \Delta y = 0$.

$$f(\Delta x, \Delta y) = \begin{cases} 0 & \text{if } \Delta x < 0 \text{ or } \Delta y < 0 \\ 1 & \text{if } \Delta x = 0 \text{ and } \Delta y \geq 0 \\ 1 & \text{if } \Delta x \geq 0 \text{ and } \Delta y = 0. \end{cases} \tag{12.4}$$

4. Derive the relationships between the complex case(s) and the simpler case(s). When $\Delta x > 0$ and $\Delta y > 0$ (the case E $\rightarrow$ F), then the driver has two options at the origin (i.e., E): Either the driver goes north first or east first. If the driver heads north, then the new origin is at $(x1, y1 + 1)$. There are $f(\Delta x, \Delta y - 1)$ possible paths from this point. If the driver goes east first, then the new origin is at $(x1 + 1, y1)$. Similarly, there are $f(\Delta x - 1, \Delta y)$ possible paths from this point. These are the only two possible options at position E and they are exclusive. Therefore, when $\Delta x > 0$ and $\Delta y > 0$, the solution can expressed as $f(\Delta x, \Delta y) = f(\Delta x, \Delta y - 1) + f(\Delta x - 1, \Delta y)$.

$$f(\Delta x, \Delta y) = \begin{cases} 0 & \text{if } \Delta x < 0 \text{ or } \Delta y < 0 \\ 1 & \text{if } \Delta x = 0 \text{ and } \Delta y \geq 0 \\ 1 & \text{if } \Delta x \geq 0 \text{ and } \Delta y = 0 \\ f(\Delta x, \Delta y - 1) + f(\Delta x - 1, \Delta y) & \text{if } \Delta x > 0 \text{ and } \Delta y > 0 \end{cases} \tag{12.5}$$

12.3 The Tower of Hanoi

FIGURE 12.5: The Tower of Hanoi. (a) Some disks are on pole A and the goal is to move all the disks to pole B, as shown in (b). A larger disk can never be placed on top of a smaller disk. A third pole, C, can be used when necessary.

Some disks of different sizes are stacked on a single pole. The disks are arranged so that smaller disks are above larger disks. The problem is to move the disks from one pole to

FIGURE 12.6: Moving one disk from A to B requires only one step.

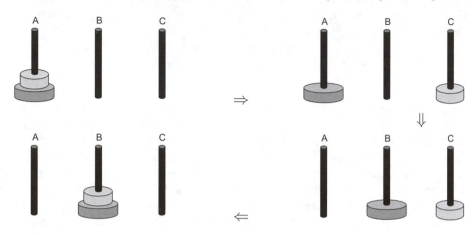

FIGURE 12.7: Moving two disks from A to B requires three steps.

another pole. Only one disk can be moved each time. A larger disk cannot be placed above a smaller disk. The third pole can be used for "temporary storage". Fig. 12.5 illustrates the problem. If there are n disks, how many steps are needed to move them to the second pole?

First consider moving only one disk from A to B. This is the simplest case and that disk can be moved directly from A to B as shown in Fig. 12.6.

Moving two disks requires more work. It is illegal to move the smaller disk to B and then move the larger disk to B. Doing so would place the larger disk above the smaller disk and violates the rules. Instead, it is necessary to move the smaller disk "somewhere else", i.e., C, before moving the larger disk to B. Then, move the larger disk from A to B and move the smaller disk from C to B. The steps are illustrated in Fig. 12.7. As illustrated, when there are two disks, the problem can be solved in three steps. Can you think of a solution that requires fewer steps for two disks?

Fig. 12.8 illustrates how to move three disks. The first three steps and the last three steps are somewhat similar. The first three steps move the top two disks from A to C. The last three steps move the top two disks from C to B. Between these steps is the fourth step, which is to move the largest disk from A to B.

What is the general strategy for moving n disks? If there is only one disk (i.e., n is one), the problem can be solved easily. Otherwise, the solution is divided into three parts:

1. Move the first $n - 1$ disks from A to C.
2. Move the largest disk from A to B.
3. Move the first $n - 1$ disks from C to B.

Now we put the steps together to solve the problem using recursion. The four-step approach for solving this problem is listed below:

1. Identify the argument (or arguments) of a problem.

   The number n is naturally the argument for the problem.

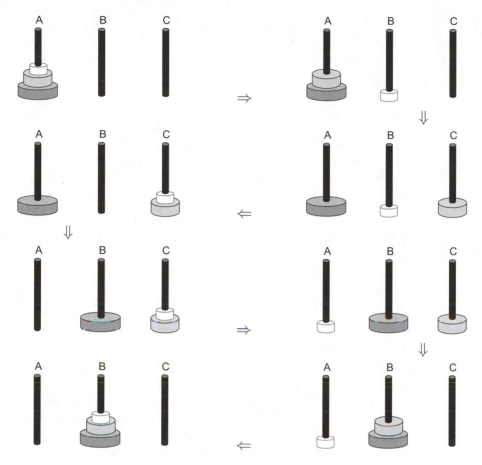

FIGURE 12.8: Moving three disks from A to B requires seven steps.

2. Express the solution based on the arguments.

   Let $f(n)$ be the answer: how many steps are needed to move n disks from A to B.

3. Determine the simple case(s) when the solutions are "obvious".

   If n is one, only one step is sufficient; thus, $f(1)$ is 1.

4. Derive the relationships between the complex case(s) and the simpler case(s).

   When n is greater than one, the problem can be divided into three parts:

   (a) Move $n-1$ disks to pole C, which requires $f(n-1)$ steps.

   (b) Move the largest disk to pole B, which requires 1 step.

   (c) Move $n-1$ disks from pole C to pole B, which requires $f(n-1)$ steps.

The following formula expresses the steps:

$$f(n) = \begin{cases} 1 & \text{if } n \text{ is } 1 \\ f(n-1)+1+f(n-1) = 2f(n-1)+1 & \text{if } n \geq 2 \end{cases} \quad (12.6)$$

This is a recursive form, meaning that the formula is defined in terms of itself. This works because the formula always references "smaller" versions of itself, until it gets to the trivial case (n is 1). For example, notice how $f(n)$ appears on one side of the = sign, and $f(n-1)$ appears on the other side. Thus, when we expand $f(n)$, we will need to expand $f(n-1)$ and then $f(n-2)$, etc., until we reach $f(1)$, which equals 1.

In this case it possible to find a *closed form* formula: $f(n)$ is expressed without $f(n-1)$ appearing on the right side of the = sign.

$$
\begin{aligned}
f(n) \; &= 2f(n-1)+1 \\
&= 4f(n-2)+2+1 \\
&= 8f(n-3)+4+2+1 \\
&= 16f(n-4)+8+4+2+1 \\
&= 2^k f(n-k)+2^{k-1}+2^{k-2}+...+4+2+1 \\
&= 2^{n-1}f(1)+2^{n-2}+2^{n-3}+...+4+2+1, \quad \text{when } k=n-1 \\
&= 2^{n-1}+2^{n-2}+2^{n-3}+...+4+2+1, \quad \text{because } f(1)=1 \\
&= 2^n - 1
\end{aligned}
\tag{12.7}
$$

It is not always possible, or easy, to find *closed form* formulas for recursive equations. Usually this requires a working knowledge of various series. Proving the answer is correct requires mathematical induction.

12.4   Calculating Integer Partitions

A positive integer can be expressed as the sum of a sequence of positive integers. An integer partition creates such a sequence of integers. For example, 5 can be broken into the sum of $1 + 2 + 2$ or $2 + 3$. These two partitions use different numbers, and thus are considered unique integer partitions. The order of the number in the partition is also important. Thus, $1 + 2 + 2$ and $2 + 1 + 2$ are considered different integer partitions because 1 appears in different positions. Below are some example integer partitions:

```
1 = 1       2 = 1 + 1       3 = 1 + 1 + 1       4 = 1 + 1 + 1 + 1
              = 2             = 1 + 2             = 1 + 1 + 2
                             = 2 + 1             = 1 + 2 + 1
                             = 3                 = 1 + 3
                                                 = 2 + 1 + 1
                                                 = 2 + 2
                                                 = 3 + 1
                                                 = 4
```

This question wants to answer the number of different partitions for a positive integer n. This problem can be solved by using the four-step approach solving recursive problems:

1. Identify the argument (or arguments) of a problem.
   The number n is naturally the argument for the problem.
2. Express the solution based on the arguments.
   Let $f(n)$ be the number of different partitions for integer n.
3. Determine the simple case(s) when the solutions are "obvious".
   When n is 1, there is only one way to partition the number: itself. When n is 2, there are two ways: $1 + 1$ and 2. Thus, $f(1) = 1$ and $f(2) = 2$.
4. Derive the relationships between the complex case(s) and the simpler case(s).
   When n is larger than 2, the solution selects the first number. It must be an integer between 1 and n inclusively. After selecting the first number, we have to partition the remaining portion of the number. Thus for each of the n possibilities for the first

number, we need to consider the number of possibilities for the remaining partition. The relationship can be expressed in this table:

Total	First Number	Remaining Value to Partition
n	1	$n-1$
n	2	$n-2$
n	3	$n-3$
	$\vdots$	
n	$n-2$	2
n	$n-1$	1
n	n	0

These are all the possible cases and they are exclusive. If the first number is 1, then the remaining value to be partitioned is $n-1$. How many ways can $n-1$ be partitioned? By definition, it is $f(n-1)$. Continuing with this logic, if the first number is 2, then the remaining value is $n-2$, and by definition there are $f(n-2)$ ways to partition it. Using recursion, we can assume that we have the answers to smaller versions of the problems. This works because the smaller versions are expressed in terms of yet smaller versions, and eventually we get to the trivial cases, i.e., $f(1) = 1$, and $f(2) = 2$.

The value of $f(n)$ is therefore the sum of all the different cases when the first number is 1, 2, 3, ..., $n-1$, or n. Now, we can express $f(n)$ as

$$f(n) = \begin{cases} 1 & \text{if } n \text{ is } 1 \\ f(n-1) + f(n-2) + \ldots f(1) + 1 = 1 + \sum_{i=1}^{n-1} f(i) & \text{if } n > 1 \end{cases} \tag{12.8}$$

There is also a convenient closed form solution to $f(n)$:

$$
\begin{array}{lll}
f(n) & = f(n-1) & +f(n-2) + f(n-3) + \ldots + 1 \\
- \quad f(n-1) & = & +f(n-2) + f(n-3) + \ldots + 1 \\
\hline
f(n) - f(n-1) & = f(n-1) & \\
f(n) & = 2f(n-1) & \\
f(n) & = 4f(n-2) & \\
f(n) & = 8f(n-3) & \\
f(n) & = 16f(n-4) & \\
& \vdots & \\
f(n) & = 2^{n-1}f(1) & \\
f(n) & = 2^{n-1} &
\end{array}
\tag{12.9}
$$

Therefore there are 2^{n-1} ways to partition the integer n.

12.4.1 Count the Number of "1"s

The partition problem has many variations. In this variation we count how many "1"s are used for partitioning n. Suppose $g(n)$ is the answer. First observe that $g(1) = 1$ and $g(2) = 2$. The more complicated cases can be related to the simpler cases with the following logic. Observe that there are 2^{n-2} partitions of n that begin with the digit "1". There may be "1"s in the partitions of the remaining value, $n-1$. Thus, when the first number is "1", we use $2^{n-2} + g(n-1)$ "1"s. Notice again how we just assume we have the answer for

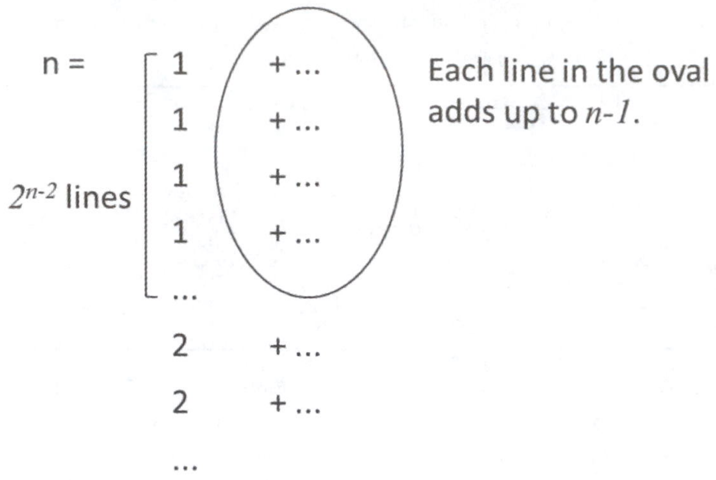

FIGURE 12.9: Count the occurrences of "1" when partitioning n.

smaller versions of the same function. We do not need to worry about the specific value of $g(n-1)$, we just use it, confident that $g(n-1)$ will be expanded to $g(n-2)$, etc., until we reach the trivial cases $g(1)$ and $g(2)$.

Continuing with this logic, when the first number is "2", "1" is not used for the first number but "1" may be used for partitioning the remaining value of $n-2$. By definition, "1" is used $g(n-2)$ times when partitioning $n-2$.

Putting this all together, we calculate $g(n)$ to be:

$$g(n) \; = \; \begin{cases} 1 & \text{when } n \text{ is } 1 \\ 2^{n-2} + g(n-1) + g(n-2) + \ldots g(1) = 2^{n-2} + \sum_{i=1}^{n-1} g(i) & \text{when } n > 1 \end{cases}$$

(12.10)

To obtain the closed form, first find the relationship between $g(n)$ and $g(n-1)$:

$$\begin{array}{rll} g(n) & = 2^{n-2} + g(n-1) & +g(n-2) + g(n-3) + \ldots + g(1) \\ - \quad g(n-1) & = 2^{n-3} & +g(n-2) + g(n-3) + \ldots + g(1) \\ \hline g(n) - g(n-1) & = 2^{n-3} + g(n-1) & \\ g(n) & = 2^{n-3} + 2g(n-1) & \end{array}$$

(12.11)

This relationship can be expanded for $g(n-2)$, $g(n-3)$, ..., $g(1)$.

$$\begin{array}{rl} g(n) & = 2^{n-3} + 2g(n-1) \\ g(n-1) & = 2^{n-4} + 2g(n-2) \\ g(n-2) & = 2^{n-5} + 2g(n-3) \\ & \vdots \\ g(n-k) & = 2^{n-k-3} + 2g(n-k-1) \\ & \vdots \\ g(3) & = 2^0 + 2g(2) \qquad \text{when } k = n-3 \end{array}$$

(12.12)

In (12.12), the coefficient for $g(n-1)$ on the right side is two. In order to cancel $g(n-1)$, the coefficient on the left size has to increase accordingly as shown below:

$$
\begin{aligned}
g(n) &= 2^{n-3} + 2g(n-1) \\
2g(n-1) &= 2^{n-3} + 4g(n-2) \\
4g(n-2) &= 2^{n-3} + 8g(n-3) \\
&\quad\vdots \\
2^k g(n-k) &= 2^{n-3} + 2^{k+1} g(n-k-1) \\
&\quad\vdots \\
+ \quad 2^{n-3} g(3) &= 2^{n-3} + 2^{n-2} g(2)
\end{aligned}
$$

$$
\begin{aligned}
g(n) + \sum_{i=3}^{n-1} 2^{n-i} g(i) &= (n-2)2^{n-3} + 2^{n-2} g(2) + \sum_{i=3}^{n-1} 2^{n-i} g(i) \\
g(n) &= (n-2)2^{n-3} + 2^{n-2} g(2) \\
g(n) &= (n-2)2^{n-3} + 2^{n-1} \\
g(n) &= (n+2)2^{n-3}
\end{aligned}
$$

(12.13)

This table shows that the value of $g(n)$ for $1 \leq n \leq 10$. If a formula does not match these cases, the formula is definitely wrong. However, matching these cases does not mean that the formula is correct. It is necessary to have a systematic way to find the formula. It is generally a bad idea to find a formula to match these finite values.

n	1	2	3	4	5	6	7	8	9
g(n)	1	2	5	12	28	64	144	320	704

12.4.2 Odd Numbers Only

In this variation of the partition problem we want to find how many ways n can be partitioned without using any even number. It may be helpful to review how Equation (12.8) is derived. What does $f(n-1)$ mean in this equation? It means the number of partitions using "1" as the first number. Similarly, what does $f(n-2)$ mean in this equation? It means the number of partitions using "2" as the first number. To restrict the partitions to odd numbers only, all partitions using even numbers must be discarded. Thus, $f(n-2)$, $f(n-4)$, $f(n-6)$, etc., must be excluded. Suppose $h(n)$ is the number of partitions for n using odd numbers only.

$$
h(n) = h(n-1) + h(n-3) + h(n-5)\ldots \text{ when } n > 1 \tag{12.14}
$$

The last few terms will be different depending on whether n itself is odd or even. If n is odd, $n-1$ is even so $h(1)$ is excluded. Also $n-1$, $n-3$, ..., are all even numbers. The complete equation is shown below:

$$
h(n) = \begin{cases} 1 & \text{when } n \text{ is } 1 \\ h(n-1) + h(n-3) + h(n-5)\ldots + h(2) + 1 & \text{when } n > 1 \text{ and } n \text{ is odd} \end{cases}
\tag{12.15}
$$

If n is even, $n-1$ is odd so $h(1)$ is included. Also $n-1$, $n-3$, ..., are all odd numbers. Therefore the complete equation is shown below:

$$h(n) = \begin{cases} 1 & \text{when } n \text{ is } 1 \\ h(n-1) + h(n-3) + h(n-5)... + h(2) + 1 & \text{when } n > 1 \text{ and } n \text{ is odd} \\ h(n-1) + h(n-3) + h(n-5)... + h(1) & \text{when } n \text{ is even} \end{cases}$$

$$(12.16)$$

12.4.3 Increasing Values

How many ways can the positive integer n be partitioned using increasing values or the number n itself? Suppose n is partitioned into the sum of k numbers:

$$n = a_1 + a_2 + a_3 + ... + a_k \tag{12.17}$$

The following conditions must be true:
- a_i $(1 \le i \le k)$ are positive integers
- $a_i < a_{i+1}$ $(1 \le i < k)$

Consider the first few cases of n:
- When n is 1, 1 is a valid partition.
- When n is 2, 2 is a valid partition but $1 + 1$ is invalid.
- When n is 3, $1 + 2$ and 3 are two valid partitions; $1 + 1 + 1$, and $2 + 1$ are invalid partitions.
- When n is 4, $1 + 3$ is a valid partition; $2 + 2$ and $3 + 1$ are invalid partitions.
- When n is 5, $1 + 4$, $2 + 3$ are valid partitions; $2 + 2 + 1$, $3 + 2$, $4 + 1$ are invalid partitions.

To solve this problem, two arguments are needed for the equation. We define $p(n, m)$ to be the number of ways to partition n where m is the smallest number used. When partitioning n, note the following:
- If 1 is used as the first number, then 2 is the smallest number that can be used when partitioning $n - 1$. There are $p(n-1, 2)$ ways to partition $n - 1$ using 2 as the smallest number.
- If 2 is used as the first number, then 3 is the smallest number that can be used to partition $n - 2$. There are $p(n-2, 3)$ ways to partition $n - 2$ using 3 as the smallest number.
- If 3 is used as the first number, then 4 is the smallest number that can be used to partition $n - 3$. There are $p(n-3, 4)$ ways to partition $n - 3$ using 4 as the smallest number.

Based on this reasoning,

$$\begin{aligned} p(n, 1) &= p(n-1, 2) + p(n-2, 3) + ... + p(n-k, k+1) + ... + p(1, n) + 1 \\ &= 1 + \sum_{i=1}^{n-1} p(n-i, i+1) \end{aligned} \tag{12.18}$$

By inspection we can tell that $p(n, n) = 1$. This means that there is one and only one way to partition n using n as the smallest number. Also, $p(n, m) = 0$ if $n < m$ because it is impossible to partition an integer using a larger integer. This problem is different from the previous ones because the recursive equations require two arguments. The fundamental recursive reasoning is the same.

12.4.4 Alternating Odd and Even Numbers

In this variation of the problem we want to find partitions that alternate between odd and even numbers. If an odd number is used, then the next must be an even number. If an even number is used, then the next must be an odd number. If only one number is used (i.e., the number to be partitioned), then this restriction does not apply and it is always a valid partition. This restriction allows only the following partitions for 1 to 7:

```
1 = 1            2 = 2            3 = 1 + 2            4 = 1 + 2 + 1
                                    = 2 + 1              = 4
                                    = 3
```

```
5 = 1 + 4        6 = 1 + 2 + 1 + 2        7 = 1 + 2 + 1 + 2 + 1
  = 2 + 1 + 2      = 1 + 2 + 3             = 1 + 6
  = 2 + 3          = 1 + 4 + 1             = 2 + 1 + 4
  = 3 + 2          = 2 + 1 + 2 + 1         = 2 + 3 + 2
  = 4 + 1          = 3 + 2 + 1             = 2 + 5
  = 5              = 6                     = 3 + 4
                                           = 4 + 1 + 2
                                           = 4 + 3
                                           = 5 + 2
                                           = 6 + 1
                                           = 7
```

The following table shows the solutions for n between 1 and 10.

n	1	2	3	4	5	6	7	8	9	10
number of partitions	1	1	3	2	6	6	11	16	22	37

This problem using alternating odd and even numbers can be solved by defining two functions as follows:

- $s(n)$ is the number of ways to partition n using an odd number as the first number.
- $t(n)$ is the number of ways to partition n using an even number as the first number.

By observation we can create the following table:

n	1	2	3	4	5
$s(n)$	1	0	2	1	3
$t(n)$	0	1	1	1	3
sum	1	1	3	2	6

To calculate $s(n)$, the first number can be 1, 3, 5, ... and the second number must be an even number. For example, when 1 is used for the first number, then the remaining $n - 1$ must start with an even number. By definition, there are $t(n-1)$ ways to partition $n - 1$ starting with an even number. When 3 is used for the first number, then there are $t(n-3)$ ways to partition $n - 3$ starting with an even number. Based on this reasoning, $s(n)$ is defined as:

$$s(n) = t(n-1) + t(n-3) + t(n-5)... \tag{12.19}$$

By definition, $s(n)$ must not start with an even number and $t(n-2)$, $t(n-4)$, ... must not be included.

It is necessary to distinguish whether n is odd or even while writing down the last few terms in this equation. If n is an even number then:

- $n - 3$ is an odd number. This means that there are $t(n - (n - 3)) = t(3)$ ways to partition n with $n - 3$ as the first number. For example, if $n = 10$, there are $t(3)$ ways to partition 10 with 7 as the first number. Note that $t(3) = 1$, because the only valid partition of 3 that starts with an even number is: $3 = 2 + 1$.
- $n - 2$ is an even number. We skip this case because $s(n)$ is only concerned with the number of ways to partition n using an odd number as the first number.
- $n - 1$ is an odd number, so $t(n - (n - 1)) = t(1)$ is included in the calculation of $s(n)$. Note, however, that $t(1) = 0$.
- n is an even number. We skip this case because $s(n)$ only concerns itself with partitions that begin with odd numbers.

Hence, when n is an even number:

$$s(n) = t(n - 1) + t(n - 3) + t(n - 5)... + t(3) + t(1) \tag{12.20}$$

Following this logic when n is an odd number:

- $n - 3$ is an even number and this case is discarded when computing $s(n)$. For example, if $n = 11$, then $n - 3 = 8$, which is even. Since $s(n)$ only concerns itself with partitions that begin with an odd number, we skip $t(3)$.
- $n - 2$ is an odd number leaving the remainder 2 to be partitioned. Thus we add $t(2)$.
- $n - 1$ is an even number and this case is discarded when computing $s(n)$.
- n is an odd number and it is a valid partition for $s(n)$. This means we add 1 to the end of the equation.

When n is an odd number, $s(n)$ can be written as:

$$s(n) = t(n - 1) + t(n - 3) + t(n - 5)... + t(2) + 1 \tag{12.21}$$

Combining these two halves together, we get:

$$s(n) = \begin{cases} t(n - 1) + t(n - 3) + t(n - 5)... + t(1) & \text{when } n \text{ is even} \\ t(n - 1) + t(n - 3) + t(n - 5)... + t(2) + 1 & \text{when } n \text{ is odd} \end{cases} \tag{12.22}$$

Using similar reasoning again, $t(n)$ can be written as follows:

$$t(n) = \begin{cases} s(n - 2) + s(n - 4) + s(n - 6)... + s(4) + s(2) + 1 & \text{when } n \text{ is even} \\ s(n - 2) + s(n - 4) + s(n - 6)... + s(3) + s(1) & \text{when } n \text{ is odd} \end{cases} \tag{12.23}$$

Since a partition may start with an odd number or an even number, $f(n) = s(n) + t(n)$ and it is the answer to the question. This is the number of ways to partition n using alternating odd and even numbers. Section 12.4.2 explains how to find the number of partitions using odd numbers only. The answer is expressed as $h(n)$. A similar procedure can be used to find the number of partitions using even numbers only. Let's call it $u(n)$. Of course, $u(n)$ is zero if n is odd.

Is $h(n) + u(n)$ the same as $s(n) + t(n)$? Why? I leave this question for you to answer. If the answer is yes, prove it. If the answer is no, explain the reason.

12.4.5   Generalizing the Integer Partition Problem

This problem has many variations, for example,
- How many "2"s are used?
- How many "3"s are used?, etc.

- How many "+" symbols are used?
- How many numbers are used, and what is the general rule?
  - When n is 1, one number is used.
  - When n is 2, three numbers are used.
  - When n is 3, eight numbers are used.
  - When n is 4, twenty numbers are used.

12.4.6   How Not to Solve the Integer Partition Problem

Sometimes people try to solve these types of problems in the following way:
1. Manually count the answers for the first several values of n.
2. Observe the relationships and write a formula that satisfies these relationships.
3. Claim this formula is the answer.

This approach is logically flawed. For any finite number of pairs of (x_1, y_1), (x_2, y_2), (x_3, y_3), ... , (x_k, y_k), there is always a polynomial $y = a_k x^k + a_{k-1} x^{k-1} + ... + a_1 x + a_0$ that passes through these points. That does not mean this polynomial is the correct formula. In fact, the previous examples show that the answers are not polynomials.

There is another explanation for why "conclusion by observation" is logically flawed. Do you have a favorite television program that is broadcast daily? By observation, this program is on air every day. Can you claim that this program will be on air forever? Of course not. The program may stop after a few seasons or a few years. Observation of finite instances is not a valid way to derive a general rule. Even after a thousand observations, you cannot guarantee that it is still true next time.

The equations in (12.8), (12.9), (12.10), and (12.12) are not derived from observation of finite cases. The equations are correct for any positive integer n. In some cases n must be greater than some specific value, for example, $n > 1$ in (12.10). The equations are general and the derivations from these equations are logically sound. When you solve this type of problem, please remember that observation is insufficient.

Recursive formulas are actually reasonably straightforward with some practice. The key is realizing that without using recursion, the problem may be really difficult. The simplicity of recursion is that you can *assume* that you already have the answer to smaller cases. Therefore if you can write $f(n)$ in terms of $f(\text{smaller than } n)$, and if you can write trivial cases like $f(0)$ and $f(1)$, then that is the entire solution.

Chapter 13

Recursive C Functions

In this chapter we convert the mathematical formulas from the previous chapter into C programs. Recall that there are four steps to solving math problems that use recursion. These steps are also used when writing C functions that use recursion.

1. Identify the argument (or arguments) of a problem. These will be, in general, the argument (or arguments) for the recursive C function.
2. Express the solution based on the arguments.
3. Determine the simple cases when the solutions are "obvious". The function has one (or several) conditions detecting whether this (or these) simple case(s) can be solved directly. This is usually referred to as the *base case*.
4. Derive the relationships between complex cases and simpler cases. We call this the *recursive case* because the function calls itself with a simplified argument (or several modified arguments).

A recursive function has the following structure:

```
 1  return_type func(arguments)
 2  {
 3      if (this is the base case) /* by checking the arguments */
 4      {
 5          solve the problem
 6      }
 7      else /* Recursive case */
 8      {
 9          func(simplified arguments) /* function calls itself */
10      }
11  }
```

A recursive function should first check whether the arguments specify a base case. A base case means that the function can immediately return the answer. For this reason, the `if` condition (or conditions) is called the *terminating condition* (or conditions) of the recursive function. The terminating conditions indicate that a base case has been reached. When the condition is true, the problem is trivial and recursive calls are unnecessary. If the problem is not simple, then the function enters the recursive case and the function calls itself with simplified versions of the arguments. The following sections implement the recursive equations in the previous chapter.

13.1   Select Balls with Restrictions

```
1  // balls.c
2  // f(1) = 2
3  // f(2) = 3
4  // f(n) = f(n-1) + f(n-2)
5  #include <stdio.h>
6  #include <stdlib.h>
7  int f(int m)
8  // use m instead of n to distinguish m in f and n in main
9  {
10    /* Base cases */
11    if (m <= 0)
12      {
13        printf("Invalid Number %d, must be positive.\n", m);
14        return -1;
15      }
16    if (m == 1)
17      {
18        return 2; // f(1) = 2
19      }
20    if (m == 2)
21      {
22        return 3; // f(2) = 3
23      }
24    /* Recursive case */
25    int a;
26    int b;
27    a = f(m - 1);
28    b = f(m - 2);
29    return (a + b);
30  }
31  int main(int argc, char * argv[])
32  {
33    int c;
34    int n;
35    if (argc < 2)
36      {
37        printf("need 1 integer.\n");
38        return EXIT_FAILURE;
39      }
40    n = (int) strtol(argv[1], NULL, 10);
41    c = f(n);
42    printf("f(%d) = %d.\n", n, c);
43    return EXIT_SUCCESS;
44  }
```

The following results were produced by executing this program with different arguments:

n	$f(n)$
1	2
2	3
3	5
4	8
5	13
6	21

Understanding how recursive functions work requires a full understanding of the call stack. If you are unsure about how the call stack works, then please review Chapter 2. Let's see what happens when n (in `main`) is 3, just after finishing line 41, and before running line 42. For simplicity, the call stack does not show `argc` and `argv`.

Frame	Symbol	Address	Value
main	n	101	3
	c	100	garbage

Calling f will change the call stack as follows:

Frame	Symbol	Address	Value
f	b	106	garbage
	a	105	garbage
	m	104	3
	value address	103	100 (c's address)
	return location	102	line 45
main	n	101	3
	c	100	garbage

Since m is greater than 2, the program will call $f(m-1)$ and assign the result in a. Recursive calls follow the same procedure as any other function call. As the function is called, the return location, value address, arguments, and local variables are pushed on to the call stack.

Frame	Symbol	Address	Value
f	b	111	garbage
	a	110	garbage
	m	109	2
	value address	108	105 (a's address)
	return location	107	line 30
f	b	106	garbage
	a	105	garbage
	m	104	3
v	value address	103	100 (c's address)
	return location	102	line 45
main	n	101	3
	c	100	garbage

The value of m is 2 now and it is a base case. The function returns 3 without calling itself again. The value 3 is written to address 105.

Frame	Symbol	Address	Value
	b	106	garbage
	a	105	garbage $\rightarrow$ 3
f	m	104	3
	value address	103	100 (c's address)
	return location	102	line 45
main	n	101	3
	c	100	garbage

Line 30 calls *f* again and m is 1 this time.

Frame	Symbol	Address	Value
	b	111	garbage
	a	110	garbage
f	m	109	1
	value address	108	106
	return location	107	line 31
	b	106	garbage
	a	105	3
f	m	104	3
	value address	103	100 (c's address)
	return location	102	line 45
main	n	101	3
	c	100	garbage

The value of m is 1 and it meets one terminating condition. The function returns 2, and this value is written to address 106.

Frame	Symbol	Address	Value
	b	106	garbage $\rightarrow$ 2
	a	105	3
f	m	104	3
	value address	103	100 (c's address)
	return location	102	line 45
main	n	101	3
	c	100	garbage

The program has returned to a previous invocation of f. The sum of a and b is 5. This value is written to the address of 100.

Frame	Symbol	Address	Value
main	n	101	3
	c	100	garbage $\rightarrow$ 5

A recursive function follows the same rules as any other function call. When a function is called, a new frame is pushed. When a function finishes, the top frame is popped. A common misconception is that the frames of a recursive function are merged into a single frame. This is wrong. The call stack handles recursive calls in the same way as non-recursive calls.

13.2   One-Way Streets

```
1   // oneway.c
2   // implement the recursive relation for calculating
3   // the number of possibilities in a city where cars can
4   // only move northbound or eastbound
5   #include <stdio.h>
6   #include <stdlib.h>
7   int f(int dx, int dy)
8   /* Do not need to worry about dx < 0 or dy < 0.
9      This is already handled in main. */
10  {
11     int a, b;
12     if ((dx == 0) || (dy == 0))
13       { /* Base case */
14         return 1;
15       }
16     /* Recursive case */
17     a = f(dx - 1, dy);
18     b = f(dx, dy - 1);
19     return (a + b);
20  }
21  int main(int argc, char * argv[])
22  {
23     int deltax, deltay;
24     int c;
25     if (argc < 3)
26       {
27         printf("need 2 positive integers.\n");
28         return EXIT_FAILURE;
29       }
30     deltax = (int) strtol(argv[1], NULL, 10);
31     deltay = (int) strtol(argv[2], NULL, 10);
32     if ((deltax < 0) || (deltay < 0))
33       {
34         printf("need 2 positive integers.\n");
35         return EXIT_FAILURE;
36       }
37     c = f(deltax, deltay);
38     printf("f(%d, %d) = %d.\n", deltax, deltay, c);
39     return EXIT_SUCCESS;
40  }
```

This program uses local variables to store the values returned from recursive calls:

```
18     a = f(dx - 1, dy);
19     b = f(dx, dy - 1);
20     return (a + b);
```

Actually, the local variables are unnecessary. Instead, the three lines can be rewritten as follows:

```
18    return f(dx - 1, dy) + f(dx, dy - 1);
```

Both of these versions do exactly the same thing. The compiler actually creates temporary variables if local variables are not used.

13.3   The Tower of Hanoi

The listing below shows how to calculate the number of moves required to move n disks in The Tower of Hanoi problem:

```
1   // hanoi1.c
2   // calculate the number of moves needed to move n disks
3   #include <stdio.h>
4   #include <stdlib.h>
5   int f(int n)
6   {
7     /* Base case */
8     if (n == 1)
9       {
10        return 1;
11      }
12    /* Recursive case */
13    return 2 * f(n - 1) + 1;
14  }
15  int main(int argc, char * argv[])
16  {
17    int n;
18    if (argc < 2)
19      {
20        printf("need one positive integer.\n");
21        return EXIT_FAILURE;
22      }
23    n = (int) strtol(argv[1], NULL, 10);
24    if (n <= 0)
25      {
26        printf("need one positive integer.\n");
27        return EXIT_FAILURE;
28      }
29    printf("f(%d) = %d.\n", n, f(n));
30    return EXIT_SUCCESS;
31  }
```

A more interesting program prints the solution—the sequence of disk moves that solves the problem. To do this, we create a function called **move** that takes four arguments:

1. The disks to move. The disks are represented by positive integers, where 1 is the smallest disk and 2 is the second smallest disk, etc.
2. The source pole
3. The destination pole
4. The additional pole

This program follows the procedure in Section 12.3: Move the top $n - 1$ disks to the additional pole (i.e., C), then move the nth disk from A to B, and then move the top $n - 1$ disk from C to B. Notice how short and simple the code is.

```c
1   // hanoi2.c
2   // print the steps moving n disks
3   #include <stdio.h>
4   #include <stdlib.h>
5   void move(int disk, char src, char dest, char additional)
6   {
7     /* Base case */
8     if (disk == 1)
9       {
10          printf("move disk 1 from %c to %c\n", src, dest);
11          return;
12        }
13    /* Recursive case */
14    move(disk - 1, src, additional, dest);
15    printf("move disk %d from %c to %c\n", disk, src, dest);
16    move(disk - 1, additional, dest, src);
17  }
18  int main(int argc, char * argv[])
19  {
20    int n;
21    if (argc < 2)
22      {
23          printf("need one positive integer.\n");
24          return EXIT_FAILURE;
25        }
26    n = (int) strtol(argv[1], NULL, 10);
27    if (n <= 0)
28      {
29          printf("need one positive integer.\n");
30          return EXIT_FAILURE;
31        }
32    move(n, 'A', 'B', 'C');
33    return EXIT_SUCCESS;
34  }
```

When the input is 3, the program's output is:

```
move disk 1 from A to B
move disk 2 from A to C
move disk 1 from B to C
move disk 3 from A to B
move disk 1 from C to A
move disk 2 from C to B
move disk 1 from A to B
```

This output matches the steps in Fig. 12.8.

13.4   Integer Partition

The implementation of formula (12.8) in C is shown below:

```
1   sum = 0;
2   for (i = 1; i < n; i ++)
3     {
4       // the first value is i
5       // f(n - i) ways for the remaining value of n - i
6       sum += f(n - i);
7     }
8   sum ++; // first value is n and the remaining is zero
```

Notice the nearly one-to-one mapping from the mathematical expression to the C code. The complete program is shown below.

```
1   // partition.c
2   // implement the recursive relation for calculating
3   // the number of partitions for a positive integer
4   #include <stdio.h>
5   #include <stdlib.h>
6   int f(int n)
7   {
8     int i;
9     int sum = 0;
10    /* Base case */
11    if (n == 1)
12      {
13        return 1; // only one way to partition 1
14      }
15    /* Recursive case */
16    for (i = 1; i < n; i ++)
17      {
18        sum += f(n - i);
19      }
20    sum ++;
21    return sum;
22  }
23  int main(int argc, char * argv[])
24  {
25    int n;
26    if (argc < 2)
27      {
28        printf("need one positive integer.\n");
29        return EXIT_FAILURE;
30      }
31    n = (int) strtol(argv[1], NULL, 10);
32    if (n <= 0)
33      {
34        printf("need one positive integer.\n");
35        return EXIT_FAILURE;
```

```
36      }
37      printf("f(%d)␣=␣%d.\n", n, f(n));
38      return EXIT_SUCCESS;
39  }
```

This program was executed with various arguments to produce the following result:

n	$f(n)$
1	1
2	2
3	4
4	8
5	16
6	32

13.5 Factorial

Many books use factorial and Fibonacci numbers to motivate the need of recursion. These are poor examples. This book does not start with these two popular examples for good reasons, as explained below. The definition of factorial for positive integers or zero is:

$$f(n) = \begin{cases} 1 & \text{when } n \text{ is } 0 \\ n \times f(n-1) & \text{when } n > 0 \end{cases} \tag{13.1}$$

It is possible to define factorial for negative values or non integers; however, that definition is beyond the scope of this book.

```
1   // factorial1.c
2   #include <stdio.h>
3   long int fac(int n)
4   {
5       if (n < 0)
6           {
7               printf("n␣cannot␣be␣negative\n");
8               return 0;
9           }
10      /* Base case */
11      if (n == 0)
12          {
13              return 1;
14          }
15      /* Recursive case */
16      return n * fac(n - 1);
17  }
```

By now, the main function should be quite easy to follow:

```
1   // mainfactorial.c
2   #include <stdio.h>
3   #include <stdlib.h>
```

```
4  #define MAXN 20
5  long int fac(int n);
6  int main(int argc, char * argv[])
7  {
8    int nval;
9    for (nval = 0; nval <= MAXN; nval ++)
10     {
11       long int fval = fac(nval);
12       printf("fac(%2d)␣=␣%ld\n", nval, fval);
13     }
14   return EXIT_SUCCESS;
15 }
```

Here is the output of this program:

```
fac( 0) = 1
fac( 1) = 1
fac( 2) = 2
fac( 3) = 6
fac( 4) = 24
fac( 5) = 120
fac( 6) = 720
fac( 7) = 5040
fac( 8) = 40320
fac( 9) = 362880
fac(10) = 3628800
fac(11) = 39916800
fac(12) = 479001600
fac(13) = 6227020800
fac(14) = 87178291200
fac(15) = 1307674368000
fac(16) = 20922789888000
fac(17) = 355687428096000
fac(18) = 6402373705728000
fac(19) = 121645100408832000
fac(20) = 2432902008176640000
```

The function `fac` returns `long int` because the values quickly get too large for `int` when n is greater than 12. The function `fac` is quite straightforward—a direct translation of the mathematical definition. Why is this a bad example for introducing recursion? The reason is that recursion is not necessary. It is possible to implement the same function *without* using recursion.

```
1  // factorial2.c
2  #include <stdio.h>
3  long int fac2(int n)
4  {
5    if (n < 0)
6      {
7        printf("n␣cannot␣be␣negative\n");
8        return 0;
9      }
10   if (n == 0)
```

```
11   {
12      return 1;
13   }
14   long int result = 1;
15   while (n > 0)
16      {
17         result *= n;
18         n --;
19      }
20   return result;
21 }
```

This function uses `while` and stores the result in a local variable called `result`.

"All right, you can use recursion but you don't have to. Why do you say that factorial is a *bad* example?" Recursion can be more flexible than iterative loops, such as `while` and `for`. Every loop can be expressed easily with recursion. However, the reverse can be difficult. Some problems can be solved naturally by recursion; solving these problems without recursion can sometimes be awkward. Why is this a bad example? The recursive solution is actually worse than the iterative solution. This brings us to the second problem: The recursive solution is slower. Why? Recursive functions must push and pop frames on the call stack. Pushing and popping frames takes time.

We compared the execution times of both functions. The iterative solution (using `while`) is 14% to 38% faster than the recursive solution. This performance difference may not seem a lot; however, in the next example (Fibonacci numbers), we will see a remarkable performance difference.

13.6   Fibonacci Numbers

Calculating Fibonacci numbers is another popular example used in teaching recursion. The numbers are defined as follows:

$$f(n) = \begin{cases} 1 & \text{if } n \text{ is } 1 \\ 2 & \text{if } n \text{ is } 2 \\ f(n-1) + f(n-2) & \text{if } n > 2. \end{cases} \tag{13.2}$$

Table 13.1 lists the values of $f(n)$ for $n \leq 10$.

This formula is similar to (12.1) in Section 12.1. The difference is the starting values of $f(1)$ and $f(2)$. Below is a straightforward implementation of the definition:

```
1  // fib1.c
2  long int fib1(int n)
3  {
4     if ((n == 1) || (n == 2)) // base case
5        {
6           return 1;
7        }
8     // recursive case
9     return fib(n - 1) + fib(n - 2);
10 }
```

n	$f(n)$
1	1
2	1
3	2
4	3
5	5
6	8
7	13
8	21
9	34
10	55

TABLE 13.1: The first ten values of Fibonacci numbers.

If we look at the definition again, we see that it is "top-down":

$$f(n) = f(n-1) + f(n-2) \qquad \text{if } n > 2 \qquad (13.3)$$

It computes $f(n)$ by using the values of $f(n-1)$ and $f(n-2)$. If n is greater than 2, then the function computes $f(n-1)$ by using the values of $f(n-2)$ and $f(n-3)$. This process continues until n is either 1 or 2.

The following implementation does not use recursion. Because the definition itself is recursive, the iterative solution must take a different approach:

```
// fib2.c
long int fib2(int n)
{
   if ((n == 1) || (n == 2))
      {
         return 1;
      }
   long int fna = 1; // as fib(0) now
   long int fnb = 1; // as fib(1) now
   long int fnc;     // to hold the latest value of fib
   n --; // starting at 1, not zero
   while (n > 1)
      {
         fnc = fnb + fna; // the new value
         fna = fnb;
         fnb = fnc;
         n --;
      }
   return fnc;
}
```

This may seem a little complex, but it simply calculates the Fibonacci numbers "bottom-up". It knows $f(1)$ and $f(2)$ first and stores the values in **fna** and **fnb** respectively. Then, the function computes $f(3)$ by using the sum of $f(1)$ and $f(2)$. This value is stored in **fnc**. After computing $f(3)$, the value in **fnc** is stored in **fnb** and the value in **fnb** is stored in **fna**. At this point **fnb** stores $f(3)$ and **fna** stores $f(2)$, and now **fnc** is free to store the fourth Fibonacci number. We are ready to compute $f(4)$, and repeat until we get to n. This is actually easier to imagine than the recursive case, because the Fibonacci sequence is built

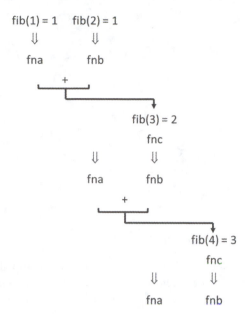

FIGURE 13.1: Computing Fibonacci numbers bottom-up without using recursion.

up from smallest to n, just as if you were doing the calculation by hand. Please spend some time to understand it. Fig. 13.1 illustrates the steps.

Why do we even bother to consider the bottom-up function? Isn't the recursive function good enough? It certainly looks simple since it is direct translation from the mathematical definition. The problem is that the recursive function does a lot of unnecessary work, and is hence rather slow. Fig. 13.2 shows the ratio of the execution time for the first (recursive, top-down) and the second (non-recursive, bottom-up) functions. It is readily apparent that the first function is slower (takes longer) than the second. Moreover, the ratio keeps rising. Please notice that the vertical axis is in the logarithmic scale. The first function takes as much as 2,000 times longer than the second when n is 20.

The data in Fig. 13.2 were generated by using the following program:

```
1   // fib.c
2   #include <stdio.h>
3   #include <stdlib.h>
4   #include <sys/time.h>
5   #define MAXN 20
6   #define REPEAT 100000
7   long int fib(int n);
8   long int fib2(int n);
9   int main(int argc, char * argv[])
10  {
11      int nval, rept;
12      struct timeval time1;
13      struct timeval time2;
14      float intv1, intv2;
15      for (nval = 1; nval <= MAXN; nval ++)
16          {
```

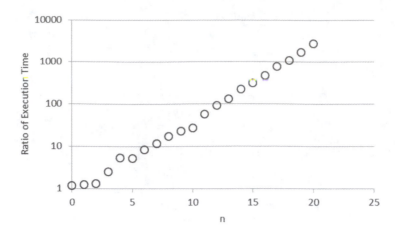

FIGURE 13.2: Ratio of the execution times of the recursive and the non-recursive versions for calculating Fibonacci numbers. The recursive function is much slower and the ratio in execution time keeps rising.

```
17        long int fval;
18        gettimeofday(& time1, NULL);
19        for (rept = 0; rept < REPEAT; rept ++)
20          {
21            fval = fib(nval);
22          }
23        gettimeofday(& time2, NULL);
24        intv1 = (time2.tv_sec - time1.tv_sec) +
25          1e-6 * (time2.tv_usec - time1.tv_usec);
26        printf("fib (%2d) = %ld, time = %f\n",
27                nval, fval, intv1);
28        gettimeofday(& time1, NULL);
29        for (rept = 0; rept < REPEAT; rept ++)
30          {
31            fval = fib2(nval);
32          }
33        gettimeofday(& time2, NULL);
34        intv2 = (time2.tv_sec - time1.tv_sec) +
35          1e-6 * (time2.tv_usec - time1.tv_usec);
36        printf("fib2(%2d) = %ld, time = %f\n",
37                nval, fval, intv2);
38        printf("ratio = %f\n", intv1/intv2);
39      }
40    return EXIT_SUCCESS;
41 }
```

This program uses `gettimeofday` to measure the execution time of the two functions. `gettimeofday` returns the time, expressed in seconds and microseconds, since 1970-01-01 00:00:00 (UTC). The two values are stored in a *structure* called **struct** in C programs. Structures will be discussed in great detail later in this book. This program measures the difference of time before and after calculating Fibonacci numbers. The basic structure of measuring a function's execution time is

1. get the current time, call it $t1$;
2. call the function;
3. get the current time, call it $t2$.

The execution time of this function is $t2 - t1$. This method of measuring execution time has limitations. The time $t1$ and $t2$ has finite precision. If this function's execution time is too short, $t2 - t1$ will be too small (possibly zero). To obtain acceptable accuracy, the execution time needs to be much longer than the precision. For `gettimeofday`, the precision is microseconds; thus, the execution time should be much longer than one microsecond. This is the reason why the program calls the functions calculating Fibonacci numbers multiple times between calling `gettimeofday`. The values may be slightly different when the program is run multiple times because your computer also runs many other programs. This is the last few lines of the program's output:

```
fib (16) = 987, time = 2.161532
fib2(16) = 987, time = 0.004730
ratio = 456.983490
fib (17) = 1597, time = 3.500462
fib2(17) = 1597, time = 0.005093
ratio = 687.308472
fib (18) = 2584, time = 5.678572
fib2(18) = 2584, time = 0.005474
ratio = 1037.371704
fib (19) = 4181, time = 9.399386
fib2(19) = 4181, time = 0.005677
ratio = 1655.696045
fib (20) = 6765, time = 15.530513
fib2(20) = 6765, time = 0.007862
ratio = 1975.389648
```

As you can see, the ratios of the execution time grow from 457 to 1975.

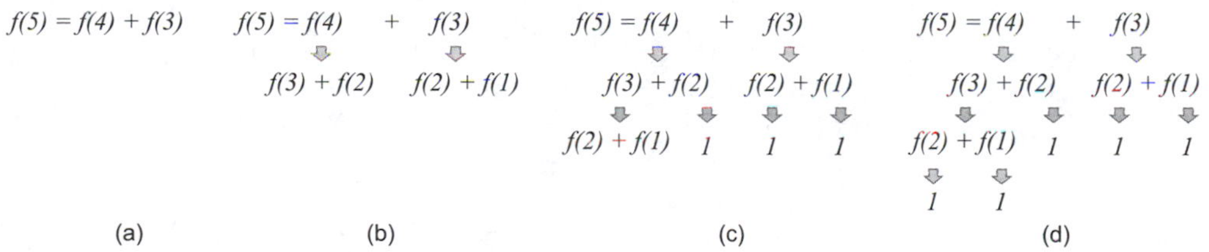

(a)   (b)   (c)   (d)

FIGURE 13.3: Computing $f(5)$ requires calling $f(4)$ and $f(3)$. Computing $f(4)$ requires calling $f(3)$ and $f(2)$.

Why is there such a large difference in the execution time? Fig. 13.3 illustrates the sequence of computation. For the first function, to compute $f(5)$, it is necessary to compute $f(4)$ and $f(3)$. To compute $f(4)$, it is necessary to compute $f(3)$ and $f(2)$. Fig. 13.4 redraws Fig. 13.3. This looks like a "tree". You need to use some imagination because the tree's "root" is at the top and the branches go downwards. Computing each value requires the sum of two values, until reaching the bottom, called *leaves*. The leaves are the base cases, where the recursion meets the terminating conditions, namely $f(1)$ or $f(2)$.

Let's do a little more mathematics here to figure out some properties of this tree. By definition,

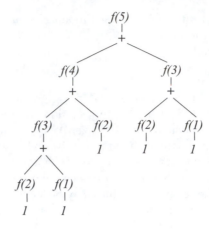

FIGURE 13.4: Redraw Fig. 13.3. This looks like a "tree": computing each value requires the sum of two values.

$$\begin{cases} f(n) = f(n-1) + f(n-2) \\ f(n-1) = f(n-2) + f(n-3) \end{cases} \tag{13.4}$$

Therefore,

$$\begin{aligned} f(n) &= f(n-1) + f(n-2) \\ &= (f(n-2) + f(n-3)) + f(n-2) \\ &= 2f(n-2) + f(n-3). \end{aligned} \tag{13.5}$$

Continuing this derivation for a few more steps we have:

$$\begin{aligned} f(n) &= f(n-1) &&+ &&f(n-2) \\ &= 2f(n-2) &&+ &&f(n-3) \\ &= 2(f(n-3) &&+ &&f(n-4)) &&+ &&f(n-3) \\ &= 3f(n-3) &&+ &&2f(n-4) \\ &= 3(f(n-4) &&+ &&f(n-5)) &&+ &&2f(n-4) \\ &= 5f(n-4) &&+ &&3f(n-5) \\ &= 5(f(n-5) &&+ &&f(n-6)) &&+ &&3f(n-5) \\ &= 8f(n-5) &&+ &&5f(n-6) \\ &= 8(f(n-6) &&+ &&f(n-7)) &&+ &&5f(n-6) \\ &= 13f(n-6) &&+ &&8f(n-7). \end{aligned} \tag{13.6}$$

Table 13.2 lists the coefficients for computing $f(n)$. When comparing this table with the values in Table 13.1, you may find that the coefficient of $f(n-k)$ is actually $f(k+1)$. Table 13.2 and Fig. 13.4 both express similar concepts. Fig. 13.4 computes $f(5)$ so n is 5 and $f(2)$ is $f(n-3)$. The coefficient for $f(n-3)$ is 3. If we count the occurrences of $f(2)$ in Fig. 13.4, we find that it is called three times.

The recursive method for calculating Fibonacci numbers is slower because it computes the same value over and over again. When computing $f(n-1)$, it has to compute $f(n-2)$. However, the recursive function in Section 13.6 does not remember the value for $f(n-2)$ and then computes the value again later. As n becomes larger, the function performs more and more redundant computations and becomes slower and slower. It is unclear why many books use Fibonacci numbers to motivate the concept of recursion.

function	coefficient	
f(n-1)	1	$f(2)$
f(n-2)	2	$f(3)$
f(n-3)	3	$f(4)$
f(n-4)	5	$f(5)$
f(n-5)	8	$f(6)$
f(n-6)	13	$f(7)$

TABLE 13.2: Coefficients for computing $f(n)$.

Does this mean recursion is bad? Does this mean that recursion is slow? Why should we even bother to learn recursion? The problem is not recursion, but the example. We cannot generalize from a bad example to say that recursion is slow. Recursion can be used to good advantage in some time-critical applications. If you have a nail and a knife, you will find that hitting the nail with a knife is difficult. Does this mean a knife is bad? If you need to hit a nail, you need a hammer. A knife is a bad tool for hitting a nail. If you want to cut paper, a knife is better than a hammer. If you have a bolt, you need a wrench. A hammer is not better than a wrench and a wrench is not better than a hammer. They are different. One is better than the other in some scenarios. If a book tells you a hammer is better than a wrench, you will say, "This doesn't make sense. In *some* cases, a wrench is better." You cannot generalize this example and conclude that recursion is slower. Some books do not explain that *this particular* top-down method is slower than *this* bottom-up method. As a result some students mistakenly think recursion is slow by generalizing this example. Some other books explain that this top-down method is slower than this bottom-up method without further explanation. These books give students the strong impression that recursion is slow. The truth is that recursion is a good approach for *some* problems, not all.

13.7   Performance Profiling with `gprof`

Many studies on software performance find that performance is generally dominated by just a few factors. This is true for both simple and complex systems. A general rule of thumb is "10% of the code consumes 90% of the time". Improving the correct 10% of code will have a noticeable impact on performance. Conversely, improving the other 90% of code will have negligible impact. The question is how to find the 10% of interest. Guessing is not a good approach. Even experienced programmers find it very hard to predict which parts of a complex program cause performance bottlenecks.

Experienced programmers know that tools can help identify that 10% of the code. A tool called `gprof` is designed specifically for this purpose. To use `gprof`, add `-pg` after `gcc` and execute the program as usual. For example:

```
$ gcc -Wall -Wshadow -pg fib.c fib1.c fib2.c -o fibprog
```

Consider the Fibonacci functions referenced earlier. After running the program, a special file called `gmon.out` is generated. This file stores the profiling information for running the program and it is not readable using a text editor. Please use the `gprof` program to view the content in `gmon.out`. The command is:

$ gprof fibprog

The output is something like this:

```
Flat profile:

Each sample counts as 0.01 seconds.
  %    cumulative    self              self     total
 time    seconds    seconds    calls  us/call  us/call  name
92.23      8.89       8.89    2000000   4.45     4.45    fib
 7.52      9.62       0.72
        frame_dummy
 0.84      9.70       0.08    2000000   0.04     0.04    fib2
 0.10      9.71       0.01                               main


granularity: each sample hit covers 2 byte(s) for 0.10% of
    9.71 seconds

index % time    self  children    called     name
                                                 <spontaneous>
[1]     92.5    0.01    8.97                   main [1]
                8.89    0.00 2000000/2000000       fib [2]
                0.08    0.00 2000000/2000000       fib2 [4]
-----------------------------------------------------------
                             3538000000              fib [2]
                8.89    0.00 2000000/2000000       main [1]
[2]     91.6    8.89    0.00 2000000+3538000000 fib [2]
                             3538000000              fib [2]
-----------------------------------------------------------
                                                 <spontaneous>
[3]      7.5    0.72    0.00                   frame_dummy [3]
-----------------------------------------------------------
                0.08    0.00 2000000/2000000       main [1]
[4]      0.8    0.08    0.00 2000000           fib2 [4]
-----------------------------------------------------------
```

This output says that 92.23% of the time is spent on the function `fib` and only 0.84% time is spent on the function `fib2`. The `main` function calls `fib` 2000000 times (REPEAT × MAXN). In [2], the report says that `fib` is called itself 3538000000 times. In contrast, [4] says that `fib2` is called 2000000 times and it does not call itself.

How can we use this information to help identify the opportunities for improving performance? First, the report says more than 90% time is spent on `fib`. This suggests that the function should be carefully inspected for better performance. Second, the report says that `main` calls `fib` 2000000 and `fib` calls itself 3538000000 times, much more than the 2000000 invocations by `main`. This also suggests that `fib` calls itself excessively and is a candidate for performance improvement.

In this example, the program requires no inputs. Complex programs usually accept inputs that specify the programs' actions. Profiling a program effectively often requires using representative inputs. If a particular line of code is not executed for a particular set of inputs, `gprof` will contain no information about that line. Moreover, `gprof` is sampling based. The top of the report says that the sampling rate is 0.01 seconds. If the execution time of a program is too short, `gprof` will not be able to give accurate results.

Chapter 14

Integer Partition

The previous two chapters explained how to obtain the formula for partitioning integers and also how to write a C program that implements the formula. This chapter explains how to print the partitions and also introduces some variations on the problem. The following program prints the partitions for an integer that is specified on the command line:

```c
// partition.c
#include <stdio.h>
#include <stdlib.h>
#include <string.h>
void printPartition(int * arr, int length)
{
  int ind;
  for (ind = 0; ind < length - 1; ind ++)
    {
      printf("%d + ", arr[ind]);
    }
  printf("%d\n", arr[length - 1]);
}

void partition(int * arr, int ind, int left)
{
  int val;
  if (left == 0)
    {
      printPartition(arr, ind);
      return; // not necessary
    }
  for (val = 1; val <= left; val ++)
    {
      arr[ind] = val;
      partition(arr, ind + 1, left - val);
    }
}
```

```
30  int main(int argc, char * argv[])
31  {
32    if (argc != 2)
33      {
34        return EXIT_FAILURE;
35      }
36    int n = (int) strtol(argv[1], NULL, 10);
37    if (n <= 0)
38      {
39        return EXIT_FAILURE;
40      }
41    int * arr;
42    arr = malloc(sizeof(int) * n);
43    partition(arr, 0, n);
44    free (arr);
45    return EXIT_SUCCESS;
46  }
```

The `partition` function is the core of this program. This function takes three arguments:
1. `arr` is an integer pointer. It is an array that stores the numbers used in a given partition.
2. `ind` is an integer. It is an index of the array. The value indicates where the next element will be written. It also gives the length of the partition so far.
3. `left` is an integer. It is the remaining value to be partitioned.

The `return` at line 21 is unnecessary. When `left` is zero, the function will not enter the `for` loop. Adding this `return` makes the program easier to read.

When `main` calls `partition`, `ind` is zero—the index of the first element of the array. The value `left` is the remaining value to be partitioned. Even though this program is short, it reviews many important concepts explained earlier. Thus, it is worth explaining in detail.

14.1   Stack and Heap Memory

Suppose the value of `n` is 4. The following table shows the stack and heap memory after running line 42 and before line 43. The table assumes that each integer occupies 4 bytes (`sizeof(int)` is 4).

Frame	Symbol	Address	Value
	arr	101	10000
main	n	100	4

(a) Stack Memory

Symbol	Address	Value
arr[3]	10012	garbage
arr[2]	10008	garbage
arr[1]	10004	garbage
arr[0]	10000	garbage

(b) Heap Memory

This is the call stack and the heap memory after entering the function `partition`. RL means return location.

Frame	Symbol	Address	Value
	val	106	garbage
	left	105	4
partition	ind	104	0
	arr	103	10000
	RL	102	line 44
main	arr	101	10000
	n	100	4

(a) Stack Memory

Symbol	Address	Value
arr[3]	10012	garbage
arr[2]	10008	garbage
arr[1]	10004	garbage
arr[0]	10000	garbage

(b) Heap Memory

The value of `left` is not zero and the terminating condition at line 18 is false. The function continues to the `for` loop at lines 23–27. In this `for` loop, we let `val` iterate from 1 to `left`. These are all the possible values that can be used. The value of `val` starts at 1. Thus line 25 first assigns 1 to `arr[0]`.

Frame	Symbol	Address	Value
	val	106	1
	left	105	4
partition	ind	104	0
	arr	103	10000
	RL	102	line 44
main	arr	101	10000
	n	100	4

(a) Stack Memory

Symbol	Address	Value
arr[3]	10012	garbage
arr[2]	10008	garbage
arr[1]	10004	garbage
arr[0]	10000	garbage → 1

(b) Heap Memory

The function then calls itself at line 26. Please notice the values of `ind` and `left`. The index has changed from 0 to 1 because line 26 uses `ind + 1`. This is the next position in `arr` for the next value. In the recursive call, the function needs to partition 3 because `left - val` is 3. That is, we wrote 1 to position 0, and now we want to partition $n - 1 = 4 - 1 = 3$ into the remaining portion of `arr`. Please pay attention to the top frame of the call stack.

Frame	Symbol	Address	Value
	val	111	garbage
	left	110	**3**
partition	ind	109	**1**
	arr	108	10000
	RL	107	line 27
	val	106	1
	left	105	4
partition	ind	104	0
	arr	103	10000
	RL	102	line 44
main	arr	101	10000
	n	100	4

(a) Stack Memory.

Symbol	Address	Value
arr[3]	10012	garbage
arr[2]	10008	garbage
arr[1]	10004	garbage
arr[0]	10000	garbage $\to$ 1

(b) Heap Memory

The `for` loop starts with `val` equal to 1. Line 25 assigns 1 to `arr[1]` because `ind` is 1.

Frame	Symbol	Address	Value
	val	111	1
	left	110	3
partition	ind	109	1
	arr	108	10000
	RL	107	line 27
	val	106	1
	left	105	4
partition	ind	104	0
	arr	103	10000
	RL	102	line 44
main	arr	101	10000
	n	100	4

(a) Stack Memory

Symbol	Address	Value
arr[3]	10012	garbage
arr[2]	10008	garbage
arr[1]	10004	garbage $\to$ 1
arr[0]	10000	garbage $\to$ 1

(b) Heap Memory

The function calls itself again at line 26.

Frame	Symbol	Address	Value
	val	116	garbage
	left	115	**2**
partition	ind	114	**2**
	arr	113	10000
	RL	112	line 27
	val	111	1
	left	110	3
partition	ind	109	1
	arr	108	10000
	RL	107	line 27
	val	106	1
	left	105	4
partition	ind	104	0
	arr	103	10000
	RL	102	line 44
main	arr	101	10000
	n	100	4

(a) Stack Memory

Symbol	Address	Value
arr[3]	10012	garbage
arr[2]	10008	garbage
arr[1]	10004	garbage $\to$ 1
arr[0]	10000	garbage $\to$ 1

(b) Heap Memory

Continuing these steps, left eventually decreases and becomes zero.

Frame	Symbol	Address	Value
	val	126	garbage
	left	125	0
partition	ind	124	4
	arr	123	10000
	RL	122	line 27
	val	121	1
	left	120	1
partition	ind	119	3
	arr	118	10000
	RL	117	line 27
	val	116	1
	left	115	2
partition	ind	114	2
	arr	113	10000
	RL	112	line 27
	val	111	1
	left	110	3
partition	ind	109	1
	arr	108	10000
	RL	107	line 27

	val	106	1
	left	105	4
partition	ind	104	0
	arr	103	10000
	RL	102	line 44
main	arr	101	10000
	n	100	4

(a) Stack Memory

Symbol	Address	Value
arr[3]	10012	1
arr[2]	10008	1
arr[1]	10004	1
arr[0]	10000	1

(b) Heap Memory

Now the value of `left` is 0 and the terminating condition at line 18 is true. This means that we have reached a base case, and line 20 calls `printPartition` and prints the 4 elements in the array. Four elements are printed because `ind` is 4. Remember, `ind` gives the next position to write an element into `arr`, and it *also* gives the length of the partition so far. If you think about it carefully, you will see that these two things are equivalent. Therefore, we can pass `ind` as the length of the array to `printPartition`. The program now prints:

```
1 + 1 + 1 + 1
```

The function then returns because of line 21. The `return` statement at line 21 is not strictly necessary, because the function will not call itself again. This is because the `for` loop starts at 1 and `val` must be smaller than or equal to `left`. Because `left` is zero the function will not enter the `for` loop, and will return normally anyway.

It is good practice to put the line 21 `return` statement. When people read recursive functions they expect the functions to be divided neatly into the base case and the recursive case. The `return` statement makes the base case clear. Clearly no recursion is going to happen. No further analysis is required. Making code as clear as possible is one of the most important parts of good programs. After meeting the terminating condition, the top frame of the call stack is popped, and the program continues at line 27.

Frame	Symbol	Address	Value
	val	121	1
	left	120	1
partition	ind	119	3
	arr	118	10000
	RL	117	line 27
	val	116	1
	left	115	2
partition	ind	114	2
	arr	113	10000
	RL	112	line 27

	val	111	1
	left	110	3
partition	ind	109	1
	arr	108	10000
	RL	107	line 27
	val	106	1
	left	105	4
partition	ind	104	0
	arr	103	10000
	RL	102	line 44
main	arr	101	10000
	n	100	4

(a) Stack Memory

Symbol	Address	Value
arr[3]	10012	1
arr[2]	10008	1
arr[1]	10004	1
arr[0]	10000	1

(b) Heap Memory

For the next iteration, `val` increments to two. This violates the condition `val <= left` and the `for` loop exists. Since the function has nothing else to do after the `for` loop, the top frame is popped. The program now continues at line 27.

Frame	Symbol	Address	Value
	val	116	1
	left	115	2
partition	ind	114	2
	arr	113	10000
	RL	112	line 27
	val	111	1
	left	110	3
partition	ind	109	1
	arr	108	10000
	RL	107	line 27
	val	106	1
	left	105	4
partition	ind	104	0
	arr	103	10000
	RL	102	line 44
main	arr	101	10000
	n	100	4

(a) Stack Memory

Symbol	Address	Value
arr[3]	10012	1
arr[2]	10008	1
arr[1]	10004	1
arr[0]	10000	1

(b) Heap Memory

Now the for loop enters the next iteration: val becomes 2 and the condition val <= left is satisfied. Line 25 assigns 2 to arr[2] and line 26 calls the function itself again.

Frame	Symbol	Address	Value
	val	121	garbage
	left	120	0
partition	ind	119	3
	arr	118	10000
	RL	117	line 27
	val	116	2
	left	115	2
partition	ind	114	2
	arr	113	10000
	RL	112	line 27
	val	111	1
	left	110	3
partition	ind	109	1
	arr	108	10000
	RL	107	line 27
	val	106	1
	left	105	4
partition	ind	104	0
	arr	103	10000
	RL	102	line 44
main	arr	101	10000
	n	100	4

(a) Stack Memory

Symbol	Address	Value
arr[3]	10012	1
arr[2]	10008	1 → 2
arr[1]	10004	1
arr[0]	10000	1

(b) Heap Memory

Because left is zero, the terminating condition at line 18 is true. The program prints the first 3 elements (because ind is 3) in arr. So the program prints:

1 + 1 + 2

Line 21 returns and the top frame is popped.

Frame	Symbol	Address	Value
	val	116	2
	left	115	2
partition	ind	114	2
	arr	113	10000
	RL	112	line 27
	val	111	1
	left	110	3
partition	ind	109	1
	arr	108	10000
	RL	107	line 27
	val	106	1
	left	105	4
partition	ind	104	0
	arr	103	10000
	RL	102	line 44
main	arr	101	10000
	n	100	4

(a) Stack Memory

Symbol	Address	Value
arr[3]	10012	1
arr[2]	10008	2
arr[1]	10004	1
arr[0]	10000	1

(b) Heap Memory

The next iteration increments `val` to 3 but the condition `val <= left` is not satisfied. The function exits the `for` loop. Since the function has nothing else to do after the `for` loop, the function returns and the top frame is popped.

Frame	Symbol	Address	Value
	val	111	1
	left	110	3
partition	ind	109	1
	arr	108	10000
	RL	107	line 27
	val	106	1
	left	105	4
partition	ind	104	0
	arr	103	10000
	RL	102	line 44
main	arr	101	10000
	n	100	4

(a) Stack Memory

Symbol	Address	Value
arr[3]	10012	1
arr[2]	10008	2
arr[1]	10004	1
arr[0]	10000	1

(b) Heap Memory

For the next iteration, `val` becomes 2 and assigns 2 to `arr[1]`.

Frame	Symbol	Address	Value
	val	111	2
	left	110	3
partition	ind	109	1
	arr	108	10000
	RL	107	line 27
	val	106	1
	left	105	4
partition	ind	104	0
	arr	103	10000
	RL	102	line 44
main	arr	101	10000
	n	100	4

(a) Stack Memory

Symbol	Address	Value
arr[3]	10012	1
arr[2]	10008	2
arr[1]	10004	$1 \rightarrow 2$
arr[0]	10000	1

(b) Heap Memory

This process may seem tedious. Fortunately, computers are good at tedious work. Please practice a few times and ensure that you fully understand the changes in the call stack and heap memory. Then, leave the details to computers.

14.2   Trace Recursive Function Calls

Another way to understand this program is to draw its *call tree*. A call tree is a graphical representation of the relationship between function calls. This tree is drawn "inverted" with the root at the top, and the leaves at the bottom. Consider the following example:

```
void f1()
{
    f2();
}
```

Fig. 14.1 illustrates the calling relation of the two functions.

Here is another example and Fig. 14.2 shows the calling relations:

FIGURE 14.1: Graphical illustration of `f1` calls `f2`.

```
1  void f1()
2  {
3      f2();
4      f3();
5  }
```

FIGURE 14.2. Graphical illustration of `f1` calls `f2` and `f3`.

This is the third example and the calling relation is shown in Fig. 14.3.

```
1  void f1()
2  {
3      f2();
4      f3();
5  }
6  void f2()
7  {
8      f3();
9  }
```

FIGURE 14.3: Graphical illustration of `f1` calls `f2` and `f3`; `f2` also calls `f3`.

Here we add a loop to the function `f1` and Fig. 14.4 shows the relation.

```
1  void f1()
2  {
3      int count;
4      for (count = 1; count < 4; count ++)
5      {
6          f2();
7      }
8      f3();
```

```
 9  }
10  void f2()
11  {
12      f3();
13  }
```

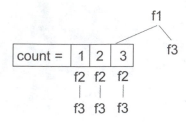

FIGURE 14.4: Graphical illustration of f1 calls f2 in a loop and f3 outside a loop; f2 calls f3.

Next, let's consider the skeleton of the `partition` function:

```
1  void partition(int * arr, int ind, int left)
2  {
3      int val;
4      for (val = 1; val <= left; val ++)
5      {
6          arr[ind] = val;
7          partition(arr, ind + 1, left - val);
8      }
9  }
```

Fig. 14.5 illustrates the calling relation.

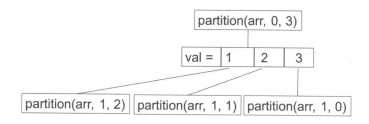

FIGURE 14.5: Graphical illustration of `partition` when the initial value of `left` is 3.

When `left` is 3, then `val` can be 1, 2, or 3.

1. When `val` is 1, `left-val` is 2. Thus, `partition(arr, 1, 2)` is called.
2. When `val` is 2, `left-val` is 1. Thus, `partition(arr, 1, 1)` is called.
3. When `val` is 3, `left-val` is 0. Thus, `partition(arr, 1, 0)` is called.

When `left` is 2, `val` can be 1 or 2. The calling relationship is illustrated in Fig. 14.6 and Fig. 14.7.

The call tree is a different way to help understand the calling relation. It is a higher level representation than the call stack because each call is represented by arguments and we do not need to examine all of the addresses and values used in each call.

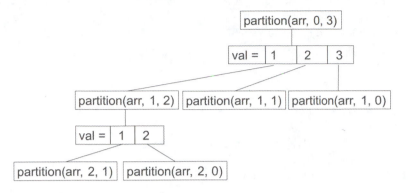

FIGURE 14.6: Graphical illustration of `partition` when the value of `left` is 2.

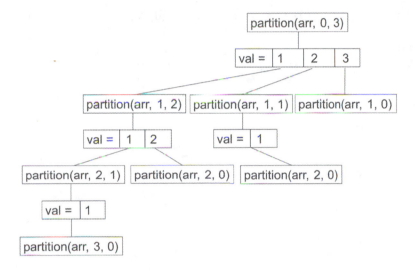

FIGURE 14.7: Graphical illustration of `partition` when the value of `left` is 1.

14.3   Generating Partitions with Restrictions

The program at the beginning of this chapter prints all possible partitions. This section explains how to change the program such that it generates partitions with restrictions, for example, partitioning with odd numbers or using sequences of increasing numbers. One simple solution is to check whether the restrictions have been satisfied before printing. Thus, in the base case, before printing anything, the function checks whether this partition is valid under the restriction. For example, if we are partitioning with odd numbers only, `printPartition` can be modified as follows:

```
void printPartition(int * arr, int length)
{
    int ind;
    // check whether any number is even
    // if an even number is used, do not print anything
    for (ind = 0; ind < length; ind ++)
```

```
 7     {
 8        if ((arr[ind] % 2) == 0)
 9          {
10            return;
11          }
12     }
13   for (ind = 0; ind < length - 1; ind ++)
14     {
15        printf("%d␣+␣", arr[ind]);
16     }
17   printf("%d\n", arr[length - 1]);
18 }
```

To check whether the numbers form an increasing sequence:

```
 1 void printPartition(int * arr, int length)
 2 {
 3   int ind;
 4   for (ind = 0; ind < length - 1; ind ++)
 5     {
 6        if (arr[ind] >= arr[ind + 1]) // not increasing
 7          {
 8            return;
 9          }
10     }
11   for (ind = 0; ind < length - 1; ind ++)
12     {
13        printf("%d␣+␣", arr[ind]);
14     }
15   printf("%d\n", arr[length - 1]);
16 }
```

However, checking before printing is inefficient because many invalid partitions have already been generated. Instead, a more efficient solution does not generate invalid partitions. This section explains how to generate valid partitions satisfying one of the following restrictions: (i) using odd numbers only, (ii) using increasing numbers, and (iii) using alternating odd and even numbers.

14.3.1   Using Odd Numbers Only

The function `partition` generates only partitions that meet the criteria. It is thus much faster than an approach where all partitions are generated and then "filtered" before being printed. If only odd numbers are used, `val` can be an odd number only.

```
 1 void partition(int * arr, int ind, int left)
 2 {
 3   int val;
 4   if (left == 0)
 5     {
 6        printPartition(arr, ind);
 7        return;
 8     }
 9   for (val = 1; val <= left; val += 2) // odd numbers only
```

```
10    {
11        arr[ind] = val;
12        partition(arr, ind + 1, left - val);
13    }
14 }
```

This will generate fewer partitions and all of them are valid.

14.3.2   Using Sequences of Increasing Numbers

To generate partitions using increasing numbers, the smallest value of `val` must be greater than the most recently used value stored in `arr`. However, if `ind` is zero, then no previously used value is stored in `arr`, and `val` can start from one.

```
1  void partition(int * arr, int ind, int left)
2  {
3      int val;
4      if (left == 0)
5          {
6              printPartition(arr, ind);
7              return;
8          }
9      int min = 1;
10     if (ind != 0)
11         {
12             min = arr[ind - 1] + 1;
13         }
14     for (val = min; val <= left; val ++)
15         {
16             arr[ind] = val;
17             partition(arr, ind + 1, left - val);
18         }
19 }
```

14.3.3   Using Alternating Odd and Even Numbers

To generate alternating odd and even numbers, the function must check whether `ind` is zero. If it is zero, `val` can be either odd or even, because `val` is being written into the first position of the partition. If `ind` is greater than zero, then the function needs to check `arr[ind - 1]`. If `arr[ind - 1]` is odd, then `val` must be an even number. If `arr[ind - 1]` is even, then `val` must be an odd number. This is checked in line 18.

```
1  void partition(int * arr, int ind, int left)
2  {
3      int val;
4      if (left == 0)
5          {
6              printPartition(arr, ind);
7              return;
8          }
9      for (val = 1; val <= left; val ++)
10         {
```

```
11    int valid = 0;
12    if (ind == 0) // no restriction for the first number
13      {
14        valid = 1;
15      }
16    else
17      {
18        valid = (arr[ind - 1] % 2) != (val % 2);
19      }
20    if (valid == 1)
21      {
22        arr[ind] = val;
23        partition(arr, ind + 1, left - val);
24      }
25  }
26 }
```

Line 18 tests whether `arr[ind - 1]` and `val` are both even or both odd. As you can see, with only a few small changes, the program can print the solutions for the integer partition problem under different restrictions.

14.3.4 Using gprof and gcov to Identify Performance Bottlenecks

Section 13.7 explains how to use `gprof` to identify opportunities for performance improvement. This section uses `gprof` to compare different ways to restrict integer partitions. In the following program, `partition1` generates only valid partitions, but `partition2` generates all possible partitions and uses `isValid` to decide whether or not to print a given partition. The function `printPartition` does nothing in this example because printing many lines can noticeably slow down a program. Since both programs print the same result, there is no reason for examining this function. We can examine the performance of `partition1` and `partition2` without the distraction of `printPartition`.

```
1  // comppartition.c
2  // partition using alternating odd and even numbers
3  // two ways to implement the partition:
4  // 1. check before recursive calls
5  // 2. generate all partitions and check before printing
6  #include <stdio.h>
7  #include <stdlib.h>
8  void printPartition(int * arr, int length)
9  {
10   /*
11   int ind;
12   for (ind = 0; ind < length - 1; ind ++)
13     {
14       printf("%d + ", arr[ind]);
15     }
16   printf("%d\n", arr[length - 1]);
17   */
18 }
19 // 1. generate only valid partitions
20 void partition1(int * arr, int ind, int left)
```

```
21  {
22    int val;
23    if (left == 0)
24      {
25        printPartition(arr, ind);
26        return;
27      }
28    for (val = 1; val <= left; val ++)
29      {
30        int valid = 0;
31        if (ind == 0) // no restriction for the first number
32          {
33            valid = 1;
34          }
35        else
36          {
37            valid = (arr[ind - 1] % 2) != (val % 2);
38          }
39        if (valid == 1)
40          {
41            arr[ind] = val;
42            partition1(arr, ind + 1, left - val);
43          }
44      }
45  }
46  // 2. before printing, check whether the partition is valid
47  // check whether the numbers are alternating odd and even
48  // return 1 if valid
49  // return 0 if invalid
50  int isValid(int * arr, int len)
51  {
52    if (len <= 1) // if only one number, it is valid
53      {
54        return 1;
55      }
56    int ind;
57    for (ind = 2; ind < len; ind += 2)
58      {
59
60        // invalid if they are different
61        if ((arr[ind] % 2) != (arr[0] % 2))
62          {
63            return 0;
64          }
65      }
66    for (ind = 1; ind < len; ind += 2)
67      {
68
69        // invalid if they are the same
70        if ((arr[ind] % 2) == (arr[0] % 2))
71          {
```

```
72            return 0;
73          }
74       }
75    return 1;
76 }
77 // generate all possible partitions, including invalid
78 // check before printing
79 void partition2(int * arr, int ind, int left)
80 {
81    int val;
82    if (left == 0)
83       {
84          if (isValid(arr, ind) == 1)
85             {
86                printPartition(arr, ind);
87             }
88          return;
89       }
90    for (val = 1; val <= left; val ++)
91       {
92          arr[ind] = val;
93          partition2(arr, ind + 1, left - val);
94       }
95 }
96
97 int main(int argc, char * argv[])
98 {
99    if (argc != 2)
100       {
101          return EXIT_FAILURE;
102       }
103    int n = (int) strtol(argv[1], NULL, 10);
104    if (n <= 0)
105       {
106          return EXIT_FAILURE;
107       }
108    int * arr;
109    arr = malloc(sizeof(int) * n);
110    printf("-----Partition␣1-----\n");
111    partition1(arr, 0, n);
112    printf("-----Partition␣2-----\n");
113    partition2(arr, 0, n);
114    free (arr);
115    return EXIT_SUCCESS;
116 }
```

This is the report from gprof when n is 30.

```
Flat profile:

Each sample counts as 0.01 seconds.
  %   cumulative   self              self     total
```

time	seconds	seconds	calls	s/call	s/call	name
55.74	6.75	6.75	1	6.75	11.99	partition2
43.28	11.99	5.24	536870912	0.00	0.00	isValid
1.50	12.17	0.18	1	0.18	0.18	partition1
0.00	12.17	0.00	202786	0.00	0.00	printPartition

index	% time	self	children	called	name
					\<spontaneous\>
[1]	100.0	0.00	12.17		main [1]
		6.75	5.24	1/1	partition2 [2]
		0.18	0.00	1/1	partition1 [4]
				1073741823	partition2 [2]
		6.75	5.24	1/1	main [1]
[2]	98.5	6.75	5.24	1+1073741823	partition2 [2]
		5.24	0.00	536870912/536870912	isValid [3]
		0.00	0.00	101393/202786	printPartition [5]
				1073741823	partition2 [2]
		5.24	0.00	536870912/536870912	partition2 [2]
[3]	43.1	5.24	0.00	536870912	isValid [3]
				308288	partition1 [4]
		0.18	0.00	1/1	main [1]
[4]	1.5	0.18	0.00	1+308288	partition1 [4]
		0.00	0.00	101393/202786	printPartition [5]
				308288	partition1 [4]
		0.00	0.00	101393/202786	partition1 [4]
		0.00	0.00	101393/202786	partition2 [2]
[5]	0.0	0.00	0.00	202786	printPartition [5]

This report shows that nearly 99% of the program's execution time is taken by partition2 (55.7%) and isValid (43.3%). Since isValid is called only by partition2, the report shows that partition2 takes 98.5% of the time. In contrast, partition1 takes only 1.5% of the time. Why is there such a large difference? The reason is that partition2 generates many invalid partitions and then uses isValid to check before printing. In contrast, partition1 generates only valid partitions. The latter approach reduces huge portions of the call tree, and is thus much more efficient.

Please notice that [4] shows printPartition is called by partition1 101393 times and by partition2 101393 times. This is expected since partition1 and partition2 should print exactly the same partitions. The function partition2 is called 1073741823 times by recursion but partition1 is called only 308288 times. The report also shows that isValid is called 536870912 times but printPartition is called only 202786 times (by both partition1 and partition2). This means that most of the generated partitions are invalid and are not printed. This is another indication that partition2 generates many invalid partitions. Notice that 55.74%, 43.28%, and 1.50% sum to 100.52%. How can it be possible that the cumulative time is above 100%? This shows a limitation of gprof: This tool is intended to be fast but the accuracy is not so great. Profiling code always interferes with the normal execution of the code, and there must be a trade-off somewhere.

When we want to improve a program's performance, then we first need to identify the functions that take the most amount of time. We can get some help by using gprof.

After finding the functions, we need to think about whether these functions are doing any unnecessary work. Eliminating unnecessary computation should be the first step in improving performance. Note that this is also the principle behind `qsort`: It uses transitivity to eliminate unnecessary comparisons.

We can also use gcov to find the opportunities for improving performance. This is primarily used to examine test coverage: It helps us understand the quality of the tests. Section 5.5 explains how to use gcov to examine test coverage. Here we show how to use gcov to look for performance bottlenecks. To run gcov, we must add `-fprofile-arcs -ftest-coverage` after `gcc`. The program can be executed normally. When the program runs, two files are generated: One has `.gcda` extension and the other has `.gcno` extension. The next step is to run the `gcov` command. It will generate another file whose extension is `.gcov`. This is the file that we want to examine. Here are the contents of the file from a sample run (suppose the value of **n** is 30).

```
     -:      0:Source:gprofeg.c
     -:      0:Graph:gprofeg.gcno
     -:      0:Data:gprofeg.gcda
     -:      0:Runs:1
     -:      0:Programs:1
     -:      1:// partition using alternating odd and even
              numbers
     -:      2:// two ways to implement the partition:
     -:      3:// 1. check before recursive calls
     -:      4:// 2. generate all partitions and check
              before printing
     -:      5:#include <stdio.h>
     -:      6:#include <stdlib.h>
     -:      7:
202786:      8:void printPartition(int * arr, int length)
     -:      9:{
     -:     10:  /*
     -:     11:  int ind;
     -:     12:  for (ind = 0; ind < length - 1; ind ++)
     -:     13:    {
     -:     14:      printf("%d + ", arr[ind]);
     -:     15:    }
     -:     16:  printf("%d\n", arr[length - 1]);
     -:     17:  */
202786:     18:}
     -:     19:
     -:     20:// 1. do not generate invalid partial
              partitions
308289:     21:void partition1(int * arr, int ind, int left)
     -:     22:{
     -:     23:  int val;
308289:     24:  if (left == 0)
     -:     25:    {
101393:     26:      printPartition(arr, ind);
409682:     27:      return;
     -:     28:    }
835786:     29:  for (val = 1; val <= left; val ++)
```

```
     -:   30:      {
628890:   31:        int valid = 0;
628890:   32:        if (ind == 0) // no restriction for the
      first number
     -:   33:          {
    30:   34:            valid = 1;
     -:   35:          }
     -:   36:        else
     -:   37:          {
628860:   38:            valid = (arr[ind - 1] % 2) != (val
      % 2);
     -:   39:          }
628890:   40:        if (valid == 1)
     -:   41:          {
308288:   42:            arr[ind] = val;
308288:   43:            partition1(arr, ind + 1, left -
      val);
     -:   44:          }
     -:   45:      }
     -:   46:}
     -:   47:
     -:   48:// 2. before printing, check whether the
      partition is valid
     -:   49:// check whether the numbers are alternating
      odd and even
     -:   50:// return 1 if valid
     -:   51:// return 0 if invalid
536870912:   52:int isValid(int * arr, int len)
     -:   53:{
536870912:   54:  if (len <= 1) // if only one number, it is
      valid
     -:   55:    {
     1:   56:      return 1;
     -:   57:    }
     -:   58:  int ind;
1304963113:   59:  for (ind = 2; ind < len; ind += 2)
     -:   60:    {
     -:   61:
     -:   62:      // invalid if they are different
1283973260:   63:      if ((arr[ind] % 2) != (arr[0] % 2))
     -:   64:        {
515881058:   65:          return 0;
     -:   66:        }
     -:   67:    }
33079750:   68:  for (ind = 1; ind < len; ind += 2)
     -:   69:    {
     -:   70:
     -:   71:      // invalid if they are the same
32978358:   72:      if ((arr[ind] % 2) == (arr[0] % 2))
     -:   73:        {
20888461:   74:          return 0;
```

```
     -:     75:              }
     -:     76:          }
101392:     77:      return 1;
     -:     78:}
     -:     79:
1073741824:    80:void partition2(int * arr, int ind, int left)
     -:     81:{
     -:     82:    int val;
1073741824:    83:    if (left == 0)
     -:     84:      {
536870912:    85:        if (isValid(arr, ind) == 1)
     -:     86:          {
101393:     87:            printPartition(arr, ind);
     -:     88:          }
1610612736:    89:        return;
     -:     90:      }
1610612735:    91:    for (val = 1; val <= left; val ++)
     -:     92:      {
1073741823:    93:        arr[ind] = val;
1073741823:    94:        partition2(arr, ind + 1, left - val);
     -:     95:      }
     -:     96:}
     -:     97:
     1:     98:int main(int argc, char * argv[])
     -:     99:{
     1:    100:    if (argc != 2)
     -:    101:      {
 #####:    102:        return EXIT_FAILURE;
     -:    103:      }
     1:    104:    int n = (int) strtol(argv[1], NULL, 10);
     1:    105:    if (n <= 0)
     -:    106:      {
 #####:    107:        return EXIT_FAILURE;
     -:    108:      }
     -:    109:    int * arr;
     1:    110:    arr = malloc(sizeof(int) * n);
     1:    111:    printf("-----Partition␣1-----\n");
     1:    112:    partition1(arr, 0, n);
     1:    113:    printf("-----Partition␣2-----\n");
     1:    114:    partition2(arr, 0, n);
     1:    115:    free (arr);
     1:    116:    return EXIT_SUCCESS;
     -:    117:}
```

Please pay special attention to lines 85 and 87. Line 85 says `isValid` is called 536870912 times but it is true only 101393 times. In other words, most generated partitions are invalid. This is another way to obtain the same information: `partition2` generates many invalid partitions.

Chapter 15

Programming Problems Using Recursion

This chapter describes several problems that can be solved using recursion.

15.1   Binary Search

A binary search is an efficient way to search for something in a sorted array. The function definition should be something like:

```
int search(int * arr, int len, int key)
```

The function **search** returns the index of **key** within **arr**. If **arr** does not contain this key, then the function returns −1. The arguments mean the following:

- **arr**: an array of integers. The elements are distinct and sorted in the ascending order.
- **len**: the length of the array, i.e., the number of elements in the array.
- **key**: the value to search for. Think of **key** as the proverbial needle in the haystack.

Since the array is already sorted, it is possible to quickly discard many elements by comparing **key** with the element at the center of the array. If **key** is larger than that element, we do not need to search the lower part of the array, i.e., the part before the center element. If **key** is smaller than that element, we do not need to search the upper part of the array. This idea can be generalized such that instead of considering the whole array, we are only considering a contiguous part of the array. As such, there are four scenarios:

- If the contiguous part of the array has no elements, then it is impossible to find **key** and the function returns −1.
- If **key** is the same as the center of the contiguous part of the array, then the index has been found, and we return that index.
- If the key is greater than the center element, then the function discards the lower half (the elements with smaller values) of the array, and considers the upper half.

- If the key is smaller than the center element, then the function discards the second half (the elements with larger values) of the array, and considers the lower half.

These steps continue until either the index is found or it is impossible to find a match. Fig. 15.1 is a graphical view of the steps:

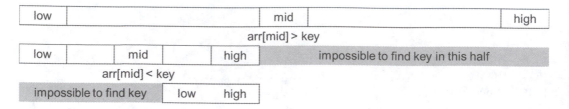

FIGURE 15.1: In each step, the binary search reduces the number of elements to search across by half. In the first step, `key` is compared with the element at the center. If `key` is smaller, then it is impossible to find `key` in the upper half of the array. If `key` is greater than the element at the center, then it is impossible to find `key` in the lower half of the array. The array must have been sorted before performing a binary search.

```c
// binarysearch.c
#include <stdio.h>
#include <stdlib.h>
#include <time.h>
#include <string.h>
#define RANGE 100
int * arrGen(int size);
// generate a sorted array of integers
static int binarySearchHelp(int * arr, int low,
                            int high, int key)
{
  if (low > high)
    {
      return -1;
    }
  int ind = (low + high) / 2;
  if (arr[ind] == key)
    {
      return ind;
    }
  if (arr[ind] > key)
    {
      return binarySearchHelp(arr, low, ind - 1, key);
    }
  return binarySearchHelp(arr, ind + 1, high, key);
}
int binarySearch(int * arr, int len, int key)
{
  return binarySearchHelp(arr, 0, len - 1, key);
}
void printArray(int * arr, int len);
int main(int argc, char * * argv)
```

```
33  {
34     if (argc < 2)
35       {
36         printf("need␣a␣positive␣integer\n");
37         return EXIT_FAILURE;
38       }
39     int num = strtol(argv[1], NULL, 10);
40     if (num <= 0)
41       {
42         printf("need␣a␣positive␣integer\n");
43         return EXIT_FAILURE;
44       }
45     int * arr = arrGen(num);
46     printArray(arr, num);
47     int count;
48     for (count = 0; count < 10; count ++)
49       {
50         int key;
51         if ((count % 2) == 0)
52           {
53             key = arr[rand() % num];
54           }
55         else
56           {
57             key = rand() % 100000;
58           }
59         printf("search(%d),␣result␣=␣%d\n",
60                 key, binarySearch(arr, num, key));
61       }
62     free (arr);
63     return EXIT_SUCCESS;
64  }
65  int * arrGen(int size)
66  {
67     if (size <= 0)
68       {
69         return NULL;
70       }
71     int * arr = malloc(sizeof(int) * size);
72     if (arr == NULL)
73       {
74         return NULL;
75       }
76     srand(time(NULL)); // set the seed
77     int ind;
78     arr[0] = rand() % RANGE;
79     for (ind = 1; ind < size; ind ++)
80       {
81         arr[ind] = arr[ind - 1] + (rand() % RANGE) + 1;
82       }
83     return arr;
```

```
84    }
85    void printArray(int * arr, int len)
86    {
87      int ind;
88      for (ind = 0; ind < len; ind ++)
89        {
90          printf("%d␣", arr[ind]);
91        }
92      printf("\n\n");
93    }
```

This program introduces the concept of *helper* functions. Helper functions are common in recursion for organizing the arguments correctly. In this example, `binarySearch` has three arguments; however, the recursive function requires four arguments. Instead of passing the array's length, two arguments indicate the contiguous part of the array that remains to be searched. The range is expressed with the two arguments: `low` and `high`.

Please pay attention to how the range changes in recursive calls: The range must shrink in each call. This ensures that the recursive call chain eventually reaches a terminating condition. Line 16 uses integer division: If `low + high` is an odd number, then the remainder is discarded because `ind` is an integer. Note carefully that line 23 uses `ind - 1` for the new high index. A common mistake is to use `ind` instead. This will cause a problem because it does not guarantee that the range shrinks in recursive calls. For example, consider the situation where the range has only one element. This occurs when `low` is the same as `high`. Their average `ind` is also the same. If line 23 were to use `ind`, then the next recursive call to the helper function would also have `low` equal to `high`. The arguments are unchanged and the recursion will not end. Similarly, in line 25 the low index must be `ind + 1` and not `ind`. Another common mistake is using `if (low >= high)` for the condition at line 12. This is wrong when the array has only one element to check. This function returns -1 without checking whether or not that single element is the same as `key`.

The source listing above includes a function to generate test cases called `arrGen`. The program calls `binarySearch` ten times. In five of the calls (when `count` is an even number at line 51), `key` is an element of the array and therefore `binarySearch` should find `key`. This program shows a strategy to test the program with known results.

15.2   Quick Sort

Section 9.2 explained how to use the `qsort` function. This section explains how quick sort works. As previously mentioned, quick sort uses the concept of transitivity: If $x > y$ and $y > z$, then $x > z$. The algorithm first selects one element from the array: It does not matter which one. This element is called the *pivot*. It can be any element in the array. Some implementations use the first or last element; some implementations use a randomly selected element. After selecting the pivot, the algorithm divides the array into three parts: (i) elements smaller than the pivot, (ii) equal to the pivot, and (iii) greater than the pivot. By dividing the elements into the three parts, the algorithm uses transitivity to avoid unnecessary comparisons among elements. This algorithm is usually faster than other sorting algorithms and is called "quick sort". After dividing the elements into the three parts, the algorithm then recursively sorts parts (i) and (iii). The program stops when all elements have been sorted. This occurs when each part has only one element or no element at all. How does the algorithm divide the array into three parts? One solution uses these steps:

1. Determine the value of the pivot. In this example, the pivot is the first element.
2. Iterate through the original array from left (smaller indexes) to right (larger indexes) using two indexes called `low` and `high`. The initial value of `low` is one higher than the index of the pivot. The initial value of `high` is the largest index of the range being considered.
3. From the left side, if an element is smaller than the pivot, `low` increments. If an element is greater than the pivot, stop changing `low`.
4. From the right side, if an element is greater than the pivot, `high` decrements. If an element is smaller than the pivot, stop changing `high`.
5. Now swap the elements whose indexes are `low` and `high`.
6. Continue steps 2 to 4 until `low` is greater than `high`.
7. Put the pivot between the two parts.

Note that by the last step, the array will be ordered such that all of the elements smaller than the pivot are together, and all of the elements larger than pivot are also together. When the pivot is placed, it is in the correct position for the final sorted array. The following figure illustrates the procedure. The pivot is 19, `low` is 1, and `high` is 11.

index	0	1	2	3	4	5	6	7	8	9	10	11
value	19	7	12	23	8	31	6	42	28	16	51	33
variable	pivot	low										high

Because 7 is smaller than 19, `low` increments.

index	0	1	2	3	4	5	6	7	8	9	10	11
value	19	7	12	23	8	31	6	42	28	16	51	33
variable	pivot		low									high

The next value, 12, is also smaller than 19, and `low` increments again. The next value is 23 and it is greater than 19. Thus, `low` stops incrementing.

index	0	1	2	3	4	5	6	7	8	9	10	11
value	19	7	12	23	8	31	6	42	28	16	51	33
variable	pivot			low								high

Following the algorithm, if the value whose index is `high` is greater than the pivot, then decrement `high`. Since 33 is greater than 19, we must decrement `high`.

index	0	1	2	3	4	5	6	7	8	9	10	11
value	19	7	12	23	8	31	6	42	28	16	51	33
variable	pivot			low							high	

Since 51 is also greater than 19, `high` decrements again.

index	0	1	2	3	4	5	6	7	8	9	10	11
value	19	7	12	23	8	31	6	42	28	16	51	33
variable	pivot			low						high		

At this moment, the value whose index is `low` is greater than the pivot. The value whose index is `high` is smaller than the pivot. Now we swap these two values.

index	0	1	2	3	4	5	6	7	8	9	10	11
value	19	7	12	16	8	31	6	42	28	23	51	33
variable	pivot			low						high		

Continuing the algorithm, the value of `low` increases because 16 is smaller than 19.

index	0	1	2	3	4	5	6	7	8	9	10	11
value	19	7	12	16	8	31	6	42	28	23	51	33
variable	pivot				low					high		

Because 8 is smaller than 19, `low` increments again.

index	0	1	2	3	4	5	6	7	8	9	10	11
value	19	7	12	16	8	31	6	42	28	23	51	33
variable	pivot					low				high		

Because 31 is greater than 19, `low` stops here. Since 23 is greater than the pivot, `high` decrements.

index	0	1	2	3	4	5	6	7	8	9	10	11
value	19	7	12	16	8	31	6	42	28	23	51	33
variable	pivot					low			high			

The index `high` decrements twice more, and the value at `high` is 6.

index	0	1	2	3	4	5	6	7	8	9	10	11
value	19	7	12	16	8	31	6	42	28	23	51	33
variable	pivot					low	high					

Now the values at `low` and `high` are swapped.

index	0	1	2	3	4	5	6	7	8	9	10	11
value	19	7	12	16	8	6	31	42	28	23	51	33
variable	pivot					low	high					

If `low` increments, it will meet `high`. This means that the array has been divided into three parts: (i) the first element, which is the pivot, (ii) the part that is smaller than the pivot, and (iii) the part that is greater than the pivot.

Now the value at `low` and the pivot are swapped.

index	0	1	2	3	4	5	6	7	8	9	10	11
value	6	7	12	16	8	19	31	42	28	23	51	33
variable						low	high					

The algorithm next sorts part (ii) using the same procedure.

index	0	1	2	3	4
value	6	7	12	16	8
variable	pivot	low			high

The algorithm also sorts part (iii) using the same procedure.

index	6	7	8	9	10	11
value	31	42	28	23	51	33
variable	pivot	low				high

A sample implementation of quick sort is shown below. The function `quickSort` takes only two arguments: the array and its length. The recursive function needs three arguments: the array and the range of indexes to be sorted. Thus, a helper function called `quickSortHelp` is created. This helper function divides the array elements in the specified range into three parts and recursively sorts the first and the third parts.

```
1   // quicksort.c
2   #include <stdio.h>
3   #include <stdlib.h>
4   #include <time.h>
5   #include <string.h>
6   #define RANGE          10000
7   int * arrGen(int size);
8   // generate a sorted array of integers
9   void swap(int * a, int * b);
10  static void quickSortHelp(int * arr, int first, int last)
11  {
12    // [first, last]: range of valid indexes (not last - 1)
13    if (first >= last) // no need to sort one or no element
14      {
15        return;
16      }
17  #ifdef DEBUG
18    printf("first = %d, last = %d\n", first, last);
19  #endif
20    int pivot = arr[first];
21    int low = first + 1;
22    int high = last;
23    while (low < high)
24      {
25        while ((low < last) && (arr[low] <= pivot))
26          {
27            // <= so that low will increment when arr[low]
28            // is the same as pivot, using < will stop
29            // incrementing low when arr[low] is the same
30            // as pivot and the outer while loop will not stop
31            low ++;
32          }
33        while ((first < high) && (arr[high] > pivot))
34          {
35            high --;
36          }
37        if (low < high)
38          {
39            swap (& arr[low], & arr[high]);
40          }
41      }
42    if (pivot > arr[high])
43      {
44        swap(& arr[first], & arr[high]);
45      }
46    quickSortHelp(arr, first, high - 1);
47    quickSortHelp(arr, low, last);
48  }
49  void quickSort(int * arr, int len)
50  {
51    quickSortHelp(arr, 0, len - 1);
```

```
52    }
53    void printArray(int * arr, int len);
54    int main(int argc, char * * argv)
55    {
56      if (argc < 2)
57        {
58          printf("need␣a␣positive␣integer\n");
59          return EXIT_FAILURE;
60        }
61      if (argc == 3)
62        {
63          srand(strtol(argv[2], NULL, 10));
64        }
65      else
66        {
67          srand(time(NULL)); // set the seed
68        }
69      int num = strtol(argv[1], NULL, 10);
70      if (num <= 0)
71        {
72          printf("need␣a␣positive␣integer\n");
73          return EXIT_FAILURE;
74        }
75      int * arr = arrGen(num);
76      printArray(arr, num);
77      quickSort(arr, num);
78      printArray(arr, num);
79      free (arr);
80      return EXIT_SUCCESS;
81    }
82    void swap(int * a, int * b)
83    {
84      int s = * a;
85      * a = * b;
86      * b = s;
87    }
88    int * arrGen(int size)
89    {
90      if (size <= 0)
91        {
92          return NULL;
93        }
94      int * arr = malloc(sizeof(int) * size);
95      if (arr == NULL)
96        {
97          return NULL;
98        }
99      int ind;
100     for (ind = 0; ind < size; ind ++)
101       {
102         arr[ind] = rand() % RANGE;
```

```
103        }
104      return arr;
105  }
106  void printArray(int * arr, int len)
107  {
108      int ind;
109      int sorted = 1;
110      for (ind = 0; ind < len; ind ++)
111          {
112  #ifdef DEBUG
113          printf("%d ", arr[ind]);
114  #endif
115          if ((ind > 0) && (arr[ind] < arr[ind -1]))
116              {
117                  sorted = 0;
118              }
119          }
120      printf("\nsorted = %d\n\n", sorted);
121  }
```

This implementation introduces a new way to debug. Lines 17 and 19 use `#ifdef DEBUG` and `#endif` to enclose debugging code. If this program is compiled the normal way, the lines between `#ifdef DEBUG` and `#endif` are skipped by the compiler. In other words, the line (or lines) between `#ifdef DEBUG` and `#endif` has (or have) no effect. This is useful if the program prints too many debugging messages. If you want to see the debugging messages, compile the program in the following way:

$ gcc -g -Wall -Wshadow -DDEBUG quicksort.c -o quicksort

When adding `-DDEBUG` (it is `-D` followed by the symbol after `#ifdef`) after `gcc`, the debugging messages are shown. This flag tells `gcc` to define the symbol `DEBUG`. You can define other symbols by adding `-D` in front of the symbol after the `gcc` command. It is also possible to add `-DDEBUG` to `CFLAGS` in `Makefile`.

You may have noticed that the function `printArray` also checks whether the array is sorted. This is another debugging technique. Visually inspecting whether an array is sorted is useful for an array with only a few elements. Instead of using visual inspection, the program automatically determines whether or not the array is sorted. Making the program check for its own correctness allows us to test `quickSort` and its helper function with an array of thousands of elements.

Another debugging technique is to use `argv[2]` to set the seed of the random numbers. To test the program, you probably want to use random numbers so that the tests can cover different scenarios. However, we need some way to repeat the test if a problem is found, and that means we must be able to control the sequence of random numbers. One solution is to use a command-line argument. If this argument is present, the random number generator is seeded correspondingly, and then the same sequence of numbers is generated. Without giving this command-line argument, the seed is determined by the system clock, and the sequence will almost certainly be different every time the program is run.

At first glance, this program may appear straightforward. A closer look, however, reveals that some common mistakes can easily occur. The helper function's second and third arguments specify the range of indexes that is being sorted. This function assumes `last` is a valid index and `quickSort` thus must use `len - 1`. If line 51 uses `len`, then the program may access an invalid memory location because `len` is not a valid index. As explained in

Section 7.2.2, sometimes accessing an invalid memory address does not seem to cause problems but the program is still wrong. If the program is compiled on different platforms, with different compilers, or if it is run enough times, then at some stage it will fail. Running `valgrind` is extraordinarily helpful in picking up these types of errors. If line 51 uses `len`, then `valgrind` reports:

```
==8895== Invalid read of size 4
==8895==    at 0x4007A0: quickSortHelp (quicksort.c:36)
```

The problem occurs when `high` is `last`. Please note that `last` can be `len`.

Now look at line 25, which uses `arr[low] <= pivot`. What happens if it is rewritten as `arr[low] < pivot`? This small difference can cause problems when some of the array's elements have the same value as the pivot. When this occurs and line 25 has no `=`, then `low` does not increment. If `arr[high]` is smaller than the pivot, then `high` does not decrement. As a result, neither `low` nor `high` change and the program enters an infinite loop because `low < high` is always true.

Some implementations of quick sort select random (not the first) array elements for the pivots. Why? Quick sort can be fast due to transitivity. If the original array is already sorted then quick sort is not faster because the first part (the part smaller than the pivot) is empty, and the program does not take advantage of transitivity. Using a random element in the array for the pivot reduces the chance when the pivot is always the smallest element in the sorted array.

15.3   Permutations and Combinations

Permutations can be generated using recursion based on the following idea: Swap the first item with any of the later locations, and then swap the second item with any of the later locations, and so on. The following example should make this clearer:

```
A   B   C   D
```

The first item, A, may appear in the first, second, third, or fourth column.

```
A
    A
        A
            A
```

Every time A moves, it is swapped with the item originally at that column. The second item, B, may also appear in the first, second, third, or fourth column. However, we need to exclude putting B in the first column because A appears in the second column by swapping A and B. Thus, B already has a chance to be moved to the first column and needs to be moved to only the second (original location), third, and fourth columns.

```
    B
        B
            B
```

Similarly, C may appear in the third or the fourth column.

$$\boxed{\begin{array}{c} \text{C} \\ \hline \text{C} \end{array}}$$

The following implementation generates all permutations of an array. It requires a command-line argument to set the array length.

```c
// permute.c
#include <stdio.h>
#include <stdlib.h>
#include <string.h>
void printArray(int * arr, int length)
{
  int ind;
  for (ind = 0; ind < length - 1; ind ++)
    {
      printf("%c␣", arr[ind]);
    }
  printf("%c\n", arr[length - 1]);
}
void swap(int * a, int * b)
{
  int s = * a;
  * a = * b;
  * b = s;
}
void permuteHelp(int * arr, int ind, int num)
{
  if (ind == num)
    {
      printArray(arr, ind);
      return;
    }
  int loc; // destination of arr[ind]
  for (loc = ind; loc < num; loc ++)
    {
      swap(& arr[ind], & arr[loc]);
      permuteHelp(arr, ind + 1, num);
      swap(& arr[ind], & arr[loc]); // swap back
    }
}
void permute(int * arr, int num)
{
  permuteHelp(arr, 0, num);
}
int main(int argc, char * argv[])
{
  if (argc != 2)
    {
      return EXIT_FAILURE;
    }
  int num = (int) strtol(argv[1], NULL, 10);
```

```
46    if (num <= 0)
47      {
48        return EXIT_FAILURE;
49      }
50    int * arr;
51    arr = malloc(sizeof(int) * num);
52    int ind;
53    for (ind = 0; ind < num; ind ++)
54      {
55        arr[ind] = ind + 'A'; // elements are 'A', 'B', ...
56      }
57    permute(arr, num);
58    free (arr);
59    return EXIT_SUCCESS;
60 }
```

Lines 28 to 33 are the core that generates the permutations. One way to understand how this works is to check the number of iterations generated. When `ind` is 0, the loop iterates `num` times. When `ind` is 1, the loop iterates `num` − 1 times. When `ind` is 2, the loop iterates `num` − 2 times. Finally, when `ind` is `num` − 1, the loop iterates only once. This program will iterate `num` × (`num` − 1) × (`num` - 2) ... 1 = `num`! times. This is the number of permutations for `num` items. If all the lines are unique then they are guaranteed to be the correct permutations.

You may be wondering why `loc` starts at `ind`, because when `loc` is `ind`, line 30,

```
1  swap(& arr[ind], & arr[loc]);
```

has no effect. It is true that swapping an element with itself has no effect. However, this is the way to keep this element at the original location. Without this line, the element will never stay in the original location. For example, if A is the first element, and `loc` starts at `ind` + 1, then A is always swapped away from the first location, and no generated permutation will begin with A. As a result, the program will fail to generate all possible permutations.

A different approach can be used to generate combinations. Instead of permuting an array storing the items, an array is used to store whether a particular item is selected or not. For example, if `arr[0]` is 0, A is not selected. If `arr[0]` is 1, then A is selected. If `arr[2]` is 0, then C is not selected. If `arr[2]` is 1, then C is selected. The helper function requires five arguments:

1. `arr` is a binary array storing whether an element is selected or not.
2. `ind` is the index of the item being decided on whether it is selected.
3. `num` is the total number of items.
4. `sel` is the number of items to be selected.
5. `sum` is the number of items already selected.

```
1  // combine.c
2  #include <stdio.h>
3  #include <stdlib.h>
4  #include <string.h>
5  void printArray(int * arr, int length)
6  {
7    int ind;
8    for (ind = 0; ind < length; ind ++)
9      {
10       if (arr[ind] == 1)
```

```
11          {
12             printf("%c␣", ind + 'A');
13          }
14       }
15    printf("\n");
16 }
17 void combineHelp(int * arr, int ind, int num,
18                   int sel, int sum)
19 {
20    if (sum == sel) // select enough items
21       {
22          printArray(arr, num);
23          return;
24       }
25    if (ind == num) // end of array, no more item to select
26       {
27          return;
28       }
29    // select this element
30    arr[ind] = 1;
31    combineHelp(arr, ind + 1, num, sel, sum + 1);
32    // do not select this element
33    arr[ind] = 0;
34    combineHelp(arr, ind + 1, num, sel, sum);
35 }
36 void combine(int * arr, int num, int sel)
37 {
38    combineHelp(arr, 0, num, sel, 0);
39 }
40 int main(int argc, char * argv[])
41 {
42    if (argc != 3) // need two numbers
43       {
44          return EXIT_FAILURE;
45       }
46    int num = (int) strtol(argv[1], NULL, 10);
47    if (num <= 0)
48       {
49          return EXIT_FAILURE;
50       }
51    int sel = (int) strtol(argv[2], NULL, 10);
52    if ((sel <= 0) || (sel > num))
53       {
54          return EXIT_FAILURE;
55       }
56    int * arr;
57    arr = malloc(sizeof(int) * num);
58    int ind;
59    for (ind = 0; ind < num; ind ++)
60       {
61          arr[ind] = 0;
```

```
62      }
63    combine(arr, num, sel);
64    free(arr);
65    return EXIT_SUCCESS;
66  }
```

When `sum` equals `sel`, enough items have been selected and the selected items are printed. When `ind` equals `num`, no more items are available for selection. Line 30 selects the item and one is added to `sum` when recursively calling `combineHelp`. Line 33 "unselects" the item and `sum` is unchanged in the recursive call. Either the item is selected or it is not. The helper function recursively calls itself to determine whether to select the remaining items. From the examples of permutations and combinations, you can see recursion is a natural way of solving these problems. **Recursion is a good approach when the solutions have "branches".** In permutation, each element can be in one of many locations. After setting one element to a particular location, the next element also can be in one of many locations. By putting recursive calls inside a loop, the solution naturally solves permutations. For combinations, each element may be selected or not and there are two branches. One reason that makes recursion a better solution is that the number of iterations changes. For both cases, the call stack keeps the values of the array indexes. The indexes indicate which element to consider next. Without using recursion, programmers have to allocate memory for keeping the values of the indexes.

15.4   Stack Sort

A stack can be used to sort a sequence of numbers, if the sequence satisfies some conditions. What is a "stack"? A stack can store information based on the "first-in, last-out" rule. The call stack is a stack that is used to control the flow of execution of a computer program. Not every stack is a call stack. The "stack" in this section is unrelated to the call stack described earlier. The stack sort algorithm is described as follows:

1. Create an empty stack.
2. Read one number from the sequence, call it x.
3. If the stack is empty, push the number x to the stack.
4. When the stack is not empty, we call the number at the top of the stack y.
5. If $y <= x$, pop y from the stack. Continue steps 4 and 5 until either the stack is empty or top of the stack is greater x.
6. If $y > x$, then push x to the stack.
7. Repeat steps 2 to 6 until finishing the input sequence.
8. If the stack is not empty, then pop all remaining numbers from the stack.
9. The sequence of numbers popped from the stack is sorted if the input sequence is "stack-sortable". The definition is described further below.

Stack sort is a theoretically interesting algorithm, because it is fast—faster than quick sort—but works only under particular circumstances. Those circumstances will be explained, but first a few examples to illustrate how stack sort works.

15.4.1   Example 1

Consider the sequence <2, 1>. When 2 is read from the sequence, the stack is empty and 2 is pushed on to the stack (step 3). Next, 1 is read from the sequence, 1 is smaller than the element on top of the stack, and is therefore pushed to the stack (step 6). Now the sequence is finished and we pop the numbers from the stack (step 8) and the result is <1, 2>. Below is a graphical illustration of the steps. The first number, 2, is read and pushed to the stack.

$$\overline{}$$
$$2$$
$$\overline{}$$

The second number, 1, is read and pushed to the stack.

$$\overline{}$$
$$1$$
$$2$$
$$\overline{}$$

The numbers are popped and the result is <1, 2>.

15.4.2 Example 2

The next example considers the sequence <1, 2>. The first number, 1, is read from the sequence and pushed to the stack.

$$\overline{}$$
$$1$$
$$\overline{}$$

The second number, 2, is read. Since 1 is smaller than 2, 1 is popped from the stack and 2 is pushed on to the stack.

$$\overline{}$$
$$2$$
$$\overline{}$$

The numbers are popped and the result is <1, 2>.

15.4.3 Example 3

The third example is the sequence <1, 3, 2>. The first number, 1, is read from the sequence and pushed on to the stack.

$$\overline{}$$
$$1$$
$$\overline{}$$

The second number, 3, is read. Since 1 is smaller than 3, 1 is popped from the stack and 3 is pushed on to the stack.

$$\overline{}$$
$$3$$
$$\overline{}$$

The third number, 2, is read. Since 2 is smaller than 3, 2 is pushed to the stack.

$$\overline{}$$
$$2$$
$$3$$
$$\overline{}$$

The numbers are popped and the result is <1, 2, 3>.

15.4.4   Example 4

In the fourth example we consider the sequence <2, 3, 1>. The first number, 2, is read and pushed on to the stack.

$$\underline{\quad 2 \quad}$$

The second number, 3, is read. Since 2 is smaller than 3, 2 is popped from the stack and 3 is pushed on to the stack.

$$\underline{\quad 3 \quad}$$

The third number, 1, is read. Since 1 is smaller than 3, 1 is pushed on to the stack.

$$\frac{1}{3}$$

The numbers are popped and the result is <2, 1, 3>.

There is a problem: The popped sequence is not sorted. Stack sort can sort some sequences of numbers but fails to sort the others. Is there a way to determine whether a sequence of numbers is "stack sortable"?

15.4.5   Stack Sortable

Let M be the largest value of the whole sequence. Without loss of generality, a sequence of numbers can be divided into three parts: $\mathbb{A}$ before M, M, and $\mathbb{B}$ after M. It is possible that the first or third parts (or both) are empty. If M is the first number in the sequence, then $\mathbb{A}$ is empty. If M is the last number in the sequence, then $\mathbb{B}$ is empty.

$\mathbb{A}$: before M	M	$\mathbb{B}$: after M

Step 5 of the algorithm pops all the numbers in the stack when M is read. Suppose $M_{\mathbb{A}}$ is the largest value in $\mathbb{A}$. All the values must obey $M_{\mathbb{A}} < M$, because M is the largest value. Suppose $m_{\mathbb{B}}$ is the smallest value in $\mathbb{B}$. When M is pushed to the stack, every number in $\mathbb{A}$ must have already been popped. If $m_{\mathbb{B}} < M_{\mathbb{A}}$, $m_{\mathbb{B}}$ should be popped before $M_{\mathbb{A}}$ is popped. However, when M is pushed, $M_{\mathbb{A}}$ has already been popped and there is no chance for $m_{\mathbb{B}}$ to be popped before $M_{\mathbb{A}}$ is popped. As a result, stack sort fails for this sequence. In the last example, <2, 3, 1>, M is 3, $M_{\mathbb{A}}$ is 2, and $m_{\mathbb{B}}$ is 1. The condition $m_{\mathbb{B}} < M_{\mathbb{A}}$ is satisfied so <2, 3, 1> is not stack sortable.

Is this sequence <1, 5, 2, 3, 5, 4> stack sortable? Note that the largest value 5 appears twice in this sequence. Following the procedure described earlier, the first number is pushed to the stack.

$$\underline{\quad 1 \quad}$$

The next number 5 is larger than 1 so 1 is popped and 5 is pushed.

$$\underline{\quad 5 \quad}$$

The third number 2 is smaller than 5 and it is pushed.

$$\frac{\begin{array}{c} 2 \\ 5 \end{array}}{}$$

The next number is 3 so 2 is popped from the stack and 3 is pushed.

$$\frac{\begin{array}{c} 3 \\ 5 \end{array}}{}$$

The next number is 5 so 3 is popped and 5 is pushed.

$$\frac{\begin{array}{c} 5 \\ 5 \end{array}}{}$$

The last number 4 is pushed.

$$\frac{\begin{array}{c} 4 \\ 5 \\ 5 \end{array}}{}$$

Finally, all numbers are popped and the output sequence is 1, 2, 3, 4, 5, 5. It is sorted. Thus, <1, 5, 2, 3, 5, 4> is stack sortable.

If the same largest value M (5 in this example) appears multiple times, which M should be chosen for breaking the sequence into $\mathbb{A}$, M, and $\mathbb{B}$? Should it be the first M, the second M, the last one, or will any one do? The answer is the first M because we compare only the smallest element in $\mathbb{B}$ and do not care about the largest element in $\mathbb{B}$. If we choose an M other than the first, then the first M is in $\mathbb{A}$ and the sequence would never be considered stack sortable, which is a mistake.

After breaking the sequence into the three parts, the same procedure is applied recursively to $\mathbb{A}$ and $\mathbb{B}$ to determine whether in turn they are stack sortable. The algorithm for checking stack sortable is described as follows:

1. An empty sequence is stack sortable. This is a base case.
2. Find the largest value in the sequence. If this value appears multiple times in the array, select the first one.
3. Divide the sequence into three parts.
4. If both $\mathbb{A}$ and $\mathbb{B}$ are empty, then the sequence is stack sortable. The sequence has only one element. This is another base case.
5. If $\mathbb{A}$ is empty ($\mathbb{B}$ must not be empty), then jump to step 9.
6. If $\mathbb{B}$ is empty ($\mathbb{A}$ must not be empty), then jump to step 8.
7. Since neither $\mathbb{A}$ nor $\mathbb{B}$ is empty, find $M_{\mathbb{A}}$ and $m_{\mathbb{B}}$. If $M_{\mathbb{A}} > m_{\mathbb{B}}$, then the sequence is not stack sortable. This is another base case.
8. Recursively check whether $\mathbb{A}$ is stack sortable.
9. Recursively check whether $\mathbb{B}$ is stack sortable.

The following implementation checks whether a sequence is stack sortable. We have used the permutation program to generate all possible test cases.

```
1  // stacksort.c
2  #include <stdio.h>
3  #include <stdlib.h>
4  #include <string.h>
5  int findIndex(int * arr, int first, int last, int maxmin)
6  // find the index of the largest or smallest element
7  // the range is expressed by the indexes [first, last]
8  // maxmin = 1: find largest, maxmin = 0: find smallest
```

```
 9  {
10     int ind;
11     int  answer = first;
12     for (ind = first + 1; ind <= last; ind ++)
13       {
14         if (((maxmin == 1) && (arr[answer] < arr[ind])) ||
15             ((maxmin == 0) && (arr[answer] > arr[ind])))
16           {
17             answer = ind;
18           }
19       }
20     return answer;
21  }
22  int findMaxIndex(int * arr, int first, int last)
23  {
24     return findIndex(arr, first, last, 1);
25  }
26  int findMinIndex(int * arr, int first, int last)
27  {
28     return findIndex(arr, first, last, 0);
29  }
30  int isStackSortable(int * arr, int first, int last)
31  // check whether the range of the array is sortable
32  // return 1 if the range of the array is sortable
33  // return 0 if the range of the array is not sortable
34  {
35     if (first >= last) // no or one element is stack sortable
36       {
37         return 1;
38       }
39     int maxIndex = findMaxIndex(arr, first, last);
40     // consider the four cases
41     // both A and B are empty
42     // The array has only one element, it is stack sortable
43     // already checked earlier
44
45     // A is empty, B is not empty
46     // check whether B is stack sortable
47     if (first == maxIndex)
48       {
49         return isStackSortable(arr, first + 1, last);
50       }
51     // A is not empty, B is empty
52     // check whether A is stack sortable
53     if (maxIndex == last)
54       {
55         return isStackSortable(arr, first, last - 1);
56       }
57     // neither is empty
58     int maxAIndex = findMaxIndex(arr, first, maxIndex - 1);
59     int minBIndex = findMinIndex(arr, maxIndex + 1, last);
```

```
60      if (arr[maxAIndex] > arr[minBIndex])
61        {
62          return 0; // not stack sortable
63        }
64      int sortA = isStackSortable(arr, first, maxIndex - 1);
65      int sortB = isStackSortable(arr, maxIndex + 1, last);
66      return (sortA && sortB); // return 1 only if both are 1
67    }
68    void printArray(int * arr, int length)
69    {
70      if (isStackSortable(arr, 0, length - 1) == 0)
71        {
72          return;
73        }
74      int ind;
75      for (ind = 0; ind < length - 1; ind ++)
76        {
77          printf("%d", arr[ind]);
78        }
79      printf("%d\n", arr[length - 1]);
80    }
81    void swap(int * a, int * b)
82    {
83      int s = * a;
84      * a = * b;
85      * b = s;
86    }
87    void permuteHelp(int * arr, int ind, int num)
88    {
89      if (ind == num)
90        {
91          printArray(arr, ind);
92          return;
93        }
94      int loc; // destination of arr[ind]
95      for (loc = ind; loc < num; loc ++)
96        {
97          swap(& arr[ind], & arr[loc]);
98          permuteHelp(arr, ind + 1, num);
99          swap(& arr[ind], & arr[loc]); // swap back
100       }
101   }
102   void permute(int * arr, int num)
103   {
104     permuteHelp(arr, 0, num);
105   }
106   int main(int argc, char * argv[])
107   {
108     if (argc != 2)
109       {
110         return EXIT_FAILURE;
```

```
111        }
112    int num = (int) strtol(argv[1], NULL, 10);
113    if (num <= 0)
114        {
115            return EXIT_FAILURE;
116        }
117    int * arr;
118    arr = malloc(sizeof(int) * num);
119    int ind;
120    for (ind = 0; ind < num; ind ++)
121        {
122            arr[ind] = ind + 1;
123        }
124    permute(arr, num);
125    free (arr);
126    return EXIT_SUCCESS;
127 }
```

For an array of n distinct numbers, there are $n!$ permutations. Among them, $\frac{1}{n+1}C_n^{2n}$ are stack sortable. This is called the *Catalan number*. The proof will be given later in this book.

15.5   Tracing a Recursive Function

This problem asks you to understand a program with a recursive function. Please solve the problem without running the program in a computer. What is the output of this program?

```
1  // trace1.c
2  #include <stdio.h>
3  #include <stdlib.h>
4  int func(int n, int * count)
5  {
6    (* count) ++;
7    if ((n == 0) || (n == 1))
8        {
9            return 1;
10        }
11    int val = 0;
12    int a = func(n - 1, count);
13    int b = func(n / 2, count);
14    val += a + b;
15    return val;
16 }
17 int main(int argc, char * * argv)
18 {
19    int count = 0;
20    int val = 4;
21    int fv = func(val, & count);
```

```
22    printf("f(%d)␣=␣%d,␣count␣=␣%d\n", val, fv, count);
23    return EXIT_SUCCESS;
24  }
```

The program prints two values at line 22: `fv` and `count`. Their values can be computed independently. Fig. 15.2 shows one way of computing both using an approach similar to that shown in Section 14.2.

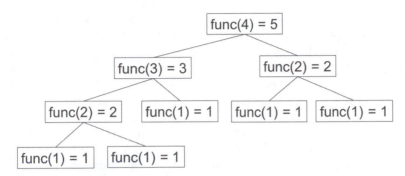

FIGURE 15.2: Determine the values of `fv` and `count` using a graphical illustration of the calling relations.

The value of `fv` is 5. The value of `count` increments every time `func` is called. The figure shows that both `func` and `count` are called 9 times.

This is a "top-down" approach to computing `func`. To compute `func(4)`, the program calls `func(3)`. To compute `func(3)`, `func(2)` is called. Computing `func(4)` calls `func(2)` three times and each time that happens it needs to call `func(1)` + `func(1)`. This is inefficient. It would be more efficient if the program remembers the values of `func(2)` so that it does not need to be recomputed. The following implementation shows a different way of computing `func`. It is a "bottom-up" approach: `func(2)` and `func(3)` are computed before computing `func(4)`. This is more efficient because the program remembers the value of `func(2)`, and therefore does not need to recompute it.

```c
1   // bottomup.c
2   #include <stdio.h>
3   #include <stdlib.h>
4   int func(int n)
5   {
6     int * arr;
7     // need n + 1 for arr[n]
8     arr = malloc(sizeof(int) * (n + 1));
9     arr[0] = 1;
10    arr[1] = 1;
11    int ind;
12    for (ind = 2; ind <= n; ind ++)
13      {
14        arr[ind] = arr[ind - 1] + arr[ind / 2];
15      }
16    int val = arr[n];
17    free (arr);
18    return val;
19  }
```

```
20  int main(int argc, char * * argv)
21  {
22      int val = 4;
23      int fv = func(val);
24      printf("f(%d) = %d\n", val, fv);
25      return EXIT_SUCCESS;
26  }
```

Some people mistakenly believe that recursion is slow. This is not true. The problem is not recursion. The problem is redundant computation: `func(2)` is recomputed multiple times. Recursion is fast when it is used correctly. Binary search and quick sort are two examples. Some problems, such as integer partition, permutations, and combinations can be solved naturally with recursion. Recursion is particularly helpful when the solution has some symmetry with smaller solutions. This is indeed the case with all our recursive examples. Solving these types of problems using `for` or `while` loops is more difficult. In each case working out the required number of iterations is non-obvious, and the implementation details would be quite complicated. What makes recursion simple is that it is possible to assume that the simpler cases are already solved. It is only necessary to figure out how to express a solution in terms of smaller solutions, and then, so long as the base cases are correct, the whole thing will work. This book puts great emphasis on recursion not because recursion is always a good strategy, but because recursion is an excellent approach for solving certain classes of problems. Attempting to solve these problems with other techniques can be difficult. If you understand recursion, then you can use it when recursion is a good approach.

15.6   A Recursive Function with a Mistake

Consider the following incorrect implementation of binary search. One line in `binarysearch` is incorrect, as marked by a comment. What is the output of this program?

```
1   // searchbug.c
2   #include <stdio.h>
3   #include <stdlib.h>
4   int binarySearch(int * arr, int key, int len);
5   #define ARRAYSIZE 10
6   int main(int argc, char * * argv)
7   {
8       int arr[ARRAYSIZE] = {1, 12, 23, 44, 65,
9                             76, 77, 98, 109, 110};
10      int ind;
11      for (ind = 0; ind < ARRAYSIZE; ind ++)
12        {
13          printf("%d\n", binarySearch(arr, arr[ind],
14                                      ARRAYSIZE));
15        }
16      return EXIT_SUCCESS;
17  }
18
19  int binarySearchHelp(int * arr, int key, int low, int high)
```

```
20  {
21     if (low >= high) /* ERROR: should be >, not >= */
22        {
23           return -1;
24        }
25     int mid = (low + high) / 2;
26     if (arr[mid] == key)
27        {
28           return mid;
29        }
30     if (arr[mid] > key)
31        {
32           return binarySearchHelp(arr, key, low, mid - 1);
33        }
34     return binarySearchHelp(arr, key, mid + 1, high);
35  }
36
37  int binarySearch(int * arr, int key, int len)
38  {
39     return binarySearchHelp(arr, key, 0, len - 1);
40  }
```

The program searches the array's elements one by one. If `binarySearchHelp` were correct, the program would print:

```
0
1
2
3
4
5
6
7
8
9
```

When searching for 1, the arguments `low` and `high` change as shown in the following:

low	high	mid	arr[mid]	key
0	9	4	65	1
0	3	1	12	1
0	0	0	1	1

The problem occurs when `low` and `high` are both zero and `binarySearchHelp` returns −1 without checking whether `arr[mid]` is the same as `key`. Does this mistake cause `binarySearchHelp` to always return −1? Consider searching for 12:

low	high	mid	arr[mid]	key
0	9	4	65	12
0	3	1	12	12

The function correctly returns 1. What will the function return when searching for 23?

low	high	mid	arr[mid]	key
0	9	4	65	23
0	3	1	12	23
2	3	2	23	23

The function correctly returns 2. The program's output is:

```
-1
1
2
-1
4
5
-1
7
8
-1
```

As you can see, this program *sometimes* produces correct results and sometimes produces incorrect results. This program has a 60% chance of producing correct results. This reinforces the need to have a strategy for testing. It is usually important to automate testing so that you can test many cases easily. A common mistake among beginning programmers is that they test several cases and then believe their programs are correct.

Part III

Structure

Chapter 16

Programmer-Defined Data Types

Section 7.1.2 mentioned several reasons for creating header files (.h files), including defining constants using #define, declaring functions, and defining new *data types*—usually referred to as "types". This chapter explains how to define new types using structures. First let us consider what makes up a type by thinking about the differences between int and double. A type specifies:

- The format for the data. For example, integers and double-precision floating-point numbers are represented differently in the computer's memory.
- The range of possible values, and the size required to store the data. A 4-byte integer stores valid values that are between the range of $-2,147,483,648$ (-2^{31}, approximately -10^9) and $2,147,483,647$ ($2^{31} - 1$). In contrast, the absolute value of a double-precision floating number (8 bytes) can be as small as 10^{-308} and as large as 10^{308} (approximately).
- The effect of operations on the data. Because the two types have different formats, when a program has a statement a + b, the actual operations depend on whether a and b are integers or floating-point numbers. Also, some operations are restricted to certain data types. For example, switch must be used with an integer; double cannot be used in switch statements.

C also supports other data types, such as char and float. C does not have a separate type for strings; instead, C uses null-terminated arrays of char for strings, as explained in Chapter 6. A natural question is whether C allows programmers to create new types. The answer is yes.

Why would programmers want to create new types? The most obvious reason is to put related data together. For example, a college student has a name (string), year (integer), grade point average (floating-point), and so on. C programmers would have to do something awkward if C did not allow the creation of new types. For example, separate arrays could be created to store the students' data: an array of strings for student names, an array of integers for years, an array of floating-point numbers for scores, etc. There is no good way to associate the elements in different arrays. There is no good way to ensure that the arrays have the same numbers of elements. Therefore, supporting programmer-defined types is essential.

16.1   Struct and Object

When multiple pieces of data are organized together, it is a *structure*. A structure is a type (similar to `int` or `char`). After creating the structure, the type can be used to create an *object* (borrowing a term from C++ and Java). An object is a specific instance of a type. For example, "bicycle" is a type describing the properties: two wheels, gears, etc. A given bicycle is an instance that has these properties. Borrowing another term used in C++ and Java, we call each piece of data an *attribute*. For a bicycle, the wheel size is an attribute. The brand is another attribute. These three terms are further described below:

- *Structure*: a data type so that multiple pieces of data can be organized together. The piece may have different types (`int`, `char`, or even other structures).
- *Object*: a specific instance of a structure. In the example below, `int` and `t` are both types. Suppose `t` is a structure. Using these types, `x` is a specific instance of integer, and `y` is a specific instance of type `t`.

```
1    int x;
2    t y;
```

- *Attribute*: A structure organizes different pieces of data together. Each piece of data is referred to as an attribute. The attributes store the information specific to the particular object. The attributes' values of different objects are likely different.

It is important to clearly distinguish these three concepts (structure, object, and attribute). Here are some more examples:

1. "Person" can be a structure. Individual people are specific instances of Person. Let's call two specific people: "Alice" and "Bob". Their names, age, height, and phone numbers are attributes. The attributes of "Alice" are different from those of "Bob". They have the same attributes, but those attributes have different values, and are stored in different locations in memory.
2. "Car" is a structure. Every car has some attributes, such as year, brand, and color. Your car is a particular instance and it is an object. That means it has a particular year, brand, and color that can be different from my car.
3. "Desk" is a structure. Every desk has attributes, such as width, height, number of drawers, weight, material, etc. The desk in your office is an instance. It is a particular desk with specific values for those attributes that can be different from the desk at your home.

Here is another way to think about the relationship between structure and object: A structure describes what attributes (age, height, color, etc.) an object has. An object has specific values for those attributes that can be distinguished from any other object of the same structure. Furthermore, an object is stored in memory somewhere. A structure has no values for its attributes, it is not stored in memory.

Now that we know what structures, objects, and attributes are, how do we create them? Below is an example that creates a new type for vectors. A vector has three components: `x`, `y`, and `z`. It is desirable to create a new type called `Vector` and put these attributes together. Programmers often create new structure types by using `typedef struct`. The structure's name is given at the end of the structure, after } and before ;.

```
1    // vector.h
2    #ifndef VECTOR_H
3    #define VECTOR_H
4    typedef struct
5    {
```

```
6    int x;
7    int y;
8    int z;
9  } Vector;  /* don't forget ; */
10 #endif
```

The type begins with `typedef struct`, which tells `gcc` that a new type is defined here. This type contains multiple attributes and they form a structure. After the closing brace, `Vector` is the name of the new type. Remember to add the semicolon after the name. This book adopts the naming convention of using a capital letter to start the name of a structure. It is common to have only one structure in each header file and the file's name is the same as the structure's name, but in lowercase. Thus, the structure `Vector` is defined in the header file `vector.h`.

In the following program, `v1` is a `Vector` object. This object has three attributes. To access an attribute, a period is needed after `v1`, such as `v1.x` and `v1.y`.

```
1  // vector.c
2  #include <stdio.h>
3  #include <stdlib.h>
4  #include <string.h>
5  #include "vector.h"
6  int main(int argc, char * argv[])
7  {
8    Vector v1;
9    v1.x = 3;
10   v1.y = 6;
11   v1.z = -2;
12   printf("The vector is (%d, %d, %d).\n",
13          v1.x, v1.y, v1.z);
14   return EXIT_SUCCESS;
15 }
```

The program's output is shown below:

```
The vector is (3, 6, -2).
```

What does line 8 actually do? It creates an object on the call stack.

Symbol	Address	Value
v1.z	108	garbage
v1.y	104	garbage
v1.x	100	garbage

The type `Vector` requires three integers and the call stack stores those three integers. Each attribute occupies 4 bytes (assuming that `sizeof(int)` is 4). The attributes are not initialized and the values are garbage. Line 9 changes the value at address 100 to 3.

Symbol	Address	Value
v1.z	108	garbage
v1.y	104	garbage
v1.x	100	garbage → 3

A `Vector` object can be copied to another `Vector` object, as the following example illustrates:

```
1  // vector2.c
2  #include <stdio.h>
3  #include <stdlib.h>
4  #include <string.h>
5  #include "vector.h"
6  int main(int argc, char * argv[])
7  {
8     Vector v1;
9     v1.x = 3;
10    v1.y = 6;
11    v1.z = -2;
12    printf("The vector is (%d, %d, %d).\n",
13           v1.x, v1.y, v1.z);
14    Vector v2 = {0};
15    printf("The vector is (%d, %d, %d).\n",
16           v2.x, v2.y, v2.z);
17    v2 = v1;
18    printf("The vector is (%d, %d, %d).\n",
19           v2.x, v2.y, v2.z);
20    v1.x = -4;
21    v2.y = 5;
22    printf("The vector is (%d, %d, %d).\n",
23           v1.x, v1.y, v1.z);
24    printf("The vector is (%d, %d, %d).\n",
25           v2.x, v2.y, v2.z);
26    return EXIT_SUCCESS;
27 }
```

The program's output is:

```
The vector is (3, 6, -2).
The vector is (0, 0, 0).
The vector is (3, 6, -2).
The vector is (-4, 6, -2).
The vector is (3, 5, -2).
```

Line 14 creates a `Vector` object and initializes every attribute to zero. Please remember that C does not initialize the attributes for you. Attributes must be initialized explicitly. Line 17 copies v1's attributes to v2's attributes. The attributes are copied from v1 to v2 one by one. The call stack is shown below:

Symbol	Address	Value
v2.z	120	-2
v2.y	116	6
v2.x	112	3
v1.z	108	-2
v1.y	104	6
v1.x	100	3

Since v1 and v2 occupy different addresses in the call stack, changing the attributes of v1 does not affect the attributes of v2 and vice versa. Line 20 changes v1.x; line 21 changes v2.y. The effects are limited to the corresponding addresses.

Symbol	Address	Value
v2.z	120	-2
v2.y	116	$6 \rightarrow 5$
v2.x	112	3
v1.z	108	-2
v1.y	104	6
v1.x	100	$3 \rightarrow -4$

As a result, lines 19 and 20 print different values.

Even though `Vector` is a type and assignment `=` is supported, the type does not have all the properties of built-in types (`int`, `char`, `double`, etc.). For example, we cannot use `==` or `!=` to compare two `Vector` objects:

```
1   Vector v1;
2   Vector v2;
3   v1.x = 1;
4   v1.y = 2;
5   v1.z = 3;
6   v2.x = 0;
7   v2.y = -1;
8   v2.z = -2;
9
10  if (v1 != v2)
11  {
12      printf("v1 and v2 are different.\n");
13  }
```

When compiling this function, gcc will say:

```
invalid operands to binary !=
```

If we want to compare two `Vector` objects, we have to write a function that compares the attributes, for example,

```
1   #include "vector.h"
2   int equalVector(Vector v1, Vector v2)
3   // return 0 if any attribute is different
4   // return 1 if all attributes are equal
5   {
6      if (v1.x != v2.x) { return 0; }
7      if (v1.y != v2.y) { return 0; }
8      if (v1.z != v2.z) { return 0; }
9      return 1;
10  }
```

The following section explains how to pass objects as function arguments.

16.2   Passing Objects as Arguments

A `Vector` object can be passed as a function argument. When passing an object as an argument, all attributes are copied to the argument of the called function. This is the same as when passing other types of arguments, such as `int` and `double`: A *copy* of the argument is passed. The following example shows a separate function for printing `Vector` objects:

```
1  // vector3.c
2  #include <stdio.h>
3  #include <stdlib.h>
4  #include <string.h>
5  #include "vector.h"
6  void printVector(Vector v)
7  {
8     printf("The vector is (%d, %d, %d).\n", v.x, v.y, v.z);
9  }
10
11 int main(int argc, char * argv[])
12 {
13    Vector v1;
14    v1.x = 3;
15    v1.y = 6;
16    v1.z = -2;
17    printVector(v1);
18    return EXIT_SUCCESS;
19 }
```

Frame	Symbol	Address	Value
	v.z	124	−2
printVector	v.y	120	6
	v.x	116	3
	return location	112	line 18
	v1.z	108	−2
main	v1.y	104	6
	v1.x	100	3

How do we know that the attributes are copied? In the following program `changeVector` changes the `Vector` object passed to it. However, inside `main`, the attributes of `v1` are unchanged.

```
1  // vector4.c
2  #include <stdio.h>
3  #include <stdlib.h>
4  #include <string.h>
5  #include "vector.h"
6  void printVector(Vector v)
7  {
8     printf("The vector is (%d, %d, %d).\n", v.x, v.y, v.z);
9  }
10
11 void changeVector(Vector v)
12 {
13    v.x = 5;
14    v.y = -3;
15    v.z = 7;
16    printVector(v);
```

```
17  }
18
19  int main(int argc, char * argv[])
20  {
21     Vector v1;
22     v1.x = 3;
23     v1.y = 6;
24     v1.z = -2;
25     printVector(v1);
26     changeVector(v1);
27     printVector(v1);
28     return EXIT_SUCCESS;
29  }
```

The output of this program is:

```
The vector is (3, 6, -2).
The vector is (5, -3, 7).
The vector is (3, 6, -2).
```

What really happens when a function's argument is an object? This can be explained by showing the call stack before calling `changeVector`:

Frame	Symbol	Address	Value
	v1.z	108	−2
main	v1.y	104	6
	v1.x	100	3

Calling `changeVector` pushes a new frame to the call stack. The argument is an object that has three attributes. The values are copied from the calling function into the new frame.

Frame	Symbol	Address	Value
	v.z	124	−2
changeVector	v.y	120	6
	v.x	116	3
	return location	112	line 27
	v1.z	108	−2
main	v1.y	104	6
	v1.x	100	3

The function `changeVector` changes the attributes of the object in its own frame.

Frame	Symbol	Address	Value
	v.z	124	7
changeVector	v.y	120	−3
	v.x	116	5
	return location	112	line 27
	v1.z	108	−2
main	v1.y	104	6
	v1.x	100	3

When `changeVector` finishes, the frame is popped and the program resumes at `main`. The call stack is shown below:

Frame	Symbol	Address	Value
	v1.z	108	−2
main	v1.y	104	6
	v1.x	100	3

Note that the attributes of v1 are unchanged.

16.3   Objects and Pointers

Is it possible to change an object's attributes inside a function and keep the changes even after the function returns? The answer is yes. To do this, we need to use pointers.

```
1   // vectorptr.c
2   #include <stdio.h>
3   #include <stdlib.h>
4   #include <string.h>
5   #include "vector.h"
6   void printVector(Vector v)
7   {
8       printf("The vector is (%d, %d, %d).\n", v.x, v.y, v.z);
9   }
10
11  void changeVector(Vector * p)
12  {
13      p -> x = 5;
14      p -> y = -3;
15      p -> z = 7;
16      printVector(* p);
17  }
18
19  int main(int argc, char * argv[])
20  {
21      Vector v1;
22      v1.x = 3;
23      v1.y = 6;
24      v1.z = -2;
25      printVector(v1);
26      changeVector(& v1);
27      printVector(v1);
28      return EXIT_SUCCESS;
29  }
```

At line 11 changeVector's argument is a pointer:

```
11  void changeVector(Vector * p)
```

This means that p is a pointer in the frame of the function changeVector. If you refer back to Table 4.1, this is the first way of using *. When calling changeVector at line 26, main must provide the address of a Vector object, i.e., & v1. This is best understood by showing the call stack:

Frame	Symbol	Address	Value
changeVector	p	116	100
	return location	112	line 27
main	v1.z	108	−2
	v1.y	104	6
	v1.x	100	3

Instead of copying the whole object, attribute by attribute, the argument p stores only the address of the object v1. This is the address of the first attribute.

What is the -> symbol inside **changeVector**? The -> symbol takes the value at the address, and then gets the attribute as if applying a . to a structure. Pointers are used with structures often and C has this special syntax. It is equivalent to saying:

13   p -> x

is the same as

13   (*p).x

This dereferences p first, and then applies . for x. Dereferencing is the second way of using * as explained in Table 4.1. Note that this means -> can only be used on a pointer to a structure. It is illegal to use it in any other circumstance. If -> is at the left hand side (LHS) of an assignment, then the attribute is modified (i.e., written). If -> is at the right hand side (RHS) of an assignment, then the attribute is read. The statement,

13   p -> x = 5;

changes the value at address 100.

Frame	Symbol	Address	Value
changeVector	p	116	100
	return location	112	line 27
main	v1.z	108	−2
	v1.y	104	6
	v1.x	100	3 → 5

14   p -> y = -3;

changes the value at address 104.

Frame	Symbol	Address	Value
changeVector	p	116	100
	return location	112	line 27
main	v1.z	108	−2
	v1.y	104	6 → -3
	v1.x	100	5

Why do we need to add * in front of p when **changeVector** calls **printVector**? In **changeVector**, p is a pointer. However, **printVector** expects an object because there is no * in the line:

6   **void printVector(Vector v)**

In **changeVector**, adding * in front of p dereferences the pointer, as explained in Table 4.1. Thus, the object stored at addresses 100–108 is copied to the argument of **printVector**. How do we know that the object is copied? In C, arguments are always copied when passed to functions. If the argument were **Vector ***, then a copy of the pointer would be passed. There is no * after `Vector` in `printVector` and the argument is an object. As a result, the object is copied. If v's attributes are changed inside `printVector`, then the changes will be lost when the function finishes. The syntax for using objects is:

- If p's value is an address of an object, use p -> x. It is allowed to put a space before or after -> but no space can be added between - and >.
- If v is an object (not an address), use v.x.

16.3.1 Returning an Object

Can a function return a `Vector` object? Yes. The following example shows a *constructor* function that creates and initializes a new object:

```c
// vector5.c
#include <stdio.h>
#include <stdlib.h>
#include <string.h>
#include "vector.h"
Vector Vector_construct(int a, int b, int c)
{
  Vector v;
  v.x = a;
  v.y = b;
  v.z = c;
  return v;
}

void Vector_print(Vector v)
{
  printf("The vector is (%d, %d, %d).\n", v.x, v.y, v.z);
}

int main(int argc, char * argv[])
{
  Vector v1 = Vector_construct(3, 6, -2);
  Vector_print(v1);
  return EXIT_SUCCESS;
}
```

What is the advantage of creating *constructor* functions? One good reason is that they make programs easier to read. The three arguments remind programmers that a `Vector` object has three attributes. Constructors should guarantee that all attributes are always initialized. Uninitialized variables can make your programs behave in surprising ways. Before calling the constructor, `v1` is already on the call stack in the frame of the `main` function. When the constructor returns the object, the attributes of v are copied to `v1`'s attributes one by one. Then, the constructor's frame is popped and v does not exist any more.

16.3.2 Objects and `malloc`

Is it possible to create an object that exists in heap memory, instead of stack memory? Yes. Here is how to do it:

```c
// vectormalloc.c
```

```
2  #include <stdio.h>
3  #include <stdlib.h>
4  #include <string.h>
5  #include "vector.h"
6  Vector * Vector_construct(int a, int b, int c)
7  // notice *
8  {
9     Vector * v;
10    v = malloc(sizeof(Vector));
11    if (v == NULL) // allocation fail
12      {
13        printf("malloc fail\n");
14        return NULL;
15      }
16    v -> x = a;
17    v -> y = b;
18    v -> z = c;
19    return v;
20 }
21 void Vector_destruct(Vector * v)
22 {
23    free (v);
24 }
25 void Vector_print(Vector * v)
26 {
27    printf("The vector is (%d, %d, %d).\n",
28           v -> x, v -> y, v -> z);
29 }
30 int main(int argc, char * argv[])
31 {
32    Vector * v1;
33    v1 = Vector_construct(3, 6, -2);
34    if (v1 == NULL)
35      {
36        return EXIT_FAILURE;
37      }
38    Vector_print(v1);
39    Vector_destruct(v1);
40    return EXIT_SUCCESS;
41 }
```

The program declares a `Vector` pointer at line 35. It will be given an address in heap memory returned by `Vector_construct`. Before calling `Vector_construct`, the call stack only has a frame for the `main` function:

Frame	Symbol	Address	Value
main	v1	100	garbage

Calling `Vector_construct` pushes a frame on to the stack:

Frame	Symbol	Address	Value
	v	124	garbage
Vector_construct	c	120	−2
	b	116	6
	a	112	3
	value address	108	100
	return location	104	line 37
main	v1	100	garbage

Calling `malloc` allocates a piece of memory that is in the heap. The size is sufficient to accommodate three integers. Suppose `malloc` returns 60000. Then the call stack becomes:

Frame	Symbol	Address	Value
	v	124	60000
	c	120	−2
	b	116	6
Vector_construct	a	112	3
	value address	108	100
	return location	104	line 37
main	v1	100	garbage

The heap memory is shown below:

Address	Value
60008	garbage
60004	garbage
60000	garbage

The pointer's value takes on the address returned by calling `malloc`. Since it is a pointer, the program uses `->` to access the attributes. The statement,

```
16  v -> x = a;
17  v -> y = b;
18  v -> z = c;
```

modifies the values at addresses 60000, 60004, and 60008 to 3, 6, and −2 respectively. The heap memory is changed to:

Address	Value
60008	garbage → −2
60004	garbage → 6
60000	garbage → 3

When `Vector_construct` returns, v's value is written to the return address 100. Therefore, the call stack becomes:

Frame	Symbol	Address	Value
main	v1	100	60000

Note that, as always, the memory allocated on heap must be released by calling `free`. This is the purpose of the destructor `Vector_destruct`.

16.4 Constructors and Destructors

Sometimes objects need to contain pointers that manage dynamically allocated memory. Consider the following example:

```
1  // person.h
2  #ifndef PERSON_H
3  #define PERSON_H
4  typedef struct
5  {
6    int year;
7    int month;
8    int date;
9    char * name;
10 } Person;
11 Person * Person_construct(int y, int m, int d, char * n);
12 void Person_destruct(Person * p);
13 void Person_print(Person * p);
14 #endif
```

Each Person object has four attributes, three for the date of birth and one for the name. The name is a pointer because the length of a person's name is unknown. If the name is created with a fixed length, this attribute must use the longest possible name and waste memory when a name is shorter. It is more efficient allocating the length of the name as needed. This is the constructor:

```
1  #include "person.h"
2  #include <stdio.h>
3  #include <string.h>
4  #include <stdlib.h>
5  Person * Person_construct(int y, int m, int d, char * n)
6  {
7    Person * p = NULL;
8    p = malloc(sizeof(Person));
9    if (p == NULL) // malloc fail
10     {
11       return NULL;
12     }
13   p -> year = y;
14   p -> month = m;
15   p -> date = d;
16   p -> name = malloc(sizeof(char) * (strlen(n) + 1));
17   // + 1 for the ending character '\0'
18   if ((p -> name) == NULL) // malloc fail
19     {
20       free (p);
21       return NULL;
22     }
23   strcpy(p -> name, n);
24   return p;
25 }
```

Notice how the constructor initializes the attributes in the same order as they are declared in the header file. This is a good programming habit. For the sake of clarity, make things as consistent as possible. This habit prevents accidentally forgetting to initialize an attribute. Below is the destructor:

```
1  #include "person.h"
2  #include <stdlib.h>
3  void Person_destruct(Person * p)
4  {
5    // p -> name must be freed before p is freed
6    free (p -> name);
7    free (p);
8  }
```

Note that the destructor releases memory in the reverse order that the constructor allocates memory. This is a general rule. If the destructor `free (p)` precedes `free (p -> name)`, then the program will have problems. Why? After `free (p)`, the object is no longer valid, and `free (p -> name)` is meaningless and dangerous. After calling `free (p)`, the program cannot access the memory that contains the pointer `free (p -> name)`. There is no guarantee that the address is still accessible. If the destructor does not call `free (p -> name)`, then the program leaks memory. Thus, as a general rule, the destructor releases memory in the reverse order that the constructor allocates memory. Please remember that every `malloc` must have a corresponding `free`.

Below is the implementation of the `Person_print` function:

```
1  #include "person.h"
2  #include <stdio.h>
3  void Person_print(Person * p)
4  {
5    printf("Name:␣%s.␣", p -> name);
6    printf("Date␣of␣Birth:␣%d/%d/%d\n",
7            p -> year, p -> month, p -> date);
8  }
```

The following is an example of using the constructor and the destructor:

```
1  #include <stdio.h>
2  #include <stdlib.h>
3  #include <string.h>
4  #include "person.h"
5
6  int main(int argc, char * argv[])
7  {
8    Person * p1 = Person_construct(1989, 8, 21, "Amy");
9    Person * p2 = Person_construct(1991, 2, 17, "Bob");
10   Person_print(p1);
11   Person_print(p2);
12   Person_destruct(p1);
13   Person_destruct(p2);
14   return EXIT_SUCCESS;
15 }
```

Some students struggle with the difference between objects and pointers to objects. A pointer stores a memory address. Consider the following example. Please notice how p2 is created.

```
1  #include <stdio.h>
2  #include <stdlib.h>
3  #include <string.h>
4  #include "person.h"
5
6  void Person_print(Person * p);
7  int main(int argc, char * argv[])
8  {
9    Person * p1 = Person_construct(1989, 8, 21, "Amy");
10   Person * p2 = p1;
11   Person_print(p1);
12   Person_print(p2);
13   Person_destruct(p1);
14   Person_destruct(p2);
15   return EXIT_SUCCESS;
16 }
```

There is no syntax error in this program, but it contains a critical mistake. If we run this program, it will likely crash. The problem reveals itself in **Person_destruct** as reported by valgrind:

```
==9344== Invalid read of size 8
==9344==    at 0x400770: Person_destruct (persondestruct.c:6)
==9344==    by 0x40069F: main (person2.c:14)
==9344== Address 0x51f2050 is 16 bytes inside a block of size 24 free'd
==9344==    at 0x4C2A739: free
              (in /usr/lib/valgrind/vgpreload_memcheck-amd64-linux.so)
==9344==    by 0x400787: Person_destruct (persondestruct.c:7)
==9344==    by 0x400693: main (person2.c:13)
```

What is wrong? To understand the problem, we need to understand what the assignment means. After the **main** function finishes line 9, this is what is in the call stack and heap memory:

Frame	Symbol	Address	Value
main	p1	100	60000

Symbol	Address	Value
p1 -> name[3]	70003	'\0'
p1 -> name[2]	70002	'y'
p1 -> name[1]	70001	'm'
p1 -> name[0]	70000	'A'
p1 -> name	60012	70000
p1 -> date	60008	21
p1 -> month	60004	8
p1 -> year	60000	1989

Line 10 assigns p1's value to p2:

Frame	Symbol	Address	Value
main	p2	104	60000
	p1	100	60000

Both **p1** and **p2** point to the same memory address 60000. Line 13 calls the destructor and releases the heap memory. This is perfectly correct. Line 14 calls the destructor again but the memory has already been released. **The same heap memory cannot be released**

twice. Assigning p1 to p2 at line 10 merely copies the pointer, and the two different pointers store the same memory address 60000.

Can the problem be solved by simply not calling the destructor for p2? Yes, but it depends on the intention of the program. When p1 and p2 have the same value, changing p1 -> name[0] (the first letter of the name) will also change p2 -> name[0]. However, in the following code:

```c
int x = 5;
int y = x;
x = 12;
```

What is the value of y? Should it be 5 or 12? Experience tells us that y should be 5. This is correct because x and y occupy different memory addresses. Even though p1 and p2 have different addresses (100 and 104), they store the same value, 60000. Thus changing p1 -> name[0] also changes p2 -> name[0]. In the next example, both p1 and p2 have distinct values generated by calling **Person_construct**. Will the following program work?

```c
#include <stdio.h>
#include <stdlib.h>
#include <string.h>
#include "person.h"
int main(int argc, char * argv[])
{
  Person * p1 = Person_construct(1989, 8, 21, "Amy");
  Person * p2 = Person_construct(1991, 2, 17, "Bob");
  p2 = p1;
  Person_print(p1);
  Person_print(p2);
  Person_destruct(p1);
  Person_destruct(p2);
  return EXIT_SUCCESS;
}
```

This is the call stack and the heap memory after line 9:

Frame	Symbol	Address	Value
main	p2	104	80000
	p1	100	60000

Symbol	Address	Value
p2 -> name[3]	85003	'\0'
p2 -> name[2]	85002	'b'
p2 -> name[1]	85001	'o'
p2 -> name[0]	85000	'B'
p2 -> name	80012	85000
p2 -> date	80008	17
p2 -> month	80004	2
p2 -> year	80000	1991
p1 -> name[3]	70003	'\0'
p1 -> name[2]	70002	'y'
p1 -> name[1]	70001	'm'
p1 -> name[0]	70000	'A'
p1 -> name	60012	70000
p1 -> date	60008	21
p1 -> month	60004	8
p1 -> year	60000	1989

Does this program work? No, `valgrind` still reports problems in `Person_destruct`. Line 10 still copies `p1`'s value to `p2` and both are 60000. This also causes a memory leak because the memory at 80000 and 85000 is no longer accessible.

Consider another scenario when the objects are not accessed through pointers:

```
1   #include <stdio.h>
2   #include <stdlib.h>
3   #include <string.h>
4   #include "person.h"
5   int main(int argc, char * argv[])
6   {
7     Person p1;
8     Person p2;
9     p1.year = 1989;
10    p1.month = 8;
11    p1.date = 21;
12    p1.name = strdup("Amy");
13    p2.year = 1991;
14    p2.month = 2;
15    p2.date = 17;
16    p2.name = strdup("Bob");
17
18    Person_print(& p1);
19    Person_print(& p2);
20    free (p1.name);
21    free (p2.name);
22    return EXIT_SUCCESS;
23  }
```

The program uses `strdup` to copy strings. In this program, both `p1` and `p2` are objects on the call stack:

Frame	Symbol	Address	Value		Symbol	Address	Value
	p2.name	128	85000		p2.name[3]	85003	'\0'
	p2.date	124	17		p2.name[2]	85002	'b'
	p2.month	120	2		p2.name[1]	85001	'o'
main	p2.year	116	1991		p2.name[0]	85000	'B'
	p1.name	112	70000		p1.name[3]	70003	'\0'
	p1.date	108	21		p1.name[2]	70002	'y'
	p1.month	104	8		p1.name[1]	70001	'm'
	p1.year	100	1989		p1.name[0]	70000	'A'

What will happen if the program has this line?

```
17      p2 = p1;
```

The assignment = copies one object's attributes to another object's attributes. After executing this line, the call stack and heap will appear as follows:

Frame	Symbol	Address	Value	Symbol	Address	Value
	p2.name	128	**70000**	p2.name[3]	85003	'\0'
	p2.date	124	21	p2.name[2]	85002	'b'
	p2.month	120	8	p2.name[1]	85001	'o'
main	p2.year	116	1989	p2.name[0]	85000	'B'
	p1.name	112	70000	p1.name[3]	70003	'\0'
	p1.date	108	21	p1.name[2]	70002	'y'
	p1.month	104	8	p1.name[1]	70001	'm'
	p1.year	100	1989	p1.name[0]	70000	'A'

Now, `p1.name` and `p2.name` have the same value (70000). The heap memory originally pointed to by `p2.name` is still in the heap but is no longer accessible because `p2.name` is no longer 85000. This causes memory leak. Moreover, lines 20 and 21 free the same heap memory at 70000 twice. As you can see, if an object's attribute is a pointer, we need to be very careful about how memory is allocated and freed. If we are not careful, then the program may leak memory or release the same memory twice, or both.

Are there general rules for handling objects that have attributes which are pointers? Fortunately, there are. When an object's attribute is a pointer, that usually indicates the need for four functions.

- *constructor*: allocates memory for the attribute and assigns the value to the attribute.
- *destructor*: releases memory for the attribute.
- *copy constructor replacing* =: by creating a new object from an existing object. This is sometimes referred to as cloning. The new object's attribute points to heap memory allocated by calling `malloc`.
- *assignment replacing* =: modifying an object that has already been created by using the constructor or the copy constructor. Since the object has already been constructed, the object's attribute stores the address of a heap memory. This memory must be released before allocating new memory.

The first two functions have already been given above. The other two functions are shown below:

```c
#include <stdio.h>
#include <stdlib.h>
#include <string.h>
#include "person.h"
Person * Person_copy(Person * p);
// create a new object by copying the attributes of p
Person * Person_assign(Person * p1, Person * p2);
// p1 is already a Person object, make its attribute
// the same as p2's attributes (deep copy)
Person * Person_copy(Person * p)
{
  return Person_construct(p -> year, p -> month,
                          p -> date, p -> name);
}
Person * Person_assign(Person * p1, Person * p2)
{
  free(p1 -> name);
  p1 -> year = p2 -> year;
  p1 -> month = p2 -> month;
  p1 -> date = p2 -> date;
```

```
21    p1 -> name = strdup(p2 -> name);
22    return p1;
23  }
24  int main(int argc, char * argv[])
25  {
26    Person * p1 = Person_construct(1989, 8, 21, "Amy");
27    Person * p2 = Person_construct(1991, 2, 17, "Jennifer");
28    Person * p3 = Person_copy(p1); // create p3
29    Person_print(p1);
30    Person_print(p2);
31    Person_print(p3);
32    p3 = Person_assign(p3, p2);
33    Person_print(p3);
34    Person_destruct(p1);
35    Person_destruct(p2);
36    Person_destruct(p3);
37    return EXIT_SUCCESS;
38  }
```

What is the difference between Person_copy and Person_assign? Person_copy creates a new **Person** object by allocating memory. **Person_assign** has to release memory for existing attributes before copying the attributes.

The copy constructor allocates separate memory space so that changing one object later does not affect the other. This is called a *deep copy*. The assignment function has to do more work, because the object already occupies memory. In our example, the original name in p3 is "Amy". When p2 is copied to p3, p3 -> **name** does not have enough memory for the longer name "Jennifer". Thus, the assignment function first releases the memory for p3 -> **name** and then allocates memory again by later calling **strdup**.

The assignment function can check whether p3 -> **name** has enough memory. If p3 -> **name** has enough memory, it is unnecessary to release p3 -> **name** and allocate memory again. Note that this would require an **if** statement and a call of **strlen**. This can marginally complicate the program. If the new name is longer, it is still necessary to free and allocate memory. Some beginner programmers want to optimize their code. However, it is often difficult for even experienced programmers to know what is slowing down a program. You should avoid making this type of unnecessary complication without first profiling the code using **gprof**. This is a very important principle to follow.

Whereas a deep copy allocates memory so that objects do not share memory, a *shallow copy* allows several objects' attributes to point to the same memory addresses. Shallow copies can be useful in some cases. For example, in a student database, every student has an attribute that points to an object representing the school. It is unnecessary for every student to have an individual copy of the school's object. There can be one school object shared by every student object. In this scenario sharing makes sense, and the copy constructor and assignment operator should perform a shallow copy of the school attribute. Another reason for using shallow copies is when objects share a very large piece of memory and few objects actually need to modify this shared memory. A copy is made only when an object intends to make changes. This is called *copy on write* and is beyond the scope of this book.

16.5   Structures within Structures

Can a structure's attribute be another structure? Yes. In this example, we move a Person's date of birth from three integers into one Date object:

```c
// dateofbirth.c
#include <stdio.h>
#include <stdlib.h>
#include <string.h>
typedef struct
{
  int year;
  int month;
  int date;
} DateOfBirth;
DateOfBirth DateOfBirth_construct(int y, int m, int d)
{
  DateOfBirth dob;
  dob.year = y;
  dob.month = m;
  dob.date = d;
  return dob;
}
void DateOfBirth_print(DateOfBirth d)
{
  printf("Date of Birth: %d/%d/%d\n",
         d.year, d.month, d.date);
}
typedef struct
{
  char * name;
  DateOfBirth dob;
} Person;
Person * Person_construct(char * n, int y, int m, int d);
void Person_destruct(Person * p);
// create a new object by copying the attributes of p
Person * Person_copy(Person * p);
// p1 is already an object, make its attribute the
// same as p2's attributes
Person * Person_assign(Person * p1, Person * p2);
void Person_print(Person * p);
int main(int argc, char * argv[])
{
  Person * p1 = Person_construct("Amy", 1989, 8, 21);
  Person * p2 = Person_construct("Jennifer", 1991, 2, 17);
  Person * p3 = Person_copy(p1); // create p3
  Person_print(p1);
  Person_print(p2);
  Person_print(p3);
  p3 = Person_assign(p3, p2); // change p3
```

```
46     Person_print(p3);
47     Person_destruct(p1);
48     Person_destruct(p2);
49     Person_destruct(p3);
50     return EXIT_SUCCESS;
51  }
52  Person * Person_construct(char * n, int y, int m, int d)
53  {
54     Person * p;
55     p = malloc(sizeof(Person));
56     if (p == NULL)
57       {
58         printf("malloc␣fail\n");
59         return NULL;
60       }
61     p -> name = malloc(sizeof(char) * (strlen(n) + 1));
62     // + 1 for the ending character '\0'
63     strcpy(p -> name, n);
64     p -> dob = DateOfBirth_construct(y, m, d);
65     return p;
66  }
67  void Person_destruct(Person * p)
68  {
69     // p must be released after p -> name has been released
70     free (p -> name);
71     free (p);
72  }
73  Person * Person_copy(Person * p)
74  {
75     return Person_construct(p -> name, p -> dob.year,
76                             p -> dob.month, p -> dob.date);
77  }
78  Person * Person_assign(Person * p1, Person * p2)
79  {
80     free(p1 -> name);
81
82     p1 -> dob = p2 -> dob;
83     p1 -> name = strdup(p2 -> name);
84
85     return p1;
86  }
87  void Person_print(Person * p)
88  {
89     printf("Name:␣%s.␣", p -> name);
90     DateOfBirth_print(p -> dob);
91  }
```

This program creates a *hierarchy* of structures. Then, Person_construct calls DateOfBirth_construct. Person_print calls DateOfBirth_print. What is the advantage of this approach? As programs become more complex, such a hierarchy becomes helpful for organization. Creating one structure that contains everything can be impractical and unclear. Instead, we should put related data together and create a structure, for example, the `DateOfBirth` structure. We can use this structure inside other structures.

Each structure should have a constructor to initialize all attributes. If a structure has pointers for dynamically allocated memory, then make sure that there is also a destructor. If deep copy is required (true in most cases), remember to write a copy constructor and an assignment function.

16.6 Binary Files and Objects

This section explains how to write an object to a file and how to read an object from a file. This section will talk about both text files and binary files. `Vector` is used as the structure for the examples in this section. The following program contains two write functions and two read functions. `Vector_writet` and `Vector_readt` use text files. `Vector_writeb` and `Vector_readb` use binary files.

When using text files, reading and writing objects is as simple as reading and writing one attribute after another. The two functions must process the attributes in the same order. If the orders are different, then the results will be wrong.

`Vector_writeb` and `Vector_readb` open files in the binary mode by adding b in the second argument when calling `fopen`. Some operating systems, including Linux, actually ignore b. It is used primarily for compatibility among different systems. Table 16.1 describes the differences of text and binary files:

Operation	Text File	Binary File
open a file	fopen	fopen
write	fprintf	fwrite
read	fgetc, fgets, or fscanf	fread

TABLE 16.1: Functions for opening, writing to, and reading from text and binary files.

```
1   // vectorfile.c
2   #include <stdio.h>
3   #include <stdlib.h>
4   #include <string.h>
5   #include "vector.h"
6   Vector Vector_construct(int a, int b, int c)
7   {
8     Vector v;
9     v.x = a;
10    v.y = b;
11    v.z = c;
12    return v;
13  }
14  void Vector_print(char * name, Vector v)
15  {
16    printf("%s is (%d, %d, %d).\n", name, v.x, v.y, v.z);
17  }
18  void Vector_writet(char * filename, Vector v)
```

```
19  // writet means write to a text file
20  {
21     FILE * fptr;
22     fptr = fopen(filename, "w");
23     if (fptr == NULL)
24        {
25           printf("Vector_writet fopen fail\n");
26           return;
27        }
28     fprintf(fptr, "%d %d %d", v.x, v.y, v.z);
29     fclose (fptr);
30  }
31  Vector Vector_readt(char * filename)
32  // readt means read from a text file
33  {
34     Vector v = Vector_construct(0, 0, 0);
35     FILE * fptr;
36     fptr = fopen(filename, "r");
37     if (fptr == NULL)
30        {
39           printf("Vector_readt fopen fail\n");
40           return v;
41        }
42     if (fscanf(fptr, "%d %d %d", & v.x, & v.y, & v.z) != 3)
43        {
44           printf("fprintf fail\n");
45        }
46     fclose (fptr);
47     return v;
48  }
49  void Vector_writeb(char * filename, Vector v)
50  // writeb means write to a binary file
51  {
52     FILE * fptr;
53     fptr = fopen(filename, "w"); // "w" same as "wb" in Linux
54     if (fptr == NULL)
55        {
56           printf("Vector_writeb fopen fail\n");
57           return;
58        }
59     if (fwrite(& v, sizeof(Vector), 1, fptr) != 1)
60        {
61           printf("fwrite fail\n");
62        }
63     fclose (fptr);
64  }
65  Vector Vector_readb(char * filename)
66  // readb means read from a binary file
67  {
68     FILE * fptr;
69     Vector v; // not initialized
```

```
70      fptr = fopen(filename, "r"); // "r" same as "rb" in Linux
71      if (fptr == NULL)
72        {
73          printf("Vector_readb␣fopen␣fail\n");
74          return v;
75        }
76      if (fread(& v, sizeof(Vector), 1, fptr) != 1)
77        {
78          printf("fread␣fail\n");
79        }
80      return v;
81  }
82  int main(int argc, char * argv[])
83  {
84    Vector v1 = Vector_construct(13, 206, -549);
85    Vector v2 = Vector_construct(-15, 8762, 1897);
86    Vector_print("v1", v1);
87    Vector_print("v2", v2);
88    printf("================================\n");
89    Vector_writet("vectort.dat", v1);
90    v2 = Vector_readt("vectort.dat");
91    Vector_print("v1", v1);
92    Vector_print("v2", v2);
93
94    v1 = Vector_construct(2089, -3357, 1234);
95    v2 = Vector_construct(7658, 0, 1876);
96    printf("================================\n");
97    Vector_print("v1", v1);
98    Vector_print("v2", v2);
99
100   Vector_writeb("vectorb.dat", v1);
101   v2 = Vector_readb("vectorb.dat");
102   printf("================================\n");
103   Vector_print("v1", v1);
104   Vector_print("v2", v2);
105   return EXIT_SUCCESS;
106 }
```

To write binary data, `fwrite` is used. This function requires four arguments:

1. The *address* of the object. If it is an object (not a pointer), & needs to be added before the object.
2. The size of the object. It can be obtained by using `sizeof` to find the size of the object or data. For this example, the size of a `Vector` object is `sizeof(Vector)`.
3. The number of objects to write. This example writes only one object so the value is 1. If a program is writing an array of objects, then this argument is the number of elements in the array.
4. The `FILE` pointer.

   The return value of `fwrite` is the number of objects written. This number can be different from the third argument because, for example, the disk may be full and only some elements are written. It is a good programming habit to check whether the return value is the same as the third argument. The data written by `fwrite` needs to be read by `fread`, not `fscanf`. Four arguments are required for `fread` and the order of the arguments is the same as that for `fwrite`.

What are advantages and disadvantages of text and binary files? If data are stored in a text file, then it can be read by using the `more` command in terminal or simply viewing it in your favorite text editor. `Vector_readt` and `Vector_writet` must handle the attributes one by one. The order in `Vector_writet` must be the same as the order in `Vector_readt`. If one more attribute is added to `Vector` (for example, `t` for time), then both `Vector_readt` and `Vector_writet` must be changed. These requirements increase the chances of mistakes: It is easy to change one place and forget to change the other. In contrast, `Vector_writeb` and `Vector_readb` automatically handle the order of attributes. If an attribute is added to `Vector`, there is no need to change `Vector_readb` and `Vector_writeb` because `sizeof` reflects the new size. The disadvantage of using binary files is that they cannot be edited and viewed directly. The data files are also specific to the platform the code is compiled on, since the size and format of the binary data can vary between computers.

Chapter 17

Programming Problems Using Structure

17.1   Sorting a Person Database

In this problem we sort a database of people. Each person is an object that has two attributes: name and age. The program sorts the people by ages or by names. To test the program, we use the 200 popular given names. The names are randomly ordered by using the Linux command `sort` with `-R`. The age of a person is a random number between 1 and 100. The database is a text file containing two columns: age and name. A few lines of the database are shown below:

```
43 Peter
87 Linda
57 Gregory
61 Larry
5 Eric
19 Dennis
56 Betty
70 Joshua
4 Donald
60 Susan
```

To test the program, we need to compare the answers of our program against the correct answers. We can use the Linux program `sort` to generate the correct answers. The correct answers are generated as follows:

- `sort -n`: sort the first column and treat the column as numbers. Without `-n`, the first column will be treated as strings and "10" is before "9" because 1 is before 9 in the dictionary.
- `sort -k 2`: sort by the second column.

This program uses the same `Person` structure defined earlier. Another structure is defined to store an array of pointers to `Person` objects. This structure also has an attribute as the number of pointers in the array. The program needs to implement the follow steps:

1. Read `Person` objects from a file.

2. Write **Person** objects to a file.

3. Sort **Person** objects by names.

4. Sort **Person** objects by ages.

5. Release memory occupied by the objects.

6. Close opened files.

Below is the header file:

```
1   // person.h
2   #ifndef PERSON_H
3   #define PERSON_H
4   typedef struct
5   {
6     int age;
7     char * name;
8   } Person;
9   typedef struct
10  {
11    int number; // number of persons
12    Person * * person; // array of pointers to Person objects
13  } PersonDatabase;
14  // read person database from a file
15  // person is an array of pointers to person objects
16  // The function returns the pointer of a database or NULL
17  // The function returns NULL if reading from the file fails
18  PersonDatabase * Person_read(char * filename);
19  void Person_sortByName(PersonDatabase * perdb);
20  void Person_sortByAge(PersonDatabase * perdb);
21  // save the database in a file
22  // return 0 if fail
23  // return 1 if succeed
24  int Person_write(char * filename, PersonDatabase * perdb);
25  // write to computer screen
26  void Person_print(PersonDatabase * perdb);
27  // release the memory of the database
28  void Person_destruct(PersonDatabase * perdb);
29  #endif
```

Here are implementations of these functions:

```
1   // person.c
2   #include "person.h"
3   #include <stdio.h>
4   #include <string.h>
5   #include <stdlib.h>
6   PersonDatabase * Person_read(char * filename)
7   {
8     FILE * fptr = fopen(filename, "r");
9     if (fptr == NULL)
10      {
11        return NULL;
12      }
13    PersonDatabase * perdb = malloc(sizeof(PersonDatabase));
14    if (perdb == NULL)
```

```
15      {
16        fclose (fptr);
17        return NULL;
18      }
19    // count the number of people in the file
20    // use the longest name for the size of the buffer
21    int numPerson = 0;
22    int longestName = 0; // length of buffer to read names
23    while (! feof(fptr))
24      {
25        int age;
26        // find a line that contains a number (age)
27        if (fscanf(fptr, "%d", & age) == 1)
28          {
29            numPerson ++;
30            // the remaning characters are the name
31            int nameLength = 0;
32            while ((!feof (fptr)) && (fgetc(fptr) != '\n'))
33              {
34                nameLength ++;
35              }
36            nameLength ++; // for '\n'
37            if (longestName < nameLength)
38              {
39                longestName = nameLength;
40              }
41          }
42      }
43    // the number of person is known now
44    perdb -> number = numPerson;
45    perdb -> person = malloc(sizeof(Person*) * numPerson);
46    // allocate a buffer to read the names
47    char * name = malloc(sizeof(char) * longestName);
48    int ind = 0;
49    // read the file again and store the data in the database
50    // return to the beginning of the file
51    fseek (fptr, 0, SEEK_SET);
52    while (! feof(fptr))
53      {
54        int age;
55        if (fscanf(fptr, "%d", & age) == 1)
56          {
57            // remove the space separating age and name
58            fgetc(fptr);
59            fgets(name, longestName, fptr);
60            // remove '\n'
61            char * chptr = strchr(name, '\n');
62            if (chptr != NULL) // last line may not have '\n'
63              {
64                * chptr = '\0';
65              }
```

```
66              perdb -> person[ind] = malloc(sizeof(Person));
67              perdb -> person[ind] -> age = age;
68              // strdup calls malloc
69              perdb -> person[ind] -> name = strdup(name);
70              ind ++;
71            }
72        }
73      free (name);
74      fclose (fptr);
75      return perdb;
76  }
77  static void Person_writeHelp(FILE * fptr,
78                               PersonDatabase * perdb)
79  {
80      int ind;
81      for (ind = 0; ind < perdb -> number; ind ++)
82        {
83          // write one person per line
84          fprintf(fptr, "%d %s\n",
85                  perdb -> person[ind] -> age,
86                  perdb -> person[ind] -> name);
87        }
88  }
89  void Person_print(PersonDatabase * perdb)
90  {
91      printf("-------------------------------------\n");
92      // stdout is a built-in FILE *
93      // stdout means the output is sent to the computer screen
94      // not a file on the disk
95      Person_writeHelp(stdout, perdb);
96  }
97  int Person_write(char * filename, PersonDatabase * perdb)
98  {
99      if (perdb == NULL)
100       {
101         // nothing in the database
102         return 0;
103       }
104     FILE * fptr = fopen(filename, "w");
105     if (fptr == NULL)
106       {
107         // cannot open the file
108         return 0;
109       }
110     Person_writeHelp(fptr, perdb);
111     fclose (fptr);
112     return 1;
113 }
114 static int comparebyName(const void * p1,
115                          const void * p2)
116 {
```

```
117    // get addresses of the array elements
118    const Person * * pp1 = (const Person * *) p1;
119    const Person * * pp2 = (const Person * *) p2;
120    // get the elements
121    const Person const * pv1 = * pp1;
122    const Person const * pv2 = * pp2;
123    // compare the attributes
124    return strcmp((pv1 -> name), (pv2 -> name));
125  }
126  void Person_sortByName(PersonDatabase * perdb)
127  {
128    qsort(perdb -> person, perdb -> number,
129          sizeof(Person *), comparebyName);
130  }
131  static int comparebyAge(const void * p1,
132                          const void * p2)
133  {
134    const Person * * pp1 = (const Person * *) p1;
135    const Person * * pp2 = (const Person * *) p2;
136    const Person * pv1 = * pp1;
137    const Person * pv2 = * pp2;
138    return ((pv1 -> age) - (pv2 -> age));
139  }
140  void Person_sortByAge(PersonDatabase * perdb)
141  {
142    qsort(perdb -> person, perdb -> number,
143          sizeof(Person *), comparebyAge);
144  }
145  void Person_destruct(PersonDatabase * perdb)
146  {
147    int ind;
148    for (ind = 0; ind < perdb -> number; ind ++)
149      {
150        free (perdb -> person[ind] -> name);
151        free (perdb -> person[ind]);
152      }
153    free (perdb -> person);
154    free (perdb);
155  }
```

This is the **main** function:

```
1   // main.c
2   #include <stdio.h>
3   #include <stdlib.h>
4   #include <string.h>
5   #include "person.h"
6   int main(int argc, char * argv[])
7   {
8     // argv[1]: name of input file
9     // argv[2]: name of output file (sort by name)
10    // argv[3]: name of output file (sort by age)
```

```
11      if (argc < 4)
12        {
13          return EXIT_FAILURE;
14        }
15      PersonDatabase * perdb = Person_read(argv[1]);
16      if (perdb == NULL)
17        {
18          return EXIT_FAILURE;
19        }
20      // Person_print(perdb);
21      Person_sortByName(perdb);
22      // Person_print(perdb);
23      if (Person_write(argv[2], perdb) == 0)
24        {
25          Person_destruct(perdb);
26          return EXIT_FAILURE;
27        }
28      Person_sortByAge(perdb);
29      // Person_print(perdb);
30      if (Person_write(argv[3], perdb) == 0)
31        {
32          Person_destruct(perdb);
33          return EXIT_FAILURE;
34        }
35      Person_destruct(perdb);
36      return EXIT_SUCCESS;
37    }
```

The example introduces a new way to debug a program. The intended output should be a file on a disk. The sorted `Person` database can be printed to the computer screen by using a pre-defined `FILE` pointer called `stdout`. It means "standard output". You do not (and cannot) `fopen` this pre-defined pointer. It already exists whenever any program runs. Writing to `stdout` is precisely what `printf` does. So you have already been using `stdout` since your first C program. The functions `Person_print` and `Person_write` both call `Person_writeHelp`, which writes the database to a file. Passing `stdout` means that the database is written to the terminal.

This is an example of the DRY (Don't Repeat Yourself) principle. Here we reuse the same code for saving the data to a file and for printing the same data to the computer screen. If something is wrong with `Person_writeHelp` or the format of the data needs changes, then you only need to make changes in one place. This saves a lot of time and reduces the chance of mistakes. The DRY principle is a characteristic of well written code.

The program calls `qsort`, passing the array of `Person *` pointers—each element of the array is a pointer to a `Person` object. Therefore, each item's size is `sizeof(Person *)`. The two comparison functions, `comparebyName` and `comparebyAge`, need some careful thought. Each argument is the address of an array element. Each element, in turn, is a pointer to a `Person` object, i.e., `Person *`. Thus, the arguments to the comparison functions are pointers to `Person *`, i.e., `Person * *`. A pointer stores a memory address. One of those `*` simply means it is a pointer. The rest, `Person *`, is what is being pointed to. The two arguments `pp1` and `pp2` in the comparison functions are `Person * *`. Inside each function `pv1` and `pv2` are the pointers to `Person` objects, i.e., `Person *`. Please notice that `*` has different meanings in the following statement:

```
1  const Person const * pv1 = * pp1;
```

Table 4.1 summarizes the different ways of using *. In this statement, the first * means that pv1 is a pointer. The second * means dereferencing pp1. Dereferencing a pointer means going to the address stored in pp1, and retrieving the value stored at that address. Since pp1 is the address of another pointer (pp1 is the address of an address), pp1's value is also an address; * pp1 is a pointer and this address is assigned to pv1. For pv1, the names and ages are obtained by using pv1 -> name and pv1 -> age. Please read this program carefully and fully understand the reasons and the purposes for each *.

17.2 Packing Decimal Digits

17.2.1 Number Systems

The minimum unit of information in a computer is called a *bit*. One bit can have two possible values: 0 or 1. A sequence of bits can be used to represent a binary number, a number in base 2. This is a *binary system*. We usually think of numbers in base ten, a *decimal system*. In base ten we form numbers with ten different values: 0, 1, 2, 3, 4, 5, 6, 7, 8, 9. What does 2783 mean in the decimal system? Two thousands + seven hundreds + eight tens + three:

$$2 \times 10^3 + 7 \times 10^2 + 8 \times 10 + 3 \times 10^0 \tag{17.1}$$

How does this relate to the binary systems? The number binary 10110 means:

$$1 \times 2^4 + 1 \times 2^2 + 1 \times 2^1 + 0 \times 2^0 \tag{17.2}$$

Another commonly used number system is the hexadecimal system. Hexadecimal numbers are in base sixteen, and thus require sixteen symbols: 0, 1, 2, 3, 4, 5, 6, 7, 8, 9, A, B, C, D, E, F. What does EA29 mean in the hexadecimal system? It means

$$E \times 16^3 + A \times 16^2 + 2 \times 16^1 + 9 \times 16^0 \tag{17.3}$$

In C programs, hexadecimal numbers start with 0x (or 0X), for example, 0xAC, 0x9B, and 0x15. Sixteen is the fourth power of two and one hexadecimal digit can express a binary number that is four bits long. A decimal number requires four bits. Table 17.1 shows the relationships between the three different number systems.

In general, if a number system is base n, n symbols are allowed: zero, one, two, ..., $n-1$. A number $a_m a_{m-1} a_{m-2}...a_1 a_0$ means

$$a_m \times n^m + a_{m-1} \times n^{m-1} + a_{m-2} \times n^{m-2} + ... + a_1 \times n^1 + a_0 \times n^0 \tag{17.4}$$

How to convert between number systems? If a decimal number is 273, what is the binary representation? $273 = 256 + 16 + 1 = 2^8 + 2^4 + 1$. Therefore, $273_d = 100010001_b$. Here, the subscripts $_d$ and $_b$ indicate the numbers are decimal and binary respectively.

In C programs, the minimum size of a variable is one byte (8 bits) and its type is **unsigned char**. The valid decimal values for **unsigned char** are 0 through 255, inclusively. It is not possible to have a one-bit variable in C programs. Also, C does not allow for the expression of binary numbers. For example, 10100110_b is expressed as 0xA6 and 11001011_b is expressed as 0xCB. Binary numbers may be used with **gcc** by prefixing 0b. For example,

Decimal	Binary	Hexadecimal
0	0	0
1	1	1
2	10	2
3	11	3
4	100	4
5	101	5
6	110	6
7	111	7
8	1000	8
9	1001	9
10	1010	A
11	1011	B
12	1100	C
13	1101	D
14	1110	E
15	1111	F
16	10000	10
17	10001	11
18	10010	12
19	10011	13

TABLE 17.1: Different number systems.

0b1010 is the number 10. This is an extension to normal C, and may not work in other compilers. Instead, binary numbers should be expressed as hexadecimal numbers.

17.2.2   Packing Two Decimal Digits into One Byte

ASCII uses 8 bits (i.e., one byte) to store characters. This is inefficient if only decimal digits (0, 1, 2, ..., 9) are needed. Only 4 bits are necessary for storing a single decimal digit. This problem asks you to implement a structure called `DecPack`, which packs two decimal digits into one single byte (`unsigned char`). Each `DecPack` object has three attributes:

- `size`: the maximum number of decimal digits that can be stored in a `DecPack` object.
- `used`: the actual number of decimal digits that are stored in a `DecPack` object.
- `data`: an array of `unsigned char`. Each element stores two decimal digits. The upper (i.e., left) 4 bits stores one decimal digit and the lower (i.e., right) 4 bits stores another decimal digit. If the attribute `size` is an even number, the size of the array should be `size / 2`. If the attribute `size` is an odd number, the size of the array should be `(size + 1) / 2`.

The following diagram shows a graphical view of a byte in the `DecPack` data structure. Each byte contains two decimal digits:

upper (left) 4 bits	lower (right) 4 bits

When inserting a decimal digit using `DecPack_insert`, the function checks whether `data` is full. If it is full, then the size of the `data` array doubles. The old array is copied to the new array and the memory for the old array is released. If a byte has not been used, then the decimal digit uses the upper 4 bits. If the upper 4 bits of a byte are already used, the decimal digit uses the lower 4 bits. When deleting a decimal digit using `DecPack_delete`, the function modifies `used` and returns the most recently inserted decimal digit. The digit's value must be between 0 and 9 (not '0' to '9'). DecPack_delete does not shrink the data array even if used is zero. The DecPack_print function prints the decimal digits stored in the object. The printed decimal digits should be between '0' and '9'—if the decimal digit is 0, then '0' is printed, if the decimal digit is 1, then '1' is printed, and so on. Finally, DecPack_destroy releases the memory.

17.2.3 Bit Operations

C provides a variety of ways to directly manipulate the bits in a byte, including:

operation	operator
bit-wise AND	&
bit-wise OR	|
shift left	<<
shift right	>>
exclusive or (XOR)	∧

The bit-wise AND operation is used between two numbers. If the bits from both numbers are 1, the resultant bit is 1. If one or both bits are zero, then the resultant bit is zero. The following shows some examples (in binary representation).

	0	1	1	0	1	0	0	1
&	1	1	0	1	0	0	1	1
	0	1	0	0	0	0	0	1

Sometimes, a program wants to keep some bits while discarding the other bits. For example, if the program wants to keep only the lower (right) four bits of a byte, then the program uses bit-wise AND with 0x0F, 0000 1111 in binary.

	-	-	-	-	a	b	c	d
&	0	0	0	0	1	1	1	1
	0	0	0	0	a	b	c	d

It does not matter whether - is 0 or 1, the first (higher, left) four bits of the result will always be 0. The other four bits: a, b, c, d are either 0 or 1 depending on the values of a, b, c, and d. This is also called a *mask*. A mask blocks some bits and allows the other bits to pass through. If a program wants to check if the leftmost bit is 1 or 0, then it can use a mask whose binary representation is $1000\ 0000_b$ (0x80 in hexadecimal). The following example checks whether the variable a's leftmost bit is 1 or 0:

```
1  unsigned char a = 161;
2  unsigned char mask = 0x80;
3  if ((a & mask) == mask)
4  {
5      // a's leftmost bit is 1
6  }
7  else
8  {
9      // a's leftmost bit is 0
10 }
```

In this example, a & mask equals mask because 161 is greater than 127 and the leftmost bit must be set to 1. Please note that the following if condition is wrong. It is a common mistake.

```
1   unsigned char a = 161;
2   unsigned char mask = 0x80;
3   if ((a & mask) == 1)
4   {
5       // a's leftmost bit is 1
6   }
7   else
8   {
9       // a's leftmost bit is 0
10  }
```

Why is this wrong? If a's leftmost bit is 1, `a & mask` equals 128, not 1.

The bit-wise AND operator `&` is useful for masking numbers—setting some bits to zero, while leaving others unaffected. The bit-wise OR operation is also used between two numbers. If the bit from either number is 1, the resultant bit is 1. If both are zero, then the resultant bit is zero. Here is an example:

$$
\begin{array}{c|cccccccc}
  & 0 & 1 & 1 & 0 & 1 & 0 & 0 & 1 \\
| & 1 & 1 & 0 & 1 & 0 & 0 & 0 & 0 \\
\hline
  & 1 & 1 & 1 & 1 & 1 & 0 & 0 & 1
\end{array}
$$

The bit-wise shift left operation moves bits to the left and adds zeros to the right. The following example shows left-shifting by two. The leftmost two bits are discarded (marked as -) and two zeros are added to the right:

$$
\begin{array}{cccccccccc}
0 & 1 & 1 & 0 & 1 & 0 & 0 & 1 & & \ll 2 \\
- & - & 1 & 0 & 1 & 0 & 0 & 1 & 0 & 0
\end{array}
$$

The next example shows shifting left by four. The leftmost four bits are discarded (marked as -) and four zeros are added to the right:

$$
\begin{array}{cccccccccc}
1 & 1 & 0 & 1 & 1 & 1 & 1 & 0 & & \ll 4 \\
- & - & - & - & 1 & 1 & 1 & 0 & 0 & 0 & 0 & 0
\end{array}
$$

Shifting left by one is equivalent to multiplying by two. If the result is greater than 255, then the leftmost bit is discarded.

The bit-wise shift left operation has a complementary bit-wise shift right operation, moving bits to the right and adding zeros to the left. The following shows an example of shifting right by two. The rightmost two bits are discarded (marked as -) and two zeros are added to the left.

$$
\begin{array}{cccccccccc}
 & & 0 & 1 & 1 & 0 & 1 & 0 & 0 & 1 & \gg 2 \\
0 & 0 & 0 & 1 & 1 & 0 & 1 & 0 & - & -
\end{array}
$$

The next example shows shifting right by four. The rightmost four bits are discarded (marked as -) and four zeros are added to the right.

$$
\begin{array}{cccccccccc}
 & & & & 1 & 1 & 0 & 1 & 1 & 1 & 1 & 0 & \gg 4 \\
0 & 0 & 0 & 0 & 1 & 1 & 0 & 1 & - & - & - & -
\end{array}
$$

Shifting right by one is equivalent to division by two.

The following program shows how to use bit-wise operations:

```
1   // bits.c
2   # include <stdio.h>
3   # include <stdlib.h>
4   # include <string.h>
5   int main ( int argc , char * * argv )
6   {
7      unsigned char a = 129;      // decimal 129, hexadecimal 0X81
8      unsigned char b = 0XF0;     // decimal 240
9      unsigned char c = a & b;    // hexadecimal 0X80, decimal 128
10     printf("%d, %X\n", c, c);   // 128, 80
11     unsigned char d = a | b;    // hexadecimal 0XF1, decimal 241
12     printf("%d, %X\n", d, d);   // 241, F1
13     unsigned char e = d << 3;   // hexadecimal 0X88, decimal 136
14     printf("%d, %X\n", e, e);   // 136, 88
15     unsigned char f = d >> 2;   // hexadecimal 0X3C, decimal 60
16     printf("%d, %X\n", f, f);   // 60, 3C
17     return EXIT_SUCCESS ;
18  }
```

The output of this program is:

```
128, 80
241, F1
136, 88
60, 3C
```

The final bit-wise operation that we will consider is the exclusive or operation, often abbreviated as XOR. With XOR, the resulting bit is 1 if and only if the two input bits are different from each other. Here is an illustrative example:

	0	1	1	0	1	0	0	1
$\wedge$	1	1	0	1	0	0	0	0
	1	0	1	1	1	0	0	1

Please note that $\wedge$ means exclusive or (XOR) in C programs. In some other languages, $\wedge$ means exponential. C uses `exp` for exponential.

17.2.4   Inserting and Retrieving Decimal Digits

In `DecPack`, a decimal digital (0 to 9) requires only 4 bits. Thus, to put this digital into the upper 4 bits, it needs to be shifted left by 4; 4 zeros will be added to the right 4 bits. To retrieve one decimal digit from the upper 4 bits, the byte is shifted right by 4 bits; 4 zeros will be added to the left 4 bits. To put one decimal digital into the lower 4 bits, it can be added to the byte. To retrieve one decimal digital from the lower 4 bits, a mask `0x0F` is used to block the upper 4 bits.

The indexes need to be carefully managed. The value of **used** means the number of digits that have been already inserted. If **used** is an even number (for example, 8), then the next inserted digit should be the 9th digit. In C programs, array indexes start from 0. The 9th digit uses the 5th byte and the index should be 4. The index is 8 / 2 (integer division). Thus, **used** / 2 is the correct index. If **used** is an odd number (for example, 11), then the next inserted digit is the 12th digit. It should be the 6th byte and the index is 5; **used** / 2 is also the correct index. Thus, **used** / 2 is the correct index for insertion; **used** should be incremented after insertion.

When deleting a digit, `used` should decrement before the retrieval. Aside from being symmetric to insertion, this can be understood by working through some examples. Suppose `used` is an even number, say 12, then six bytes are used. The last digit is at the 6th byte and the index is 5. If `used` decrements first, it becomes 11 and `used` / 2 is 5. If `used` is an odd number, say 9, then we are using five bytes. The last digit is at the 5th byte and the index is 4. If `used` decrements first, it becomes 8 and `used` / 2 is 4. In both cases, `used` should decrement before deletion.

17.2.5   DecPack Program

The header file `decpack.h` is listed below:

```
// decpack.h
#ifndef DECPACK_H
#define DECPACK_H
typedef struct
{
  int size; // how many digits can be stored
  int used; // how many digits are actually stored
  unsigned char * data; // store the digits
  // size should be 2 * the actually allocated memory because
  // each byte can store two digits
} DecPack;
// create a DecPack object with the given size
DecPack * DecPack_create(int sz);
// Insert a decimal value into the DecPack object. The new
// value is at the end of the array
void DecPack_insert(DecPack * dp, int val);
// delete and return the last value in the DecPack object
// do not shrink the data array even if nothing is stored
// The returned value should be between 0 and 9
// return -1 if no digit can be deleted
int DecPack_delete(DecPack * dp);
// print the values stored in the object, the first inserted
// value should be printed first
// the printed values are between '0' and '9'
void DecPack_print(DecPack * dp);
// destroy the whole DecPack object, release all memory
void DecPack_destroy(DecPack * dp);
#endif
```

Here are sample implementations of the functions in `decpack.c`:

```
// decpack.c
# include <stdio.h>
# include <stdlib.h>
# include <string.h>
# include "decpack.h"
DecPack * DecPack_create(int sz)
{
  // allocate memory for DecPack
  DecPack * dp = malloc(sizeof(DecPack));
```

```
10    // check whether allocation fails
11    if (dp == NULL)
12      {
13        return NULL;
14      }
15    // initialize size to sz and used to 0
16    dp -> size = sz;
17    dp -> used = 0;
18    // allocate memory for data, should be only sz/2 because
19    // each byte can store two digits
20
21    // if sz is odd, increment sz by one
22    if ((sz % 2) == 1) { sz ++; }
23    dp -> data = malloc(sizeof(unsigned char) * (sz / 2));
24    // check whether allocation fails
25    if (dp -> data == NULL)
26      {
27        free (dp);
28        return NULL;
29      }
30    // return the allocate memory
31    return dp;
32  }
33  void DecPack_insert(DecPack * dp, int val)
34  {
35    // if the object is empty, do nothing
36    if (dp == NULL) { return; }
37
38    // if val < 0 or val > 9, ignore and do nothing
39    if ((val < 0) || (val > 9)) { return; }
40
41    // If the allocated memory is full, double the size,
42    // allocate memory for the new size, copy the data,
43    // and insert the new value
44    int used = dp -> used;
45    if (used == dp -> size)
46      {
47        unsigned char * newdata =
48          malloc(sizeof(unsigned char) * (dp -> size));
49        int iter;
50        for (iter = 0; iter < used; iter ++)
51          {
52            newdata[iter / 2] = dp -> data[iter / 2];
53          }
54        (dp -> size) *= 2;
55        free (dp -> data);
56        dp -> data = newdata;
57      }
58    // If used is an even number, the inserted value should
59    // use the upper (left) 4 bits.
60    // If used is an odd number, the inserted value should
```

```
61      // use the lower (right) 4 bits.
62      //
63      // careful: do not lose the data already stored in DecPack
64      if ((used % 2) == 0)
65        {
66          // shifting left adds zeros for the lower bits
67          dp -> data[used / 2] = (val << 4);
68        }
69      else
70        {
71          // reset the lower four bits, may be left from delete
72          unsigned char upper = dp -> data[used / 2] & 0XF0;
73          dp -> data[used / 2] = upper + val;
74        }
75      (dp -> used) ++;
76   }
77   int DecPack_delete(DecPack * dp)
78   {
79      // if the object is empty, do nothing
80      if (dp == NULL) { return -1; }
81      // return -1 if the DecPack object stores no data
82      if ((dp -> used) == 0) { return -1; }
83      // If used is even, the returned value is the upper
84      // (left) 4 bits. Make sure the returned value is between
85      // 0 and 9. If used is odd, the returned value is the
86      // lower (right) 4 bits. Make sure the returned value
87      // is between 0 and 9.
88      int val;
89      // decrement the used attribute in the DecPack object
90      (dp -> used) --;
91      int used = dp -> used;
92      if ((used % 2) == 0)
93        {
94          val = dp -> data[used / 2] >> 4;
95        }
96      else
97        {
98          val = (dp -> data[used / 2]) & 0X0F;
99        }
100     // return the value
101     return val;
102  }
103  void DecPack_print(DecPack * dp)
104  {
105     // if the object is empty, do nothing
106     if (dp == NULL) { return; }
107     int iter;
108     int used = dp -> used;
109
110     // go through every value stored in the data attribute
111     for (iter = 0; iter < used; iter ++)
```

```
112     {
113         if  ((iter % 2) == 0)
114             {
115                 printf("%d", (dp-> data[iter / 2] >> 4));
116             }
117         else
118             {
119                 printf("%d", (dp-> data[iter / 2] & 0X0F));
120             }
121     }
122     printf("\n");
123 }
124 void DecPack_destroy(DecPack * dp)
125 {
126     // if the object is empty, do nothing
127     if (dp == NULL) { return; }
128     // release the memory for the data
129     free (dp -> data);
130     // release the memory for the object
131     free (dp);
132 }
```

This is the **main** function:

```
1  // main.c
2  #include <stdio.h>
3  #include <stdlib.h>
4  #include "decpack.h"
5  int main ( int argc , char * * argv )
6  {
7      DecPack * dp = DecPack_create(5);
8      int iter;
9      for (iter = 0; iter < 21 ; iter ++)
10         {
11             DecPack_insert(dp, iter % 10);
12         }
13     DecPack_print(dp);
14     for (iter = 0; iter < 7 ; iter ++)
15         {
16             printf("delete %d\n", DecPack_delete(dp));
17         }
18     DecPack_print(dp);
19     for (iter = 0; iter < 6 ; iter ++)
20         {
21             DecPack_insert(dp, iter % 10);
22         }
23     DecPack_print(dp);
24     for (iter = 0; iter < 6 ; iter ++)
25         {
26             printf("delete %d\n", DecPack_delete(dp));
27         }
28     DecPack_print(dp);
```

```
29    DecPack_destroy(dp);
30    return EXIT_SUCCESS ;
31  }
```

Here is the Makefile:

```
1  GCC = gcc
2  CFLAGS = -g -Wall -Wshadow
3  VALGRIND = valgrind --tool=memcheck --verbose --log-file
4
5  decpack: decpack.c decpack.h main.c
6          $(GCC) $(CFLAGS) decpack.c main.c -o $@
7          $(VALGRIND)=valgrindlog ./decpack
8
9  clean:
10         /bin/rm -f *.o decpack *log
```

17.3   Binary File and Pointer

Section 16.6 describes how to use `fread` and `fwrite` to read and write the attributes of an object. What happens if the object contains one or more pointers? Consider the following example:

```
1  // structfile.c
2  #include <stdio.h>
3  #include <stdlib.h>
4  #include <time.h>
5  #pragma pack(1) // tell compiler not to pad any space
6  typedef struct
7  {
8    int length;
9    int * data;
10  } Array;
11  // for simplicity, this program does not check errors
12  int main(int argc, char **argv)
13  {
14    int length = 10;
15    char * filename = "data";
16    // create an object
17    Array * aptr1 = NULL;
18    printf("sizeof(aptr1) = %d\n", (int) sizeof(aptr1));
19    aptr1 = malloc(sizeof(Array));
20    printf("sizeof(aptr1) = %d, sizeof(Array) = %d\n",
21           (int) sizeof(aptr1), (int) sizeof(Array));
22    // allocate memory for the data
23    aptr1 -> length = length;
24    aptr1 -> data = malloc(sizeof(int) * (aptr1 -> length));
25    printf("sizeof(aptr1): %d, sizeof(aptr1 -> data): %d\n",
26           (int) sizeof(aptr1), (int) sizeof(aptr1 -> data));
```

```
27    // initialize the values of the array
28    int ind;
29    for (ind = 0; ind < (aptr1 -> length); ind ++)
30      {
31        aptr1 -> data[ind] = ind;
32      }
33    // save the data to a file
34    FILE * fptr = fopen(filename, "w");
35    // write the data to the file
36    if (fwrite(aptr1, sizeof(Array), 1, fptr) != 1)
37      {
38        // fwrite fail
39        return EXIT_FAILURE;
40      }
41    printf("ftell(fptr)_=_%d\n", (int) ftell(fptr));
42    fclose (fptr);
43
44    // fill the array with random numbers
45    // ensure the heap contains garbage before releasing it
46    srand(time(NULL)); // set the seed of the random number
47    for (ind = 0; ind < (aptr1 -> length); ind ++)
48      {
49        aptr1 -> data[ind] = rand();
50      }
51
52    // release memory
53    free(aptr1 -> data);
54    free(aptr1);
55    // read the data from the file
56    Array * aptr2 = NULL;
57    aptr2 = malloc(sizeof(Array));
58    fptr = fopen(filename, "r");
59    if (fread(aptr2, sizeof(Array), 1, fptr) != 1)
60      {
61        // fread fail
62        return EXIT_FAILURE;
63      }
64    // add the data
65    int sum = 0;
66    for (ind = 0; ind < (aptr2 -> length); ind ++)
67      {
68        sum += aptr2 -> data[ind];
69      }
70    printf("sum_=_%d\n", sum);
71    // release memory
72    free(aptr2);
73    return EXIT_SUCCESS;
74  }
```

Assume this program runs on a 64-bit (8 bytes) machine and furthermore, that each integer uses 4 bytes. Also assume that the program never returns EXIT_FAILURE. What is the output of this program? Here is a sample output:

```
sizeof(arrptr1) = 8
sizeof(arrptr1) = 8, sizeof(Array) = 12
sizeof(arrptr1) = 8, sizeof(arrptr1 -> data) = 8
ftell(fptr) = 12
sum = 1289469162
```

The value of sum changes if the program is run again. The array's elements are set to random values (line 49) after the data has been written to the file (line 36). When line 59 reads the data, the elements' values should be 0, 1, 2, ..., right? Wrong. If we run this program with valgrind, it will tell us that the program has an "Invalid read" at line 68. Why? The reason is that we cannot use fwrite to save the value of a pointer because this value is a memory address. The address is meaningless when saved into a file. Instead of saving the address, the program must save the data stored at the address. To summarize, it makes no sense to write memory addresses to a file; nor does it make sense to read memory addresses from a file.

Chapter 18

Linked Lists

18.1   Expandable Types

In the previous chapters we described two common ways to allocate memory. The first is static allocation. The advantage of static allocation is that there can be no memory leaks; however, the size of the array must be known at the time when the program is written. For example

```
1  int arr[100];
```

This creates an array with 100 elements.

In many cases, the size is unknown when the program is compiled; however, it is known after the program starts executing. This is the second scenario. An example is shown below, where the size is given by the user:

```
1  int * arr2;
2  int length;
3  printf("Please enter the length of the array: ");
4  scanf("%d", & length);
5  arr2 = malloc(length * sizeof(int));
```

This scenario is often used when reading data from a file. One common strategy is to:

1. Read the file once to determine how much memory is needed.
2. Allocate the required memory.
3. Call **fseek** to return to the beginning of the file.
4. Read the file again and store the data in the allocated memory.

This chapter describes how to handle another common scenario: when it is impractical or impossible to know the size even after the program starts. Memory must be allocated and released on an as-needed basis. This is a very common scenario.

Imagine that you are creating a social network system. How many users will register? It is possible that there will be millions of users but we have no direct control over who signs up. We cannot have a pre-determined number, say five million users, and reject registrations after there are already five million users. Perhaps we could allocate enough memory for a few billions users, enough for the foreseeable future. It is wasteful. Moreover, users may come and go. Some users register but forget their passwords and then create new accounts.

It may be necessary to remove accounts that have not been used for more than one year. To manage this type of application, we must be able to allocate memory on an as-needed basis. Memory usage must grow and shrink as the demands of the application require. This chapter describes how to use *dynamic structures*. The book covers only the basic concepts and does not give enough knowledge required to actually build a social network site. The information in this chapter, however, provides a foundation.

If data structures, such as arrays, need to change size as programs run, we can create a new larger (or smaller) array, copy the data, and then free the old array. Section 17.2 gives an example of an auto-resizing array: If too many digits are inserted, the array's size doubles. This chapter explains how to create a simple data structure that is designed to grow without copying the existing data. It supports the following functions:

- Insert: add new data, and allocate memory as needed.
- Search: determine whether a piece of data has already been inserted.
- Delete: remove data and release memory if it is no longer needed.
- Print: print the stored data.
- Destroy: delete everything before the program ends.

The simple data structure is called a *linked list*, and is an example of dynamic structures and is also an example of *container structures*. Such structures may contain different types of data (`int`, `char`, `Person` ...). The code to `insert`, `search`, `delete`, `print`, and `destroy` is quite similar for each different type. The next chapter will describe another type of container structure called the *binary tree*.

18.2   Linked Lists

A linked list is a collection of *nodes* that are linked together by pointers. Each node is an object with at least two *attributes*:

- A pointer to another node. By convention, this attribute is called `next`. If a given node does not have a "next" node, then the `next` attribute stores `NULL`.
- Some data. This attribute may be a pointer, an object, or a primitive type such as `int`, `char`, or `double`.

Below is an example structure, with two attributes, used as a node in a linked list. For simplicity, the data attribute is an integer.

```
1  typedef struct listnode
2  {
3    struct listnode * next;
4    int value;
5  } Node; // do not forget ;
```

This introduces the concept of a "self-referring structure". Notice how `next` is a pointer to `struct listnode`? That is what makes it self-referring. Because the C compiler reads source files from top to bottom, it cannot see the type name `Node` at the time `next` is declared. Thus, we assign a temporary type name: `struct listnode`. It is possible to refer to the nodes as `struct listnode`; however, the structure is called `Node` from now on. Fig. 18.1 shows three views for the first operation in creating a linked list.

The diagrammatic view in (b) is the most commonly used. In (b), when a pointer's value is `NULL`, it is common to make it point to the "Ground" symbol used in electronics. My experience working with students suggests that some students are more comfortable with

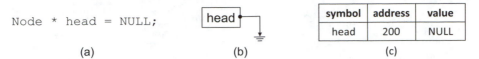

```
Node * head = NULL;
```

(a)   (b)   (c)

symbol	address	value
head	200	NULL

FIGURE 18.1: A linked list starts empty, i.e., without any `Node`. This figure shows three views: (a) the source code view, (b) a diagram, and (c) the stack memory.

one particular view than with other views. The three views are shown simultaneously so that we can see the relationships between the different representations.

18.3 Inserting Data

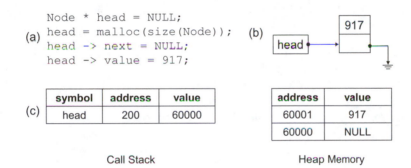

(a)
```
Node * head = NULL;
head = malloc(size(Node));
head -> next = NULL;
head -> value = 917;
```

(b)

(c)

symbol	address	value
head	200	60000

address	value
60001	917
60000	NULL

Call Stack   Heap Memory

FIGURE 18.2: Creating a `Node` object whose value is 917. Please note that `head` is a pointer.

Fig. 18.2 shows how to create the very first node in a linked list, and assign a number to the `value` attribute. Calling `malloc` will allocate space in heap memory for the two attributes. Suppose `malloc` returns address 60000, then this value is assigned to the value of `head`. The next line is:

```
head -> next = NULL;
```

This line assigns `NULL` to the node's `next` attribute. Then, we assign 917 to the `value` attribute, which is the data:

```
head -> value = 917;
```

Add space before or after `->` makes no difference. We create a function `List_insert` that can make inserting nodes much more straightforward. The function can
  • allocate memory for a new node.
  • assign an address to the `next` attribute.
  • assign a value to the `value` attribute.

Fig. 18.3 shows that the function can simplify inserting a node. Calling `List_insert` with −504 as the argument creates one more list node and it is inserted at the beginning of the list. Later, we will explain how to insert −504 at the end of the list. It is simpler to insert nodes onto the front of a linked list. Please note that this means that the value stored

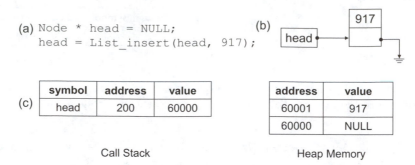

FIGURE 18.3: Replacing the three lines by using `List_insert`.

at `head` must change. This is because `head` must be the newly inserted node that we just allocated. Note that there is no guarantee that when calling `malloc` twice we will obtain consecutive addresses. Fig. 18.4 shows a gap between the memory allocated to the two list nodes. Fig. 18.5 shows three nodes.

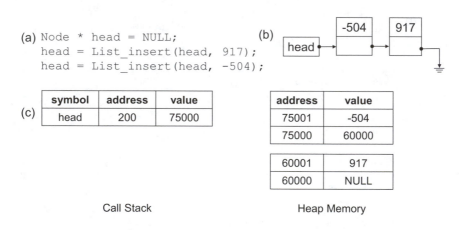

FIGURE 18.4: Calling `List_insert` again to insert another list node.

Here is a sample implementation of the insert function:

```c
// A static function can be called by functions in this
// file only. Functions outside this file cannot call it.
static Node * Node_construct(int val)
{
  Node * nd = malloc(sizeof(Node));
  nd -> value = val;
  nd -> next = NULL;
  return nd;
}

Node * List_insert(Node * head, int val)
{
  printf("insert %d\n", val);
  Node * ptr = Node_construct(val);
```

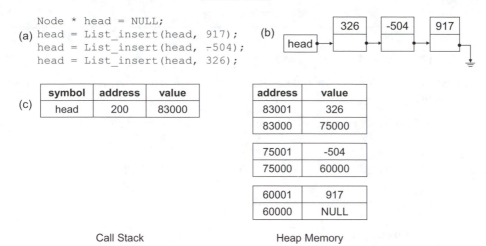

Call Stack   Heap Memory

FIGURE 18.5: Insert the third object by calling `List_insert` again.

```
15    ptr -> next = head; // insert at the beginning
16    return ptr;
17  }
```

In the insert function we use a **static** function called **Node_construct**. Prefixing a function with **static** means that the function can only be used within the current file. We mark the function **static** because it is called by **List_insert** only. This constructor ensures that **next** is always initialized to NULL. Even though **List_insert** immediately changes **next** after calling **Node_construct**, it is a good habit to always initialize **next**. Later on, the program tests whether **next** is NULL to determine whether a node is the last node in the list. Some students are eager to make their programs faster and do not always initialize the **next** pointer inside **Node_construct**. Forgetting to initialize **next** to NULL is a common and easily avoidable mistake.

In **List_insert**, the newly constructed node is called **ptr**. Sometimes students call this variable **new**. This is discouraged because **new** has a special meaning in C++. This is important when C and C++ programs are integrated together, which happens quite often.

Referring back to the code, line 15 puts the newly created node in front of the head of the old list. Line 16 returns the newly created node. This makes **head** point to the newly created node. Thus, the most recently added node is at the beginning of the list. When **List_insert** is called again, a new list node is created and it is the beginning of the list. The value stored at **head** changes again. We assume there is a gap between this new object and the other two existing objects.

Pushing new elements onto the front of the list is rather like a "stack". The end of the list is always the first inserted value, and the beginning of the list is always the most recently inserted value. To remove the first inserted value (at the very end of the list), it is necessary to go through the entire list. If we always remove from the front, then we indeed meet the property of a stack: first-in, last-out.

18.4   Searching a Linked List

The next function searches a linked list for the node whose value is the same as the given argument.

```
1  Node * List_search(Node * head, int val)
2  {
3    Node * ptr = head;
4    while (ptr != NULL)
5      {
6        if ((ptr -> value) == val)
7          {
8            return ptr;
9          }
10         ptr = ptr -> next;
11     }
12   return ptr; // must be NULL
13 }
```

The function starts from the first node in the list. Before the function does anything, the function has to check whether the list is empty. This is the purpose of line 4. If the value is found at line 6, then the function returns the node. Otherwise, `ptr` moves to the next node. If multiple nodes store the value matching the argument `val`, then this function returns the first match. Line 12 returns `ptr` and it should always be NULL. If `ptr` is not NULL, then the `while` loop should continue. This example shows the importance of initializing `next` to NULL to indicate the end of the list.

18.5   Deleting from a Linked List

The `List_delete` function deletes the `Node` object whose `value` is the same as the second argument. Suppose the program needs to delete the second `Node` object in the list. After calling `List_delete`, the first and the third nodes must remain in the linked list. The first node's `next` must point to the third node (now second). This ensures that the node is still reachable from the `head`. Fig. 18.6 shows the new list and Fig. 18.7 to Fig. 18.10 show the steps.

How do we implement `List_delete`? First, the function creates a new pointer `p` and makes its value the same as `head`'s value. The list is accessible from the head. The function has to keep `head`'s value, because if `head`'s value is changed, then we lose the entire list.

```
1  Node * List_delete(Node * head, int val)
2  {
3    printf("delete %d\n", val);
4    Node * p = head;
5    if (p == NULL) // empty list, do nothing
6      {
7        return p;
8      }
```

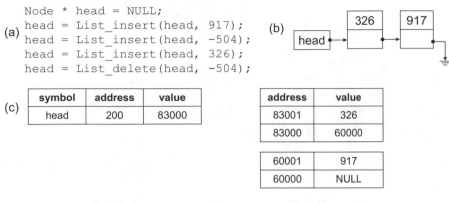

FIGURE 18.6: Delete the node whose value is −504.

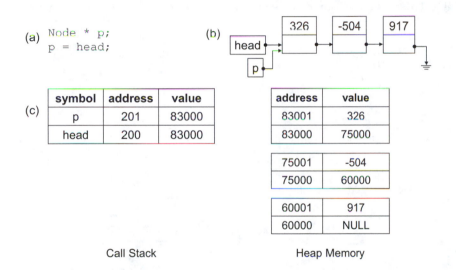

FIGURE 18.7: To delete a list node, first create a pointer p that points to the same memory address as head.

```
9
10    // delete the first node (i.e., head node)?
11    if ((p -> value) == val)
12      {
13        p = p -> next;
14        free (head);
15        return p;
16      }
17
18    // not deleting the first node
19    Node * q = p -> next;
20    while ((q != NULL) && ((q -> value) != val))
```

(a)
```
Node * p;
p = head;
Node * q;
q = p -> next;
```

(b)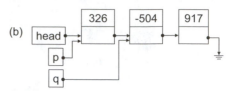

(c)

symbol	address	value
q	202	75000
p	201	83000
head	200	83000

address	value
83001	326
83000	75000

address	value
75001	-504
75000	60000

address	value
60001	917
60000	NULL

Call Stack   Heap Memory

FIGURE 18.8: The function creates another pointer q. Its value is the same as `p->next`.

(a)
```
Node * p;
p = head;
Node * q;
q = p -> next;
p -> next = q -> next;
```

(b)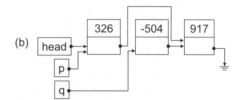

(c)

symbol	address	value
q	202	75000
p	201	83000
head	200	83000

address	value
83001	326
83000	60000

address	value
75001	-504
75000	60000

address	value
60001	917
60000	NULL

Call Stack   Heap Memory

FIGURE 18.9: Modify `p->next` to bypass the node that is about to be deleted.

```
21      {
22        // check whether q is NULL before checking q -> value
23        p = p -> next;
24        q = q -> next;
25      }
26    if (q != NULL)
27      {
28        // delete the node whose value is val
29        p -> next = q -> next;
30        free (q);
31      }
```

(a)
```
Node * p;
p = head;
Node * q;
q = p -> next;
p -> next = q -> next;
free (q);
```

(b)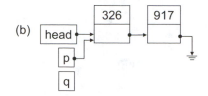

(c)

symbol	address	value
q	202	-
p	201	83000
head	200	83000

address	value
83001	326
83000	60000

60001	917
60000	NULL

Call Stack　　　　　　　　　　Heap Memory

FIGURE 18.10: Release the memory pointed to by q.

```
32    return head;
33  }
```

If head's value (head -> value) is the same as val, the first node is deleted. This is achieved by storing head -> next in p at line 14. In this case, the function returns p as the new head of the list. It is possible that p is set to NULL. This occurs when the list has only one node and its value is the same as val. After deleting this node, the list is empty.

If head's value is different from val, then the node to be deleted, if it exists, is after head somewhere. When we find this node, we must make the previous node point to the next node. As we will see below, the List_delete function uses another pointer q for this purpose, and its value is p -> next.

Lines 20 to 25 find the node whose value is val. The while loop stops in one of two conditions: either q is NULL or q -> value is val. To avoid a memory error, the function must check the first condition before checking the second condition. If q is NULL, then the second condition is not checked. When q is NULL, the first part of the logical AND (&&) expression is false and the entire logical AND expression is false. The program does check whether q -> value is the same as val. This is called *short-circuit* evaluation and C programs often rely on it. Lines 23 and 24 move p and q to their next nodes. Since q is initialized to p -> next, the code inside the entire block always keeps q as p -> next.

What does it means when q is NULL at line 26? It means that no node in the linked list stores val, and therefore no node needs to be deleted. If q is not NULL, then a node whose value is val has been located. The function changes p -> next to q -> next. This bypasses the node q that is about to be deleted. In this method, q is the node to be deleted and p is the node before q. It is necessary to keep p because it is not possible to go backward from q to p. The purpose of keeping both p and q is that we cannot go back one node from q without p. The function then releases the memory pointed to by q. The value stored in q is still a memory address but that address is no longer valid. Using q's value after free(q) will cause segmentation fault. It is also possible to implement List_delete with recursion. Below is a sample implementation. Lines 19 to 31 above can be replaced by a single line as shown below.

```
1  Node * List_delete2(Node * head, int val)
```

```
2  {
3    printf("delete %d\n", val);
4    if (head == NULL)
5      {
6        return NULL;
7      }
8
9    if ((head -> value) == val)
10     {
11       Node * p = head -> next;
12       free (head);
13       return p;
14     }
15
16   head -> next = List_delete2(head -> next, val);
17   return head;
18 }
```

How does this work? The function checks whether the list is empty (line 4) and then checks whether the first node is the node to be deleted (lines 9 to 14). How can line 16 in List_delete2 replace lines 19 to 31 in List_delete? Line 16 calls List_delete2 recursively, passing head -> next. This means that every time List_delete2 is called, one node (the head) is excluded. Thus, the list being considered shrinks in every recursive call, and eventually reaches NULL (checked at line 4) if val is not stored in the list. This ensures that List_delete2 terminates.

This function has three places that call return. Line 6 returns when the list is empty and nothing can be deleted. Line 13 returns the node after head because head is the node to be deleted. Line 17 returns head if head is not the node to be deleted.

Consider the scenario when val is not stored in any node. Line 16 assigns head -> next to what is returned by calling List_delete2(head -> next, val). Since val is not in the list, the condition at line 9 is never true in any of the recursive calls. The function will always return the first argument. This means that line 16 will reduce to head -> next = head -> next and the list remains unchanged.

Next consider the case when the list does contain a node whose value is val. In this case, the condition at line 9 will become true in one recursive call. The function then returns the node after head, skipping head. This is equivalent to line 15 in List_delete. Thus, List_delete2 can delete the node whose value is val. List_delete2 does not need to use q because the call stack stores the value of each node (as head) as the function moves forward along the list.

18.6   Printing a Linked List

List_print is more straightforward than the previous functions because it does not need to change the list. The function simply goes through the nodes one-by-one and prints the values. The listing below gives two implementations: one iterative, and one recursive.

```
1  void List_print(Node * head)
2  {
3    printf("\nPrint the whole list:\n");
```

```
4    while (head != NULL)
5      {
6        printf("%d␣", head -> value);
7        head = head -> next;
8      }
9    printf("\n\n");
10 }
11
12 static void List_print2Help(Node * head)
13 {
14   if (head == NULL)
15     {
16       return;
17     }
18   printf("%d␣", head -> value);
19   List_print2Help(head -> next);
20 }
21
22 void List_print2(Node * head)
23 {
24   printf("\nPrint␣the␣whole␣list:\n");
25   List_print2Help(head);
26   printf("\n\n");
27 }
```

List_print2 is the recursive function. It prints the message and then calls a helper function. The helper function goes through the nodes one by one until reaching the end of the list.

18.7   Destroying a Linked List

List_destroy destroys the whole list, releasing the memory for each node. The non-recursive method keeps a pointer p for the node after the node to be deleted. The recursive method uses the call stack to keep the value of head. Note that line 18 must be after line 17 because head -> next does not exist after free (head).

```
1  void List_destroy(Node * head)
2  {
3    while (head != NULL)
4      {
5        Node * p = head -> next;
6        free (head);
7        head = p;
8      }
9  }
10
11 void List_destroy2(Node * head)
12 {
13   if (head == NULL)
```

```
14        {
15            return;
16        }
17     List_destroy2(head -> next);
18     free (head); // must be after the recursive call
19  }
```

The following `main` function shows how to use the linked list functions we have developed in this chapter.

```
1   // file: main.c
2   #include "list.h"
3   #include <stdlib.h>
4   #include <stdio.h>
5   int main(int argc, char * argv[])
6   {
7     Node * head = NULL; /* must initialize it to NULL */
8     head = List_insert(head, 917);
9     head = List_insert(head, -504);
10    head = List_insert(head, 326);
11    List_print(head);
12    head = List_delete(head, -504);
13    List_print(head);
14    head = List_insert(head, 138);
15    head = List_insert(head, -64);
16    head = List_insert(head, 263);
17    List_print(head);
18    if (List_search(head, 138) != NULL)
19      {
20        printf("138 is in the list\n");
21      }
22    else
23      {
24        printf("138 is not in the list\n");
25      }
26    if (List_search(head, 987) != NULL)
27      {
28        printf("987 is in the list\n");
29      }
30    else
31      {
32        printf("987 is not in the list\n");
33      }
34    head = List_delete(head, 263); // delete the first Node
35    List_print(head);
36    head = List_delete(head, 917); // delete the last Node
37    List_print(head);
38    List_destroy(head);    // delete all Nodes
39    return EXIT_SUCCESS;
40  }
```

The output of this program is:

```
insert 917
insert -504
insert 326

Print the whole list:
326 -504 917

delete -504

Print the whole list:
326 917

insert 138
insert -64
insert 263

Print the whole list:
263 -64 138 326 917

138 is in the list
987 is not in the list
delete 263

Print the whole list:
-64 138 326 917

delete 917

Print the whole list:
-64 138 326
```

Chapter 19

Programming Problems Using Linked List

19.1   Queues

The function List_insert in Section 18.3 always inserts the new value at the beginning of the list. If we always delete nodes from the front of the list, then the linked list is a stack. In this problem we change the insert function so that the first inserted value is at the beginning of the list and the latest inserted value is at the end of the list. If we still remove elements from the beginning of the list we have created a *queue*, like a line at a store waiting for service. The implementation below uses recursion.

```
Node * List_insert(Node * head, int val)
{
   if (head == NULL)
      {
         return Node_construct(val);
      }
   head -> next = List_insert(head -> next, val);
   return head;
}
```

When the if condition is (when head is NULL), the list is empty. Every recursive call moves forward by following the next link. This condition can be true if the function has reached the end of the list. When the frame from the call stack is popped, the previous node's next is set to a pointer to the newly created node. For nodes not at the end, line 7 is essentially head -> next = head -> next without changing the list.

You may have noticed that this particular linked list implementation of a queue is not efficient. Every time a node is inserted, the function has to go through the entire list to reach the end of the list. This is unavoidable because the program only tracks the beginning of the list. One solution is to keep track of both the beginning (the head) and the end (the tail) of the list. This requires two pointers.

Another problem is that the links are uni-directional. When deleting a node, it is necessary to keep track of the node before the node to be deleted. This inconvenience can be solved by using two links in each node: next and previous. If q is p -> next, then p is q -> previous. The head of the list has no previous node so its previous points to NULL. The tail of the list has no next node so its next points to NULL. This is called a *doubly linked list*. The structure definition for a node in a doubly linked list is shown below:

```
1  typedef struct listnode
2  {
3    struct listnode * next;
4    struct listnode * previous;
5    int value;
6  } Node;
```

19.2   Sorting Numbers

This problem asks you to modify `List_insert` so that the values in the list are sorted in the ascending order. This function is similar to the previous one, except for lines 8 to 12. If `val` is smaller, it should be inserted before `head`. Otherwise, it should be inserted after `head`, as handled by line 13.

```
1  Node * List_insert(Node * head, int val)
2  {
3    Node * ptr = Node_construct(val);
4    if (head == NULL)
5      {
6        return ptr;
7      }
8    if ((head -> value) > val)
9      {
10       ptr -> next = head;
11       return ptr;
12     }
13   head -> next = List_insert(head -> next, val);
14   return head;
15 }
```

This and the previous problems use the call stack to keep `head`. When the recursive function returns, `head` is unchanged.

19.3   Sparse Arrays

Arrays are widely used in many applications, but sometimes most of the elements are zeros. Storing these elements wastes memory. A sparse array stores only those elements whose values are non-zero. This problem asks you to write a program managing spare arrays: Each node stores one pair of index and value. The program reads two sparse arrays from two files, merges the arrays, and stores the new array in a file. How are two arrays merged?

- If one index exists in one array and is not in the other array, then this element is added to the new array.
- If the same index exists in both arrays, the values are added. If the value is zero, then

the element is deleted. If the value is not zero, then the element is added to the new array.

The diagram below illustrates what happens when we join two sparse arrays. Each element is expressed by an index–value pair.

Array 1	index	0			102	315
	value	5			−5	8
Array 2	index			11	102	315
	value			2	5	2
Array 1 + Array 2	index	0		11		315
	value	5		2		10

The index 102 is not in the new array because the value becomes zero after the two arrays are joined. To test this implementation, we want to read sparse arrays from disk. For simplicity, we can assume that in each input file the indexes are distinct. Each line of the file contains two integers: index and value. The two integers are separated by space. The indexes stored in a file are not necessarily sorted. The header file is shown below. The header file declares four functions:

```
1  // sparse.h
2  #ifndef SPARSE_H
3  #define SPARSE_H
4  typedef struct linked {
5     int index;
6     int value;
7     struct linked * next;
8  } Node;
9  // read a sparse array from a file and return the array
10 // return NULL if reading fails
11 Node * List_read(char * filename);
12 // write a sparse array to a file
13 // return 1 if success, 0 if fail
14 int List_save(char * filename, Node * arr);
15 // merge two sparse arrays
16 // the two input arrays are not changed and the new array
17 // does not share memory with the input arrays
18 Node * List_merge(Node * arr1, Node * arr2);
19 // release all nodes in a sparse array
20 void List_destroy(Node * arr);
21 #endif
```

Below is a sample implementation of these four functions. Even though the indexes from input files are not sorted, the linked lists are sorted by the indexes.

```
1  // sparse.c
2  #include "sparse.h"
3  #include <stdio.h>
4  #include <stdlib.h>
5  static Node * Node_create(int ind, int val);
6  static Node * List_insert(Node * head, int ind, int val);
7  static Node * List_copy(Node * head);
8  Node * List_read(char * filename)
9  {
```

```
10      FILE * fptr = fopen(filename, "r");
11      if (fptr == NULL)
12        {
13          return NULL;
14        }
15      int ind;
16      int val;
17      Node * head = NULL;
18      while (fscanf(fptr, "%d␣%d", & ind, & val) == 2)
19        {
20          head = List_insert(head, ind, val);
21        }
22      fclose(fptr);
23      return head;
24    }
25    int List_save(char * filename, Node * arr)
26    {
27      FILE * fptr = fopen(filename, "w");
28      if (fptr == NULL)
29        {
30          return 0;
31        }
32      while (arr != NULL)
33        {
34          fprintf(fptr, "%d␣%d\n", arr -> index, arr -> value);
35          arr = arr -> next;
36        }
37      fclose(fptr);
38      return 1;
39    }
40    Node * List_merge(Node * arr1, Node * arr2)
41    {
42      Node * arr3 = List_copy(arr1);
43      while (arr2 != NULL)
44        {
45          arr3 = List_insert(arr3, arr2 -> index,
46                             arr2 -> value);
47          arr2 = arr2 -> next;
48        }
49      return arr3;
50    }
51    void List_destroy(Node * arr)
52    {
53      if (arr == NULL)
54        {
55          return;
56        }
57      while (arr != NULL)
58        {
59          Node * ptr = arr -> next;
60          free(arr);
```

```c
61          arr = ptr;
62      }
63  }
64  static Node * Node_create(int ind, int val)
65  {
66    Node * nd = malloc(sizeof(Node));
67    if(nd == NULL)
68      {
69        return NULL;
70      }
71    nd -> index = ind;
72    nd -> value = val;
73    nd -> next = NULL;
74    return nd;
75  }
76  // If the same index appears again, add the value
77  // The returned list is sorted by the index.
78  static Node * List_insert(Node * head, int ind, int val)
79  {
80    if (val == 0) // do not insert zero value
81      {
82        return head;
83      }
84    if (head == NULL)
85      {
86        return Node_create(ind, val);
87      }
88    if ((head -> index) > ind)
89      {
90        // insert the new node before the list
91        Node * ptr = Node_create(ind, val);
92        ptr -> next = head;
93        return ptr;
94      }
95    if ((head -> index) == ind)
96      {
97        // merge the nodes
98        head -> value += val;
99        if ((head -> value) == 0)
100          {
101            // delete this node
102            Node * ptr = head -> next;
103            free (head);
104            return ptr;
105          }
106        return head;
107      }
108    head -> next = List_insert(head -> next, ind, val);
109    return head;
110  }
111  Node * List_copy(Node * arr)
```

```
112  {
113    Node * arr2 = NULL;
114    while (arr != NULL)
115      {
116        arr2 = List_insert(arr2, arr -> index, arr -> value);
117        arr = arr -> next;
118      }
119    return arr2;
120  }
```

Below is a sample `main` function that we can use to test our implementation.

```
1   // main.c
2   #include <stdio.h>
3   #include <stdlib.h>
4   #include "sparse.h"
5   int main(int  argc, char ** argv)
6   {
7     if (argc != 4)
8       {
9         return EXIT_FAILURE;
10      }
11    Node * arr1 = List_read(argv[1]);
12    if (arr1 == NULL)
13      {
14        return EXIT_FAILURE;
15      }
16    Node * arr2 = List_read(argv[2]);
17    if (arr2 == NULL)
18      {
19        List_destroy(arr2);
20        return EXIT_FAILURE;
21      }
22    Node * arr3 = List_merge(arr1, arr2);
23    int ret = List_save(argv[3], arr3);
24    List_destroy(arr1);
25    List_destroy(arr2);
26    List_destroy(arr3);
27    if (ret == 0)
28      {
29        return EXIT_FAILURE;
30      }
31    return EXIT_SUCCESS;
32  }
```

Here is a `Makefile` that combines the compiling and testing.

```
1   GCC = gcc
2   CFLAGS = -g -Wall -Wshadow
3   LIBS =
4   SOURCES = sparse.c main.c
5   TARGET = main
6   VALGRIND = valgrind --tool=memcheck --verbose --log-file
```

```
7  TEST0 = inputs/input0A inputs/input0B outputs/output0
8  TEST1 = inputs/input1A inputs/input1B outputs/output1
9
10 main: $(SOURCES)
11         $(GCC) $(CFLAGS) $(SOURCES) -o $@
12         ./main $(TEST0)
13         diff -w outputs/output0 expected/expected0
14         ./main $(TEST1)
15         diff -w outputs/output1 expected/expected1
16         $(VALGRIND)=outputs/valgrindlog0 ./main $(TEST0)
17         $(VALGRIND)=outputs/valgrindlog1 ./main $(TEST1)
18
19 clean:
20         /bin/rm -f main outputs/*
```

Let's assume that we have inputs input0A and input0B as shown below. The expected0 column shows the result of merging the two arrays.

input0A:

```
1  76 1615
2  115 -1970
3  164 281
4  495 883
5  912 116
6  1124 458
7  1396 70
8  1468 -1100
9  1777 1772
10 2064 2093
11 2333 -1163
12 2418 -1683
13 2943 -2078
14 3545 -538
15 3678 -2260
16 3700 -131
17 3708 -1596
18 3933 2050
19 4031 -408
20 4287 -728
21 4363 2244
22 4857 -2293
23 4951 -1737
```

input0B:

```
1  1502 1794
2  2545 -1387
3  2872 2035
4  3133 2339
5  3164 -1373
6  4218 713
7  4934 -1539
```

expected0:

```
1  76 1615
2  115 -1970
3  164 281
4  495 883
5  912 116
6  1124 458
7  1396 70
8  1468 -1100
9  1502 1794
10 1777 1772
11 2064 2093
12 2333 -1163
13 2418 -1683
14 2545 -1387
15 2872 2035
16 2943 -2078
17 3133 2339
18 3164 -1373
19 3545 -538
20 3678 -2260
21 3700 -131
22 3708 -1596
23 3933 2050
24 4031 -408
25 4218 713
26 4287 -728
27 4363 2244
28 4857 -2293
29 4934 -1539
30 4951 -1737
```

Below is a second set of sample inputs and outputs. Some elements (indexes = 54 and 4019) are eliminated in the output because the values add to zero.

input1A:

1	1769	-1121
2	1859	2170
3	4879	-2440
4	1994	911
5	3123	2169
6	4441	784
7	54	-1185
8	4735	2350
9	4931	1454
10	3811	2088
11	4019	1227

input1B:

1	54	1185
2	2328	-2473
3	2379	2207
4	886	-642
5	1765	-1694
6	2226	-1542
7	3103	-700
8	2304	2324
9	2308	-369
10	4019	-1227

expected1:

1	886	-642
2	1765	-1694
3	1769	-1121
4	1859	2170
5	1994	911
6	2226	-1542
7	2304	2324
8	2308	-369
9	2328	-2473
10	2379	2207
11	3103	-700
12	3123	2169
13	3811	2088
14	4441	784
15	4735	2350
16	4879	-2440
17	4931	1454

19.4   Reversing a Linked List

This program asks you to write a function that reverses a linked list by reversing the individual links between the nodes. The function's input argument is the head of the linked list and returns the head of the reversed linked list. This function should not call `malloc` directly or indirectly (i.e., calling another function that calls `malloc`), because it is unnecessary and slow.

```
1  Node * List_reverse(Node * head);
```

Fig. 19.1 shows an example list and its reversed form.

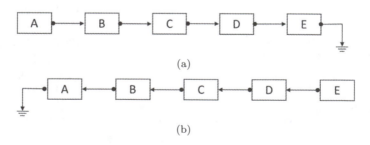

(a)

(b)

FIGURE 19.1: (a) The original linked list. The list's head points to A. (b) The reversed linked list. The list's head points to E.

Fig. 19.2 shows how to reverse a linked list. Suppose the first two nodes have already been reversed: `revhead` points to the head of the partially reversed list; `orighead` points to the head of the remaining original list; `origsec` points to the second node of the remaining list.

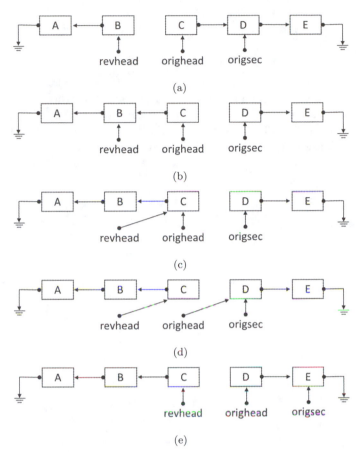

FIGURE 19.2: (a) Three pointers are used. (b) Change `orighead -> next` and make it point to `revhead`. (c) Update `revhead` to the new head of the reversed list. (d) Update `orighead` to the new head of the remaining list. (e) Update `origsec` to the second node of the remaining list.

Below is a sample implementation that reverses a linked list as desired. It essentially implements the four steps depicted in the figure.

```
Node * List_reverse(Node * head)
{
   if (head == NULL)
      {
         // empty list, nothing to do
         return NULL;
      }
   Node * orighead = head;
   Node * revhead = NULL; // must initialize to NULL
   Node * origsec; // will be assigned before using
   while (orighead != NULL)
```

```
12      {
13          origsec = orighead -> next;
14          orighead -> next = revhead;
15          revhead = orighead;
16          orighead = origsec;
17      }
18    return revhead;
19 }
```

The order of the four steps inside `while` is important. It would be wrong if the order were different. For example, reversing lines 13 and 14 would lose the remaining list because `orighead -> head` has already been changed and `origsec` is the same as `revhead`. Remember to initialize `revhead` to `NULL` because it will be the end of the reversed list. It is unnecessary to initialize `origsec` because it is `orighead -> next` before it is used.

Chapter 20

Binary Search Trees

The previous chapter explained linked lists. Each `Node` has precisely one link called `next`. Traversing the list to find a given node means starting at the first node—usually called the head—and visiting each node in turn. In a doubly linked list, each `Node` has two links (`next` and `previous`). A doubly linked list allows for traversing forward using `next` and backward using `previous`. Even though doubly linked lists are more convenient, they still have the same limitations of singly linked lists. If the list is long, then finding particular nodes may require visiting many nodes. If we want to efficiently add and remove data, a linked list is insufficient.

Section 15.1 provides an example of quickly locating data in an array by skipping large portions of it. This is a step in the right direction. Note, however, that the array must be sorted before a binary search can be applied. Furthermore, the array's size is fixed. Inserting an element in an array can be expensive, because there may not be enough memory available. It is necessary to allocate a new array and copying data before freeing the old array. If the new element is inserted at the beginning, all the elements must be moved. This is inefficient.

Can a dynamic structure support the efficient searching properties of binary searching, but still preserve the ability to quickly add and remove elements? *Binary search trees* are designed to do precisely that. A binary search tree can typically discard half of the data in a single comparison. This makes search efficient. A binary search tree is one type of binary tree. A binary search tree is always a binary tree, but a binary tree may not necessarily be a binary search tree. We will start exploring binary search trees and then generalize to binary trees.

Like a linked list, a binary search tree is composed of nodes that are linked together. The tree is a single root node similar to the head node in a linked list. Every node in a binary tree has two links called `left` and `right`. A binary tree is different from a doubly linked list. In a doubly linked list, if `p -> next` is `q`, then `q -> previous` must be `p`. It is possible to reach `p` from `q` and it is also possible to reach `q` from `p`. Even though each node has two links, they form a single chain.

The situation is fundamentally different in binary trees. Although each node has two links, the links point to distinct nodes. This means that if `q` is `p -> left` or `p -> right`, neither `q -> left` nor `q -> right` is `p`. It is possible to reach `q` from `p` but it is impossible to reach `p` from `q`.

The following are some terms used for binary trees. If q is p -> left, then q is called p's *left child*. If r is p -> right, then r is p's *right child*. We call p the parent of q and r. We also say that q and r are siblings. If a node has no child, then it is called a *leaf node*. All the nodes on the left side of p are called p's left *subtree*. All the nodes on the right side of p are called p's right *subtree*. The top node is called the *root* of the tree, and the root can reach every node in the tree.

Fig. 20.1 shows an example of a binary tree. The root stores the value 8. The value 4 is stored in the left child of the root. The nodes storing 1, 4, 5, and 7 are the left subtree of the root. The nodes storing 9, 10, 11, 12, and 15 are the right subtree of the root.

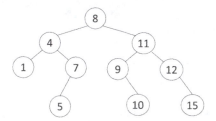

FIGURE 20.1: An example of a binary search tree.

The *distance* of a node from the root is the number of links between the root and the node. For example, the distance between the node 7 and the root is 2. The *height* of a binary tree is one plus the longest distance in the tree. The height of the tree above is 4. In a *full* binary tree, each node has either two children or no children. The tree in Fig. 20.1 is not full because some nodes (nodes 7, 9, and 12) have only one child. In a *complete* binary tree, each node, except the nodes just above the leaf nodes, has two children. Fig. 20.1 is complete but not full.

It is possible for a node in a complete binary tree to have only one child, and thus not be a full binary tree. It is also possible that a full binary tree is incomplete. If a binary tree is full and complete and its height is n (i.e., the distance between a leaf node and the root is $n-1$), then the tree has precisely $2^n - 1$ nodes and 2^{n-1} leaf nodes. In a *balanced* binary tree, the difference between the height of the left subtree and the height of the right subtree is at most one. A binary tree is *degenerated* if each node has at most one child. In this case, the binary tree is essentially a linked list.

We can create tree structures in which each object has three or more links. For example, many computer games take advantage of *octrees* where each node has eight children. In this case, octrees are used to partition three-dimensional space, and are thus useful for indexing the objects in 3D worlds. This book focuses on binary trees because they are useful for a wide array of problems.

20.1   Binary Search Tree

A binary *search* tree is a binary tree and satisfies the following conditions:
- Each node has two links and one data attribute. This data attribute can be a primitive type (int, double, char, etc.) or an object.
- The data attributes store values that must be distinct.
- The data attributes must be *totally ordered*. If a and b are the values stored in two different nodes, then either $a < b$ or $a > b$ must be true. Transitivity must be satisfied

(if $a < b$ and $b < c$, then $a < c$). For example, integers, characters, floating-point numbers, and strings all support total ordering. Complex numbers are not totally ordered and cannot be used as the attributes for binary search trees.

- For every node p in a tree, if p has a left child node q, then q -> value must be smaller than p -> value. Similarly, if p has a right child node r, then r -> value must be greater than p -> value.

Fig. 20.1 is an example of a binary search tree. Below is the header file for a binary search tree. It shows the structure definition for a tree node, and gives function declarations for binary search trees.

```
1   // tree.h
2   #ifndef TREE_H
3   #define TREE_H
4   #include <stdio.h>
5   typedef struct treenode
6   {
7     struct treenode * left;
8     struct treenode * right;
9     int value;
10  } TreeNode;
11  // insert a value v to a binary search tree starting
12  // with root, return the new root
13  TreeNode * Tree_insert(TreeNode * root, int v);
14  // search a value in a binary search tree starting
15  // with root, return the node whose value is v,
16  // or NULL if no such node exists
17  TreeNode * Tree_search(TreeNode * root, int v);
18  // delete the node whose value is v in a binary search
19  // tree starting with root, return the root of the
20  // remaining tree, or NULL if the tree is empty
21  TreeNode * Tree_delete(TreeNode * root, int v);
22  // print the values stored in the binary search tree
23  void Tree_print(TreeNode * root);
24  // delete every node
25  void Tree_destroy(TreeNode * root);
26  #endif
```

A binary search tree has similar functionality to a linked list. For example, both structures support insert, search, and delete. The differences are the *internal organization* and the efficiency of these operations. Note that a linked list can be considered a special case of a binary tree where every node uses only one link, and the other link is always NULL.

20.2   Inserting Data into a Binary Search Tree

As in the chapter on linked lists, we will present the three views of a binary search tree. Fig. 20.2 illustrates an empty binary tree (in three ways). Remember that the starting point of a binary tree is called root instead of head. Fig. 20.3 creates the first tree TreeNode. It is better to create a function Tree_insert than write these three statements over and over again. (Remember, DRY code means Don't Repeat Yourself.)

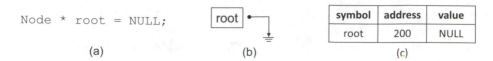

FIGURE 20.2: An empty tree has one pointer called `root` and its value is NULL; `root` is a pointer and it is not a tree node.

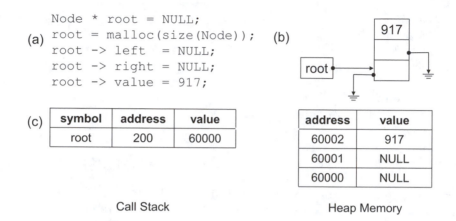

FIGURE 20.3: A binary tree with only one tree node. Both `left` and `right` are NULL. This node is called the root because it has no parent. It is also a leaf node because it has no children.

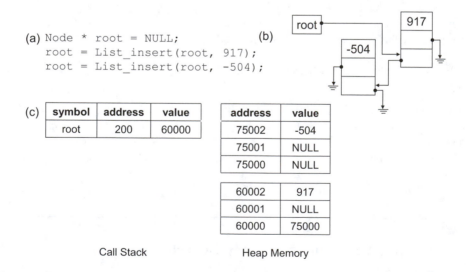

FIGURE 20.4: A binary tree with two nodes. The node with value 917 remains the root. It is no longer a leaf node because it has one child. The node with value −504 is a leaf node because it has no children.

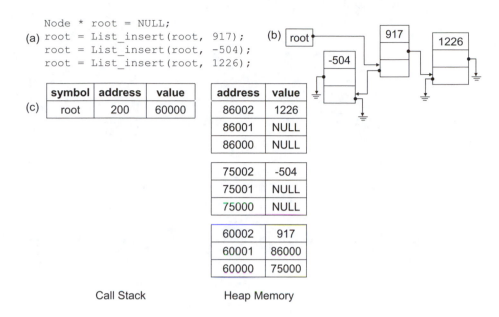

FIGURE 20.5: A binary tree with three nodes.

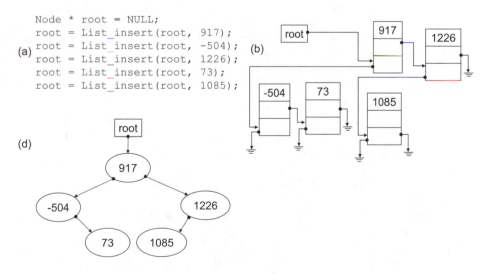

FIGURE 20.6: A binary tree with five tree nodes. A new view (d) simplifies the representation of the tree.

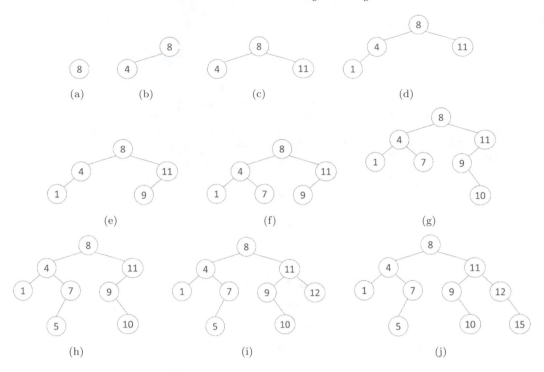

FIGURE 20.7: Insert values 8, 4, 11, 1, 9, 7, 10, 5, 12, 15.

Fig. 20.4 shows the tree after inserting two nodes. Since -504 is smaller than 917, the second node is inserted to the left of the first node. This is an essential property of binary search trees. Also, note that the **root**'s value (the address of the root node) does not change after inserting the first node. In this example, the value remains 60000.

Fig. 20.5 shows that another tree node is inserted. The value is 1226 and it is larger than 917. Thus, it is inserted to the right side of the first node. Fig. 20.6 shows a tree with five tree nodes. The second view in (b) quickly becomes complicated as more nodes are inserted. The memory view is also getting quite long. Thus, a different representation is more convenient, as shown in Fig. 20.6 (d). In this view, each tree node is represented as an oval. Note that "tree"s are drawn upside down, i.e., the root is at the top. This is different from the trees seen in forests.

The values -504 and 73 are smaller than the value at **root**, so both tree nodes are at the left side of **root**. Because 73 is larger than -504, 73 is at the right side of -504. Binary search tree has an important property: For any tree node whose value is **val**, all tree nodes on the left side have values smaller than **val**. Furthermore, all tree nodes on the right side have values larger than **val**. Fig. 20.7 shows a binary search as values are inserted. The first inserted value is the tree's root.

The following code listing gives an implementation **Tree_insert**, as well as an auxiliary function **TreeNode_construct**. It is **static** because it should not be called by any function outside this file. When inserting a new value into a binary search tree, a new leaf node is created. That means that the new node never has any children. **Tree_insert** is similar to the insert function in Section 19.1, where a linked list is used as a queue, and the newly created node is placed at the end.

```
1  // treeinsert.c
2  #include "tree.h"
```

```
3   #include <stdlib.h>
4   static TreeNode * TreeNode_construct(int val)
5   {
6       TreeNode * tn;
7       tn = malloc(sizeof(TreeNode));
8       tn -> left = NULL;
9       tn -> right = NULL;
10      tn -> value = val;
11      return tn;
12  }
13
14  TreeNode * Tree_insert(TreeNode * tn, int val)
15  {
16      if (tn == NULL)
17          {
18              // empty, create a node
19              return TreeNode_construct(val);
20          }
21      // not empty
22      if (val == (tn -> value))
23          {
24              // do not insert the same value
25              return tn;
26          }
27      if (val < (tn -> value))
28          {
29              tn -> left = Tree_insert(tn -> left, val);
30          }
31      else
32          {
33              tn -> right = Tree_insert(tn -> right, val);
34          }
35      return tn;
36  }
```

20.3 Searching a Binary Search Tree

To find whether a given number is stored in a binary search tree, the search function compares the number with the value stored at the root. If the two values are the same, then we know that the value is stored in the tree. If the number is greater than the value stored at the root, then it is impossible to find the value on the left side of the tree. If the number is smaller than the value stored at the root, then it is impossible to find the value on the right side of the tree. This property is applied recursively until either (1) there is nothing to search or (2) it is found. This is precisely why a binary search tree is called a *binary - search - tree*: It is a tree that naturally supports searches. It is called binary search because in each step, either the left subtree or the right subtree is discarded. In general, searching binary search trees is far more efficient than searching linked lists. It is most efficient when the left side and the right side of each node have the same number of nodes. In this case, half of the search space is discarded after each comparison, because we no longer need to consider half of the nodes in the tree. The following shows how to implement `Tree_search`.

```c
// treesearch.c
#include "tree.h"
TreeNode * Tree_search(TreeNode * tn, int val)
{
  if (tn == NULL)
    {
      // cannot find
      return NULL;
    }
  if (val == (tn -> value))
    {
      // found
      return tn;
    }
  if (val < (tn -> value))
    {
      // search the left side
      return Tree_search(tn -> left, val);
    }
  return Tree_search(tn -> right, val);
}
```

Note the similarities to the binary search over an array as described in Section 15.1. A binary search tree is more flexible than a sorted array because a binary search tree supports efficient insertion and deletion.

When I teach binary search trees, I always get this question: Why do we use binary search trees (two links per node)? Why don't we use ternary search trees (three links)? Or quaternary search trees (4 links)? Earlier, I said the main problem of linked lists (one link per node) is that finding a node needs to visit many nodes. Do binary search trees solve this problem? Why?

There is a fundamental difference between one and two. For any positive number n, it is possible to find a number k (maybe negative or irrational) such that 2^k is n. For example, if n is 0.5, k is -1. If n is 3.7, k is approximately 1.8875. If n is 191.6, k is approximately 7.5819. In contrast, one does not have this property. For any number m, 1^m is still one. What does this mean? It is possible to accomplish something by using two but it cannot be accomplished by using one. The most important difference between linked lists and binary trees is that the latter may discard large amounts of data very quickly. This is impossible if only one link is used. For the same positive number n, it is possible to find another number p such that 3^p is n. Thus, two can do what three can do and vice versa. Moving from one link (linked list) to two links (binary tree) is a fundamental improvement. However, moving from two links to three (or four) links is not a fundamental improvement. Ternary search trees can be better in some scenarios but there is no fundamental advantage.

20.4   Printing a Binary Tree

`Tree_print` can be implemented in three characteristically different ways. In each case, the function has three steps:

(1) Visiting the node's left side (subtree).
(2) Visiting the node's right side.
(3) Printing the node's value.

Visiting every node in a tree is also called *traversing* the tree. Every node is visited once, and only once. There are $3! = 6$ ways to order these three steps but (1) usually precedes (2). Thus, the three ways to implement `Tree_print` are:

- Pre-order traversal.   The three steps are ordered as $(3) \rightarrow (1) \rightarrow (2)$.
- In-order traversal.   The three steps are ordered as $(1) \rightarrow (3) \rightarrow (2)$.
  For a binary search tree, in-order will print the values in the ascending order.
- Post-order traversal.   The three steps are ordered as $(1) \rightarrow (2) \rightarrow (3)$.

It is important to understand these three traversal methods, because each one is useful in different circumstances, as will become apparent later in this book. The code listing below shows an example of printing a tree using pre-order, in-order, and post-order traversals.

```c
// treeprint.c
#include "tree.h"
static void TreeNode_print(TreeNode *tn)
{
   printf("%d ",tn -> value);
}

static void Tree_printPreorder(TreeNode *tn)
{
   if (tn == NULL)
     {
        return;
     }
   TreeNode_print(tn);
   Tree_printPreorder(tn -> left);
   Tree_printPreorder(tn -> right);
}

static void Tree_printInorder(TreeNode *tn)
{
   if (tn == NULL)
     {
        return;
     }
   Tree_printInorder(tn -> left);
   TreeNode_print(tn);
   Tree_printInorder(tn -> right);
}

static void Tree_printPostorder(TreeNode *tn)
```

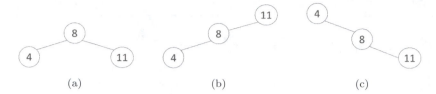

FIGURE 20.8: Three differently shaped binary search trees.

```
31  {
32    if (tn == NULL)
33      {
34        return;
35      }
36    Tree_printPostorder(tn -> left);
37    Tree_printPostorder(tn -> right);
38    TreeNode_print(tn);
39  }
40
41  void Tree_print(TreeNode *tn)
42  {
43    printf("\n\n=====Preorder=====\n");
44    Tree_printPreorder(tn);
45    printf("\n\n=====Inorder=====\n");
46    Tree_printInorder(tn);
47    printf("\n\n=====Postorder=====\n");
48    Tree_printPostorder(tn);
49    printf("\n\n");
50  }
```

Consider the different shapes of binary search trees in Fig. 20.8. How do the outputs differ for each of the three traversal methods?

These three trees store the same values. They have different shapes due to the order of insertion. In (a), 8 is inserted first. In (b), 11 is inserted first. In (c), 4 is inserted first. The outputs of the three traversal methods are shown below.

	(a)			(b)			(c)		
pre-order	8	4	11	11	8	4	4	8	11
in-order	4	8	11	4	8	11	4	8	11
post-order	4	11	8	4	8	11	11	8	4

The pattern in in-order traversal is the easiest to see—the values are always visited in the ascending order. In other words, this is a method of traversing the values in a sorted ordering. Hence the name *in-order* traversal. One consequence of this is that in-order traversal has the same outputs for the three differently shaped trees. Thus in-order traversal cannot distinguish between different shapes of trees. In contrast, pre-order and post-order traversals *do* distinguish the different shapes. If we want to describe the shape of a tree, then in-order will not work. Pre-order and post-order traversals make this possible.

What are the outputs when printing with different traversal methods on the trees shown in Fig. 20.9?

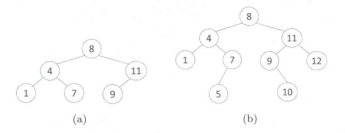

FIGURE 20.9: Examples of binary search trees.

	(a)						(b)								
pre-order	8	4	1	7	11	9	8	4	1	7	5	11	9	10	12
in-order	1	4	7	8	9	11	1	4	5	7	8	9	10	11	12
post-order	1	7	4	9	11	8	1	5	7	4	10	9	12	11	8

Answering this question helps visualize the different traversal techniques. To write the output of a pre-order traversal for (b), write the value of the root first:

$$8$$

It is followed by the outputs of the left subtree and then the right subtree.

8 | pre-order of left subtree | pre-order of right subtree |

The pre-order traversal of the left subtree starts with 4. The pre-order traversal of 4's left subtree is 1 and the pre-order traversal of 4's right subtree is 7 5.

The pre-order traversal of the right subtree starts with 11. The pre-order traversal of 11's left subtree is 9 10 and the pre-order traversal of 11's right subtree is 12.

Thus, the output is

8 | 4 1 7 5 | 11 9 10 12

20.5 Deleting from a Binary Search Tree

Deleting a node from a binary search tree is more complex than inserting because insertion adds only leaf nodes. Deleting a non-leaf node must maintain the tree's ordering property. When deleting a node, there are three different scenarios, as shown in Fig. 20.10.

1. If the node has no children, then release the memory occupied by this node. The pointer that originally points to this child is set to NULL. Fig. 20.10 (b) illustrates this scenario.

2. If the node has only one child, then the node's parent points to the node's only child and releases the memory occupied by the node. Fig. 20.10 (c) illustrates this scenario.

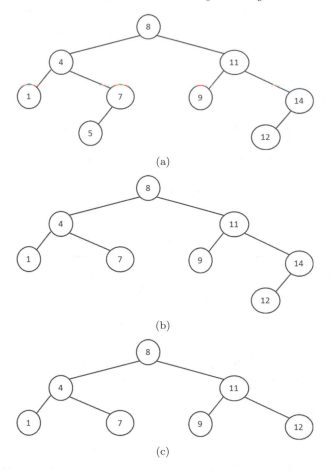

FIGURE 20.10: (a) The original binary search tree. (b) Deleting the node "5". The node is a leaf node (has no children). This is the first case. The left child of node "7" becomes NULL. (c) Deleting the node "14". This node has one child. This is the second case. The parent of "14" points to the only child of "14", i.e., "12".

3. If the node has two children, then find this node's immediate successor. The immediate successor is the node that appears immediately after this node in an in-order traversal. The successor must be on the right side of the node. Exchange the values of the node with its immediate successor. Then delete the successor. Fig. 20.11 (a) and (b) illustrates this scenario. Note that the successor cannot not have the left child. Why?

Below is a sample implementation of the delete function. Lines 39–43 finds **tn**'s immediate successor. The immediate successor is at the right side of **tn** and hence **su** starts with **tn -> right**. The immediate successor must also be the leftmost node on **tn**'s right side. The immediate successor cannot have a left child. Otherwise it would not be the immediate successor. Note that the immediate successor may have the right child. It is also possible to use the immediate predecessor but this book uses the successor.

```
1  // treedelete.c
2  #include "tree.h"
3  #include <stdlib.h>
4  TreeNode * Tree_delete(TreeNode * tn, int val)
```

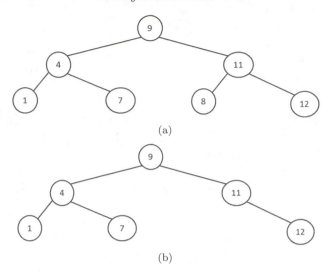

(a)

(b)

FIGURE 20.11: (a) The node "8" has two children. This is the third case. Exchange the values of this node and its successor. The tree temporarily loses its ordering property. (b) Deleting the node "8" restores the property of the binary search tree.

```
5   {
6      if (tn == NULL) { return NULL; }
7      if (val < (tn -> value))
8         {
9            tn -> left = Tree_delete(tn -> left, val);
10           return tn;
11        }
12     if (val > (tn -> value))
13        {
14           tn -> right = Tree_delete(tn -> right, val);
15           return tn;
16        }
17     // v is the same as tn -> value
18     if (((tn -> left) == NULL) && ((tn -> right) == NULL))
19        {
20           // tn has no child
21           free (tn);
22           return NULL;
23        }
24     if ((tn -> left) == NULL)
25        {
26           // tn -> right must not be NULL
27           TreeNode * rc = tn -> right;
28           free (tn);
29           return rc;
30        }
31     if ((tn -> right) == NULL)
32        {
33           // tn -> left must not be NULL
```

```
34        TreeNode * lc = tn ->  left;
35        free (tn);
36        return lc;
37      }
38    // tn have two children
39    // find the immediate successor
40    TreeNode * su = tn ->  right; // su must not be NULL
41    while ((su -> left) != NULL)
42      {
43        su = su -> left;
44      }
45    // su is tn's immediate successor
46    // swap their values
47    tn ->  value = su -> value;
48    su -> value = val;
49    // delete su
50    tn ->  right = Tree_delete(tn ->  right , val);
51    return tn;
52  }
```

After swapping the values, Fig. 20.11 (a) is temporarily not a binary search tree. This is because the value "8" is now on the right side of "9", a violation of the binary search tree's properties. When "8" is deleted, then the tree becomes a binary search tree again.

A common mistake at line 49 is calling `Tree_delete(tn, val)`. This is wrong because "8" is smaller than "9". Using `Tree_delete(tn, val)` causes the function to search for (and attempt to delete) "8" from the left side of "9". Since "8" is not on the left side, the function will fail to do anything. If nothing is deleted, the function returns the root `tn` and this line becomes `tn -> right = tn`. A node that is its own parent creates many problems and furthermore all nodes to the right side ("8", "11", and "12") are lost.

Another common mistake is to write `while (su != NULL)` at line 40. The `while` loop will continue until `su` is `NULL`, and the program will have segmentation fault at line 46 when it attempts to read `su -> value`.

20.6   Destroying a Binary Search Tree

The `Tree_destroy` function destroys the whole tree by releasing the memory occupied by all the tree nodes.

```
1   // treedestroy.c
2   #include "tree.h"
3   #include <stdlib.h>
4   void Tree_destroy(TreeNode * n)
5   {
6     if (n == NULL)
7       {
8         return;
9       }
10    Tree_destroy(n -> left);
11    Tree_destroy(n -> right);
```

```
12    free(n);
13  }
```

Note that every node must be destroyed once, and only once. Thus it is necessary to traverse the tree. Also note that both `left` and `right` must be destroyed before this tree node's memory is released. Can you tell what type of traversal this is?

20.7 main

Below is a `main` function that inserts and deletes random values into a binary search tree:

```
1   // main.c
2   #include "tree.h"
3   #include <time.h>
4   #include <stdlib.h>
5   #include <stdio.h>
6   int main(int argc, char * argv[])
7   {
8       TreeNode * root = NULL;
9       int num = 0;
10      int iter;
11      unsigned int seed = time(NULL);
12      seed = 0;
13      srand(seed);
14      if (argc >= 2)
15          {
16              num = (int) strtol(argv[1], NULL, 10);
17          }
18      if (num < 8)
19          {
20              num = 8;
21          }
22      int * array = malloc(sizeof(int) * num);
23      for (iter = 0; iter < num; iter ++)
24          {
25              array[iter] = rand() % 10000;
26          }
27      for (iter = 0; iter < num; iter ++)
28          {
29              int val = array[iter];
30              printf("insert %d\n", val);
31              root = Tree_insert(root, val);
32              Tree_print(root);
33          }
34      for (iter = 0; iter < num; iter ++)
35          {
36              int index = rand() % (2 * num);
37              if (index < num)
```

```
38          {
39              int val = array[index];
40              printf("delete %d\n", val);
41              root = Tree_delete(root, val);
42              Tree_print(root);
43          }
44      }
45      Tree_destroy(root);
46      free (array);
47      return EXIT_SUCCESS;
48  }
```

20.8 Makefile

The following listing is an example `Makefile` for compiling and running the code under valgrind.

```
1  CFLAGS = -g -Wall -Wshadow
2  GCC = gcc $(CFLAGS)
3  SRCS = treemain.c treesearch.c treedestroy.c treeinsert.c
4  SRCS += treeprint.c treedelete.c
5  OBJS = $(SRCS:%.c=%.o)
6
7  tree: $(OBJS)
8          $(GCC) $(OBJS) -o tree
9
10 memory: tree
11          valgrind --leak-check=yes --verbose ./tree 10
12
13 .c.o:
14          $(GCC) $(CFLAGS) -c $*.c
15
16 clean:
17          rm -f *.o a.out tree
```

20.9 Counting the Different Shapes of a Binary Tree

How many unique shapes can a binary tree with n nodes possibly have? This is the definition of shapes. Two binary trees have the same shape if each node has the same number of left offsprings and the same number of right offsprings. This rule is applied recursively until reaching leaf nodes. Fig. 20.12 shows the different shapes of trees with two or three nodes. Table 20.1 gives the number of uniquely shaped binary trees with 1 through 10 nodes.

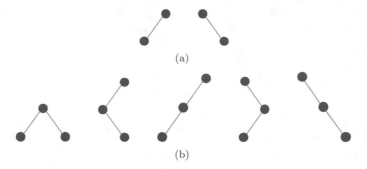

(a)

(b)

FIGURE 20.12: (a) There are two uniquely shaped binary trees with 2 nodes. (b) There are five uniquely shaped binary trees with 3 nodes.

n	1	2	3	4	5	6	7	8	9	10
number of shapes	1	2	5	14	42	132	429	1430	4862	16796

TABLE 20.1: The numbers of shapes for binary trees of different sizes.

Suppose there are $f(n)$ shapes for a binary tree with n nodes. First note that by observation we can tell that $f(1) = 1$ and $f(2) = 2$ We can use this as a base case for a recursive function.

If there are k nodes on the left side of the root node, then there must be $n - k - 1$ nodes on the right side or the root node. Here k can be 0, 1, 2, ..., $n - 1$. By definition, the left subtree has $f(k)$ possible shapes and the right side has $f(n - k - 1)$ possible shapes. The shapes on the two sides are independent of each other. This means that for every possible shape in the left subtree, we count every shape in the right subtree. Thus, if the left subtree has k nodes, then the total possible number of shapes is: $f(k) \times f(n - k - 1)$. The value of k is between 0 and $n - 1$ nodes. The total number of shapes is the sum of all the different possible values of k.

$$f(n) = \sum_{k=0}^{n-1} f(k) \times f(n - k - 1) \tag{20.1}$$

Using recursion is easier because we can assume that simpler (smaller) cases have already been solved. This formula gives the *Catalan numbers* in Section 15.4. To prove the equivalence, let us consider the six possible permutations of 1, 2, 3:

1. $< 1, 2, 3 >$
2. $< 1, 3, 2 >$
3. $< 2, 1, 3 >$
4. $< 2, 3, 1 >$
5. $< 3, 1, 2 >$
6. $< 3, 2, 1 >$

Among these six permutations, $< 2, 3, 1 >$ is not stack sortable as shown in Section 15.4. Thus, five permutations are stack sortable. Next, consider binary search trees that store the three numbers.

It is not possible to have $< 2, 3, 1 >$ as the result of pre-order traversal of a binary search tree that stores 1, 2, and 3. This is not a coincidence. Suppose $s(n)$ is the number of possible stack-sortable permutations of 1, 2, 3, ..., n. It turns out $s(n)$ is the *Catalan*

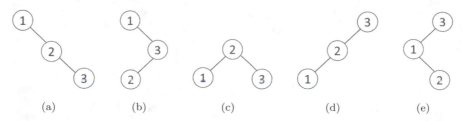

FIGURE 20.13: Five different shapes for the pre-order traversals of binary search trees storing 1, 2, and 3. (a) $< 1, 2, 3 >$, (b) $< 1, 3, 2 >$, (c) $< 2, 1, 3 >$, (d) $< 3, 2, 1 >$, (e) $< 3, 1, 2 >$.

numbers as well. As illustrated by the example above, $s(n) \leq n!$ because there are $n!$ possible permutations of 1, 2,..., n. If $n > 2$, $s(n)$ must be smaller than $n!$. We have already seen that $s(3) = 5 \leq 3! = 6$

Below is a proof that $s(n)$ defines the sequence of *Catalan numbers*. Suppose a sequence of numbers $< a_1, a_2, a_3, ...a_n >$ is a particular permutation of 1, 2, ..., n and the sequence is stack-sortable. Any prefix $< a_1, a_2, a_3, ...a_k >$, $k < n$ must be stack-sortable. Suppose a_i $(1 \leq i \leq n)$ is n (the largest number in the entire sequence). Then the sequence $< a_1, a_2, a_3, ...a_n >$ can be divided into three parts:

$$< a_1, a_2, ..., a_{i-1} > \quad a_i = n \quad < a_{i+1}, a_{i+2}, ..., a_n >$$

What is the condition that makes a sequence stack-sortable? Section 15.4 explained that $\max(a_1, a_2, ..., a_{i-1})$ must be smaller than $\min(a_{i+1}, a_{i+2}, ..., a_n)$. Therefore, the first sequence must be a permutation of 1, 2, ..., $i - 1$ and the second sequence must be a permutation of i, $i + 1$, ..., $n - 1$. Moreover, the two sequences $< a_1, a_2, ..., a_{i-1} >$ and $< a_{i+1}, a_{i+2}, ..., a_n >$ must also be stack-sortable; otherwise, the entire sequence cannot be stack-sortable. Therefore the entire sequence includes two stack-sortable sequences divided by $a_i = n$. By definition, there are $s(i - 1)$ stack-sortable permutations of 1, 2, 3, ..., $i - 1$. There are $s(n - i)$ stack-sortable permutations of i, ..., $n - 1$. The permutations in these two sequences are independent so there are $s(i - 1) \times s(n - i)$ possible permutations of the two sequences. The value of i is between 1 and n. When i is 1, the first value in the sequence is n and this corresponds to the tree in which the root has no left child. When i is n, the last value is n and this corresponds to the tree in which the root has no right child. Thus, the total number of stack-sortable permutations is:

$$s(n) = \sum_{i=1}^{n} s(i - 1) \times s(n - i) = \sum_{i=0}^{n-1} s(i) \times s(n - i - 1). \tag{20.2}$$

This is the Catalan number.

Chapter 21

Parallel Programming Using Threads

Multi-core processors are everywhere: high-end desktops have multiple cores. Even mobile phones also have multi-core chips. It has become difficult to make individual cores faster, but adding more cores is easier. More cores do not necessarily mean faster programs, because many factors affect a computer's performance. The number of cores is one factor, but the software is also important. If a program does not take advantage of multiple cores, then it may as well be running on a single core processor. If a program is written for multiple cores, then the program can be referred to as a *parallel program*. If a program is not written for multiple cores, then it is called a *sequential program*. All programs so far in this book are sequential programs. This chapter provides an introduction to writing parallel programs using *threads*.

21.1   Parallel Programming

There are many ways to write parallel programs. A parallel program performs multiple operations at the same time. Parallel programs are often classified into three categories:

1. SIMD: single instruction, multiple data. This is commonly used in signal processing, such as manipulating data in arrays. When adding two arrays, the same instruction (addition) is applied to all array elements at once.

2. MISD: multiple instructions, single data. Different operations are performed on the same piece of data. As an example, census data are widely studied for various purposes. The same data may be processed simultaneously by different threads of execution, in order to find, for example, the average and median age of a population at once.

3. MIMD: multiple instructions, multiple data. This is the most general case. Different operations are performed on different pieces of data.

A sequential program is SISD: At any moment, the program is performing one operation on one piece of data.

21.2   Multi-Tasking

If parallel programs take advantage of multiple cores, then does this mean that parallel programs cannot run on single-core processors? Yes, they can. The operating system is between the program and the cores, and provides an abstraction so that programs do not need to be too concerned about the number of cores. For example, how many computer programs are running simultaneously on your computer right now? There could be a web browser, a text editor, a music player, instant messaging, and many other programs, including various system services.

How many cores does your computer have? One? Two? Four? It is the operating system that makes sure everything works—every program gets a turn to execute some of its code in a timely fashion. Specifically, the operating system gives each program a short time interval (usually several milliseconds) in which one or several cores execute the program and the program makes some progress. After this interval, the operating system suspends the program, and then allows another program to run. By giving every program a short time interval to make some progress, the operating system gives the user the impression that every program makes progress. If a processor has only one core, then only one program can run at any given moment. This is called *multi-tasking* and is analogous to several children sharing a slide in a playground. Even though only one person can slide down at any moment (for safety), everyone gets a turn, and everyone enjoys the slide.

In order to improve the overall performance, the operating system may change the lengths of the time intervals depending on what particular programs are doing. For example, when a program wants to read data from a file, this program has to wait for the disk to get the data. During this waiting period, the operating system shortens the program's time interval so that another program can use the processor. If a program waits for a user to enter something on the keyboard, then the operating system also shortens the program's time interval while the program is waiting for the user's input. Shortened intervals also occur when a program is waiting on data from the network. Because the lengths of the time intervals can change, it is difficult to predict exactly which program is executing at any given moment of time.

21.3   POSIX Threads

Threading is one way to write parallel programs. Each thread in a program may execute the code in parallel. A sequential program can be thought of as having a single thread of execution. Parallel programs have two or more threads. This book uses *POSIX* threads, also called *pthread*. POSIX stands for Portable Operating System Interface and it is a standard that most operating systems support.

A typical multi-thread program starts with only one thread, called the main thread or the first thread. The main thread creates one or several threads by calling the `pthread_create` function. This function requires four arguments:

1. The first argument is an address of a structure called `pthread_t`. This is a structure defined in `pthread.h` and it stores information about the newly created thread. You do not need to know precisely what information the pthread library stores in `pthread_t`. Pthreads needs to manage *some* data on each thread of execution, and this data is

stored in **pthread_t**. This is similar to the **FILE** pointer: it stores some information about an opened file.

2. The second argument is the address of a structure called **pthread_attr_t**. This specifies optional attributes for initializing a thread. If this argument is **NULL**, the thread is initialized with default values.

3. The third argument is the name of a function. Section 9.2 explains how to use a function as an argument to another function (**qsort**). There are some differences here. For **pthread_create**, the function's return type must be **void*** and the function takes precisely one argument. For **qsort**, it expects a function that returns an integer and the function takes two pointers as arguments.

4. The fourth argument is the argument passed to the function specified in the third argument.

After calling **pthread_create**, a new thread (the second thread) is created and executes the function specified in the third argument. The main thread and the new thread may now run simultaneously (if there are two or more cores). If the program equally divides its tasks between the first thread and the second thread, then the program can be about twice as fast. On a single core machine, the two threads take turns and there is no performance improvement.

The main thread should call **pthread_join** on the second thread before terminating. This function causes the calling (main) thread to wait until another thread terminates. After the call to **pthread_join**, there will only be one thread executing. If the main thread does not wait for the second thread to finish, and the main thread terminates, then the second thread will also be terminated. Below is a code listing for a simple program creating one thread:

```c
// thread1.c
#include <pthread.h>
#include <stdio.h>
#include <stdlib.h>
void * printHello(void *arg)
{
  int* intptr = (int *) arg;
  int val = * intptr;
  printf("Hello World! arg = %d\n", val);
  return NULL;
}
int main (int argc, char *argv[])
{
  pthread_t second;
  int rtv; // return value of pthread_create
  int arg = 12345;
  rtv = pthread_create(& second, NULL,
                       printHello, (void *) & arg);
  if (rtv != 0)
    {
      printf("ERROR; pthread_create() returns %d\n", rtv);
      return EXIT_FAILURE;
    }
  rtv = pthread_join(second, NULL);
  if (rtv != 0)
    {
```

```
27          printf("ERROR;␣pthread_join()␣returns␣%d\n", rtv);
28          return EXIT_FAILURE;
29        }
30      return EXIT_SUCCESS;
31    }
```

To compile this file into an executable program, we need to add `-lpthread` at the end of the `gcc` command in this way:

$ gcc -g -Wall -Wshadow thread1.c -o thread1 -lpthread

This will link the `pthread` library to the executable program. When the program runs, it prints the following output:

Hello World! arg = 12345

How does this program work? Let's start at line 17 where `pthread_create` is called. The first argument is the address of a `pthread_t` object created at line 14. The second argument is `NULL`, and thus the thread is initialized with the default attributes. The third argument is `printHello`. This is the address of the `printHello` function and pthread will use this address to execute `printHello` of lines 4 to 10. The function's return type must be `void *`. The function must take one and only one argument and the type must be `void *`. The fourth argument to `pthread_create` is the argument that pthreads will in turn pass to `printHello` when it calls this function. In this case, it is the address of an integer. If `pthread_create` succeeds, it returns zero. This indicates that the thread is created normally. There are now two parallel threads in the program.

Inside `printHello`, the argument is cast to the correct type. Since line 18 uses the address of an integer, the correct type is `int *`. Line 7 dereferences the address to get the integer value. The `printHello` has no useful information to return so it returns `NULL` at line 9. The main thread calls `pthread_join` to wait for the second thread to finish executing before `main` terminates. If `pthread_join` is not called, the main thread may terminate and destroy the second thread before it gets a chance to print anything to the terminal.

21.4   Subset Sum

The subset sum problem is commonly encountered when studying cryptography. This problem can be defined in different ways. Here is one definition. Consider a positive integer k and a set of positive integers $\mathbb{A} = \{a_1, a_2, ..., a_n\}$. Is it possible to find a subset $\mathbb{B} = \{b_1, b_2, ..., b_m\} \subset \mathbb{A}$ such that $k = b_1 + b_2 + ... + b_m$? Note that $\mathbb{B}$ cannot be the empty set because $k > 0$. Since $\mathbb{B}$ is a subset of $\mathbb{A}$, m must be less than or equal to n.

Consider the following example: $\mathbb{A} = \{19, 10, 2, 9, 8\}$ and $k = 20$. We have $k = 10+2+8$, and thus there is a solution. Consider another example, $\mathbb{A} = \{3, 5, 1, 2, 6\}$ and $k = 21$. In this case, the sum of all elements in $\mathbb{A}$ is $3 + 5 + 1 + 2 + 6 = 17$, which is smaller than k. Hence there is no solution. Sometimes multiple solutions are possible. For example, if $\mathbb{A} = \{1, 2, 3, 4, 5\}$ and k is 7. Here we have the solutions: $\{1, 2, 4\}$, $\{3, 4\}$, and $\{2, 5\}$.

This problem asks you to write a program that counts the number of subsets whose sum equals to the value of k. For a set of n elements, there are 2^n subsets. This program restricts the size of sets to 31 so that the number of subsets does not exceed 2^{31}.

21.4.1 Generate Test Cases

As always, it is good practice to think about testing a program before it is written. In this case we can write a program that generates test cases. This generator program takes three command-line arguments:

- `argv[1]` is the number of elements. For this program, the value must be between 3 and 31.
- `argv[2]` is "1" if the set is valid, and "0" if the set is invalid. A valid set must contain distinct positive integers. If an element is zero or negative, then the set is invalid. If two or more elements have the same value, then the set is also invalid.
- `argv[3]` is "1" if there is a solution for the test case. It is "0" if there is no solution.

The program first generates an array of positive integers. The values are guaranteed to be distinct because each element is larger than the previous element. If we want to generate an invalid set, then the program chooses one of the two possibilities: Either it makes an element zero or negative, or it makes two elements have the same value. If the set is invalid, then the value of k is irrelevant and the generator chooses a random number for k.

For a valid set with a solution, k is the sum of some elements. Each element has a one-third chance of being part of the sum equal to k. It is possible that no element is added. In this case, k will be zero and the generator program corrects this situation by setting k to the first element. If the set is valid but the generator creates a test case with no solution, then k is greater than the sum of all elements. The output or the generator program prints k first, and then the set elements one after another. The complete generator program is shown below:

```c
// testgen.c
#include <stdio.h>
#include <stdlib.h>
#include <time.h>
// command line arguments
//      argv[1]: the number of elements
//               must be between 3 and 31
//      argv[2]: "1" the array is valid
//               "0" the array is invalid
//      argv[3]: "1" if there is a solution
//               "0" if there is no solution
void swap(int * a, int * b)
{
    int t = * a;
    * a = * b;
    * b = t;
}
void shuffleArray(int * arr, int num)
{
    int ind1, ind2, ind3;
    for (ind1 = 0; ind1 < 1000; ind1 ++)
    {
        ind2 = rand() % num;
        ind3 = rand() % num;
        swap(& arr[ind2], & arr[ind3]);
    }
}
void printArray(int * arr, int num, int kval)
```

```
29   {
30      printf("%d\n", kval);
31      int ind;
32      for (ind = 0; ind < num; ind ++)
33         {
34            printf("%d\n", arr[ind]);
35         }
36   }
37   int main(int argc, char ** argv)
38   {
39      if (argc < 4)
40         {
41            return EXIT_FAILURE;
42         }
43      int numInt  = (int) strtol(argv[1], NULL, 10);
44      int isValid = (int) strtol(argv[2], NULL, 10);
45      int hasSol  = (int) strtol(argv[3], NULL, 10);
46      if ((numInt < 3) || (numInt > 31))
47         {
48            return EXIT_FAILURE;
49         }
50      if ((hasSol != 0) && (hasSol != 1))
51         {
52            return EXIT_FAILURE;
53         }
54      if ((hasSol != 0) && (hasSol != 1))
55         {
56            return EXIT_FAILURE;
57         }
58      srand(time(NULL)); // set the seed
59      int kval = 0;
60      int * arr = malloc(sizeof(int) * numInt);
61      int ind;
62      // the array is increasing and all elements are distinct
63      arr[0] = rand() % 100;
64      for (ind = 1; ind < numInt; ind ++)
65         {
66            arr[ind] = arr[ind - 1] + (rand() % 10000) + 1;
67         }
68      if (isValid == 0)
69         {
70            if ((rand() % 2) == 0)
71               {
72                  // make two elements the same
73                  arr[numInt - 1] = arr[0];
74               }
75            else
76               {
77                  // make an element negative or zero
78                  arr[0] = - (rand() % 10000);
79               }
```

```
80        // kval irrelevant when the array is invalid
81        kval = rand() % 10000 + 1;
82      }
83    else
84      {
85        for (ind = 0; ind < numInt; ind ++)
86          {
87            if (hasSol == 0)
88              {
89                // kval > sum of all elements
90                kval += arr[ind] + 1;
91              }
92            else
93              {
94                if ((rand() % 3) == 1)
95                  {
96                    kval += arr[ind];
97                  }
98              }
99          }
100       if (kval == 0) // only if hasSol is 1
101         {
102           kval = arr[0];
103         }
104     }
105   shuffleArray(arr, numInt);
106   printArray(arr, numInt, kval);
107   free(arr);
108   return EXIT_SUCCESS;
109 }
```

It is important to understand the value of a test generator. Writing test generators is often necessary. Creating test cases by hand is really too much work. The main problem of hand-generated tests is that only a few cases can be produced. As a result, the tests often miss some important cases.

21.4.2   Sequential Solution

One obvious solution to the subset sum problem is to enumerate each subset of A and then check each to see if the sum of the elements is k. This will take exponential time since a set of size n has 2^n subsets. The number of possible subsets becomes really large. For example, a set of size 400 has 2^{400} subsets; this is more than the number of atoms in the observable universe.

There is no known "quick" way of solving the subset sum problem. In computer science, "quick" usually means that there is a polynomial-time algorithm that solves the problem. A polynomial-time algorithm is an algorithm whose execution time is bounded by a polynomial function of the input size. For example, if we are searching a linked list for a given value, then we may need to traverse the entire list. If the list has n elements (the input data) then the execution time of the search is bounded by a polynomial function of n. For a polynomial of degree p, the largest term is n^p. For any constant $p > 1$, the following statement is true:

$$\lim_{n \to \infty} \frac{2^n}{n^p} = \infty. \tag{21.1}$$

This means that the exponential function eventually grows faster than any polynomial. There is always a value of n such that 2^n is larger than n^p, no matter what p is. This can be proved by using the L'Hospital's Rule from calculus.

This section asks you to write a program that counts the number of subsets whose sums are equal to the given value k. Instead of finding a sophisticated algorithm, the section uses a simple solution that enumerates all subsets (excluding the empty set). The program must read the value of k and then the set's elements from a file. After reading the data from the file, the program checks whether the set is valid. The set is invalid if any element is zero or negative, or if two elements have the same value. If the set is invalid, then the program does not attempt to solve the subset sum problem.

If the set is valid, then the program generates all possible subsets of the given set. This program first calculates the number of possible subsets. If a set has n elements, then there are 2^n subsets including the empty set. If each subset is given a number, then the subsets are numbers between 0 and $2^n - 1$ inclusively. The empty set is not considered because $k \neq 0$, and thus we only need to consider the subsets labeled 1 to $2^n - 1$. Note that since each number corresponds to a subset, and we will check to total sum of the numbers in that subset, we have each number corresponding to a subset sum. The following table explains how the numbers are related to the subset sums:

Value	Sum
1	a_1
2	a_2
3	$a_1 + a_2$
4	a_3
5	$a_1 + a_3$
6	$a_2 + a_3$
7	$a_1 + a_2 + a_3$
8	a_4
$\vdots$	$\vdots$
$2^n - 1$	$a_1 + a_2 + a_3 + ... + a_n$

The test generator is restricted to at most 31 elements so that 2^n can fit in a four-byte integer. This following is a sample implementation of the sequential program as described above. First is the main function:

```
1   // main.c
2   #include <pthread.h>
3   #include <stdio.h>
4   #include <stdlib.h>
5   #include "subsetsum.h"
6   int main (int argc, char *argv[])
7   {
8     // read the data from a file
9     if (argc < 2)
10      {
11        printf("Need input file name\n");
12        return EXIT_FAILURE;
13      }
14    FILE * fptr = fopen(argv[1], "r");
```

```
15    if (fptr == NULL)
16      {
17        printf("fopen fail\n");
18        return EXIT_FAILURE;
19      }
20    int numInt = countInteger(fptr);
21    // go back to the beginning of the file
22    fseek (fptr, 0, SEEK_SET);
23    int kval; // the value equal to the sum
24    if (fscanf(fptr, "%d", & kval) != 1)
25      {
26        printf("fscanf error\n");
27        fclose(fptr);
28        return EXIT_FAILURE;
29      }
30    numInt --; // kval is not part of the set
31    int * setA = malloc(sizeof(int) * numInt);
32    int ind = 0;
33    for (ind = 0; ind < numInt; ind ++)
34      {
35        int aval;
36        if (fscanf(fptr, "%d", & aval) != 1)
37          {
38            printf("fscanf error\n");
39            fclose(fptr);
40            return EXIT_FAILURE;
41          }
42        setA[ind] = aval;
43      }
44    fclose (fptr);
45    if (isValidSet(setA, numInt) == 1)
46      {
47        printf("There are %d subsets whose sums are %d\n",
48               subsetSum(setA, numInt, kval), kval);
49      }
50    else
51      {
52        printf("Invalid set\n");
53      }
54    free(setA);
55    return EXIT_SUCCESS;
56 }
```

This **main** function calls several other functions that are declared in this header file.

```
1 // subsetsum.h
2 #ifndef SUBSETSUM_H
3 #define SUBSETSUM_H
4 #include <stdio.h>
5 int subsetEqual(int * setA, int sizeA, int kval,
6                 unsigned int code);
7 // return 1 if the subset expressed by the code sums to kval
```

```
8   // return 0 if the sum is different from kval
9   int subsetSum(int * setA, int sizeA, int kval);
10  // the number of subsets in setA equal
11  int isValidSet(int * setA, int sizeA);
12  // valid if elements are positive and distinct
13  // return 1 if valid, 0 if invalid
14  int countInteger(FILE * fptr);
15  // how many integers in a file
16  // fptr must not be NULL, checked by the caller
17  #endif
```

The functions `isValid` and `countInt` should be straightforward:

```
1   // isvalid.c
2   #include <stdio.h>
3   int isValidSet(int * setA, int sizeA)
4   // valid if every element is positive and distinct
5   // return 1 if valid, 0 if invalid
6   {
7     int ind1;
8     int ind2;
9     for (ind1 = 0; ind1 < sizeA; ind1 ++)
10      {
11        if (setA[ind1] <= 0)
12          {
13            return 0;
14          }
15        for (ind2 = ind1 + 1; ind2 < sizeA; ind2 ++)
16          {
17            if (setA[ind1] == setA[ind2])
18              {
19                return 0;
20              }
21          }
22      }
23    return 1;
24  }
```

```
1   // countint.c
2   #include <stdio.h>
3   int countInteger(FILE * fptr)
4   {
5     int numInt = 0; // how many integers
6     int value;
7     while (fscanf(fptr, "%d", & value) == 1)
8       {
9         numInt ++;
10      }
11    return numInt;
12  }
```

The function `subsetSum` counts the number of subsets:

```
1  // sequential.c
2  #include "subsetsum.h"
3  int subsetSum(int * setA, int sizeA, int kval)
4  {
5    unsigned int maxCode = 1;
6    unsigned int ind;
7    for (ind = 0; ind < sizeA; ind ++)
8      {
9        maxCode *= 2;
10     }
11   int total = 0;
12   for (ind = 1; ind < maxCode; ind ++)
13     {
14       total += subsetEqual(setA, sizeA, kval, ind);
15     }
16   return total;
17 }
```

The function `subsetEqual` determines whether a specific subset sums to the value of k:

```
1  // subsetequal.c
2  #include <stdio.h>
3  int subsetEqual(int * setA, int sizeA, int kval,
4                  unsigned int code)
5  {
6    int sum = 0;
7    int ind = 0;
8    unsigned int origcode = code;
9    while ((ind < sizeA) && (code > 0))
10     {
11       if ((code % 2) == 1)
12         {
13           sum += setA[ind];
14         }
15       ind ++;
16       code >>= 1;
17     }
18   if (sum == kval)
19     {
20       printf("equal: sum = %d, code = %X\n",
21              sum, origcode);
22       return 1;
23     }
24   return 0;
25 }
```

21.4.3   Multi-Threaded Solution

The sequential program can be parallelized in a variety of ways. We need to figure out how to distribute the work evenly across several threads. Each thread can be responsible for checking the sums of some of the subsets. To be more precise, suppose a set has n elements and t threads are used to solve the subset sum program (excluding the main thread). One solution to distribute the work is to have the first thread check the subsets between 1 and $\lfloor \frac{2^n}{t} \rfloor$. The second thread simultaneously checks the subsets between $\lfloor \frac{2^n}{t} \rfloor + 1$ and $2 \times \lfloor \frac{2^n}{t} \rfloor$. It is important to handle the last thread with caution. If t is not a factor of 2^n, then the program must ensure that the thread includes the last set (value is $2^n - 1$).

The new subsetSum function contains three steps:

1. Create an object as the argument to each thread. This object contains multiple attributes to a function. The attributes are put together into a single structure because a thread can take only one argument. In this case, each object specifies the range of subsets checked by the individual thread. The object includes (i) the range of the subsets to be examined, (ii) the set, (iii) the set's size, (iv) the value of k, and (v) the number of subsets whose sums equal to k. It is necessary to give each thread all relevant information because using global variables is strongly discouraged.

2. Create the threads. Each thread checks some subsets and computes the number of subsets whose sums equal to k.

3. The main thread waits for every thread to complete and then adds the number subsets that each thread reports.

The checkRange function is used by each thread, and is an argument of pthread_create. This is a SIMD program because the same function is used in every thread. Below is the code listing for the subsetSum function using threads:

```c
// threaddata.h
#ifndef THREADDATA_H
#define THREADDATA_H
typedef struct
{
  unsigned int minval;
  unsigned int maxval;
  int numSol;
  int * setA;
  int sizeA;
  int kval;
} ThreadData;
#endif
```

```c
// parallel.c
#include <pthread.h>
#include <stdio.h>
#include <stdlib.h>
#include "threaddata.h"
#include "subsetsum.h"
#define NUMBER_THREAD 16
void * checkRange(void * range)
{
  ThreadData * thd = (ThreadData *) range;
  unsigned int minval = thd -> minval;
  unsigned int maxval = thd -> maxval;
  // printf("minval = %d, maxval = %d\n", minval, maxval);
  unsigned int ind;
  // caution: need to use <= for max
  for (ind = minval; ind <= maxval; ind ++)
    {
```

```
18      thd -> numSol +=
19          subsetEqual(thd -> setA, thd -> sizeA,
20                      thd -> kval, ind);
21      }
22   return NULL;
23 }
24
25 int subsetSum(int * setA, int sizeA, int kval)
26 // This function does not allocate memory (malloc)
27 // No need to free memory if failure occurs
28 {
29
30   pthread_t tid[NUMBER_THREAD];
31   ThreadData thd[NUMBER_THREAD];
32   // set the values for the thread data
33   unsigned int maxCode = 1;
34   unsigned int ind;
35   for (ind = 0; ind < sizeA; ind ++)
36     {
37        maxCode *= 2;
38     }
39   int total = 0;
40   unsigned int minval = 1;
41   unsigned int size = maxCode / NUMBER_THREAD;
42   unsigned int maxval = size;
43   for (ind = 0; ind < NUMBER_THREAD - 1; ind ++)
44     {
45        thd[ind].minval = minval;
46        thd[ind].maxval = maxval;
47        thd[ind].numSol = 0;
48        thd[ind].setA = setA;
49        thd[ind].sizeA = sizeA;
50        thd[ind].kval = kval;
51        minval = maxval + 1;
52        maxval += size;
53     }
54   // ind should be NUMBER_THREAD - 1 now
55   // handle the last thread differently because
56   // maxCode may not be a multiple of NUMBER_THREAD
57   thd[ind].minval = minval;
58   thd[ind].maxval = maxCode - 1; // remember -1
59   thd[ind].numSol = 0;
60   thd[ind].setA = setA;
61   thd[ind].sizeA = sizeA;
62   thd[ind].kval = kval;
63
64   // create the threads
65   for (ind = 0; ind < NUMBER_THREAD; ind ++)
66     {
67        int rtv;
68        rtv = pthread_create(& tid[ind], NULL,
```

```
69                              checkRange, (void *) & thd[ind]);
70          if (rtv != 0)
71            {
72                printf("ERROR:_pthread_crate()_fail\n");
73            }
74        }
75
76      // wait for the threads to complete
77      for (ind = 0; ind < NUMBER_THREAD; ind ++)
78        {
79          int rtv;
80          rtv = pthread_join(tid[ind], NULL);
81          if (rtv != 0)
82            {
83                printf("ERROR;_pthread_join()_returns_%d\n", rtv);
84                return EXIT_FAILURE;
85            }
86          total += thd[ind].numSol;
87        }
88      return total;
89    }
```

There are a few details worth noting. First, the ranges checked by the threads must be mutually exclusive. If one subset is checked by two or more threads and this subset's sum happens to equal to k, then this subset is counted multiple times and the total is wrong. Second, the threads combined should check all subsets (excluding the empty set). Also, checkRange needs to be consistent with the ranges assigned in subsetSum. In particular, if checkRange uses <= maxval, then the maximum value checked by the last thread must be maxCode - 1, not maxCode. You may notice that the individual threads share some data. In each object, the attribute setA is a pointer to an array. This means that every thread uses the same piece of memory. This is acceptable because the threads do not modify the array. The other attributes are unique to each thread, because the object stores unshared attributes (the int and unsigned int data).

21.5   Interleaving the Execution of Threads

The threads in the subset sum program shared a common array setA. Being able to share memory between different threads is a characteristic of threaded programming; however, it can sometimes be problematic. In the subset sum case, the threads never modify the shared memory (i.e., setA), but only read the elements from the array. The only memory that the threads modify is the attribute numSol, and each thread has a unique copy of this variable. The main thread waits until all the threads are complete by calling pthread_join on each thread. Then the main thread adds the numSol values. The threads never intend to modify any piece of *shared* memory. What happens if threads share memory that may be read and written? The following listing is a simple and instructive example:

```
1  // outsync.c
2  #include <pthread.h>
3  #include <stdio.h>
```

```
4   #include <stdlib.h>
5   #define NUMBER_THREAD 16
6   void * threadfunc(void *arg)
7   {
8     int * intptr = (int *) arg;
9     while (1)
10      {
11        (* intptr) ++;
12        (* intptr) --;
13        if ((* intptr) != 0)
14          {
15            printf("value is %d\n", * intptr);
16            return NULL;
17          }
18      }
19    return NULL;
20  }
21
22  int main (int argc, char *argv[])
23  {
24    pthread_t tid[NUMBER_THREAD];
25    int rtv; // return value of pthread_create
26    int ind;
27    int arg = 0;
28    for (ind = 0; ind < NUMBER_THREAD; ind ++)
29      {
30        rtv = pthread_create(& tid[ind], NULL,
31                             threadfunc, (void *) & arg);
32        if (rtv != 0)
33          {
34            printf("pthread_create() fail %d\n", rtv);
35            return EXIT_FAILURE;
36          }
37      }
38    for (ind = 0; ind < NUMBER_THREAD; ind ++)
39      {
40        rtv = pthread_join(tid[ind], NULL);
41        if (rtv != 0)
42          {
43            printf("pthread_join() fail %d\n", rtv);
44            return EXIT_FAILURE;
45          }
46      }
47    return EXIT_SUCCESS;
48  }
```

This program creates some threads that share the address of the same integer variable (`arg` in main). Each thread increments and decrements the value stored at that address (i.e., the integer). If a thread finds that the value is not zero, then it prints a message and terminates. Otherwise the thread will continue indefinitely. Can the threads ever print the message? Will any thread return NULL and terminate? There is no good way to answer this question, because the execution of this program is unpredictable. When we executed this program three different times, the program printed three different values:

```
value is 1
value is -1
value is 0
```

How can this be possible? If a thread increments and decrements the value before checking, how can it be possible that the value is anything other than zero? It can be even more surprising when we see the output that includes:

```
value is 0
```

This makes no sense because the program should print the message only if the value is non-zero, based on the condition at line 12.

```
12  if ((* intptr) != 0)
```

The program prints the value only when `*intptr` is not zero. However, the program ends up printing zero. What is wrong with this program? To understand what this means, we must understand this statement: *the operating system may change the lengths of the time intervals*. The operating system gives each thread a short time interval to execute some code. If the program has multiple threads, then each thread gets some time intervals. Due to many reasons, the operating system may decide to suspend a thread (or a program) so that another thread (or another program) can run and make progress. There is no guarantee when a thread is suspended. The operating system needs to manage all programs and threads so that no single program or thread can occupy the processor for too long. If a processor has multiple cores, two or more threads may be executing simultaneously. It is possible that one thread is executing the machine instructions for line 10, while another thread is executing the machine instructions for line 12. The microsecond differences in what hundreds of different programs are doing at different times makes it impossible in general to predict what any given thread is doing at any given time.

Let us look deeper into how this relates to the program. How specifically does this make the value of `* intptr` anything other than zero after the increment and decrement operations? What happens when the program executes this statement?

```
10  (* intptr) ++;
```

Because `intptr` stores `arg`'s address, this statement increments the value stored in `arg`. To execute this statement, the computer must do the following:

1. Read the value of `arg`.
2. Increment the value.
3. Write the new value to `arg`.

Please note that `arg`'s value is changed only at the last step. During the first and the second steps, the value is stored in a temporary location (called *register*) inside the processor. Threads may share memory space but they do not share registers. The operating system may suspend a thread anywhere in these three steps. The following diagram shows one possible interleaving of the execution of two threads. In this diagram, time progresses downwards. We use - to indicate that a thread is currently suspended. If thread 1 is suspended right after `arg` increments, then the value is 1 when thread 2 reads it. As a result, when thread 2 checks the value, it is not zero and it prints the message. Table 21.1 explains why the program may print the value 1.

If we change the ordering, Table 21.2 shows why it is possible to see the value 0 printed. In this scenario, thread 2 is suspended after it checks `arg`'s value and it is one. When

thread 1	thread 2	arg's value
read arg	-	0
increment arg	-	0
write arg	-	1
-	read arg	1
-	increment arg	1
-	write arg	2
-	read arg	2
-	decrement arg	2
-	write arg	1
-	check arg's value	1
-	print arg's value	1

TABLE 21.1: Interleaving scenario 1.

thread 1	thread 2	arg's value
read arg	-	0
increment arg	-	0
write arg	-	1
-	read arg	1
-	increment arg	1
-	write arg	2
-	read arg	2
-	decrement arg	2
-	write arg	1
-	check arg's value	1
read arg	-	1
decrement arg	-	1
write arg	-	0
-	print arg's value	0

TABLE 21.2: Interleaving scenario 2.

thread 2 prints the value, it has already been changed to 0. Due to the subtle interleaving of the threads, it is possible that arg's value is nonzero when the condition is checked and is 0 when the value is printed.

Is it possible for the program to print 2? Yes. This is one scenario: Thread 1 increments and decrements arg and arg is 0 when it is suspended just before the if statement. The thread enters the if statement, but is suspended before it does any printing. Now thread 2 increments arg and is then suspended. The value is now 1. Thread 3 increments arg and the thread is then suspended. The value is 2 now. Thread 1 gets another turn on the processor, and prints the value of arg and it is 2. If the threads always increment before decrementing, how is it possible to print −1? Consider the scenario in Table 21.3.

How contrived is this example? Do scenarios like this happen when solving real world problems? It happens almost always.

We can find analogous examples in the real world. For example, when several people try to purchase tickets for the same flight, the shared variable is the total number of tickets sold for the flight. If only one seat is available and several people buy the ticket at once, then the flight is oversold (also called overbooked). How can it be possible to oversell one flight? Suppose two customers check the flight at almost the same time (reading the shared variable). The flight still has one seat available and both buy the tickets. Now, the flight

thread 1	thread 2	arg's value
read arg	-	0
increment arg	-	0
write arg	-	1
read arg	-	1
decrement arg	-	1
-	read arg	1
-	increment arg	1
-	write arg	2
write arg	-	0
-	read arg	0
-	decrement arg	0
-	write arg	−1
-	check arg's value	−1
-	print arg's value	−1

TABLE 21.3: Interleaving scenario 3.

is oversold. Airline companies often do this on purpose because some people buy tickets but never show up for their flight. It can save money, including the customer, if airlines do this. Airlines can make reasonable accommodations in the unlikely scenario that everyone actually checks in for the flight. One common solution is to give a voucher to a volunteer for taking a later flight.

In some other real world cases, we need a solution that strictly prevents this type of problem occurring altogether. Consider the following scenario: Two people share a bank account and the current balance is $900. One day, they go to two ATMs (automatic teller machine) side-by-side. Each withdraws $100 simultaneously. The two people stand next to each other and attempt to hit the keys on the ATMs at the same time. The correct remaining balance should be $700. However, subtle interleaving could make the remaining balance $800 as illustrated below:

Customer 1	Customer 2	Balance
read balance	-	$900
-	read balance	$900
subtract $100	-	$900
-	subtract $100	$900
write balance	-	$800
-	write balance	$800

The bank gives each customer $100 and the remaining balance is $800 so the bank loses $100. No bank would allow this to happen.

How could the designers of threads allow this to happen? First, it is not a flaw in the specification of threads. The source of the problem is that there is no simple way to predict the order in which multiple threads execute their instructions. Thus it allows operating systems to manage the computer resources more efficiently.

The solution to the problem is to prevent any interleaving of the withdrawal operations. If two requests come in simultaneously, then one must wait until the other request finishes in its entirety. The entire withdrawal operation is said to be *atomic*: it cannot be divided into parts, i.e., it is irreducible. Threads would not be particularly useful if they did not support atomic operations, and this is the topic of the next section. Atom comes from the Greek word *atomon* which means uncuttable. Such irreducible components of matter have been hypothesized since at least the beginning of recorded history. Now we know that an atom *can* be divided to electrons, neutrons, and protons. Nevertheless, we still use "atomic operation" to describe a computer operation that cannot be divided.

21.6 Thread Synchronization

The previous section described a problem in multi-threaded programs. The problem occurs because there is no good way to predict the order in which multiple threads may read and modify the same shared variable. There is no problem when threads do not share data. There is no problem when they share read-only data. For the subset sum problem, the threads share the array but it is read-only. No thread modifies the array and there is no problem. The problem only occurs when threads are writing to, or reading from and writing to, the same piece of memory, and the operations are interleaved in specific ways. When we test the program, the problem will occur sometimes, and frustratingly, will not occur at other times. This adds a significant challenge to testing threaded programs. The only way to be sure is to use a clear mind to reason logically about how multi-thread programs work.

Threads can specify which operations must be atomic. An atomic operation is called a *critical section*. Critical sections cannot interleave. In the previous example, the critical section should include the code where the variable is read or written. If the threads takes turns to increment and decrement the variable atomically, then the value will always remain zero. Thus, the question becomes how to ensure that the threads take turns executing the critical section of code. Only one thread can start a critical section at a time, and once it starts, no other thread can enter the critical section until it finishes. The threads must be *synchronized*. *Synchronization* restricts how threads' operations may interleave. This is achieved by using a *mutually exclusive lock*, also called *mutex lock* or *mutex* for short.

Consider an analogy of a library study room with the following rules:

- The room has a lock and only one key.
- Before a student enters the room, the student must obtain the key from the library's reception desk.
- Only one student can enter the room. The student must keep the key while inside the room.
- When the student enters the room, the student must immediately lock the door.
- When the student leaves the room, the door is unlocked and the key is returned to the library's reception desk.
- If a student wants to use the study room but does not have the key, the student has to wait.

A mutex comes with a pair of lock and unlock statements. The code between this pair of statements is the *critical section*. A mutex lock is very similar to the lock of the library's study room.

- Before a thread enters the critical section, the thread must obtain the key from the operating system.
- Only one thread can enter the critical section. The thread must lock the door and keep the key while running the code in the critical section.
- When the thread leaves the critical section, the thread unlocks the door and returns the key to the operating system.
- If a thread wants to enter the critical section but does not have the key, then the thread has to wait for the key.

The following example shows how to lock and unlock a mutex in order to create a critical section of code.

```
1   // sync.c
2   #include <pthread.h>
3   #include <stdio.h>
4   #include <stdlib.h>
5   #define NUMBER_THREAD 16
6   typedef struct
7   {
8     int * intptr;
9     pthread_mutex_t * mlock;
10  } ThreadData;
11
12  void * threadfunc(void *arg)
13  {
14    ThreadData * td = (ThreadData *) arg;
15    int * intptr = td -> intptr;
16    pthread_mutex_t * mlock = td -> mlock;
17    while (1)
18      {
19        int rtv;
20        rtv = pthread_mutex_lock(mlock); // lock
21        // beginning critical section
22        if (rtv != 0)
23          {
24            printf("mutex_lock fail\n");
25            return NULL;
26          }
27        (* intptr) ++;
28        (* intptr) --;
29        if ((* intptr) != 0)
30          {
31            printf("value is %d\n", * intptr);
32            return NULL;
33          }
34        // end critical section
35        rtv = pthread_mutex_unlock(mlock); // unlock
36        if (rtv != 0)
37          {
38            printf("mutex_unlock fail\n");
39            return NULL;
40          }
41      }
42    return NULL;
43  }
44
45  int main (int argc, char *argv[])
46  {
47    pthread_mutex_t mlock;
48    pthread_mutex_init(& mlock, NULL);
```

```
49    int val = 0;
50    ThreadData arg;
51    arg.intptr = & val;
52    arg.mlock  = & mlock;
53    pthread_t tid[NUMBER_THREAD];
54    int rtv; // return value of pthread_create
55    int ind;
56    for (ind = 0; ind < NUMBER_THREAD; ind ++)
57      {
58        rtv = pthread_create(& tid[ind], NULL,
59                             threadfunc, (void *) & arg);
60        if (rtv != 0)
61          {
62            printf("pthread_create()␣fail␣%d\n", rtv);
63            return EXIT_FAILURE;
64          }
65      }
66    for (ind = 0; ind < NUMBER_THREAD; ind ++)
67      {
68        rtv = pthread_join(tid[ind], NULL);
69        if (rtv != 0)
70          {
71            printf("pthread_join()␣fail␣%d\n", rtv);
72            return EXIT_FAILURE;
73          }
74      }
75    pthread_mutex_destroy(& mlock);
76    return EXIT_SUCCESS;
77  }
```

The program has a structure `ThreadData` that includes two pointers: one for the integer's address (i.e., the shared memory) and the other for the mutex's address. For a critical section to work as intended, all the threads must attempt to lock and unlock the **same mutex**. Hence a pointer to the mutex is passed in `ThreadData`. If each thread has its own mutex, then this would be like the library having a key available for every student, even though there is only one study room. All of them can enter the room and this will create problems.

The critical section includes the code that reads and writes the shared variable. Each thread obtains the lock by calling `pthread_mutex_lock` right after entering the `while` block. If the thread cannot lock the mutex (because some other thread is in the critical section), then that thread will be waiting at `pthread_mutex_lock` until the thread can obtain a lock. The mutex is unlocked by calling `pthread_mutex_unlock` at the end of the `while` block.

The `main` function creates a single `ThreadData` object shared by all threads. Before calling `pthread_mutex_lock` or `pthread_mutex_unlock`, the lock must be initialized by calling `pthread_mutex_init`. This is done in the `main` function. What is the output of this program? Nothing. The `if` condition in `threadfunc` is never true and nothing is printed. This means that all threads keep running indefinitely.

There is much more to say about critical sections of code, and thread synchronization. This chapter is only an introduction, and covers the most important concepts. Writing correct multi-threaded programs can be challenging, and developing better tools and programming languages for this purpose is an ongoing topic of research. When writing multi-threaded programs, it is important to identify critical sections and make them atomic.

Failure to do so will result in unpredictable and difficult-to-reproduce bugs. It is usually difficult to test and detect synchronization problems. You must think very carefully before writing the programs.

21.7   Amdahl's Law

A typical multi-thread program starts with one thread (the main thread). This thread may do some work (such as reading data from a file) before creating more threads. Then, multiple threads are created for computing the results. The results from multiple threads are later combined into the final result. If a program is structured this way, then there is an obvious problem: The initialization and the finalization steps are sequential and can become the bottleneck.

Consider the following scenario. A sequential (single threaded) program takes 100 seconds. The program runs on a computer with an infinite number of cores. The initialization and the finalization steps account for 1% of the execution time. The remaining 99% of execution time is divided between two threads. What is the performance improvement of the two-threads solution? The new execution time is $1 + \frac{99}{2} = 50.5$ seconds. Now suppose that the remaining 99% of execution time is divided between three threads. The execution time becomes $1 + \frac{99}{3} = 34$ seconds.

What is the execution time when 99 threads are used? $1 + \frac{99}{99} = 2$ seconds. How about 990 threads? $1 + \frac{99}{990} = 1.1$ seconds. The reduction in execution is less than 50% (2 seconds → 1.1 seconds) after increasing the number of threads by an order of magnitude. In fact, if the program uses an infinite number of threads, the execution is still 1 second.

What does this mean? The initialization and the finalization steps seem like a small portion of the total execution for the single-thread program. They dominate the total execution time as more and more threads are created. As more threads are used, the initialization and the finalization steps become the bottleneck. The mathematical model for this is called *Amdahl's Law*. The model says that adding more threads has diminishing returns. In this model, the total execution time becomes shorter as more threads are used. In reality, doubling the number of threads rarely shortens the total execution time by half. Consider the subset sum program again. We ran this program on a 32-core server using different numbers of threads. As the number of threads is increased from one to 32, the program's total execution time is reduced by 72%. Even though this is noticeable improvement, it is far from the ideal improvement of $(1 - \frac{1}{32} = 97\%$ reduction).

This chapter provides an introduction to the subject of parallel programming using threads. You can find many books and courses about this important topic.

Part IV

Applications

Chapter 22

Finding the Exit of a Maze

The following chapters use problems and reference solutions to integrate what you have learned in earlier chapters. The first problem is to develop a computer algorithm that finds a way to get out of a maze.

Imagine that you are an adventurer looking for hidden treasure in far-off caves, perhaps the remnants of a lost civilization. Unfortunately you become trapped in an underground maze. Only walls are visible, and you must develop a strategy to find the exit. You need to write a program that finds the path from your current location to the exit.

22.1 Maze File Format

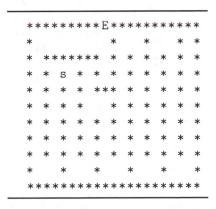

TABLE 22.1: An example of a maze.

A maze is described by a file like the one shown in Table 22.1. This is the input to the program. The characters represent:

- '*': brick
- ' ': (space) corridor

- 'E': exit, i.e., the destination
- 's': starting location

The maze is divided into cells. Each cell is represented by a coordinate, (row, column). Both rows and columns are referred to by integers, and are stored in a two-dimensional array. As shown in Fig. 22.1, the top left corner is $(0,0)$, and not $(1,1)$. After moving right one step, the coordinate becomes $(0, 1)$. From $(0, 1)$, moving down one step reaches coordinate $(1, 1)$. In C programs, array indexes start from zero. Thus making the upper left corner $(0, 0)$ simplifies the indexes. This is consistent with the convention used in computer graphics.

$$(0, 0) \quad (0, 1) \quad (0, 2)$$

$$(1, 0) \quad (1, 1) \quad (1, 2)$$

$$(2, 0)$$

$$(3, 0)$$

FIGURE 22.1: Coordinates (row, column). The upper left corner is (0, 0). Moving right increases the column; moving down increases the row.

This chapter considers only valid mazes meeting the following properties:
- There is one and only one exit.
- There is one and only one starting location.
- There is one and only one route from the starting location to the exit.
- The maze is enclosed by bricks, except for the exit.

For the example in Fig. 22.1, the starting coordinate is (3, 4) and the exit is at (0, 9). The output of the program is the path from the starting location to the exit, and is printed in the following format:

```
Move to (3,3)              Move to (4,1)
Move to (4,3)              Move to (3,1)
Move to (5,3)              Move to (2,1)
Move to (6,3)              Move to (1,1)
Move to (7,3)              Move to (1,2)
Move to (8,3)              Move to (1,3)
Move to (9,3)              Move to (1,4)
Move to (9,2)              Move to (1,5)
Move to (9,1)              Move to (1,6)
Move to (8,1)              Move to (1,7)
Move to (7,1)              Move to (1,8)
Move to (6,1)              Move to (1,9)
Move to (5,1)              Move to (0,9)
```

Each line is one step and the two numbers give the coordinates that are stepped to. The maze is very dark and you can see only one step in front of you. You do not know if a corridor is a dead end until you reach the end. As a result, you may need to move backward after discovering that a corridor is a dead end.

Consider the sequence of steps below:

```
Move to (5,19)
Move to (4,19)
```

```
Move to (3,19)
Move to (2,19)
Move to (1,19)
Move to (2,19)
Move to (3,19)
Move to (4,19)
Move to (5,19)
```

Column 19 is the corridor at the right end of the maze. The top of this corridor is cell $(1, 19)$. After reaching this cell, you discover that it is a dead end. Then you have to turn around and continue the search for the exit. This is called *backtracking*. As a result, the coordinates $(2, 19)$, $(3, 19)$, ..., are repeated showing backtracking.

This chapter provides an opportunity using several topics covered in this book so far:
- Reading data from a file.
- Creating a structure to hold the data of the maze.
- Allocating memory to store the maze cells.
- Using recursion to move around the maze and find the exit.

22.2   Reading the Maze File

A maze file uses four characters to represent bricks, corridors, the exit, and the starting point. In addition, each line ends with a new line character (i.e., '\n'). Fig. 22.1 is an example of a maze file. The following program reads a maze file and prints some information about it. The information includes:
- The number of rows and the number of columns in the maze. The maze must be rectangular, i.e., all rows have the same number of columns.
- The location (row, column) of the exit.
- The location (row, column) of the starting point.

Please remember that the coordinate of the upper left corner is $(0, 0)$. Moving right increases the column, and moving down increases the row.

```
1   /* read a maze file, print the size, the coordinates of
2      the exit and the starting point. */
3   #include <stdio.h>
4   #include <stdlib.h>
5   int main(int argc, char * * argv)
6   {
7     FILE * fptr;
8     int ch;
9     int row = 0;
10    int column = 0;
11    int numberBrick = 0;
12    int exitRow, exitColumn;
13    int startRow, startColumn;
14    int numberColumn;
15    if (argc < 2)
16       {
17          printf("Need to provide the file's name.\n");
```

```
18        return EXIT_FAILURE;
19      }
20    fptr = fopen(argv[1], "r");
21    if (fptr == NULL)
22      {
23        printf("fopen fail.\n");
24        return EXIT_FAILURE;
25      }
26    numberColumn = 0;
27    do
28      {
29        ch = fgetc(fptr);
30        switch (ch)
31          {
32          case '*':
33            numberBrick ++;
34            break;
35          case 'E':
36            exitRow = row;
37            exitColumn = column;
38            break;
39          case 's':
40            startRow = row;
41            startColumn = column;
42            break;
43          }
44        if (ch != EOF)
45          {
46            if (ch == '\n')
47              {
48                row ++;
49                numberColumn = column;
50                column = 0;
51              }
52            else
53              {
54                column ++;
55              }
56          }
57      } while (ch != EOF);
58    fclose(fptr);
59    printf("The maze has %d rows and %d columns.\n",
60            row, numberColumn);
61    printf("The file has %d bricks.\n", numberBrick);
62    printf("The exit is at (%d, %d).\n",
63            exitRow, exitColumn);
64    printf("The starting location is at (%d, %d).\n",
65            startRow, startColumn);
66    return EXIT_SUCCESS;
67  }
```

This is the output of the program when loading the file displayed in Fig. 22.1:

```
The maze has 11 rows and 21 columns.
The file has 131 bricks.
The exit is at (0, 9).
The starting location is at (3, 4).
```

The program can be modified to handle mazes that are not rectangular. To do this, replace:

```
49    numberColumn = column;
```

with,

```
49    if (numberColumn < column)
50      {
51        numberColumn = column;
52      }
```

If a maze is not rectangular, then **numberColumn** stores the size of the widest row.

To get out of the maze, the program needs to know where the bricks are. The program creates a two-dimensional array to remember the maze cells. The program uses the following procedure to read a maze from the file and store the information in a two-dimensional array.

1. Read the file once to determine the size (number of rows and number of columns) of the maze.
2. Allocate enough memory to store the maze.
3. Use **fseek** to return to the beginning of the file.
4. Read the file again and store the maze in the allocated memory.

The previous program completes the first step. After finding the maze's width and height, a two-dimensional array can be allocated to store each cell of the maze. Section 8.4 explained how to allocate a two-dimensional array.

As illustrated in Fig. 10.1, calling **fgetc** each time removes one character from the stream and eventually reaches the end of the file. If the program wants to read the file again, then the program can call **fclose** and then **fopen** again. The second call to **fopen** will start from the beginning of the file. Another solution is to use **fseek** to go back to the beginning of a file stream. The program then reads the characters from the file again.

```
1   // readmaze.c
2   // read a maze file and store it in a two-dimensional array
3
4   #include <stdio.h>
5   #include <stdlib.h>
6   int main(int argc, char * argv[])
7   {
8     FILE * fptr;
9     int ch;
10    int row = 0;
11    int column = 0;
12    int numberRow, numberColumn;
13    int * * mazeArr;
14    if (argc < 2)
15      {
16        printf("Need to provide the file's name.\n");
17        return EXIT_FAILURE;
```

```
18        }
19    fptr = fopen(argv[1], "r");
20    if (fptr == NULL)
21       {
22          printf("fopen fail.\n");
23          return EXIT_FAILURE;
24       }
25    numberColumn = 0;
26    // get the numbers of rows and columns
27    do
28       {
29          ch = fgetc(fptr);
30          if (ch != EOF)
31             {
32                if (ch == '\n')
33                   {
34                      row ++;
35                      numberColumn = column;
36                      column = 0;
37                   }
38                else
39                   {
40                      column ++;
41                   }
42             }
43       } while (ch != EOF);
44    numberRow = row;
45    // allocate memory for the mazeArr
46    mazeArr = malloc(numberRow * sizeof (int *));
47    for (row = 0; row < numberRow; row ++)
48       {
49          mazeArr[row] = malloc(numberColumn * sizeof (int));
50       }
51    // return to the beginning of the file
52    fseek(fptr, 0, SEEK_SET);
53    // read the file again and fill the two-dimensional array
54    row = 0;
55    column = 0;
56    do
57       {
58          ch = fgetc(fptr);
59          if (ch != EOF)
60             {
61                if (ch == '\n')
62                   {
63                      row ++;
64                      column = 0;
65                   }
66                else
67                   {
68                      mazeArr[row][column] = ch;
```

```
69              column ++;
70          }
71      }
72    } while (ch != EOF);
73   fclose(fptr);
74   printf("The mazeArr has %d rows and %d columns.\n",
75          numberRow, numberColumn);
76   for (row = 0; row < numberRow; row ++)
77     {
78       for (column = 0; column < numberColumn; column ++)
79         {
80            printf("%c", mazeArr[row][column]);
81         }
82       printf("\n");
83     }
84   // release the memory
85   for (row = 0; row < numberRow; row ++)
86     {
87       free (mazeArr[row]);
88     }
89   free (mazeArr);
90   return EXIT_SUCCESS;
91 }
```

The program stores the maze in a two-dimensional array called `mazeArr`. With `mazeArr`, it is easier to determine whether a particular cell is a brick by giving the row and column indexes. There is a fundamental problem, however: Several pieces of information are not stored anywhere with the array. For example, the size of the maze, the location of the exit, and the location of the starting point. It is better to create a structure so that all of this related information can be better organized.

22.3 The Maze Structure

A structure is defined to store relevant information about a maze. This structure stores the maze's size (number of rows and number of columns), the starting location, the exit location, and the current location during movement. The structure also has a two-dimensional array to store the information for each cell in the maze. A constructor function creates and initializes the maze object by reading a file. The destructor function releases the memory used in the maze object, and is called before the program ends.

Below is the code listing for the header file. It includes the definition for `Maze` structure, as well as the constructor and destructor functions.

```
1  /* maze.h */
2  #ifndef MAZE_H
3  #define MAZE_H
4  #define STARTSYMBOL      's'
5  #define EXITSYMBOL       'E'
6  #define BRICKSYMBOL      '*'
7  #define CORRIDORSYMBOL   ' '
```

```
 8  #define INVALIDSYMBOL   '-'
 9  typedef struct
10  {
11    int numRow, numCol;      // size of the maze
12    int startRow, startCol;  // starting location
13    int exitRow, exitCol;    // exit location
14    int curRow, curCol;      // current location
15    // brick? exit? starting point? corridor? 2-dimensional
16    // array storing the cells
17    int * * cells;
18  } Maze;
19  // directions, ORIGIN marks the starting point
20  enum {ORIGIN, EAST, SOUTH, WEST, NORTH};
21  // move forward, backward, or found exit alread
22  enum {FORWARD, BACKWARD, DONE};
23  // read the maze from a file
24  Maze * Maze_construct(char * fileName);
25  // release memory before the program ends
26  void Maze_destruct(Maze * mz);
27  // print the maze's properties (mainly for debugging)
28  void Maze_print(Maze * mz);
29  #endif
```

The following listing gives sample implementations for the functions declared in the header file.

```
 1  // mazeread.c
 2  #include "maze.h"
 3  #include <stdio.h>
 4  #include <stdlib.h>
 5  // A static function can be called by another function
 6  // in the same file. A static function cannot be called
 7  // by any function outside this file.
 8  // If ptr is NULL, print an error message and exit
 9  static void checkMalloc(void * ptr, char * message);
10  // find the length of a line in a file (EOF or '\n')
11  static int findLineLength(FILE * fh);
12  // Find the numbers of rows and columns. If the maze is not
13  // rectangular, use the widest row
14  static void Maze_findSize(FILE * fh, int * numRow,
15                            int * numCol);
16  static void checkMalloc(void * ptr, char * message)
17  {
18    if (ptr == NULL) // malloc fail
19      {
20        printf("malloc for %s fail\n", message);
21      }
22  }
23  static int findLineLength(FILE * fh)
24  {
25    int ch;
26    int length = 0;
```

```
27    if (feof(fh)) { return -1; }
28    do
29      {
30        ch = fgetc(fh); // read one character
31        length ++;
32      } while ((ch != '\n') && (ch != EOF));
33    return length;
34 }
35 static void Maze_findSize(FILE * fh, int * numRow, int *
36    numCol)
37 {
38    int row = 0;
39    int col = 0;
40    int maxCol = 0;
41    // find the maximum number of columns. This allows the
42    // program to handle a maze that is not rectangular.
43    do
44      {
45        col = findLineLength(fh);
46        if (col != -1)
47          {
48            if (maxCol < col) { maxCol = col; }
49            row ++;
50          }
51      } while (col != -1);
52    * numRow = row;
53    * numCol = maxCol;
54 }
55 Maze * Maze_construct(char * fileName)
56 {
57    int numRow = 0;
58    int numCol = 0;
59    int row, col;
60    int ch;
61    FILE * fptr = fopen(fileName, "r");
62    if (fptr == 0)
63      {
64        fprintf(stderr, "open %s fail\n", fileName);
65        return NULL;
66      }
67    Maze_findSize(fptr, & numRow, & numCol);
68    Maze * mzptr = malloc(sizeof(Maze));
69    checkMalloc(mzptr, "mzptr");
70    mzptr -> numRow = numRow;
71    mzptr -> numCol = numCol;
72    // create a two-dimensional array to store the cells
73    mzptr -> cells = malloc(numRow * sizeof(int *));
74    checkMalloc(mzptr -> cells, "mzptr -> cells");
75    for (row = 0; row < numRow; row ++)
76      {
77        mzptr -> cells[row] = malloc(numCol * sizeof(int));
```

```
78      checkMalloc(mzptr -> cells[row],
79                      "mzptr_->_cells[row]");
80      // initialize the cells to invalid
81      for (col = 0; col < numCol; col ++)
82        {
83          (mzptr -> cells)[row][col] = INVALIDSYMBOL;
84        }
85    }
86  // move fptr to the beginning
87  fseek(fptr, 0, SEEK_SET);
88  // read the file again and fill the two-dimensional array
89  row = 0;
90  while ((! feof(fptr)) && (ch != EOF) && (row < numRow))
91    {
92      // fill one row
93      col = 0;
94      do
95        {
96          ch = fgetc(fptr);
97          if (ch != EOF)
98            {
99              // notice that '\n' is also stored
100             (mzptr -> cells)[row][col] = ch;
101             switch (ch)
102               {
103               case STARTSYMBOL:
104                 mzptr -> startRow = row;
105                 mzptr -> startCol = col;
106                 mzptr -> curRow = row;
107                 mzptr -> curCol = col;
108                 break;
109               case EXITSYMBOL:
110                 mzptr -> exitRow = row;
111                 mzptr -> exitCol = col;
112                 break;
113               }
114             col ++;
115            }
116        } while ((ch != EOF) && (ch != '\n'));
117      // checking '\n" to handle non-rectangular mazes
118      row ++;
119    }
120  fclose(fptr);
121  return mzptr;
122 }
123 // release the memory
124 void Maze_destruct(Maze * mzptr)
125 {
126  int row;
127  for (row = 0; row < (mzptr -> numRow); row ++)
128    { free ((mzptr -> cells)[row]); }
```

```
129      free (mzptr -> cells);
130      free(mzptr);
131  }
132  void Maze_print(Maze * mzptr)
133  {
134      int row;
135      int col;
136      for (row = 0; row < (mzptr -> numRow); row ++)
137        {
138          for (col = 0; col < (mzptr -> numCol); col ++)
139            {
140              if (((mzptr -> curRow) == row) &&
141                  ((mzptr -> curCol) == col))
142                {
143                  if (((mzptr -> curRow) ==
144                       (mzptr -> startRow))
145                      &&
146                      ((mzptr -> curCol) ==
147                       (mzptr -> startCol)))
148                    {
149                      printf("s");
150                    }
151                  else
152                    {
153                      printf("c");
154                    }
155                }
156              else
157                {
158                  printf("%c", (mzptr -> cells)[row][col]);
159                }
160            }
161          printf("\n");
162        }
163  }
```

22.4   An Escape Strategy

Your GPS (Global Positioning System) is not working—it cannot receive the satellite signal. Your compass is, fortunately, working. Therefore it is possible to tell the directions: east, south, west, north. Using just a compass and some memory, it is possible to solve a maze using the following strategy:

- Inside a corridor, go as far as possible. This is shown in Fig. 22.2 (a) and (b). The dotted line behind the 1 arrow indicates that you cannot move backwards.
- After reaching a dead end, turn around and move backward along the same corridor. This is shown in Fig. 22.2 (c). In "backward mode", the dotted line is no longer applicable.

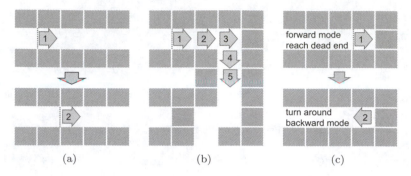

(a)   (b)   (c)

FIGURE 22.2: Strategy to get out of a maze. Suppose ↑ is north and → is east. A gray square is a brick. (a) If moving east in step 1 does not reach a dead end, then keep moving east in step 2. (b) If the corridor has a turn, then follow the turn and keep moving forward. (c) After encountering a dead end, turn around (i.e., backtrack) and move back along the corridor.

- At an intersection, try to go east if that is possible. It is, of course, arbitrary to prefer east. The solution would be similar if we preferred south first, or west first, or north first. This example strategy chooses to go east first. If that is not possible, then try to go south. If going south is not an option, then try to go west. The last preference is to attempt to go north. Fig. 22.3–Fig. 22.6 illustrate the strategy. Fig. 22.3 (a) shows that you are about to enter an intersection.
- After encountering a dead end, return to the previous intersection and choose another direction.
- If all possible directions at an intersection lead to dead ends, then return to the *previous* intersection and choose another direction.

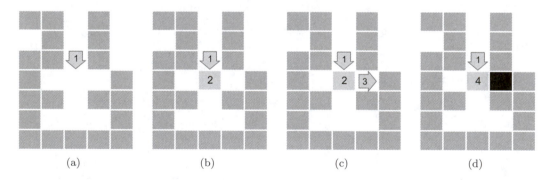

(a)   (b)   (c)   (d)

FIGURE 22.3: Strategy at an intersection. (a) About to enter an intersection. (b) At the intersection (marked as "2"), try to go east first. (c) It is a dead end. Turn around and return to the previous intersection. (d) The mark "2" now becomes "4", indicating that it is the fourth visited cell. Since cell "3" is a dead end, it is marked black.

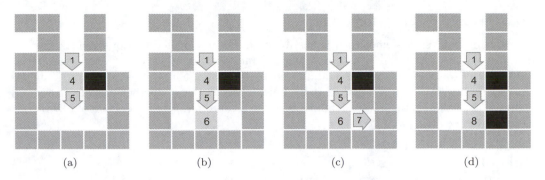

FIGURE 22.4: (a) Since east is a dead end, try to go south. (b) Enter another intersection, marked as "6". (c) Go east and find that it is another dead end. (d) Turn around to the previous intersection, now marked as "8". (This is the eighth move in the sequence of moves.) The dead end is replaced by black.

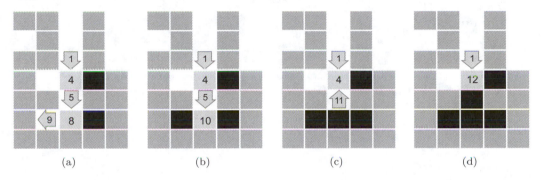

FIGURE 22.5: (a) It is not possible to go south at this intersection. Move west and mark the cell as "9". (b) This is another dead end. Turn around and mark the intersection as "10". (c) Since both options lead to dead ends, we return to the previous intersection. The visited cells are marked black. (d) Back at the first intersection.

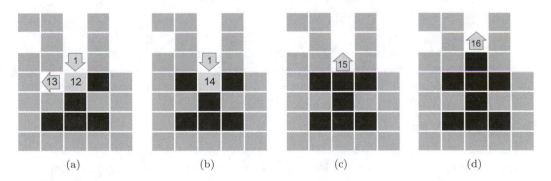

FIGURE 22.6: (a) Going west is an option. (b) It is another dead end. Return to the previous intersection. (c),(d) All options at this intersection lead to dead ends, so it should return along the corridor.

22.5 Implementing the Strategy

How can such a strategy be implemented in C? We will explain step by step.

22.5.1   canMove **Function**

This function reports whether it is possible to move in a given direction from the current location. If the destination is a brick, then the move is not allowed. As explained earlier in Fig. 22.1, moving east means adding one to the column index. Moving north means subtracting one from the row index. It is unnecessary to check whether indexes (rows and columns) are valid (in the maze's bounds) because a valid maze is always enclosed by bricks, except for the exit.

```
1   // canmove.c
2   #include "maze.h"
3   int canMove(Maze * mzptr, int row, int col, int dir)
4   {
5     /* (row, col) is the current location */
6     switch (dir)
7       {
8       case NORTH:
9         row --;
10        break;
11      case SOUTH:
12        row ++;
13        break;
14      case WEST:
15        col --;
16        break;
17      case EAST:
18        col ++;
19        break;
20      }
21    int dest = (mzptr->cells)[row][col];
22    if ((dest == '␣') || (dest == 'E'))
23      { return 1; } /* corridor or exit, can move to */
24    return 0; /* cannot move to */
25  }
```

Modifying the function arguments (`row` and `col`) does not result in a move, because the function arguments are copied onto the frame of `canMove` in the call stack. Modifying them only changes the values in `camMove`'s frame and does not modify the values in the caller.

22.5.2   getOut **Function**

This function finds the exit, and is thus called `getOut`. We will build this function up by gradually adding more code and explanation. Let's start with a simple function that stops when the exit is found:

```
1   void getOut(Maze * mzptr, int row, int col)
2   {
3     if ((mzptr -> maze)[row][col] == 'E') // found exit
4       {
5         printf("Found␣the␣exit!\n");
6         return;
7       }
8   }
```

That is easy enough. This does not solve the entire problem but it is a good stepping stone. Good programmers always take small steps toward solutions. What should the function do if the current location is not the exit? If the current location is not the exit, then the function checks whether it is possible to move east. If this is possible (because `canMove` returns 1), then the function moves east by adding 1 to the column index and calls `getOut` again. This is a recursive call. Why should the function be recursive? The reason is that we adopt the same strategy at each cell, until the exit is found.

```
1  void getOut(Maze * mzptr, int row, int col)
2  {
3    if ((mzptr -> maze)[row][col] == 'E') // found exit
4      {
5        printf("Found the exit!\n");
6        return;
7      }
8    if (canMove(mzptr, row, col, EAST))
9      {
10       getOut(mzptr, row, col + 1);
11       // moving east means adding 1 to the column index
12      }
13 }
```

What should the function do if moving east is not possible? An example is shown in Fig. 22.3 (a). In this case, the function tries to go south.

```
1  void getOut(Maze * mz, int row, int col)
2  {
3    if ((mz -> maze)[row][col] == 'E') // found exit
4      {
5        printf("Found the exit!\n");
6        return;
7      }
8    if (canMove(mz, row, col, EAST))
9      {
10       getOut(mz, row, col + 1);
11       // moving east means adding 1 to the column index
12      }
13   if (canMove(mz, row, col, SOUTH))
14      {
15       getOut(mz, row + 1, col);
16       // moving south means adding 1 to the row index
17      }
18 }
```

What is the method to determine which of the four possible directions can be taken? The order of calling `canMove` determines which direction is considered first. If the order of these calls is changed, then the function tries another direction first. The other two directions (west and north) are also checked using the following function:

```
1  void getOut(Maze * mzptr, int row, int col)
2  {
3    if ((mzptr -> maze)[row][col] == 'E') // found exit
4      {
5        printf("Found the exit!\n");
```

```
 6          return;
 7      }
 8      if (canMove(mzptr, row, col, EAST))
 9      {
10          getOut(mzptr, row, col + 1);
11          // moving east : adding 1 to the column index
12      }
13      if (canMove(mzptr, row, col, SOUTH))
14      {
15          getOut(mzptr, row + 1, col);
16          // moving south : adding 1 to the row index
17      }
18      if (canMove(mzptr, row, col, WEST))
19      {
20          getOut(mzptr, row, col - 1);
21          // moving west : subtracting 1 from the column index
22      }
23      if (canMove(mzptr, row, col, NORTH))
24      {
25          getOut(mzptr, row - 1, col);
26          // moving north : subtracting 1 from the row index
27      }
28 }
```

This function implements the basic concepts of our strategy, however, it still needs a few improvements. A common question from students is whether this function can handle a corridor with an intersection. To answer this question, we need to understand the difference between a corridor and an intersection. A corridor is enclosed by bricks on two sides. Therefore, two of the `if` conditions are false. At an intersection, more than two `if` conditions are true. It is possible to have a four-way intersection as shown in Fig. 22.7. There is nothing special about corridors and intersections. If it is possible to move in a particular direction, then the program moves in that direction. Thus, the same code can handle corridors and intersections because along a corridor only two `if` conditions are true.

What about dead ends? If it is a dead end, then only one `if` condition is true.

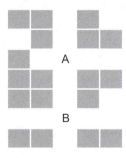

FIGURE 22.7: Two four-way intersections at A and B. At a four-way intersection, all four `if` conditions are true.

How does the program determine if a cell is a dead end? Fig. 22.3–22.6 mark visited cells as bricks. Marking visited cells seems a reasonable approach. If a cell is a dead end, then the cell should be visited only once. If a cell is a corridor, then the cell may be visited twice. If a cell is an intersection, then the cell may be visited more than twice. We need to distinguish between these conditions. If we simply mark a cell as visited, then we may inadvertently eliminate an intersection. Therefore, the function does not mark cells that have already been visited. Without marking visited cells, won't the function revisit the same cells over and over again and get stuck? Is marking visited cells necessary? Before answering this question, let's consider how the function handles dead ends.

Fig. 22.8 shows an example of a dead end. After discovering the dead end, we turn around and move west. However, after moving one step to the west, the function finds that it is possible to move east again. After moving east, we find the dead end and turn around to move west. Again we find we can move east again and do so. This function has problems because it gets stuck.

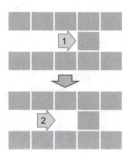

FIGURE 22.8: After reaching a dead end, we should turn around and move west. At location 2, moving east is an option again. We will get stuck here in these two cells and need a solution to prevent this from happening.

If you take a closer look of Fig. 22.2, you will find something different between Fig. 22.2 and Fig. 22.8. There are dotted lines in Fig. 22.2 as a barrier that prevents moving backward. How can we write code for this? The function goes east if the two conditions are satisfied:

1. It is not a brick.
2. The previous location was not going west.

These two conditions prevent going back and forth as illustrated in Fig. 22.8. Similarly, the function considers south if there is no brick to the south, and the previous step was not north. To make this work, one more argument is needed for the `getOut` function. This argument is `dir` and it tells the function the direction taken in the previous step.

```
void getOut(Maze * mzptr, int row, int col, int dir)
{
    if ((mzptr -> maze)[row][col] == 'E') // found exit
        {
            printf("Found the exit!\n");
            return;
        }
    if (canMove(mzptr, row, col, EAST) && (dir != WEST))
        {
            // move east if it is not a brick and
            // the last step was not moving west
            getOut(mzptr, row, col + 1, EAST);
        }
    if (canMove(mzptr, row, col, SOUTH) && (dir != NORTH))
        {
            getOut(mzptr, row + 1, col, SOUTH);
        }
```

```
18    if (canMove(mzptr, row, col, WEST) && (dir != EAST))
19      {
20        getOut(mzptr, row, col - 1, WEST);
21      }
22    if (canMove(mzptr, row, col, NORTH) && (dir != SOUTH))
23      {
24        getOut(mzptr, row - 1, col, NORTH);
25      }
26  }
```

This function prevents going back and forth by checking whether the previous step was in the opposite direction.

The function does not turn around after reaching a dead end. It needs a way to distinguish between "forward" and "backward" mode. In forward mode, it does not revisit cells. In backward mode after turning around, it is necessary to revisit cells.

What does a dead end mean? It means that none of the four forward directions are available. In other words, all the four if (canMove ...&& (dir != ...)) conditions are false. Why? If one of them were true, then the function would have taken that direction and moved forward. Thus, if the function reaches the bottom without calling itself, the cell is a dead end. The mode variable is set to BACKWARD. It must be a pointer in order to keep this change when the function returns to the caller after the top frame is popped.

```
1   void getOut(Maze * mzptr, int row, int col,
2               int dir, int * mode)
3   {
4     if ((mzptr -> maze)[row][col] == 'E')
5       {
6         printf("Found the exit!\n");
7         return;
8       }
9     if (canMove(mzptr, row, col, EAST) && (dir != WEST))
10      {
11        getOut(mzptr, row, col + 1, EAST, mode);
12      }
13    if (canMove(mzptr, row, col, SOUTH) && (dir != NORTH))
14      {
15        getOut(mzptr, row + 1, col, SOUTH, mode);
16      }
17    if (canMove(mzptr, row, col, WEST) && (dir != EAST))
18      {
19        getOut(mzptr, row, col - 1, WEST, mode);
20      }
21    if (canMove(mzptr, row, col, NORTH) && (dir != SOUTH))
22      {
23        getOut(mzptr, row - 1, col, NORTH, mode);
24      }
25    // reaching this point means the cell is a dead end
26    // turn around and move backward
27    (* mode) = BACKWARD;
28  }
```

In the forward mode, getOut calls itself and new frames are pushed onto the call stack. In the backward mode, frames are popped from the call stack. This means returning to the previously visited cells because `row` and `col` are stored in the frames. This is an example of using the call stack to store information. How many frames should be popped? When will this `*` `mode` variable be changed back to `FORWARD`? The answer is after returning to a location where another direction is possible and has not been taken. This is, by definition, an intersection. Remember, intersections have at least two `if` conditions that are true.

In Fig. 22.3–22.6, when moving backward, the visited cells are marked black. This is unnecessary in the function because the four `if` conditions already keep track of which remaining options are available. In Fig. 22.3, number 2 is an intersection and the program moves east when the first `if` condition is true. After finding that it is a dead end and turning around, the function continues from the return location stored in the call stack. This is the line after the first `if` condition. When returning to the previous location (now marked as 4), the first `if` condition has already been tested and will not be tested again.

This can be explained in a different way. Consider the following example:

```
void f(int x, int y)
{
   if (x == 1)
     {
        /* do A */
     }
   /* do B */
   if (y == 1)
     {
        /* do C */
     }
}
```

When the function reaches location B, the function will not test `x == 1` again and the function will not execute A again. This is the same even if A calls `f` itself. In Fig. 22.3, when returning to the previous location, currently marked 4, the function has already checked and taken the option of moving east. The function will not check whether moving east is an option any more. Instead, the function will check the remaining three `if` conditions for going south, west, and north. Each `if` condition uses `dir !=` to prevent going back to the previous cell. Thus, when an `if` condition is true, there must be an unexplored direction and the function changes `*` `mode` to `FORWARD`. The `getOut` function is changed as follows:

```
void getOut(Maze * mzptr, int row, int col,
            int dir, int * mode)
{
   if ((mzptr -> maze)[row][col] == 'E')
     {
        printf("Found the exit!\n");
        return;
     }
   if (canMove(mzptr, row, col, EAST) && (dir != WEST))
     {
        (* mode) = FORWARD;
        getOut(mzptr, row, col + 1, EAST, mode);
     }
   if (canMove(mzptr, row, col, SOUTH) && (dir != NORTH))
     {
        (* mode) = FORWARD;
        getOut(mzptr, row + 1, col, SOUTH, mode);
```

```
18      }
19   if (canMove(mzptr, row, col, WEST) && (dir != EAST))
20     {
21       (* mode) = FORWARD;
22       getOut(mzptr, row, col - 1, WEST, mode);
23     }
24   if (canMove(mzptr, row, col, NORTH) && (dir != SOUTH))
25     {
26       (* mode) = FORWARD;
27       getOut(mz, row - 1, col, NORTH, mode);
28     }
29   (* mode) = BACKWARD;
30 }
```

22.5.3   Printing Visited Locations

We still need to print the moves as shown in Section 22.1. How can getOut do that, especially when moving backward? Fortunately, the call stack remembers the visited cells because row and col are stored for each recursive call in the function's frame on the call stack. When getOut is called, the function prints the location, row and col. If a cell is revisited, then the function must be in BACKWARD mode after popping the call stack and the cell's location is printed again. After finding the exit, * mode is set to DONE and this prevents any further if conditions from being true. Thus, after finding the exit, there are no more recursive calls. The frames will pop from the call stack all the way back to the beginning of the first call to getOut.

```
1  // getout.c
2  #include <stdio.h>
3  #include "maze.h"
4  int canMove(Maze * mzptr, int row, int col, int dir);
5  void getOut(Maze * mzptr, int row, int col,
6              int dir, int * mode)
7  {
8    printf("Move to (%d,%d)\n", row, col);
9    if ((mzptr -> cells)[row][col] == 'E') /* found exit */
10     {
11       printf("Found the exit!\n");
12       (* mode) = DONE;
13     }
14   if (((*mode) != DONE) &&
15       canMove(mzptr, row, col, EAST) &&
16       (dir != WEST))
17     {
18       (* mode) = FORWARD;
19       getOut(mzptr, row, col + 1, EAST, mode);
20       if ((*mode) == BACKWARD)
21         {
22           printf("Move to (%d,%d)\n", row, col);
23         }
24     }
25   if (((*mode) != DONE) &&
```

```
26              canMove(mzptr, row, col, SOUTH) &&
27              (dir != NORTH))
28          {
29              (* mode) = FORWARD;
30              getOut(mzptr, row + 1, col, SOUTH, mode);
31              if ((*mode) == BACKWARD)
32                  {
33                      printf("Move to (%d,%d)\n", row, col);
34                  }
35          }
36      if (((*mode) != DONE) &&
37              canMove(mzptr, row, col, WEST) &&
38              (dir != EAST))
39          {
40              (* mode) = FORWARD;
41              getOut(mzptr, row, col - 1, WEST, mode);
42              if ((*mode) == BACKWARD)
43                  {
44                      printf("Move to (%d,%d)\n", row, col);
45                  }
46          }
47      if (((*mode) != DONE) &&
48              canMove(mzptr, row, col, NORTH) &&
49              (dir != SOUTH))
50          {
51              (* mode) = FORWARD;
52              getOut(mzptr, row - 1, col, NORTH, mode);
53              if ((*mode) == BACKWARD)
54                  {
55                      printf("Move to (%d,%d)\n", row, col);
56                  }
57          }
58      if ((*mode) != DONE)
59          {
60              (* mode) = BACKWARD;
61          }
62  }
```

This is the final version of the `getOut` function. This final version `getOut` solves the maze. It can be driven by the `main` function as shown below:

```
1  #include <stdio.h>
2  #include "maze.h"
3  void getOut(Maze * mzptr, int row, int col,
4              int dir, int * mode);
5  int main(int argc, char * argv[])
6  {
7      if (argc < 2)
8          {
9              fprintf(stderr, "need a file name\n");
10             return -1;
11         }
```

```
12   Maze * mzptr = Maze_construct(argv[1]);
13   if (mzptr == 0) { return -1; }
14   /* Maze_print(mzptr); */
15   int progress = FORWARD;
16   getOut(mzptr, mzptr -> startRow, mzptr -> startCol,
17           ORIGIN, & progress);
18   Maze_destruct(mzptr);
19   return 0;
20 }
```

This program shows how to use structures and recursion together. By using recursion, the visited locations are stored in the call stack as function arguments. This allows the program to backtrack after visiting dead ends.

Chapter 23

Image Processing

The rapid growth of digital photography is one of the most important technological changes in the past fifteen years. Cameras are now standard on mobile phones, tablets, and laptops. There is also a proliferation of webcams and surveillance cameras. All of these digital images call for clever applications to improve our lives. For example, social media websites use facial recognition in order to make it easier to see photos of your friends. Future applications may be able to determine what people are doing in images, or sequences of images.

This chapter introduces some basics of image processing. The main goal of this chapter is to explain how to read and write images, as well as how to modify the colors in the image pixels. For simplicity, this chapter considers only one image format: *bitmap* (BMP). BMP files are not normally compressed and the pixels are independently stored. A more commonly used format is called Joint Photographic Experts Group, also known as *JPEG*. JPEG files are compressed using the discrete cosine transform (DCT). This compression algorithm is beyond the scope of this book.

23.1   Structure for Image

An image includes many *pixels*. Each pixel is a dot in the image and it has one single color. The colors of the pixels are called the "data" of the image. In addition to the colors, an image has additional information about the image. For example, if it is a photograph, the file may have the date when the photo was taken, the brand of the camera, etc. The additional information is separate from the pixel colors, but describes something that may be interesting about the pixels. This additional information is called "metadata". When taking a photograph with a digital camera, the camera records a wide range of metadata. Fig. 23.1 shows the metadata of a photograph taken by a Nikon Coolpix S3500 camera. A different camera model or a different brand may produce different types of metadata.

A bitmap image file has two parts. The first part is the metadata (also called *header*). The second part is the data. The header has 54 bytes in length and the size of the data depends on the number of pixels.

The header is defined as:

FIGURE 23.1: Example of metadata: the exposure time, the focal length, the time and the date, etc.

```c
// bmpheader.h
#ifndef _BMPHEADER_H_
#define _BMPHEADER_H_
#include <stdint.h>
// tell compiler not to add space between the attributes
#pragma pack(1)
// A BMP file has a header (54 bytes) and data

typedef struct
{
  uint16_t type;              // Magic identifier
  uint32_t size;              // File size in bytes
  uint16_t reserved1;         // Not used
  uint16_t reserved2;         // Not used
  uint32_t offset;            //
  uint32_t header_size;       // Header size in bytes
  uint32_t width;             // Width of the image
  uint32_t height;            // Height of image
  uint16_t planes;            // Number of color planes
  uint16_t bits;              // Bits per pixel
  uint32_t compression;       // Compression type
  uint32_t imagesize;         // Image size in bytes
  uint32_t xresolution;       // Pixels per meter
  uint32_t yresolution;       // Pixels per meter
  uint32_t ncolours;          // Number of colors
  uint32_t importantcolours;  // Important colors

} BMP_Header;
#endif
```

This header file introduces several new concepts. The sixth line tells the compiler not to add any padding between the attributes of a structure. This ensures that the size of a header object is precisely 54 bytes. Without this line, the compiler may align the attributes for better performance.

Another new concept is including the file `<stdint.h>`. This file contains definitions of integer types that are guaranteed to have the same sizes on different machines. The `int` type on one machine may have a different size from the `int` type on another machine. When reading a 54 byte head from disk, we need to use the same size for the header regardless of the machine. These types defined in `<stdint.h>` all have `int` in them, followed by the number of bits, and `_t`. Thus, a 32-bit integer is `int32_t`. If the type is unsigned, then it is prefixed with a `u`. An unsigned 16-bit integer is `uint16_t`.

In the bitmap header structure, some attributes are 16 bits and the others are 32 bits. They are all unsigned, because none of the attributes can take on negative values. The order of the attributes is important because the order must meet the bitmap specification. Reordering the attributes will cause errors. The size of the header is calculated as follows:

Attribute	Type	Size (Bytes)	Cumulative Size (Bytes)
type	uint16_t	2	2
size	uint32_t	4	6
reserved1	uint16_t	2	8
reserved2	uint16_t	2	10
offset	uint32_t	4	14
header_size	uint32_t	4	18
width	uint32_t	4	22
height	uint32_t	4	26
planes	uint16_t	2	28
bits	uint16_t	2	30
compression	uint32_t	4	34
imagesize	uint32_t	4	38
xresolution	uint32_t	4	42
yresolution	uint32_t	4	46
ncolours	uint32_t	4	50
importantcolours	uint32_t	4	54

To read the image header from file, call `fread` as follows:

```
FILE *fptr = fopen(filename, "r");
if (fptr == NULL)
  {
    return NULL;
  }
BMP_Header header;
if (fread(& header, sizeof(BMP_Header), 1, fptr) != 1)
  {
    // error
  }
```

The header has a "magic number" whose value must be 0X4D42. This is an easy way to check whether or not the file is a valid BMP file. If the value is not 0X4D42, then it cannot be a BMP file. Using the magic number is a quick, but imperfect, solution for determining whether it is a BMP file. The `size` attribute in the header is the size of the entire file, including the header. Each pixel has three color values: red, green, and blue. Each color uses one byte. Thus, the value of `bits` is 24 bits per pixel. The images considered in this chapter have only one image plane and compression is not used. The correct value for `planes` should be 1; the correct value for `compression` should be 0.

We cannot store the image pixels in the header struct, because the header has a fixed size. The header merely tells us how to read the rest of the file. To store the pixels in memory, we need to use another type of structure. We will call this structure BMP_Image, as shown below.

```
1  // bmpimage.h
2  #ifndef _BMPIMAGE_H
3  #define _BMPIMAGE_H
4  #include "bmpheader.h"
5  typedef struct
6  {
7    BMP_Header header;
8    unsigned int data_size;
9    unsigned int width;
10   unsigned int height;
11   unsigned int bytes_per_pixel;
12   unsigned char * data;
13  } BMP_Image;
14 #endif
```

A BMP_Image includes the header, data_size, width and height (duplicated from the header), the number of bytes per pixel, and a pointer to the pixel data. The data_size is the size of the file after subtracting the size of the header, i.e., sizeof(BMP_Header). Even though sizeof(BMP_Header) is 54, it is bad to write 54 directly. The size can be derived from sizeof(BMP_Header). Few people reading the code will know what 54 means, but every C programmer will instantly understand sizeof(BMP_Header). Therefore, you should not use "54". The number of bytes per pixel is the number of bits per pixel divided by 8. because one byte is 8 bits. The following listing shows the header file and an implementation of reading and saving image files.

```
1  // bmpfile.h
2  #ifndef _BMPFILE_H_
3  #define _BMPFILE_H_
4  #include "bmpimage.h"
5  // open a BMP image given a filename
6  // return a pointer to a BMP image if success
7  // returns NULL if failure.
8  BMP_Image *BMP_open(const char *filename);
9  // save a BMP image to the given a filename
10 // return 0 if failure
11 // return 1 if success
12 int BMP_save(const BMP_Image *image, const char *filename);
13 // release the memory of a BMP image structure
14 void BMP_destroy(BMP_Image *image);
15 #endif
```

```
1  // bmpfile.c
2  #include <stdio.h>
3  #include <stdlib.h>
4  #include "bmpfile.h"
5  // correct values for the header
6  #define MAGIC_VALUE     0X4D42
7  #define BITS_PER_PIXEL 24
```

```
8   #define NUM_PLANE        1
9   #define COMPRESSION      0
10  #define BITS_PER_BYTE    8
11
12  // return 0 if the header is invalid
13  // return 1 if the header is valid
14  static int checkHeader(BMP_Header * hdr)
15  {
16    if ((hdr -> type) != MAGIC_VALUE)
17      {
18        return 0;
19      }
20    if ((hdr -> bits) != BITS_PER_PIXEL)
21      {
22        return 0;
23      }
24    if ((hdr -> planes) != NUM_PLANE)
25      {
26        return 0;
27      }
28    if ((hdr -> compression) != COMPRESSION)
29      {
30        return 0;
31      }
32    return 1;
33  }
34  // close opened file and release memory
35  BMP_Image * cleanUp(FILE * fptr, BMP_Image * img)
36  {
37    if (fptr != NULL)
38      {
39        fclose (fptr);
40      }
41    if (img != NULL)
42      {
43        if (img -> data != NULL)
44          {
45            free (img -> data);
46          }
47        free (img);
48      }
49    return NULL;
50  }
51  BMP_Image *BMP_open(const char *filename)
52  {
53    FILE * fptr    = NULL;
54    BMP_Image *img = NULL;
55    fptr = fopen(filename, "r"); // "rb" unnecessary in Linux
56    if (fptr == NULL)
57      {
58        return cleanUp(fptr, img);
```

```
59       }
60    img = malloc(sizeof(BMP_Image));
61    if (img == NULL)
62      {
63        return cleanUp(fptr, img);
64      }
65    // read the header
66    if (fread(& (img -> header), sizeof(BMP_Header),
67            1, fptr) != 1)
68      {
69        // fread fails
70        return cleanUp(fptr, img);
71      }
72    if (checkHeader(& (img -> header)) == 0)
73      {
74        return cleanUp(fptr, img);
75      }
76    img -> data_size =
77      (img -> header).size - sizeof(BMP_Header);
78    img -> width    = (img -> header).width;
79    img -> height   = (img -> header).height;
80    img -> bytes_per_pixel =
81      (img -> header).bits / BITS_PER_BYTE;
82    img -> data =
83      malloc(sizeof(unsigned char) * (img -> data_size));
84    if ((img -> data) == NULL)
85      {
86        // malloc fail
87        return cleanUp(fptr, img);
88      }
89    if (fread(img -> data, sizeof(char), img -> data_size,
90            fptr) != (img -> data_size))
91      {
92        // fread fails
93        return cleanUp(fptr, img);
94      }
95    char onebyte;
96    if (fread(& onebyte, sizeof(char), 1, fptr) != 0)
97      {
98        // not at the of the file but the file still has data
99        return cleanUp(fptr, img);
100     }
101   // everything successful
102   fclose (fptr);
103   return img;
104 }
105 int BMP_save(const BMP_Image *img, const char *filename)
106 {
107   FILE * fptr     = NULL;
108   fptr = fopen(filename, "w");
109   if (fptr == NULL)
```

```
110      {
111        return 0;
112      }
113    // write the header first
114    if (fwrite(& (img -> header), sizeof(BMP_Header), 1,
115               fptr) != 1)
116      {
117        // fwrite fails
118        fclose (fptr);
119        return 0;
120      }
121    if (fwrite(img -> data, sizeof(char), img -> data_size,
122               fptr) != (img -> data_size))
123      {
124        // fwrite fails
125        fclose (fptr);
126        return 0;
127      }
128    // everything successful
129    fclose (fptr);
130    return 1;
131  }
132  void BMP_destroy(BMP_Image *img)
133  {
134    free (img -> data);
135    free (img);
136  }
```

23.2   Processing Images

In this BMP file format, each pixel uses three bytes representing the three primary colors of the visible spectrum: red, green, and blue. This is commonly referred to as the RGB color space. Other color spaces exist and are used for various purposes. Another common color space is HSV, which stands for hue, saturation, and value, and is useful for certain transformations. For example, changing the saturation value changes the vibrancy of the color. The RGB color space is a convenient color space to start because computer monitors use RGB values. It is not a particularly useful color space for producing natural blending effects, or for specifying the patterns and amounts of inks to be sprayed when printing. RGB is simple and can be used for displaying pixels on computer monitors. BMP images store their pixels in the RGB color space. RGB is an *additive* color space. When red and green are combined, the resulting color is yellow. When red and blue are combined, the resulting color is magenta. When green and blue are combined, the resulting color is cyan. White is generated by combining all of the colors.

This section explains several methods for processing BMP images. Let's see some examples before explaining how they work. Fig. 23.2–Fig. 23.7 are in the color insert.

23.2.1   Image Pixels and Colors

The image's colors are stored in the `data` attribute. Every pixel uses three consecutive bytes. For example, the first pixel uses the first three bytes: `data[0]`, `data[1]`, and `data[2]`. The second pixel uses `data[3]`, `data[4]`, and `data[5]`. Among the three elements, the first byte represents blue, the second represents green, and the third represents red. Thus, the order is actually BGR (not RGB).

Each `data` element is a byte and has a value between 0 and 255 (inclusive). Larger values mean brighter colors. If a given pixel is pure blue, then the first element is non-zero and the other two elements are zero. If a given pixel is pure red, then the red element is non-zero and the other two elements are both zero. If all three elements are 255, then the pixel is the brightest white. If all three elements are 0, then the pixel is black.

Even though an image is two-dimensional, `data` stores the pixels in a one-dimensional array. This is the most common method because managing one-dimensional arrays is simpler than managing two-dimensional arrays.

Each pixel has an (x, y) coordinate. In high school geometry, the origin (0, 0) is the lower left corner of a graph, the X coordinate increases to the right, and the Y coordinate increases upward. Computer graphics is generally done with a different coordinate system. The origin (0, 0) is the top left corner of the image. The X coordinate increases to the right, and the Y coordinate increases downward. In this coordinate system, we can access the color values of pixels (x, y) by calculating their index in `data`. The formula is:

- $3 \times (y \times width + x)$ for blue
- $3 \times (y \times width + x) + 1$ for green
- $3 \times (y \times width + x) + 2$ for red

23.2.2   Processing Functions

The following listing is a header file that declares the functions we will consider in the rest of this chapter.

```
1   // bmpfunc.h
2   #ifndef _BMPFUNC_H_
3   #define _BMPFUNC_H_
4   #include "bmpimage.h"
5   // keep only one color,
6   // clr = 2, keep red
7   // clr = 1, keep green
8   // clr = 0, keep blue
9   void BMP_color(BMP_Image *image, int clr);
10  // Invert all of the image data in a BMP image
11  // (value = 255 - value)
12  void BMP_invert(BMP_Image *image);
13  // calculate vertical edges using the given threshold value
14  void BMP_edge(BMP_Image *image, int thrshd);
15  // convert an RGB image to a gray-level image
16  void BMP_gray(BMP_Image *image);
17  // calculate the histogram of each color
18  void BMP_histogram(BMP_Image *image);
19  // make a checkerboard
20  void BMP_checker(BMP_Image *image);
21  // mix the colors
22  void BMP_mix(BMP_Image *image);
```

```
23  // equalize by making the darkest to and brightest to 255
24  void BMP_equalize(BMP_Image *image);
25  #endif
```

23.2.3 Applying a Color Filter

The first processing function is the color filter BMP_Color. The method takes a BMP image and an integer between 0 and 2. The integer indicates which color will be selected. If the integer is 0, then blue is selected. Likewise, 1 selects green, and 2 selects red. If a color is not selected, it is set to zero.

```
1   // bmpcolor.c
2   #include "bmpfunc.h"
3   void BMP_color(BMP_Image *img, int clr)
4   {
5      int pxl;
6      for (pxl = clr; pxl < (img -> data_size); pxl ++)
7         {
8            // set the other color components to zero
9            if ((pxl % 3) != clr)
10              {
11                 img -> data[pxl] = 0;
12              }
13         }
14  }
```

As shown in Fig. 23.2 selecting one color sets the other two colors to zeros, revealing the contribution of the selected color to the overall image. If the selected color was zero in the original image, then the resultant pixel becomes black. For example, the upper left of Fig. 23.2 is green. If red or blue is selected, then the upper left pixels become black, as shown in Fig. 23.2 (b) and (d). Similarly, the upper right pixels of Fig. 23.2 are pure blue. This means that these pixels become black if red or green is selected—shown in Fig. 23.2 (b) and (c). In most images, for example Fig. 23.3, each pixel is a mixture of all three colors. After applying a color filter, the corresponding color stands out while the other two colors are removed.

23.2.4 Inverting the Image Colors

The next method, BMP_invert, inverts the color of each pixel. Fig. 23.4 shows the result of this effect.

```
1   // bmpinvert.c
2   #include "bmpfunc.h"
3   void BMP_invert(BMP_Image *img)
4   {
5      int pxl;
6      for (pxl = 0; pxl < (img -> data_size); pxl ++)
7         {
8            img -> data[pxl] = 255 - (img -> data[pxl]);
9         }
10  }
```

23.2.5   Edge Detection

Detecting edges in an image is not easy because human brains have complex methods using past experience and inferred knowledge. This book gives only a simple algorithm and the results may be unsatisfactory in some ways. Part of the difficulty is that high level features about objects must be known in order to determine where the edges are. That is well beyond today's state of the art. The problem *looks* simple because we, as humans, have been seeing edges our entire lives. Commonly used computer edge detectors have no notion of objects and attempt to detect edges from pixels. This chapter gives a very simple (but still useful) method in the following steps:

1. Convert the RGB values to gray levels. This is the formula for converting an RGB value to its corresponding gray level: $0.2989 \times \text{red} + 0.5870 \times \text{green} + 0.1140 \times \text{blue}$. This formula is used because of the perceptual properties of the RGB color space.
2. Find the difference in the gray levels between two adjacent pixels.
3. If the difference is greater than a threshold value, then an edge has been detected.

Selecting the correct threshold depends on many factors. As shown in Fig. 23.5, if the threshold is too high, then some edges are not detected. If the threshold is too low, then the detection is sensitive to noise. In this example we set the threshold to 140. The code listing below gives the function for detecting vertical edges using this simple setup.

```
1   // bmpedge.c
2   #include "bmpfunc.h"
3   #include <stdlib.h>
4   static int RGB2Gray(char red, char green, char blue)
5   {
6     // this is a commonly used formula
7     double gray = 0.2989 * red + 0.5870 * green + 0.1140 * blue;
8     return (int) gray;
9   }
10  void BMP_edge(BMP_Image *img, int thrshd)
11  {
12    // create a two-dimension array for the gray level
13    int width  = img -> width;
14    int height = img -> height;
15    char * * twoDGray = malloc(sizeof(char *) * height);
16    int row;
17    int col;
18    for (row = 0; row < height; row ++)
19      {
20        twoDGray[row] = malloc(sizeof(char *) * width);
21      }
22    // convert RGB to gray
23    int pxl = 0;
24    for (row = 0; row < height; row ++)
25      {
26        for (col = 0; col < width; col ++)
27          {
28            twoDGray[row][col] = RGB2Gray(img -> data[pxl + 2],
29                                          img -> data[pxl + 1],
30                                          img -> data[pxl]);
31            pxl += 3;
32          }
```

```
33        }
34   // detect edges and save the edges in the image
35   pxl = 0;
36   for (row = 0; row < height; row ++)
37      {
38        pxl += 3; // skip the first pixel in each row
39        for (col = 1; col < width; col ++)
40           {
41              int diff = twoDGray[row][col] -
42                twoDGray[row][col - 1];
43              // take the absolute value
44              if (diff < 0)
45                 {
46                    diff = - diff;
47                 }
48              if (diff > thrshd) // an edge
49                 {
50                    // set color to white
51                    img -> data[pxl + 2] = 255;
52                    img -> data[pxl + 1] = 255;
53                    img -> data[pxl]     = 255;
54                 }
55              else // not an edge
56                 {
57                    // set color to black
58                    img -> data[pxl + 2] = 0;
59                    img -> data[pxl + 1] = 0;
60                    img -> data[pxl]     = 0;
61                 }
62              pxl += 3;
63           }
64      }
65   for (row = 0; row < height; row ++)
66      {
67        free(twoDGray[row]);
68      }
69   free (twoDGray);
70 }
```

23.2.6 Color Equalization

Sometimes an image is over exposed (too bright) or under exposed (too dark). The image can usually be enhanced by using *color equalization* using the following steps:

1. Find the maximum and the minimum values of the colors.
2. If the maximum and the minimum values are different, scale the maximum value to 255 and the minimum value to 0.
3. Scale the color based on a formula.

There are many ways to scale the pixel's colors. One simple method is called linear scaling: using a linear equation to express the relationship between the original color and the new color. Let x and y be the old and the new colors, then a linear equation has two coefficients: a and b.

$$y = ax + b \tag{23.1}$$

Suppose M and m are the original minimum and the maximum values. They should become 0 and 255 after the scaling. The following two equations are used to determine the correct values for a and b.

$$\begin{aligned} 0 &= am + b \\ 255 &= aM + b \end{aligned} \tag{23.2}$$

$$a = \frac{255}{M - m} \text{ and } b = -\frac{255m}{M - m} \tag{23.3}$$

The code listing below implements this color equalization scheme.

```c
// bmpequalize.c
#include "bmpfunc.h"
void BMP_equalize(BMP_Image *img)
{
    int pxl;
    unsigned char redmin   = 255;
    unsigned char redmax   = 0;
    unsigned char greenmin = 255;
    unsigned char greenmax = 0;
    unsigned char bluemin  = 255;
    unsigned char bluemax  = 0;
    // find the maximum and the minimum values of each color
    for (pxl = 0; pxl < (img -> data_size); pxl += 3)
    {
        unsigned char red   = img -> data[pxl + 2];
        unsigned char green = img -> data[pxl + 1];
        unsigned char blue  = img -> data[pxl];
        if (redmin > red) { redmin = red; }
        if (redmax < red) { redmax = red; }
        if (greenmin > green) { greenmin = green; }
        if (greenmax < green) { greenmax = green; }
        if (bluemin > blue) { bluemin = blue; }
        if (bluemax < blue) { bluemax = blue; }
    }
    // calculate the scaling factors
    // max and min must be different to prevent
    // divided by zero error
    double redscale   = 1.0;
    double greenscale = 1.0;
    double bluescale  = 1.0;
    if (redmax > redmin)
    {
        redscale = 255.0 / (redmax - redmin);
    }
    if (greenmax > greenmin)
    {
```

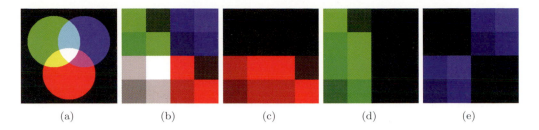

(a)   (b)   (c)   (d)   (e)

FIGURE 23.2: (a) The RGB color space, showing the primary colors and their mixtures. White is produced by mixing all three primary colors together. Color filters. (b) original images. (c) red only, (d) green only, (e) blue only.

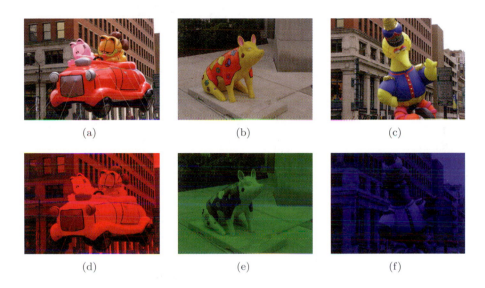

FIGURE 23.3: Color filters. (a)–(c) original images. (d) red only, (e) green only, (f) blue only.

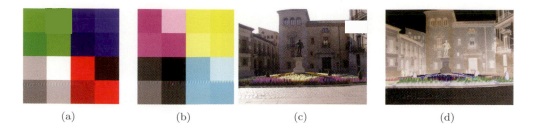

|(a)|(b)|(c)|(d)|

FIGURE 23.4: Color inversion. (a),(c): original. (b),(d): inverted.

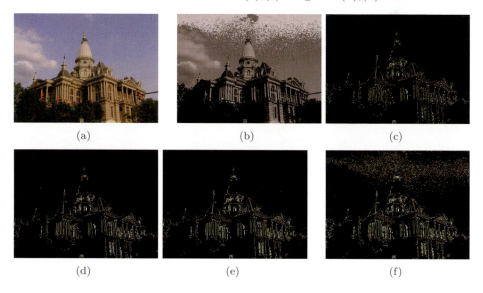

|(a)|(b)|(c)|

|(d)|(e)|(f)|

FIGURE 23.5: Detecting vertical edges. (a) The original image. (b) Gray-scale image. The detected edges use different threshold values. (c) 120. (d) 100. (e) 80. (f) is 60. Many vertical edges are not detected when the threshold is too high. When the threshold is too low, there are many false-positive edges (like the sky).

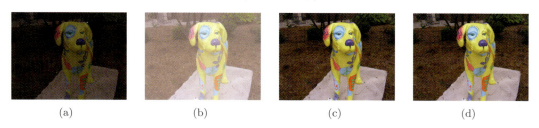

|(a)|(b)|(c)|(d)|

FIGURE 23.6: Equalization. (a),(b): original images. (c),(d): processed images.

|(a)|(b)|(c)|(d)|

FIGURE 23.7: Equalization. (a),(b): original images. (c),(d): processed images.

```
37      greenscale = 255.0 / (greenmax - greenmin);
38    }
39  if (bluemax > bluemin)
40    {
41      bluescale = 255.0 / (bluemax - bluemin);
42    }
43
44  // equalize the pixels
45  for (pxl = 0; pxl < (img -> data_size); pxl += 3)
46    {
47      if (redmax > redmin)
48        {
49          img -> data[pxl + 2] = (int) (redscale *
50                    (img -> data[pxl + 2] - redmin));
51        }
52      if (greenmax > greenmin)
53        {
54          img -> data[pxl + 1] = (int) (greenscale *
55                    (img -> data[pxl + 1] - greenmin));
56        }
57      if (bluemax > bluemin)
58        {
59          img -> data[pxl] = (int) (bluescale *
60                    (img -> data[pxl] - bluemin));
61        }
62    }
63  }
```

This chapter gives a starting point for image processing. Image processing is a rich subject and there are many books on the topic and related topics.

Chapter 24

Huffman Compression

Section 10.4 introduced binary trees through the example of binary search trees. This chapter describes another way to use binary trees in a popular compression technique called *Huffman Compression* or *Huffman Coding*. Huffman Coding was developed by David Huffman in the early 1950s, while he was still a graduate student at MIT. After more than 60 years, Huffman Coding remains one of the best general-purpose compression algorithms available, fast and widely used.

It is easier to understand Huffman Coding by comparing it to ASCII. ASCII is a "fixed-length code" using 8 bits for each letter, even though some letters (such as e and s) are more common than some others (such as q and z). In contrast, Huffman Compression uses "variable-length code". If a letter appears frequently, then it is encoded with fewer bits. If a letter appears infrequently, then more bits are used. This means that the average length of all letters is shorter—the information is compressed. Huffman Coding is *lossless compression* because the original data can be fully recovered. *Lossy compression* means the original data cannot be fully recovered. Lossy compression may achieve higher *compression ratios* than lossless compression, and is useful when full recovery of the original data is unnecessary. Lossy compression is frequently used to compress images and JPEG is an example of lossy compression. A compression ratio is defined as:

$$\frac{\text{size of uncompressed file}}{\text{size of compressed file}} \tag{24.1}$$

This chapter uses Huffman Coding to compress articles written in English. Given a set of letters (or symbols) and their frequencies, Huffman Coding is optimal because Huffman Coding uses the fewest bits on average.

24.1   Example

Consider an article with only eight different characters: E, N, G, T, g, p, d, and h. To encode these characters, only 3 bits are sufficient because $2^3 = 8$. That means that each character can be assigned to a unique 3-bit sequence. Next consider the situation when the letters' frequencies are quite different, as shown in this table:

character	frequencies
E	0.56%
N	1.12%
G	3.93%
T	3.93%
g	10.67%
p	12.92%
d	25.84%
h	41.01%

Consider the following codes (bit sequences) for the characters. We will explain how to generate these codes (called a "code book") in the next section.

character	code	length
E	1110100	7
N	1110101	7
G	111011	6
T	11100	5
g	1111	4
p	110	3
d	10	2
h	0	1

The average number of bits is $7 \times 0.0056 + 7 \times 0.0112 + 6 \times 0.0393 + 5 \times 0.0393 + 4 \times 0.1067 + 3 \times 0.1292 + 2 \times 0.2584 + 1 \times 0.4101 = 2.29$. This is $1 - \frac{2.29}{3} \approx 1 - 0.76 = 24\%$ reduction in the total length over using 3-bit codes. The code book can be displayed as a tree, as shown in Fig. 24.1. At any tree node, 0 means moving left and 1 means moving right.

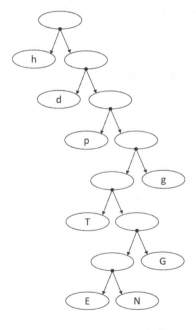

FIGURE 24.1: Graphical representation of the code book.

The code book tree has several important properties:

- Characters are stored only at leaf nodes. Non-leaf nodes do not store any characters. If a non-leaf node stores a character, then ambiguity arises. For example, if the root's right child stores the character 'm', does 10 mean 'mh' or 'd'? To put it in a different way, no code is the *prefix* of another code.
- If a character is more frequent, then its distance to the root is shorter. This means that its bit sequence will be shorter and the average total length will be shorter.
- If the entire article contains only one character (perhaps repeated many times), then the code book has only one row in the table and the tree has one node—the root node.
- If the article contains n different characters ($n > 1$), then the tree has n leaf nodes and each non-leaf node has two children. It is impossible to have a non-leaf node that has only one child.

24.2 Encoding

To compress a file, the following steps are needed:

1. Count the frequencies of the characters.
2. Sort the characters by frequencies
3. Build a tree similar to Fig. 24.1.
4. Build the code book.
5. Use the code book to compress the file.

The chapter uses "encoder" and "compressor" interchangeably. Similarly, "decoder" and "decompresser" are used interchangeably.

24.2.1 Count Frequencies

The first step of Huffman Coding is to determine the frequencies of each letter in the document being compressed. We will use the charter of the United Nations as an example:

```
The Charter of the United Nations was signed on 26 June 1945, in San
Francisco, at the conclusion of the United Nations Conference on
International Organization, and came into force on 24 October
1945. The Statute of the International Court of Justice is an
integral part of the Charter.

Amendments to Articles 23, 27 and 61 of the Charter were adopted by
the General Assembly on 17 December 1963 and came into force on 31
August 1965. A further amendment to Article 61 was adopted by the
General Assembly on 20 December 1971, and came into force on 24
September 1973. An amendment to Article 109, adopted by the General
Assembly on 20 December 1965, came into force on 12 June 1968.

The amendment to Article 23 enlarges the membership of the Security
Council from eleven to fifteen. The amended Article 27 provides that
decisions of the Security Council on procedural matters shall be made
by an affirmative vote of nine members (formerly seven) and on all
other matters by an affirmative vote of nine members (formerly
seven), including the concurring votes of the five permanent members
of the Security Council.
```

The amendment to Article 61, which entered into force on 31 August 1965, enlarged the membership of the Economic and Social Council from eighteen to twenty-seven. The subsequent amendment to that Article, which entered into force on 24 September 1973, further increased the membership of the Council from twenty-seven to fifty-four.

The amendment to Article 109, which relates to the first paragraph of that Article, provides that a General Conference of Member States for the purpose of reviewing the Charter may be held at a date and place to be fixed by a two-thirds vote of the members of the General Assembly and by a vote of any nine members (formerly seven) of the Security Council. Paragraph 3 of Article 109, which deals with the consideration of a possible review conference during the tenth regular session of the General Assembly, has been retained in its original form in its reference to a "vote,␣of␣any␣seven␣members␣of the␣Security␣Council", the paragraph having been acted upon in 1955 by the General Assembly, at its tenth regular session, and by the Security Council.

The table below shows the frequencies of the characters in the UN charter:

V: ASCII value						**C**: character (if printable)			**F**: frequency		
V	**C**	**F**	**V**	**C**	**F**	**V**	**C**	**F**	**V**	**C**	**F**
10		38	11		0	12		0	13		0	14		0
30		0	31		0	32		340	33	!	0	34	"	2
35	#	0	36	$	0	37	%	0	38	&	0	39	'	0
40	(| 3 | 41 |)	3	42	*	0	43	+	0	44	,	20
45	-	4	46	.	11	47	/	0	48	0	5	49	1	22
50	2	11	51	3	8	52	4	5	53	5	7	54	6	9
55	7	6	56	8	1	57	9	14	58	:	0	59	;	0
60	<	0	61	=	0	62	>	0	63	?	0	64	@	0
65	A	21	66	B	0	67	C	15	68	D	3	69	E	1
70	F	1	71	G	7	72	H	0	73	I	2	74	J	3
75	K	0	76	L	0	77	M	1	78	N	2	79	O	2
80	P	1	81	Q	0	82	R	0	83	S	12	84	T	7
85	U	2	86	V	0	87	W	0	88	X	0	89	Y	0
90	Z	0	91	[	0	92	\	0	93	]	0	94	^	0
95	_	0	96	`	0	97	a	105	98	b	38	99	c	64
100	d	46	101	e	263	102	f	58	103	g	19	104	h	73
105	i	96	106	j	0	107	k	0	108	l	56	109	m	64
110	n	140	111	o	121	112	p	23	113	q	1	114	r	119
115	s	71	116	t	157	117	u	37	118	v	21	119	w	13
120	x	1	121	y	30	122	z	1	123	{	0	124	—	0
125	}	0	126		0	127		0						

The important point is that some characters appear much more frequently than the others. For example, the letter 'e' appears 263 times and 't' appears 157 times. In contrast, 'z' appears only once and 'B' is not in the article at all. Note that there are some invisible characters. For example, 10 is the newline character ('\n') and it is used 38 times (there are 38 lines in the charter). The ASCII code 32 is used for a space character, and it is used 340 times.

24.2.2 Sort by Frequency

After finding the frequencies of the characters, the frequencies are sorted in the ascending order. The table below shows the characters sorted by their frequencies. If a character (for example, 'B' and 'H') does not appear in the article, then it is discarded. If two characters have the same frequency, then their order does not matter. When this occurs, we order the letters of the same frequency by their ASCII value. For example, 'E' and 'F' appear once and 'E' is before 'F' in this table.

V: value			C: character			F: frequency								
V	C	F	V	C	F	V	C	F	V	C	F	V	C	F
56	8	1	69	E	1	70	F	1	77	M	1	80	P	1
113	q	1	120	x	1	122	z	1	34	"	2	73	I	2
78	N	2	79	O	2	85	U	2	40	(	3	41	)	3
68	D	3	74	J	3	45	-	4	48	0	5	52	4	5
55	7	6	53	5	7	71	G	7	84	T	7	51	3	8
54	6	9	46	.	11	50	2	11	83	S	12	119	w	13
57	9	14	67	C	15	103	g	19	44	,	20	65	A	21
118	v	21	49	1	22	112	p	23	121	y	30	117	u	37
10		38	98	b	38	100	d	46	108	l	56	102	f	58
99	c	64	109	m	64	115	s	71	104	h	73	105	i	96
97	a	105	114	r	119	111	o	121	110	n	140	116	t	157
101	e	263	32		340									

The following code gives a sample implementation for determining the frequency of each character, and then sorting the characters by their frequencies. This is the header file:

```
// freq.h
#ifndef FREQ_H
#define FREQ_H
typedef struct
{
  char value;
  int freq;
} CharFreq;
// count the frequencies of the letters
// NUMLETTER is a constant (128) defined in constant.h
// frequencies is an array of NUMLETTER elements
// The function returns the number of characters in the file
// The function returns 0 if cannot read from the file
int countFrequency(char * filename, CharFreq * frequencies);
// print the array
void printFrequency(CharFreq * frequencies);
// sort the array
void sortFrequency(CharFreq * frequencies);
#endif
```

This listing defines the function implementations.

```
// freq.c
#include "constant.h"
#include "freq.h"
#include <stdio.h>
#include <stdlib.h>
```

```
 6  #include <strings.h>
 7  int countFrequency(char * filename, CharFreq * freq)
 8  {
 9    FILE * fptr = fopen(filename, "r");
10    int count = 0;
11    if (fptr == NULL)
12      {
13        return 0;
14      }
15    while (! feof (fptr))
16      {
17        int onechar = fgetc(fptr);
18        if (onechar != EOF)
19          {
20            count ++;
21            freq[onechar].value = (char) onechar;
22            freq[onechar].freq ++;
23          }
24      }
25    fclose (fptr);
26    return count;
27  }
28  void printFrequency(CharFreq * freq)
29  {
30    int ind;
31    for (ind = 0; ind < NUMLETTER; ind ++)
32      {
33        printf("%d %d\n", freq[ind].value,
34                freq[ind].freq);
35      }
36    printf("-----------------------\n");
37  }
38  static int compareFreq(const void * p1, const void * p2)
39  {
40    const CharFreq * ip1 = (const CharFreq *) p1;
41    const CharFreq * ip2 = (const CharFreq *) p2;
42    const int iv1 = ip1 -> freq;
43    const int iv2 = ip2 -> freq;
44    return (iv1 - iv2);
45  }
46  void sortFrequency(CharFreq * freq)
47  {
48    qsort(freq, NUMLETTER, sizeof(CharFreq), compareFreq);
49  }
```

24.2.3 Build a Code Tree

Let's revisit the small example from the first section of this chapter. Fig. 24.2 to Fig. 24.7 illustrate the procedure for building the tree. First, the characters (**C**) are sorted by the frequencies (**F**). Then, a linked list is created and the nodes are sorted by the character

C	F
E	1
N	2
G	7
T	7
g	19
p	23
d	46
h	73

(a)

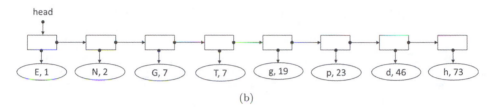

(b)

FIGURE 24.2: (a) The characters are sorted by the frequencies. (b) A linked list is created. List nodes are expressed by rectangles. Tree nodes are expressed by ovals.

frequencies. Each list node points to a tree node. At the beginning of the algorithm, none of the tree nodes have children.

Fig. 24.3 shows how to merge the first two list nodes. The first two list nodes, $\mathbb{L}$ and $\mathbb{R}$, are taken. A new tree node $\mathbb{N}$ is created and its left and right children are $\mathbb{L}$ and $\mathbb{R}$. The frequency of the newly created tree node is the sum of the frequencies of the two children. The newly created tree node is not a leaf node so its character is irrelevant. A new list node is created and points to the newly created tree node. The list nodes must remain sorted in the ascending order by the tree nodes' frequencies. These three steps have removed the two trees from the list with the smallest frequencies, combined them into a single tree, and then placed the new tree back onto the list, keeping the list sorted by the frequencies.

Fig. 24.4 to Fig. 24.6 repeat the same steps: (i) taking the first two tree nodes, (ii) creating a parent node (the node's frequency is the sum of the frequencies of the two children), (iii) creating a list node, and (iv) inserting the list node and keeping the list sorted. As a result, two nodes are moved from the list, and one is added, giving a net change of removing one list node. The linked list becomes shorter.

It is important to understand the concept that is described in the figures. The first part of the program is described below.

1. A tree structure is created. Each tree node stores a character and the character's frequency.

```
1   // tree.h
2   #ifndef TREE_H
3   #define TREE_H
4   typedef struct treenode
5   {
6       struct treenode * left;
7       struct treenode * right;
```

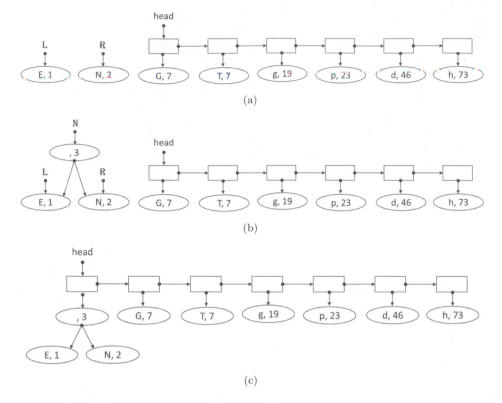

FIGURE 24.3: (a) Take the tree nodes, $\mathbb{L}$ and $\mathbb{R}$, from the first two list nodes. (b) Create a tree node $\mathbb{N}$ whose left and right children are $\mathbb{L}$ and $\mathbb{R}$. (c) Create a new list node pointing to the newly created tree node. The list nodes are sorted in the ascending order by the tree nodes' frequencies.

```
8       char value;  // character
9       int freq;    // frequency
10    } TreeNode;
11    #endif
```

2. A list structure is created. Each list node has a pointer to the tree node and a link to the next list node.

```
1    // list.h
2    #ifndef LIST_H
3    #define LIST_H
4    typedef struct listnode
5    {
6      struct listnode * next;
7      TreeNode * tnptr;
8    } ListNode;
9    #endif
```

3. A linked list is created. Each list node points to a tree node. The linked list is sorted by the frequencies. If two characters have the same frequency, then they are sorted alphabetically.

4. Repeat the following steps until the linked list has only one node left.

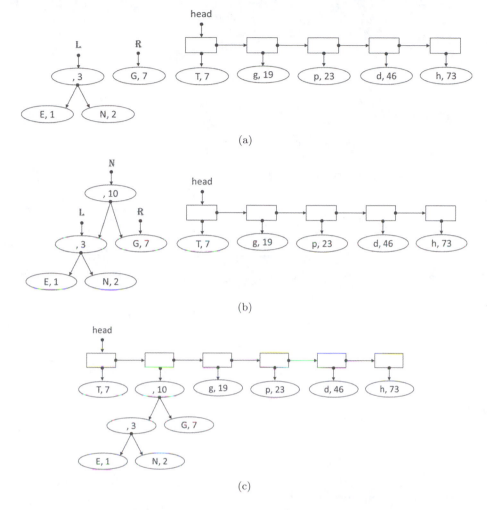

FIGURE 24.4: Continue the procedure.

5. Take the first two nodes from the linked list (the head and the node after the head). Take the two tree nodes pointed to by these two list nodes. Call these two tree nodes $\mathbb{L}$ and $\mathbb{R}$. Create a new tree node $\mathbb{N}$ whose left and right children are $\mathbb{L}$ and $\mathbb{R}$. $\mathbb{N}$'s frequency is the sum of $\mathbb{L}$'s and $\mathbb{R}$'s frequencies. The character stored in this non-leaf node is irrelevant.

6. Remove the first two list nodes and discard them. They are no longer needed.

7. Create a new list node pointing to $\mathbb{N}$. Insert this list node so that the list nodes remain sorted by the tree nodes' frequencies.

Below is the program for building the tree.

```
// constant.h
#ifndef CONSTATNT_H
#define CONSTATNT_H
#define NUMLETTER 128
#define TEXT 1
#define BINARY 2
#endif
```

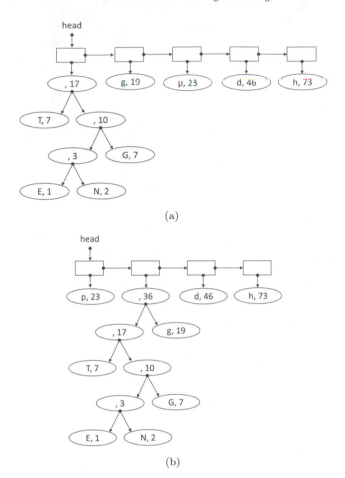

FIGURE 24.5: At every step, two tree nodes are removed, combined into a single tree, and then the new tree is added into the list.

```
// extend the previous tree.h
TreeNode * TreeNode_create(char val, int freq);
TreeNode * Tree_merge(TreeNode * tn1, TreeNode * tn2);
void Tree_print(TreeNode * tn, int level);
```

```
// extend the previous list.h
#include "tree.h"
#include "constant.h"
#include "freq.h"
#include <stdio.h>
ListNode * List_build(CharFreq * frequencies);
ListNode * ListNode_create(TreeNode * tn);
ListNode * List_insert(ListNode * head, ListNode * ln);
void List_print(ListNode * head);
```

```
// encode.h
#ifndef ENCODE_H
#define ENCODE_H
```

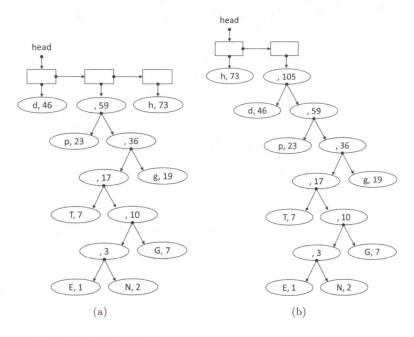

FIGURE 24.6: Continue the procedure shortening the linked list.

```
4  // encode the text in the input file
5  // save the result in the output file
6  // mode: TEXT or BINARY
7  // return 0 if cannot read from file or write to file
8  // return 1 if success
9  int encode(char * infile, char * outfile, int mode);
10 #endif
```

```
1  // tree.c
2  #include "tree.h"
3  #include <stdio.h>
4  #include <stdlib.h>
5  TreeNode * TreeNode_create(char val, int freq)
6  {
7    TreeNode * tn = malloc(sizeof(TreeNode));
8    tn -> left = NULL;
9    tn -> right = NULL;
10   tn -> value = val;
11   tn -> freq = freq;
12   return tn;
13 }
14 TreeNode * Tree_merge(TreeNode * tn1, TreeNode * tn2)
15 {
16   TreeNode * tn = malloc(sizeof(TreeNode));
17   tn -> left = tn1;
18   tn -> right = tn2;
19   tn -> value = 0; // do not care
20   tn -> freq = tn1 -> freq + tn2 -> freq;
```

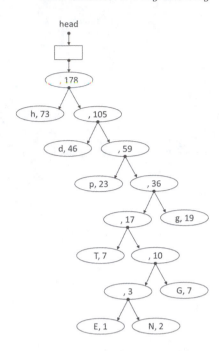

FIGURE 24.7: Now the linked list has only one node. The tree has been built, and it is in the only remaining list node.

```c
21    return tn;
22  }
23  // post-order
24  void Tree_print(TreeNode * tn, int level)
25  {
26    if (tn == NULL)
27      {
28        return;
29      }
30    TreeNode * lc = tn -> left;   // left child
31    TreeNode * rc = tn -> right;  // right child
32    Tree_print(lc, level + 1);
33    Tree_print(rc, level + 1);
34    int depth;
35    for (depth = 0; depth < level; depth ++)
36      {
37        printf("␣␣␣␣");
38      }
39    printf("freq␣=␣%d␣", tn -> freq);
40    if ((lc == NULL) && (rc == NULL))
41      {
42        // a leaf node
43        printf("value␣=␣%d,␣'%c'", tn -> value, tn -> value);
44      }
45    printf("\n");
46  }
```

```
1   // list.c
2   #include "list.h"
3   #include "freq.h"
4   #include <stdlib.h>
5   ListNode * ListNode_create(TreeNode * tn)
6   {
7     ListNode * ln = malloc(sizeof(ListNode));
8     ln -> next = NULL;
9     ln -> tnptr = tn;
10    return ln;
11  }
12  // head may be NULL
13  // ln must not be NULL
14  // ln -> next must be NULL
15  ListNode * List_insert(ListNode * head, ListNode * ln)
16  {
17    if (head == NULL)
18      {
19        return ln;
20      }
21    if (ln == NULL)
22      {
23        printf("ERROR! ln is NULL\n");
24      }
25    if ((ln -> next) != NULL)
26      {
27        printf("ERROR! ln -> next is not NULL\n");
28      }
29    int freq1 = (head -> tnptr) -> freq;
30    int freq2 = (ln -> tnptr) -> freq;
31    if (freq1 > freq2)
32      {
33        // ln should be the first node
34        ln -> next = head;
35        return ln;
36      }
37    // ln should be after head
38    head -> next = List_insert(head -> next, ln);
39    return head;
40  }
41  // frequencies must be sorted
42  ListNode * List_build(CharFreq * frequencies)
43  {
44    // find the first index whose frequency is nonzero
45    int ind = 0;
46    while (frequencies[ind].freq == 0)
47      {
48        ind ++;
49      }
50    if (ind == NUMLETTER)
51      {
```

```
52        // no letter appears
53        return NULL;
54      }
55    // create a linked list, each node points to a tree node
56    ListNode * head = NULL;
57    while (ind < NUMLETTER)
58      {
59        TreeNode * tn =
60          TreeNode_create(frequencies[ind].value,
61                          frequencies[ind].freq);
62        ListNode * ln = ListNode_create(tn);
63        head = List_insert(head, ln);
64        ind ++;
65      }
66    return head;
67  }
68  void List_print(ListNode * head)
69  {
70    if (head == NULL)
71      {
72        return;
73      }
74    Tree_print(head -> tnptr, 0);
75    List_print(head -> next);
76  }
```

The following function implements the concept depicted earlier.

```
1  // encode.c
2  #include "encode.h"
3  #include "constant.h"
4  #include "freq.h"
5  #include "list.h"
6  #include <stdio.h>
7  #include <strings.h>
8  #include <stdlib.h>
9  int encode(char * infile, char * outfile, int mode)
10 {
11   CharFreq frequencies[NUMLETTER];
12   // set the array elements to zero
13   bzero(frequencies, sizeof(CharFreq) * NUMLETTER);
14   if (countFrequency(infile, frequencies) == 0)
15     {
16       return 0;
17     }
18   // printFrequency(frequencies);
19   sortFrequency(frequencies);
20   // printFrequency(frequencies);
21   ListNode * head = List_build(frequencies);
22   if (head == NULL)
23     {
24       // the article is empty
```

```
25        return 0;
26      }
27    // merge the top two list nodes until only one list node
28    while ((head -> next) != NULL)
29      {
30        List_print(head); printf("-----------\n");
31        ListNode * second = head -> next;
32        // second must not be NULL, otherwise, will not enter
33        ListNode * third  = second -> next;
34        // third may be NULL
35        // get the tree nodes of the first two list nodes
36        TreeNode * tn1 = head -> tnptr;
37        TreeNode * tn2 = second -> tnptr;
38        // remove the first two nodes
39        free (head);
40        free (second);
41        head = third;
42        TreeNode * mrg = Tree_merge(tn1, tn2);
43        ListNode * ln = ListNode_create(mrg);
44        head = List_insert(head, ln);
45      }
46    List_print(head);
47    return 1;
48  }
```

Line 46 prints the linked list, and it should have only one list node. Otherwise, the function should continue inside `while`. Calling `Tree_print` prints the tree nodes using a post-order traversal. Below is the output. Note that it matches Fig. 24.7.

```
freq = 73 value = 104, 'h'
    freq = 46 value = 100, 'd'
        freq = 23 value = 112, 'p'
                freq = 7 value = 84, 'T'
                            freq = 1 value = 69, 'E'
                            freq = 2 value = 78, 'N'
                    freq = 3
                    freq = 7 value = 71, 'G'
                freq = 10
            freq = 17
            freq = 19 value = 103, 'g'
        freq = 36
    freq = 59
    freq = 105
freq = 178
```

Fig. 24.8 shows the list of tree nodes as displayed in the debugging program DDD. DDD can help you visualize how the list nodes and the tree nodes change as the program makes progress. Fig. 24.9 shows the tree in DDD after the tree has been completely built. It is the same tree as Fig. 24.7. The visualization function in DDD can help you see the nodes of the tree.

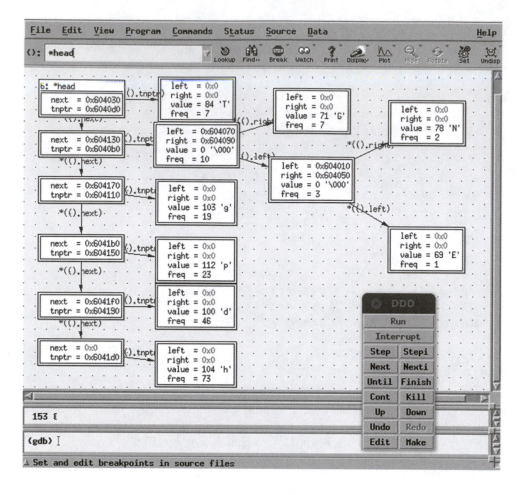

FIGURE 24.8: A list of tree nodes. This figure shows the list as it is being built. The tree is the same as the one shown in Fig. 24.4 (c).

24.2.4 Build a Code Book

The next step creates the code book from the tree. We use a two-dimensional array to store the code book. In each row, the first column stores the character. The remaining columns store the code, i.e., the bit-sequence for the character. The maximum length of a code is the tree's height minus one since the root itself is counted as one when computing the height. The number of rows is the number of leaf nodes. For the tree in Fig. 24.7, the height is 8 and there are 8 leaf nodes. In general, the tree's height is much smaller than the number of leaf nodes. For example, the tree for the Charter of the United Nations has 57 leaf nodes but the tree's height is only 12. The following table shows the two-dimensional array for the code book. Since the codes' lengths are different, -1 is used to terminate a sequence of bits.

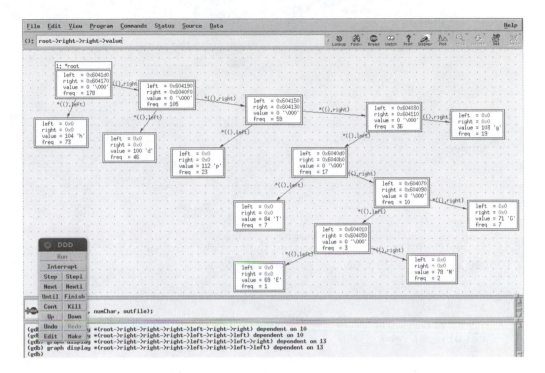

FIGURE 24.9: Display the tree in DDD.

index		character		code						
[0]	→	h	0	−1						
[1]	→	d	1	0	−1					
[2]	→	p	1	1	0	−1				
[3]	→	T	1	1	1	0	0	−1		
[4]	→	E	1	1	1	0	1	0	0	−1
[5]	→	N	1	1	1	0	1	0	1	−1
[6]	→	G	1	1	1	0	1	1	−1	
[7]	→	g	1	1	1	1	−1				

Do you notice that only one row (for 'h') has 0 in the first column? The reason for this is that there is only one node on the left side of the root. There are seven nodes on the right side of the root and ones are filled to the first column of seven rows. From the root, after moving down to the right child, there is only one node on the left side (for 'd'). As a result, only one row has zero in column 2. The other six rows have ones in column 2.

Fig. 24.10 shows the general rule. If there are n leaf nodes on the left side of a node, zeros are filled in n rows. The column of the zeros is determined by the distance to the root. If the node is the root itself, then the first column is used. Similarly, if there are m leaf nodes on the right side, ones are filled in m rows.

The following functions compute the height of a tree and the number of leaf nodes. To determine a tree's height, the function recursively computes the heights of the left subtree and the right subtree. Then the function chooses the taller of the two subtrees. To determine the number of leaf nodes, the function increments a counter when a leaf node is encountered. A leaf node is a node that has no children nodes.

```
static int Tree_heightHelper(TreeNode * tn, int height)
{
```

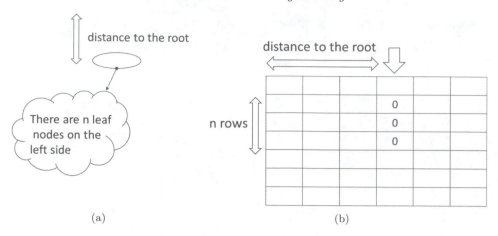

(a)   (b)

FIGURE 24.10: If there are n leaf nodes on the left side, zeros should be filled in n rows. The column is determined by the distance from the root.

```
3     if (tn == 0)
4       {
5         return height;
6       }
7     int lh = Tree_heightHelper(tn -> left, height + 1);
8     int rh = Tree_heightHelper(tn -> right, height + 1);
9     if (lh < rh)
10      {
11        return rh;
12      }
13    if (lh > rh)
14      {
15        return lh;
16      }
17    return lh;
18  }
19
20  int Tree_height(TreeNode * tn)
21  {
22    return Tree_heightHelper(tn, 0);
23  }
24
25  static void Tree_leafHelper(TreeNode * tn, int * num)
26  {
27    if (tn == 0)
28      {
29        return;
30      }
31    // if it is a leaf node, add one
32    TreeNode * lc = tn -> left;
33    TreeNode * rc = tn -> right;
34    if ((lc == NULL) && (rc == NULL))
35      {
```

```
36          (* num) ++;
37          return;
38       }
39     Tree_leafHelper(lc, num);
40     Tree_leafHelper(rc, num);
41  }
42
43  int Tree_leaf(TreeNode * tn)
44  {
45     int num = 0;
46     Tree_leafHelper(tn, & num);
47     return num;
48  }
```

The following listing is part of the **encode** function after the code tree has been built.

```
1   // the linked list is no longer needed
2   TreeNode * root = head -> tnptr;
3   free (head);
4
5   // build the code book
6   // get the number of leaf nodes
7   int numRow = Tree_leaf(root);
8   // get the tree's height
9   int numCol = Tree_height(root);
10  // numCol should add 1 to accommodate the ending -1
11  numCol ++;
12  // create a 2D array initialize the codes to -1
13  int * * codebook = malloc(sizeof(int*) * numRow);
14  int row;
15  for (row = 0; row < numRow; row ++)
16     {
17        codebook[row] = malloc(sizeof(int) * numCol);
18        int col;
19        // initialize to -1
20        for (col = 0; col < numCol; col ++)
21           {
22              codebook[row][col] = -1;
23           }
24     }
25  buildCodeBook(root, codebook);
26  printCodeBook(codebook, numRow);
27  return 1;
28  }
```

The following listing shows the function **buildCodeBook**. It uses a recursive helper function to traverse the tree. When a leaf node is encountered, the character is stored. At line 14, the function uses the very first column (with index zero) to store the characters. The code book codes start from the second index (i.e., index 1), which is passed as the fourth argument to **buildCodeBookHelper** at line 44.

```
1   void buildCodeBookHelper(TreeNode * tn, int * * codebook,
2                            int * row, int col)
```

```
3   {
4     if (tn == NULL)
5       {
6         return;
7       }
8     // is it a leaf node?
9     TreeNode * lc = tn -> left;
10    TreeNode * rc = tn -> right;
11    if ((lc == NULL) && (rc == NULL)) // it is a leaf node
12      {
13        // finish one code
14        codebook[*row][0] = tn -> value; // the character
15        (* row) ++; // finish one row
16        return;
17      }
18    if (lc != NULL)
19      {
20        // populate this column of the entire subtree
21        int numRow = Tree_leaf(lc);
22        int ind;
23        for (ind = * row; ind < (* row) + numRow; ind ++)
24          {
25            codebook[ind][col] = 0;
26          }
27        buildCodeBookHelper(lc, codebook, row, col + 1);
28      }
29    if (rc != NULL)
30      {
31        int numRow = Tree_leaf(rc);
32        int ind;
33        for (ind = * row; ind < (* row) + numRow; ind ++)
34          {
35            codebook[ind][col] = 1;
36          }
37        buildCodeBookHelper(rc, codebook, row, col + 1);
38      }
39  }
40  void buildCodeBook(TreeNode * root, int * * codebook)
41  {
42    int row = 0;
43    // column start at 1, column = 0 stores the character
44    buildCodeBookHelper(root, codebook, & row, 1);
45  }
46
47  void printCodeBook(int * * codebook, int numRow)
48  {
49    int row;
50    for (row = 0; row < numRow; row ++)
51      {
52        // print the character
53        printf("%c:␣", codebook[row][0]);
```

```
54    int col = 1;
55    // print the code
56    while (codebook[row][col] != -1)
57      {
58        printf("%d␣", codebook[row][col]);
59        col ++;
60      }
61    printf("\n");
62    }
63  }
```

After the code book has been built, it is printed. Below is the output of `printCodeBook`.

```
h: 0
d: 1 0
p: 1 1 0
T: 1 1 1 0 0
E: 1 1 1 0 1 0 0
N: 1 1 1 0 1 0 1
G: 1 1 1 0 1 1
g: 1 1 1 1
```

24.2.5 Compress a File

The file can be compressed once the code book has been created. The compressed file must include the code book because it is required to decode the file. The code book is dependent on the characters, and the frequencies of the characters, within the file, and thus each code book is unique to a given file. Thus, a compressed file has two parts: a header that represents the code book and the data immediately after the code book. The code can be expressed in different ways as long as the compression program and the decompression program agree to the format. This book uses the following way to express the code book:

- The tree is traversed using post-order traversal. As explained earlier, in-order traversal cannot distinguish different shapes of binary trees. Thus, in-order traversal cannot be used.
- When encountering a leaf node, '1' is printed before printing the character. This '1' is a "command" for describing the tree.
- When encountering a non-leaf node, one '0' is printed. This is the other "command". Commands can be either 1 or 0. Remember, the non-leaf node is encountered after visiting both the left subtree and the right subtree—this is what a post-order traversal means.
- One 0 is added after visiting the root. After that, a new line '\n' is added.

Fig. 24.11 shows several examples that express the code trees using this format. Note that if '\n' appears in an article, then it is a leaf node in the code tree, and the node is expressed as 1'\n'. This method can also handle '1' and '0' in the article. They become 11 and 10. For Fig. 24.1, the header is 1h1d1p1T1E1N01G001g00000.

After the header, the rest of the compressed file is the data. If 'h' appears in the original uncompressed file, then it is replaced by the code 0. If 'g' appears in the original uncompressed file, then it is replaced by the code 1111. To do this efficiently, the program can build a mapping table from the ASCII value to the indexes in the code book. Below is the mapping to the code book.

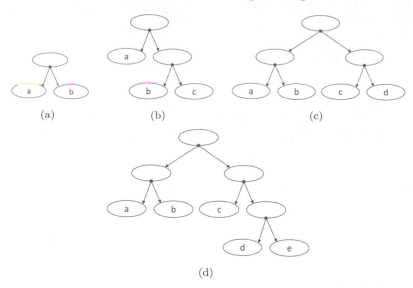

FIGURE 24.11: The expressions for the code trees are (a) 1a1b00, (b) 1a1b1c000, (c) 1a1b01c1d000, (d) 1a1b01c1d1e0000. For each tree, the number of 1s is the same as the number of leaf nodes. The number of 0s is one plus the number of non-leaf nodes.

Character	index
E	4
G	6
N	5
T	3
d	1
g	7
h	0
p	2

The listing below shows a sample implementation that makes the header and compresses the data.

```
// compress.c
#include <stdio.h>
#include "tree.h"
#include "constant.h"
static void Tree_headerHelper(TreeNode * tn, FILE * outfptr)
{
  if (tn == NULL)
    {
      return; // should not get here
    }
  TreeNode * lc = tn -> left;
  TreeNode * rc = tn -> right;
  if ((lc == NULL) && (rc == NULL))
    {
      // leaf node
      fprintf(outfptr, "1%c", tn -> value);
      return;
```

```
18          }
19      Tree_headerHelper(lc, outfptr);
20      Tree_headerHelper(rc, outfptr);
21      fprintf(outfptr, "0");
22   }
23   void Tree_header(TreeNode * tn, char * outfile)
24   {
25      FILE * outfptr = fopen(outfile, "w");
26      if (outfptr == NULL)
27          {
28              return;
29          }
30      Tree_headerHelper(tn, outfptr);
31      fprintf(outfptr, "0\n");
32      fclose (outfptr);
33   }
34   int compress(char * infile, char * outfile,
35                  int * * codebook, int * mapping)
36   {
37      FILE * infptr = fopen(infile, "r");
38      if (infptr == NULL)
39          {
40              return 0;
41          }
42      FILE * outfptr = fopen(outfile, "a"); // append
43      if (outfptr == NULL)
44          {
45              fclose (outfptr);
46              return 0;
47          }
48      while (! feof(infptr))
49          {
50              int onechar = fgetc(infptr);
51              if (onechar != EOF)
52                  {
53                      int ind = mapping[onechar];
54                      int ind2 = 1;
55                      while (codebook[ind][ind2] != -1)
56                          {
57                              fprintf(outfptr, "%d", codebook[ind][ind2]);
58                              ind2 ++;
59                          }
60                  }
61          }
62      fclose(infptr);
63      fclose(outfptr);
64      return 1;
65   }
66   // ******************************************
67      // continue encode ...
68      Tree_header(root, outfile);
```

```
69    // mapping from ASCII to the indexes of the code book
70    int mapping[NUMLETTER];
71    int ind;
72    for (ind = 0; ind < NUMLETTER; ind ++)
73      {
74        mapping[ind] = -1; // initialized to invalid index
75        int ind2;
76        for (ind2 = 0; ind2 < numRow; ind2 ++)
77          {
78            if (codebook[ind2][0] == ind)
79              {
80                mapping[ind] = ind2;
81              }
82          }
83      }
84    compress(infile, outfile, codebook, mapping);
```

If this is the input file:

ENNGGGGGGGGTTTTTTTTggggggggggggggggggggggPPPPPPPPPPPPPPPPPPPPPPPPPPd
ddddddddddddddddddddddddddddddddddddddddddddddhhhhhhhhhhhhhhhh
hhhhhhhhhhhhhhhhhhhhhhhhhhhhhhhhhhhhhhhhhhhhhhhhhhhhhhhhhhhhhhh

This is the compressed file:

1h1d1p1T1E1N01G001g00000
1110100111010111101011110111110111110111110111110111110111110
1111100111001110011100111001110011100111111111111111111111111
1111111111111111111111111111111111111111111111111110110110
11011011011011011011011011011011011011011011011011011011011101101101
0101010101010101010101010101010101010101010101010101010101010
10101010101010101010101010100000000000000000000000000000000000
000000000000000000000000000000000000000000

There is only one newline '\n', which appears after the header. Line breaks are added so that the very long sequence of 1s and 0s can fit on this page. Please notice that the header does not include the characters' frequencies because this information is unnecessary for decoding.

24.2.6   Compress with Bits

You may have noticed that the "compressed" file is actually longer than the original file. The original file has 178 bytes and the "compressed" file has 433 bytes. Why? Because the compressed file uses '1' and '0' (8-bit characters) to represent single bits. That is a lot of waste. In order to actually compress the file, only single bits should be used. This will not reduce the file size to one eighth or the original; however, it should be smaller than 178 bytes. The compressed file contains more than the bits describing the data. The compressed file starts with the header that describes the code book. The header includes the "commands" 1 or 0 to indicate whether the following information is a leaf node or not. If a command bit is 1, it must be followed by an ASCII character. ASCII codes go from 0 to 127 (this book ignores the characters whose values are greater than 128), and $2^7 = 128$, which means that 7 bits is sufficient to store a character. This allows us to put a command bit and a character into a single byte. Note, however, that if the command bit is 0, then the rest of the header needs to be shifted right by one bit. If some bits in the last byte are unused, then these bits are zero. The header in the ASCII format is:

```
1h1d1p1T1E1N01G001g00000
```

If each letter uses 7 bits, then the header in the binary format becomes:

```
11101000 11100100 11110000 11010100 11000101
11001110 01100011 10011100 11100000
```

For clarity, we have added space between every byte. The first four bytes are generated by the following rules:

1. The letter 'h' is 0x68 in hexadecimal and the 7-bit representation is 1101000. The first byte is 11101000.
2. The letter 'd' is 0x64 and the 7-bit representation is 1100100. The second byte is 11100100.
3. The letter 'p' is 0x70 and the 7-bit representation is 1110000. The third byte is 11110000.
4. The letter 'T' is 0x54 and the 7 bit representation is 1010100. The fourth byte is 11010100.

The first zero appears after 'N' and it is the seventh byte. This zero is followed by 1. Thus, the first two bits are 01. The next character is 'G'. It is 0x47 and the 7-bit representation is 01000111. Only six bits can be accommodated in the seventh byte and this byte is 010100011. The remaining (rightmost) bit enters the leftmost part of the eighth byte. The following table shows the bits for the header:

C: command								D: data								U: Unused							
1	1	1	0	1	0	0	0	1	1	1	0	0	1	0	0								
C	←			'h'			→	C	←			'd'			→								
1	1	1	1	0	0	0	0	1	1	0	1	0	1	0	0								
C	←			'p'			→	C	←			'T'			→								
1	1	0	0	0	1	0	1	1	1	0	0	1	1	1	0								
C	←			'E'			→	C	←			'N'			→								
0	1	1	0	0	0	1	1	1	0	0	1	1	1	0	0								
C	C	←			'G'			→	C	C	C	←			'g'								
1	1	1	0	0	0	0	0																
	→	C	C	C	C	U																	

One major problem of using bits is that the minimum unit of memory in C is a byte (**unsigned char**). The following is a function for writing one bit to a file. This function accumulates 8 bits in a buffer, and then writes to the file. It is called whenever a bit needs to be written to the file. The function uses **curbyte** to keep all of the written bits and when 8 bits have been sent, the function writes a single byte to the file.

```
1  #include "utility.h"
2  // function for debugging purpose
3  static void printByte(unsigned char onebyte)
4  {
5    unsigned char mask = 0x80;
6    while (mask > 0)
7      {
8        printf("%d", (onebyte & mask) == mask);
9        mask >>= 1;
```

```
10        }
11     printf("\n");
12   }
13   // write one bit to a file
14   //
15   // whichbit indicates which bit this is written to
16   // (0 means leftmost, 7 means rightmost)
17   //
18   // curbyte is the current byte
19   //
20   // if whichbit is zero, curbyte is reset and bit is put
21   // to the leftmost bit
22   //
23   // when whichbit reaches 7, this byte is written to the
24   // file and whichbit is reset
25   //
26   // the function returns 1 if a byte is written to the file
27   //                 returns 0 if no byte is written
28   //                      -1 if it tries to write and fails
29   int writeBit(FILE * fptr, unsigned char bit,
30                unsigned char * whichbit,
31                unsigned char * curbyte)
32   {
33     if ((* whichbit) == 0)
34       {
35         // reset
36         * curbyte = 0;
37       }
38     // shift the bit to the correct location
39     unsigned char temp = bit << (7 - (* whichbit));
40     * curbyte |= temp; // store the data
41     int value = 0;
42     if ((* whichbit) == 7)
43       {
44         int ret;
45         ret = fwrite(curbyte, sizeof(unsigned char), 1, fptr);
46         // printByte(* curbyte); // for debugging
47         if (ret == 1)
48           {
49             value = 1;
50           }
51         else
52           {
53             value = -1;
54           }
55       }
56     * whichbit = ((* whichbit) + 1) % 8;
57     return value;
58   }
```

This function writes the tree (the header of the file) to the file. When a leaf node is visited, one command bit (value is 1) is written to the file, followed by the 7 bits of the character. When a non-leaf node is visited, one commend bit (value is 0) is written to the file. If some bits of the last byte are not used, these bits are set to zero. The new line character ends the header.

```c
// print the 7 bits of an ASCII character
static void char2bits(FILE * outfptr, int ch,
                      unsigned char * whichbit,
                      unsigned char * curbyte)
{
  unsigned char mask = 0x40; // only 7 bits
  while (mask > 0)
    {
      writeBit(outfptr, (ch & mask) == mask,
               whichbit, curbyte);
      mask >>= 1;
    }
}
static void Tree_headerHelper(TreeNode * tn, FILE * outfptr,
                              unsigned char * whichbit,
                              unsigned char * curbyte)
{
  if (tn == NULL)
    {
      return;
    }
  TreeNode * lc = tn -> left;
  TreeNode * rc = tn -> right;
  if ((lc == NULL) && (rc == NULL))
    {
      // leaf node
      writeBit(outfptr, 1, whichbit, curbyte);
      char2bits(outfptr, tn -> value, whichbit, curbyte);
      return;
    }
  Tree_headerHelper(lc, outfptr, whichbit, curbyte);
  Tree_headerHelper(rc, outfptr, whichbit, curbyte);
  writeBit(outfptr, 0, whichbit, curbyte);
}
void Tree_header(TreeNode * tn, char * outfile)
{
  FILE * outfptr = fopen(outfile, "w");
  if (outfptr == NULL)
    {
      return;
    }
  unsigned char whichbit = 0;
  unsigned char curbyte = 0;
  Tree_headerHelper(tn, outfptr, & whichbit, & curbyte);
  while (whichbit != 0)
```

```
46        {
47          // if the current byte has unused bits
48            writeBit(outfptr, 0, & whichbit, & curbyte);
49        }
50      unsigned char newline = '\n'; // add '\n' at the end
51      fwrite(& newline, sizeof(unsigned char), 1, outfptr);
52      fclose (outfptr);
53    }
```

This is the compress function. It writes the bits to the file. If some bits of the last byte is unused, these bits are zero.

```
1  int compress(char * infile, char * outfile,
2                 int * * codebook, int * mapping)
3  {
4    FILE * infptr = fopen(infile, "r");
5    if (infptr == NULL)
6      {
7        return 0;
8      }
9    FILE * outfptr = fopen(outfile, "a"); // append
10   if (outfptr == NULL)
11     {
12       fclose (outfptr);
13       return 0;
14     }
15   unsigned char whichbit = 0;
16   unsigned char curbyte = 0;
17   while (! feof(infptr))
18     {
19       int onechar = fgetc(infptr);
20       if (onechar != EOF)
21         {
22           int ind = mapping[onechar];
23           int ind2 = 1;
24           while (codebook[ind][ind2] != -1)
25             {
26               writeBit(outfptr, (codebook[ind][ind2] == 1),
27                       & whichbit, & curbyte);
28               ind2 ++;
29             }
30         }
31     }
32   while (whichbit != 0)
33     {
34       // if the current byte has unused bits
35       writeBit(outfptr, 0, & whichbit, & curbyte);
36     }
37   fclose(infptr);
38   fclose(outfptr);
39   return 1;
40 }
```

After writing the code book, the header uses the next 4 bytes (32 bits) to write the length of the article. This is an unsigned integer and can be as large as $2^{32} - 1$, more than four billion. A 1000-page novel has about 500,000 words, a few million characters. Thus, 32 bits are sufficient. After the length, a new line character is written to the file, signifying the end of the header.

The output file cannot be viewed easily in a text editor, because the data is compressed in bit representations. We can use the xxd program in Linux to see the hexadecimal values that represent each byte in the file. The following shows the compressed file in hexadecimal format using xxd.

```
0000000: e8e4 f0d4 c5ce 639c e0b2 0000 000a e9d7  ......c.........
0000010: af7d f7df 7df7 ce73 9ce7 3fff ffff ffff  .}..}..s..?.....
0000020: ffff ffff 6db6 db6d b6db 6db6 d555 5555  ....m..m..m..UUU
0000030: 5555 5555 5555 5554 0000 0000 0000 0000  UUUUUUT........
0000040: 00
```

The following shows the compressed file in binary format using

```
0000000: 11101000 11100100 11110000 11010100 11000101 11001110  ......
0000006: 01100011 10011100 11100000 10110010 00000000 00000000  c.....
000000c: 00000000 00001010 11101001 11010111 10101111 01111101  .....}
0000012: 11110111 11011111 01111101 11110111 11001110 01110011  ..}..s
0000018: 10011100 11100111 00111111 11111111 11111111 11111111  ..?...
000001e: 11111111 11111111 11111111 11111111 11111111 11111111  ......
0000024: 01101101 10110110 11011011 01101101 10110110 11011011  m..m..
000002a: 01101101 10110110 11010101 01010101 01010101 01010101  m..UUU
0000030: 01010101 01010101 01010101 01010101 01010101 01010101  UUUUUU
0000036: 01010101 01010100 00000000 00000000 00000000 00000000  UT....
000003c: 00000000 00000000 00000000 00000000 00000000           .....
```

24.3   Decoding

Decoding is the reverse of encoding. The decoder first reconstructs the code tree from the file header, and then reads the compressed codes of the characters. From the codes, the decompresser traverses the code tree and outputs the characters stored in the tree's leaf nodes. To reconstruct the tree, the decoder needs to know how the tree is represented in the header. In our case, the code book is encoded using the rules described in Section 24.2.5. The header contains both commands (1 bit, either 0 or 1) and characters (7 bits). To build the code tree, the decoder does the following:

- The first bit is a command bit and it is always 1.
- If a command is 1, then the next 7 bits are the value stored in a leaf node. Create a tree node to store this value. Add this tree node to the beginning of the list. This tree node is a single-node tree.
- If a command is 0 and the list has only one node, then the complete tree has been built. If a command is 0 and the list has two or more nodes, then take the first two nodes from the list, create a tree node as the parent. Add this parent node to the list.
- After the tree is completely built, then read one more bit. If this is not the last (rightmost) bit of the byte, discard the remaining bits in the byte. The next four

bytes (an **unsigned int**) store the number of characters in the article. This number is followed by a new line '\n' character.

Consider the header in Section 24.2.6. The decoder reads one bit from the compressed file. This bit is 1 and then the decoder reads another 7 bits. Fig. 24.12 to Fig. 24.15 show how to reconstruct the tree from the header. The first character is 'h'. One tree node is created and it is pointed to by one list node as shown in Fig. 24.12 (a). For decoding, as long as the tree can be rebuilt, the frequencies of the characters are not needed. Fig. 24.12 (b) shows the list after reading the first two bytes. Fig. 24.12 (c) shows the list after reading the first six bytes. In Fig. 24.12 (d), the first two tree nodes share the same parent. The first tree node becomes the right child and the second tree node is the left child, making E and N share a parent node. This is because the code book was encoded using a post-order traversal. Please notice the symmetry between this figure and Fig. 24.3. In Fig. 24.12 (e), this command is followed by 7 bits of data for the character G. Another tree node for G is added to the list.

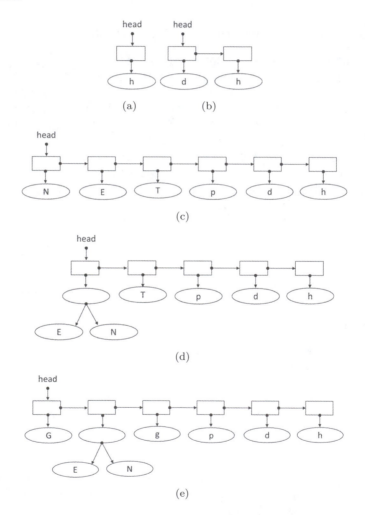

FIGURE 24.12: (a) One tree node is added after reading the first command and the first character. (b) After reading two bytes. (c) After reading six bytes. (d) The first bit in the seventh byte is a command and it is 0. (e) The next command bit (the second bit in the seventh byte) is 1.

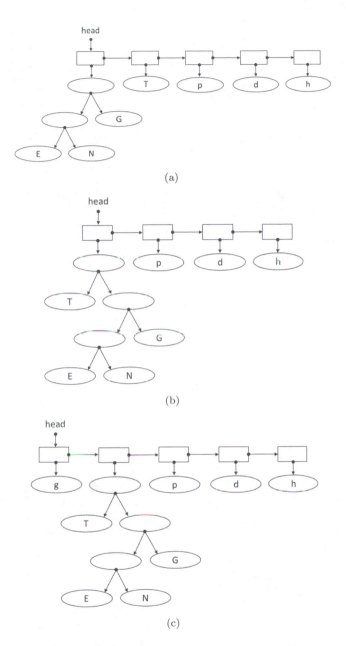

FIGURE 24.13: (a) The next command (the second bit in the eighth byte) is 0. This will create a common parent for the first two tree nodes. (b) The next command (the third bit in the eighth byte) is also 0. This will create a common parent for the first two tree nodes. (c) The next command (the fourth bit in the eighth byte) is 1. This will create a tree node to store the value g.

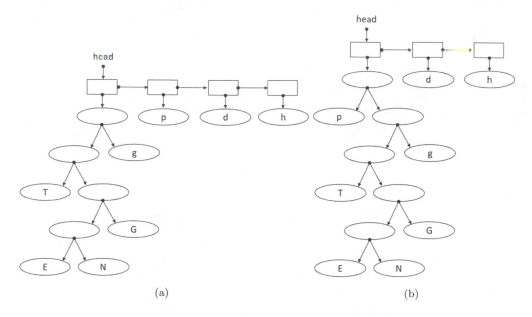

(a)   (b)

FIGURE 24.14: The remaining commands are 0. Continue building the tree.

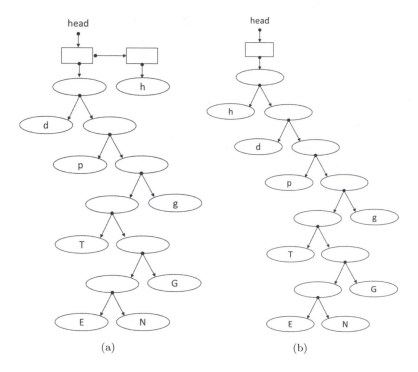

(a)   (b)

FIGURE 24.15: Finish building the tree.

The following is the final version of the complete program, for both compression and decompression.

```c
// main.c
#include "encode.h"
#include "constant.h"
#include <stdlib.h>
#include <string.h>
int main(int argc, char ** argv)
{
   // argv[1]: "e" encode
   //          "d" decode
   // argv[2]: name of input file
   // argv[3]: name of output file
   if (argc != 4)
     {
        return EXIT_FAILURE;
     }
   if (strcmp(argv[1], "e") == 0)
     {
        encode(argv[2], argv[3]);
     }
   if (strcmp(argv[1], "d") == 0)
     {
        decode(argv[2], argv[3]);
     }
   return EXIT_SUCCESS;
}
```

```c
// encode.h
#ifndef ENCODE_H
#define ENCODE_H
// encode the input (text) file
// save the result in the output (binary) file
// return 0 if cannot read from file or write to file
// return 1 if success
int encode(char * infile, char * outfile);
// decode the input (binary) file
// save the result in the output (text) file
// return 0 if cannot read from file or write to file
// return 1 if success
int decode(char * infile, char * outfile);
#endif
```

```c
// encode.c
#include "encode.h"
#include "constant.h"
#include "freq.h"
#include "list.h"
#include "utility.h"
#include <stdio.h>
#include <strings.h>
```

```
 9  #include <stdlib.h>
10  #include <values.h>
11  #define ENCODEMODE 0
12  #define DECODEMODE 1
13  void printFrequencyLatex(CharFreq * frequencies);
14  void buildCodeBookHelper(TreeNode * tn, int * * codebook,
15                             int * row, int col)
16  {
17    if (tn == NULL)
18      {
19        return;
20      }
21    // is it a leaf node?
22    TreeNode * lc = tn -> left;
23    TreeNode * rc = tn -> right;
24    if ((lc == NULL) && (rc == NULL))
25      {
26        // finish one code
27        codebook[*row][0] = tn -> value;
28        (* row) ++;
29        return;
30      }
31    if (lc != NULL)
32      {
33        // populate this column of the entire subtree
34        int numRow = Tree_leaf(lc);
35        int ind;
36        for (ind = * row; ind < (* row) + numRow; ind ++)
37          {
38            codebook[ind][col] = 0;
39          }
40        buildCodeBookHelper(lc, codebook, row, col + 1);
41      }
42    if (rc != NULL)
43      {
44        int numRow = Tree_leaf(rc);
45        int ind;
46        for (ind = * row; ind < (* row) + numRow; ind ++)
47          {
48            codebook[ind][col] = 1;
49          }
50        buildCodeBookHelper(rc, codebook, row, col + 1);
51      }
52  }
53  void buildCodeBook(TreeNode * root, int * * codebook)
54  {
55    int row = 0;
56    // column start at 1 because [0] stores the character
57    buildCodeBookHelper(root, codebook, & row, 1);
58  }
59  void printCodeBook(int * * codebook, int numRow)
```

```
60  {
61     int row;
62     for (row = 0; row < numRow; row ++)
63       {
64         // print the character
65         printf("%c:␣", codebook[row][0]);
66         int col = 1;
67         while (codebook[row][col] != -1)
68           {
69             printf("%d␣", codebook[row][col]);
70             col ++;
71           }
72         printf("\n");
73       }
74  }
75  int compress(char * infile, char * outfile,
76               int * * codebook, int * mapping)
77  {
78     FILE * infptr = fopen(infile, "r");
79     if (infptr == NULL)
80       {
81         return 0;
82       }
83     FILE * outfptr = fopen(outfile, "a"); // append
84     if (outfptr == NULL)
85       {
86         fclose (outfptr);
87         return 0;
88       }
89     unsigned char whichbit = 0;
90     unsigned char curbyte = 0;
91     while (! feof(infptr))
92       {
93         int onechar = fgetc(infptr);
94         if (onechar != EOF)
95           {
96             int ind = mapping[onechar];
97             int ind2 = 1;
98             while (codebook[ind][ind2] != -1)
99               {
100                writeBit(outfptr, (codebook[ind][ind2] == 1),
101                         & whichbit, & curbyte);
102                // fprintf(outfptr, "%d", codebook[ind][ind2]);
103                ind2 ++;
104              }
105          }
106      }
107    padZero(outfptr, & whichbit, & curbyte);
108    fclose(infptr);
109    fclose(outfptr);
110    return 1;
```

```
111    }
112    // if endec is 0: encode, if it is 1: decode
113    // encoded and decode must flip the order of the two
114    // subtrees
115    static ListNode * MergeListNode(ListNode * head, int endec)
116    {
117      ListNode * second = head -> next;
118      // second must not be NULL, otherwise, will not enter
119      ListNode * third  = second -> next;
120      // third may be NULL
121      // get the tree nodes of the first two list nodes
122      TreeNode * tn1 = head -> tnptr;
123      TreeNode * tn2 = second -> tnptr;
124      // remove the first two nodes
125      free (head);
126      free (second);
127      head = third;
128      TreeNode * mrg;
129      if (endec == ENCODEMODE)
130        {
131          mrg = Tree_merge(tn1, tn2);
132        }
133      else
134        {
135          mrg = Tree_merge(tn2, tn1);
136        }
137      ListNode * ln = ListNode_create(mrg);
138      if (endec == ENCODEMODE)
139        {
140          head = List_insert(head, ln, SORTED);
141        }
142      else
143        {
144          head = List_insert(head, ln, STACK);
145        }
146      return head;
147    }
148    // merge the top two list nodes until only one list node
149    static TreeNode * list2Tree(ListNode * head)
150    {
151      // merge the top two list nodes until only one list node
152      while ((head -> next) != NULL)
153        {
154          List_print(head); printf("-----------\n");
155          head = MergeListNode(head, ENCODEMODE);
156        }
157      List_print(head);
158      // the linked list is no longer needed
159      TreeNode * root = head -> tnptr;
160      // the linked list is no longer needed
161      free (head);
```

```
162    return root;
163  }
164  int encode(char * infile, char * outfile)
165  {
166    CharFreq frequencies[NUMLETTER];
167    // set the array elements to zero
168    bzero(frequencies, sizeof(CharFreq) * NUMLETTER);
169    unsigned int numChar =
170      countFrequency(infile, frequencies);
171    if (numChar == 0)
172      {
173        return 0;
174      }
175    // printFrequency(frequencies);
176    sortFrequency(frequencies);
177    // printFrequency(frequencies);
178    ListNode * head = List_build(frequencies);
179    if (head == NULL)
180      {
181        // the article is empty
182        return 0;
183      }
184    TreeNode * root = list2Tree(head);
185    // build the code book
186    // get the number of leaf nodes
187    int numRow = Tree_leaf(root);
188    // get the tree's height
189    int numCol = Tree_height(root);
190    // numCol should add 1 to accommodate the ending -1
191    numCol ++;
192    // create a 2D array and initialize the codes to -1
193    int * * codebook = malloc(sizeof(int*) * numRow);
194    int row;
195    for (row = 0; row < numRow; row ++)
196      {
197        codebook[row] = malloc(sizeof(int) * numCol);
198        int col;
199        // initialize to -1
200        for (col = 0; col < numCol; col ++)
201          {
202            codebook[row][col] = -1;
203          }
204      }
205    buildCodeBook(root, codebook);
206    printCodeBook(codebook, numRow);
207    // mapping from ASCII to the indexes of the code book
208    int mapping[NUMLETTER];
209    int ind;
210    for (ind = 0; ind < NUMLETTER; ind ++)
211      {
212        mapping[ind] = -1; // initialized to invalid index
```

```
213        int ind2;
214        for (ind2 = 0; ind2 < numRow; ind2 ++)
215          {
216            if (codebook[ind2][0] == ind)
217              {
218                mapping[ind] = ind2;
219              }
220          }
221      }
222    for (ind = 0; ind < NUMLETTER; ind ++)
223      {
224        if (mapping[ind] != -1)
225          {
226            printf("%c:%d\n", ind, mapping[ind]);
227          }
228      }
229    Tree_header(root, numChar, outfile);
230    compress(infile, outfile, codebook, mapping);
231    // release memory
232    for (ind = 0; ind < numRow; ind ++)
233      {
234        free (codebook[ind]);
235      }
236    free (codebook);
237
238    Tree_destroy(root);
239    return 1;
240  }
241  static TreeNode * readHeader(FILE * infptr)
242  {
243    int done = 0;
244    unsigned char whichbit = 0;
245    unsigned char curbyte  = 0;
246    unsigned char onebit   = 0;
247    ListNode * head = NULL;
248    // decreasing to ensure the list is a stack
249    while (done == 0)
250      {
251        readBit(infptr, & onebit, & whichbit, & curbyte);
252        if (onebit == 1)
253          {
254            // a leaf node, get 7 move bits
255            int bitcount;
256            unsigned char value = 0;
257            for (bitcount = 0; bitcount < 7; bitcount ++)
258              {
259                value <<= 1; // shift left by one
260                readBit(infptr, & onebit, & whichbit, &
261                    curbyte);
262                value |= onebit;
263              }
```

```
264        // push a tree node into the list
265        TreeNode * tn = TreeNode_create(value, 0);
266        ListNode * ln = ListNode_create(tn);
267        head = List_insert(head, ln, STACK);
268      }
269    else
270      {
271        if (head == NULL)
272          {
273            printf("ERROR, head should not be NULL\n");
274          }
275        if ((head -> next) == NULL)
276          {
277            // the tree has been completely built
278            done = 1;
279          }
280        else
281          {
282            head = MergeListNode(head, DECODEMODE);
283          }
284      }
285    }
286  // unnecessary to read the remaining unused bits
287  TreeNode * root = head -> tnptr;
288  // the linked list is no longer needed
289  free (head);
290  return root;
291 }
292 int decode(char * infile, char * outfile)
293 {
294  FILE * infptr = fopen(infile, "r");
295  if (infptr == NULL)
296    {
297      return 0;
298    }
299  TreeNode * root = readHeader(infptr);
300  Tree_print(root, 0);
301  // read the number of characters
302  unsigned int numChar = 0;
303  fread(& numChar, sizeof(unsigned int), 1, infptr);
304  printf("numChar = %d\n", numChar);
305  // read '\n'
306  unsigned char newline;
307  fread(& newline, sizeof(unsigned char), 1, infptr);
308  if (newline != '\n')
309    {
310      printf("ERROR!\n");
311    }
312  unsigned char whichbit = 0;
313  unsigned char onebit = 0;
314  unsigned char curbyte = 0;
```

```
315    FILE * outfptr = fopen(outfile, "w");
316    while (numChar != 0)
317      {
318        TreeNode * tn = root;
319        while ((tn -> left) != NULL)
320          {
321            // tn is not a leaf node
322            readBit(infptr, & onebit, & whichbit, & curbyte);
323            if (onebit == 0)
324              {
325                tn = tn -> left;
326              }
327            else
328              {
329                tn = tn -> right;
330              }
331          }
332        // tn is a leaf node
333        printf("%c", tn -> value);
334        fprintf(outfptr, "%c", tn -> value);
335        numChar --;
336      }
337    Tree_destroy(root);
338    fclose(infptr);
339    fclose(outfptr);
340    return 1;
341  }
```

```
1   // tree.h
2   #ifndef TREE_H
3   #define TREE_H
4   typedef struct treenode
5   {
6     struct treenode * left;
7     struct treenode * right;
8     char value; // character
9     int freq;   // frequency
10  } TreeNode;
11  TreeNode * TreeNode_create(char val, int freq);
12  TreeNode * Tree_merge(TreeNode * tn1, TreeNode * tn2);
13  void Tree_print(TreeNode * tn, int level);
14  // find the maximum height of the leaf nodes
15  int Tree_height(TreeNode * tn);
16  // find the number of leaf nodes
17  int Tree_leaf(TreeNode * tn);
18  // save the header of a compressed file
19  void Tree_header(TreeNode * tn, unsigned int numChar, char *
20      outfile);
21  void Tree_destroy(TreeNode * tn);
22  #endif
```

```
1  // tree.c
2  #include "tree.h"
3  #include "utility.h"
4  #include <stdio.h>
5  #include <stdlib.h>
6  TreeNode * TreeNode_create(char val, int freq)
7  {
8    TreeNode * tn = malloc(sizeof(TreeNode));
9    tn -> left = NULL;
10   tn -> right = NULL;
11   tn -> value = val;
12   tn -> freq = freq;
13   return tn;
14 }
15 TreeNode * Tree_merge(TreeNode * tn1, TreeNode * tn2)
16 {
17   TreeNode * tn = malloc(sizeof(TreeNode));
18   tn -> left = tn1;
19   tn -> right = tn2;
20   tn -> value = 0; // do not care
21   tn -> freq = tn1 -> freq + tn2 -> freq;
22   return tn;
23 }
24 // post-order
25 void Tree_print(TreeNode * tn, int level)
26 {
27   if (tn == NULL)
28     {
29       return;
30     }
31   TreeNode * lc = tn -> left;  // left child
32   TreeNode * rc = tn -> right; // right child
33   Tree_print(lc, level + 1);
34   Tree_print(rc, level + 1);
35   int depth;
36   for (depth = 0; depth < level; depth ++)
37     {
38       printf("    ");
39     }
40   printf("freq = %d ", tn -> freq);
41   if ((lc == NULL) && (rc == NULL))
42     {
43       // a leaf node
44       printf("value = %d, '%c'", tn -> value, tn -> value);
45     }
46   printf("\n");
47 }
48 static int Tree_heightHelper(TreeNode * tn, int height)
49 {
50   if (tn == 0)
51     {
```

```
52      return height;
53    }
54   int lh = Tree_heightHelper(tn -> left, height + 1);
55   int rh = Tree_heightHelper(tn -> right, height + 1);
56   if (lh < rh)
57     {
58       return rh;
59     }
60   if (lh > rh)
61     {
62       return lh;
63     }
64   return lh;
65 }
66 int Tree_height(TreeNode * tn)
67 {
68   return Tree_heightHelper(tn, 0);
69 }
70 static void Tree_leafHelper(TreeNode * tn, int * num)
71 {
72   if (tn == 0)
73     {
74       return;
75     }
76   // if it is a leaf node, add one
77   TreeNode * lc = tn -> left;
78   TreeNode * rc = tn -> right;
79   if ((lc == NULL) && (rc == NULL))
80     {
81       (* num) ++;
82       return;
83     }
84   Tree_leafHelper(lc, num);
85   Tree_leafHelper(rc, num);
86 }
87 int Tree_leaf(TreeNode * tn)
88 {
89   int num = 0;
90   Tree_leafHelper(tn, & num);
91   return num;
92 }
93 // print the 7 bits of an ASCII character
94 static void char2bits(FILE * outfptr, int ch,
95                       unsigned char * whichbit,
96                       unsigned char * curbyte)
97 {
98   unsigned char mask = 0x40; // only 7 bits
99   while (mask > 0)
100     {
101       writeBit(outfptr, (ch & mask) == mask,
102               whichbit, curbyte);
```

```
103        mask >>= 1;
104      }
105 }
106 static void Tree_headerHelper(TreeNode * tn,
107                               FILE * outfptr,
108                               unsigned char * whichbit,
109                               unsigned char * curbyte)
110 {
111   if (tn == NULL)
112     {
113       return; // should not get here
114     }
115   TreeNode * lc = tn -> left;
116   TreeNode * rc = tn -> right;
117   if ((lc == NULL) && (rc == NULL))
118     {
119       // leaf node
120       writeBit(outfptr, 1, whichbit, curbyte);
121       char2bits(outfptr, tn -> value, whichbit, curbyte);
122       return;
123     }
124   Tree_headerHelper(lc, outfptr, whichbit, curbyte);
125   Tree_headerHelper(rc, outfptr, whichbit, curbyte);
126   writeBit(outfptr, 0, whichbit, curbyte);
127 }
128 void Tree_header(TreeNode * tn, unsigned int numChar,
129                  char * outfile)
130 {
131   FILE * outfptr = fopen(outfile, "w");
132   if (outfptr == NULL)
133     {
134       return;
135     }
136   unsigned char whichbit = 0;
137   unsigned char curbyte = 0;
138   Tree_headerHelper(tn, outfptr, & whichbit, & curbyte);
139   // add one more 0 to end the header
140   writeBit(outfptr, 0, & whichbit, & curbyte);
141   padZero(outfptr, & whichbit, & curbyte);
142   // write the number of characters
143   fwrite(& numChar, sizeof(unsigned int), 1, outfptr);
144   // add '\n' at the end of the header
145   unsigned char newline = '\n';
146   fwrite(& newline, sizeof(unsigned char), 1, outfptr);
147   fclose(outfptr);
148 }
149 void Tree_destroy(TreeNode * tn)
150 {
151   if (tn == NULL)
152     {
153       return;
```

```
154        }
155      Tree_destroy(tn -> left);
156      Tree_destroy(tn -> right);
157      free (tn);
158    }
```

```
1    // list.h
2    #ifndef LIST_H
3    #define LIST_H
4    #include "tree.h"
5    #include "constant.h"
6    #include "freq.h"
7    #include <stdio.h>
8    #define QUEUE   0
9    #define STACK   1
10   #define SORTED  2
11   typedef struct listnode
12   {
13     struct listnode * next;
14     TreeNode * tnptr;
15   } ListNode;
16   ListNode * List_build(CharFreq * frequencies);
17   ListNode * ListNode_create(TreeNode * tn);
18   // The mode is QUEUE, STACK, or SORTED
19   ListNode * List_insert(ListNode * head, ListNode * ln, int
20      mode);
21   void List_print(ListNode * head);
22   #endif
```

```
1    // list.c
2    #include "list.h"
3    #include "freq.h"
4    #include <stdlib.h>
5    ListNode * ListNode_create(TreeNode * tn)
6    {
7      ListNode * ln = malloc(sizeof(ListNode));
8      ln -> next = NULL;
9      ln -> tnptr = tn;
10     return ln;
11   }
12   // head may be NULL
13   // ln must not be NULL
14   // ln -> next must be NULL
15   ListNode * List_insert(ListNode * head, ListNode * ln,
16                          int mode)
17   {
18     if (ln == NULL)
19       {
20          printf("ERROR!␣ln␣is␣NULL\n");
21          return NULL;
22       }
```

```
23    if ((ln -> next) != NULL)
24      {
25        printf("ERROR!_ln_->_next_is_not_NULL\n");
26      }
27    if (head == NULL)
28      {
29        return ln;
30      }
31    if (mode == STACK)
32      {
33        ln -> next = head;
34        return ln;
35      }
36    if (mode == QUEUE)
37      {
38        head -> next = List_insert(head -> next, ln, mode);
39        return head;
40      }
41    // insert in increasing order
42    int freq1 = (head -> tnptr) -> freq;
43    int freq2 = (ln -> tnptr) -> freq;
44    if (freq1 > freq2)
45      {
46        // ln should be the first node
47        ln -> next = head;
48        return ln;
49      }
50    // ln should be after head
51    head -> next = List_insert(head -> next, ln, mode);
52    return head;
53  }
54  // frequencies must be sorted
55  ListNode * List_build(CharFreq * frequencies)
56  {
57    // find the first index whose frequency is nonzero
58    int ind = 0;
59    while (frequencies[ind].freq == 0)
60      {
61        ind ++;
62      }
63    if (ind == NUMLETTER)
64      {
65        // no letter appears
66        return NULL;
67      }
68    // create a linked list, each node points to a tree node
69    ListNode * head = NULL;
70    while (ind < NUMLETTER)
71      {
72        TreeNode * tn =
73          TreeNode_create(frequencies[ind].value,
```

```
74                     frequencies[ind].freq);
75      ListNode * ln = ListNode_create(tn);
76      head = List_insert(head, ln, SORTED);
77      ind ++;
78    }
79   return head;
80 }
81 void List_print(ListNode * head)
82 {
83   if (head == NULL)
84     {
85       return;
86     }
87   Tree_print(head -> tnptr, 0);
88   List_print(head -> next);
89 }


1  // utility.h
2  #ifndef UTILITY_H
3  #define UTILITY_H
4  #include <stdio.h>
5  // write one bit to a file
6
7  // whichbit indicates which bit this is written to (0 means
8  // leftmost, 7 means rightmost)
9  // curbyte is the current byte
10 //
11 // if whichbit is zero, curbyte is reset and bit is put
12 // to the leftmost bit
13 //
14 // when which bit reaches 7, this byte is written to the
15 // file and whichbit is reset
16 //
17 // the function returns 1 if a byte is written to the file
18 //              returns 0 if no byte is written
19 //                    -1 if it tries to write and fails
20 int writeBit(FILE * fptr, unsigned char bit,
21              unsigned char * whichbit, unsigned char *
22              curbyte);
23 // if * whichbit is not 0, some bits of * curbyte are not used
24 // fill these bits by 0 and write the byte to the file
25 int padZero(FILE * fptr, unsigned char * whichbit,
26             unsigned char * curbyte);
27
28 int readBit(FILE * fptr, unsigned char * bit,
29             unsigned char * whichbit,
30             unsigned char * curbyte);
31 #endif


1  // utility.c
2  #include <stdio.h>
```

```
3   #include "utility.h"
4   int padZero(FILE * fptr, unsigned char * whichbit,
5                unsigned char * curbyte)
6   {
7     int rtv;
8     while ((* whichbit) != 0)
9       {
10        rtv = writeBit(fptr, 0, whichbit, curbyte);
11        if (rtv == -1)
12          {
13            return -1;
14          }
15      }
16    return rtv;
17  }
18  int readBit(FILE * fptr, unsigned char * bit,
19               unsigned char * whichbit, unsigned char * curbyte)
20
21  {
22    int ret = 1;
23    if ((* whichbit) == 0)
24      {
25        // read a byte from the file
26        ret = fread(curbyte, sizeof(unsigned char), 1, fptr);
27      }
28    if (ret != 1)
29      {
30        // read fail
31        return -1;
32      }
33    // shift the bit to the correct location
34    unsigned char temp = (* curbyte) >> (7 - (* whichbit));
35    temp = temp & 0X01; // get only 1 bit, ignore the others
36    // increase by 1
37    * whichbit = ((* whichbit) + 1) % 8;
38    * bit = temp;
39    return 1;
40  }
```

This is the Makefile for the program.

```
1   CFLAGS = -g -Wall -Wshadow
2   GCC = gcc $(CFLAGS)
3   SRCS = main.c encode.c freq.c tree.c list.c utility.c
4   OBJS = $(SRCS:%.c=%.o)
5   VALGRIND = valgrind --leak-check=full --tool=memcheck
6     --verbose --log-file
7
8   code: $(OBJS)
9         $(GCC) $(OBJS) -o code
10
11  test1: code
```

```
12              ./code e input1 compress1
13              $(VALGRIND)=logenc1 ./code e input1 compress1
14              ./code d compress1 output1
15              $(VALGRIND)=logdec1 ./code d compress1 output1
16              echo # add a blank line
17              diff input1 output1
18
19   test2: code
20              ./code e input2 compress2
21              $(VALGRIND)=logenc2 ./code e input2 compress2
22              ./code d compress2 output2
23              $(VALGRIND)=logdec2 ./code d compress2 output2
24              echo # add a blank line
25              diff input2 output2
26
27   test3: code
28              ./code e input3 compress3
29              $(VALGRIND)=logenc3 ./code e input3 compress3
30              ./code d compress3 output3
31              $(VALGRIND)=logdec3 ./code d compress3 output3
32              echo # add a blank line
33              diff input3 output3
34
35   .c.o:
36              $(GCC) $(CFLAGS) -c $*.c
37
38   clean:
39              rm -f *.o a.out code log*
```

This is the most complex program in this book. It integrates almost all topics in this book. Please study this program carefully. It is a bridge for you from being an intermediate programmer to becoming an advanced programmer.

Appendix A

Linux

All examples in this book are tested in the Linux programming environment. Linux is a widely used operating system. It is free in two senses. First there is no need to pay anyone to get the operating system and many tools for Linux. Second, all the source code for Linux and many associated tools is freely available. Furthermore, this code can be modified and used by anyone, for personal or business reasons. Google's Search Engine uses Linux. So does the software on the International Space Station. The mobile operating system Android is based on Linux. Some estimate that over 60% of web servers run UNIX-based operating systems, and among them Linux dominates.

Sometimes people are surprised by how widely Linux is used. Consider Amazon EC2 (elastic cloud computing). It gives the options for Linux and Windows. For the same capabilities (measured by the number of virtual processors and the amount of memory), the price for a Linux instance is about half of the price for Windows. Many software companies, such as Oracle and SAP, sell programs running on Linux. Why? Because many customers prefer to use Linux for a variety of reasons. If a company does not support Linux, then this company forgoes a large market segment. Linux is widely used in universities and companies. The skills learned using Linux are widely applicable. Learning Linux is important for developing an understanding of computing in general, and is especially important in some business and scientific fields.

A.1   Options for Installing Linux

There are several options for setting up a Linux programming environment:
- Buy a computer that already has Linux installed. Many computer vendors have this option. This is the easiest solution.
- Build your own desktop computer: You can buy a motherboard, a processor, a hard disk, a display, ... After assembling the hardware, then install Linux. This is great experience for understanding the components of a computer. You will know precisely what is inside your computer.
- Install Linux side-by-side with an existing operating system (also called *dual boot*). This is possible if your computer already has another operating system (such as Microsoft Windows or MacOS). MacOS and Linux are both "UNIX-based" but some of the fundamentals are different. As of writing this book, some programming tools are

more stable in Linux than in MacOS. Therefore, I recommend installing Linux even if you already have MacOS. The advantage of dual booting is that each operating system has the resources of the entire computer. The disadvantage is that it is more difficult for the operating systems to share data and co-operate, since only one operating system can be used at a time. Changing the operating system requires restarting the computer.

- Dual booting used to be more popular than it is today. Now we have access to high quality and affordable (or free) *virtual machines* that are well supported by special hardware. This is my preferred option because of the convenience, and also the widespread usage in industry. A virtual machine is a computer program that runs an operating system inside of it. The operating system thinks it is running directly on the hardware, but it is actually embedded in a type of container. The vast majority of modern computers have special hardware to support virtual machines. The two operating systems run simultaneously, and it is often easy to move data between the two "computers"—either moving files, or simply using the clipboard to copy data from a Windows or MacOS program and paste it into a running Linux program. The two operating systems must share the resources of your computer. If your computer has less than 4GB of memory, you may notice occasional slowdown and you should consider dual booting.

  Assuming that your computer has 4GB or more memory, and is currently running Windows, then when we install a virtual machine, Windows is called the *host operating system*. The operating system (Linux) inside the virtual machine is called the *guest operating system*. There are several choices for a virtual machine. *VirtualBox* from Oracle is an excellent choice and it is free.

If you choose dual boot or virtual machine, you should always save the files already in your computer before installing Linux. It is possible (even though unlikely) that something may be wrong and you may lose the files in your computer.

After choosing how to install Linux, you now have to choose which distribution of Linux you want to use. The common choices are: Fedora, Ubuntu, Mint, and SUSE. This chapter uses Ubuntu as an example, but all of the distributions listed above are good choices. The following sections explain how to install Linux as dual boot and how to install Linux inside Virtualbox.

A.2   Getting Ubuntu Linux

To install Linux, first download the most recent *image*. An image contains all the files needed for installation. The file should have an `.iso` extension. Please go to web site `www.ubuntu.com`. Select the correct `iso` file and click "Download". The size of a CD `iso` file is approximately 700 MB. It is helpful to find a fast network connection before downloading the file. Please select the correct version for your computer. If your computer is bought after 2009, then it is likely to use a 64-bit CPU and thus you should download the 64-bit installation ISO file.

If you want to make the computer dual boot, then you need to find a flash drive that is at least 700 MB. The `iso` file *cannot* be copied onto the flash drive. Instead a special program is needed to rewrite all of the data on the flash drive such that it looks like what the `iso` file specifies. This will make the flash drive *bootable*. If you search on-line "ISO to USB", then you can easily find a program to do this. After you make the flash drive bootable, keep the flash drive plugged into the computer and restart the computer. When the computer restarts, and for a few seconds, press F2 (or F10 or F12, depending on the computer's firmware or BIOS, namely basic input/output system) to change the computer's settings. You will need to select the flash drive as the first choice for booting the computer. Save the change and restart the computer. Skip the next section and go directly to Section A.4.

A.3   Downloading and Installing VirtualBox

The following pages explain how to install VirtualBox. Please go to the web site `www.virtualbox.org`. Click "Downloads" and choose the correct program for your computer. For example, if your computer runs Windows, then you should select "Windows hosts". After downloading the VirtualBox program, run the program. In most cases, you can use the default settings by clicking "Next" or "Yes". Your computer will disconnect from the network for a short moment during installation. This is expected.

A.4   Install and Update Linux

If you use VirtualBox, you need to start the virtual machine. It will ask for the location of the `iso` file downloaded earlier. The virtual machine boots with a starting page. If you do not see this page, try to download a 32-bit `iso` file and use it in the previous step. Click "Install Ubuntu". If you use dual boot, you will see the same starting page, without the VirtualBox window. Follow the instructions to install Linux. In VirtualBox, install the "Guest Additions". The Guest Additions allows Linux to use the full screen of your computer. It also allows for seamless use of the mouse between the guest and host operating systems. Ubuntu will inform you if any of the installed programs needs an update. In some cases, after installing the updates and restarting the virtual computer, you will need to install the Guest Addition again.

A.5   Install Programming Tools

This book introduces some programming tools. Please install the following tools: emacs, valgrind, ddd, and git. Click the "Software Center" at the toolbar on the left side. Search "emacs" and install it. I use `emacs` because it can automatically indent C programs and makes the programs easier to read. This is another example when using the right tools is important. Correct indentation helps prevent careless mistakes, such as forgetting to add the closing braces }. To indent your program in `emacs`, follow this procedure: Select "Edit" at the menubar → click "Select All" → press the Tab key → save the file. These steps are all you need to do for indenting your programs.

Now you have a computer running Linux, and have also installed some programming tools. This chapter gives a quick overview about how to install and update Linux, as well as to install new programs. There is a lot of information available on-line. Be aware that instructions change over time, and the Internet keeps a lot of old and outdated information around. It is important to find up-to-date instructions when managing Linux. Linux is widely used in business and science for good reasons: Linux is powerful and flexible. Spend some time to become familiar with Linux and the knowledge can help you understand computers more deeply.

Appendix B

Version Control

A complex program cannot be finished in a single day. Furthermore, it is usually released to customers in stages by creating different versions of the same program. *Version control* is a method keeping track of all of the different versions of the many files used in a software project. Version control can back up files and can also manage the files written by a team of people. Many tools for version control have been developed, for example: CVS, SVN, mercurial, SourceSafe, and git.

B.1   Github.com

This book uses `github.com` because it is a popular web site that offers free version control service for students and teachers. After creating an account, use the web interface to create a new repository (also called repo).

B.2   Cloning a Repository and Modifying a File

After creating a repository, start a terminal in Linux and type:

$ git clone https://account:password@github.com/.../demorepo.git

Here `account` is your account name and `password` is your password. Replace `github.com/.../demorepo.git` with the correct path for your repository. You will see something like the following on the Linux terminal:

```
Cloning into 'demorepo'...
remote: Counting objects: 4, done.
remote: Compressing objects: 100% (4/4), done.
remote: Total 4 (delta 0), reused 0 (delta 0)
Unpacking objects: 100% (4/4), done.
```

Type the `ls` command in terminal and you can see the `demorepo` directory and the `README` file. There is also a hidden file called `.gitignore`. When a file begins with a period,

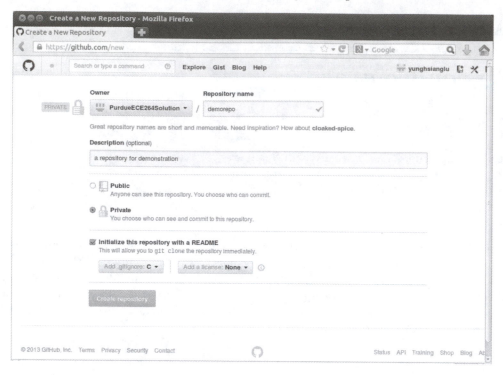

FIGURE B.1: Create a new repository. In this example, I call it "demorepo". As a teacher, I can create a free private repository. Check the box of "Initialize this repository with a README". Add .gitignore for C. This will ignore files that are not supposed to be in the repository. Click "Create repository".

the file is hidden. To see hidden files, please type `ls -a`. Use your preferred text editor to add one line into `README`. Type the `git diff` command and the difference is shown between the edited file, and the version of the file before changes. In particular, the line just added appears with the "+" in front of it. Type this command to commit the change:

    $ git commit README.md

Please give a meaningful comment. The comment becomes a part of the history in the repository. Meaningful comments are required when working with a team. Comments help document the progression of the program, and also make it easier to track old versions of files. After committing the changes, the new version is stored. You can see the history using this command:

    $ git log

Creating a new version allows you to roll back to previous versions when necessary. However, if your computer is broken, then you will lose everything in the computer. To protect your programs, you want to keep another copy outside of your computer. You can use `github.com` to store the repository using this command:

    $ git push

If you are the only person working on the project and you have only one computer, you can push right after commit. If you are working on a team project or you have several computers, you should do

$ git pull

before push to ensure that you have the latest version before pushing. Now you can go to `github.com` and see the history of the repository in github.com.

B.3 Adding Files and Directories

You can add files and directories by using the `git add` command. The following commands add a file (called `prog1.c`) to the repository and push it to `github.com`.

$ git add prog1.c
$ git commit -m "add a program" prog1.c
$ git push

B.4 Revising a Program

Version control is designed to keep track of changes. Try adding two lines to `prog1.c` and then type the following commands:

$ git commit -m "added two lines" prog1.c
$ git push

Now remove some lines and type the following commands:

$ git commit -m "changed some lines" prog1.c
$ git push

The history of changes can be seen at `github.com`. If a line is added, then a "+" sign appears in front of the line. If a line is deleted, then a "−" sign appears in front of the line. Using `git`, you can keep track of changes line-by-line. It is necessary to take small steps to build a complex program. A professional programmer adds one function at a time, makes sure it works, and commits a new version before adding another function. Sometimes, the functions written earlier require improvement. Perhaps the function no longer works as expected due to some other changes. If you do not use version control, you are out of luck. It is difficult to remember what changes have been made. Version control can show which lines have been changed since the previous commit, and thus saves a lot of time. Version control is very helpful when you learn a new programming language. You can change your programs without the fear of losing previously working functions. If you make a mistake, you can easily roll back to an earlier version. Version control can help only if you commit often. It is quite reasonable if you commit every hour, or even every few minutes. If you work in a team, you may need to create a *branch* so that you can commit incomplete functions without affecting the other people. You can find many tutorials on the Internet about how to use `git`. Spend some time learning `git` and you can save a lot of time managing your software projects.

Appendix C

Integrated Development Environments (IDE)

An Integrated Development Environment (IDE) is a program that integrates different programming tools together into a unified user interface. In this chapter we illustrate the notion of an IDE with Eclipse. Fig. C.1 shows the web site. This chapter uses many screenshots to visually explain various steps when using Eclipse.

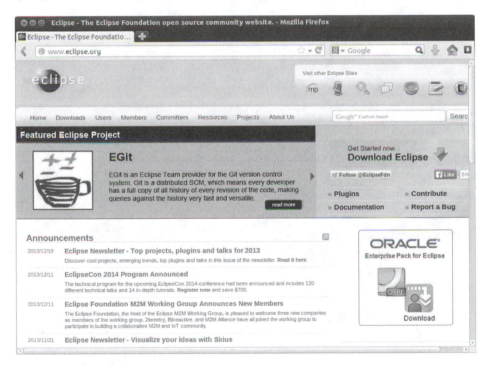

FIGURE C.1: Eclipse (`www.eclipse.org`) is one of the most popular IDEs.

C.1   Eclipse

There are several ways to install Eclipse. One is to download Eclipse from the web site. Another is to use Ubuntu's Software Center. After starting Eclipse, it asks you for the location of a "workspace". This is a folder where you keep your Eclipse programming projects. The default location is a directory called `workspace`. Eclipse has a *plug-in* architecture for adding features. This is one reason (possibly the most important) why Eclipse is a popular IDE. To install a plug-in, click Help at the menubar and select Install New Software. Select Programming Languages and C/C++ Development Tools, as shown in Fig. C.2. Eclipse does not support the C programming language until this plugin is installed.

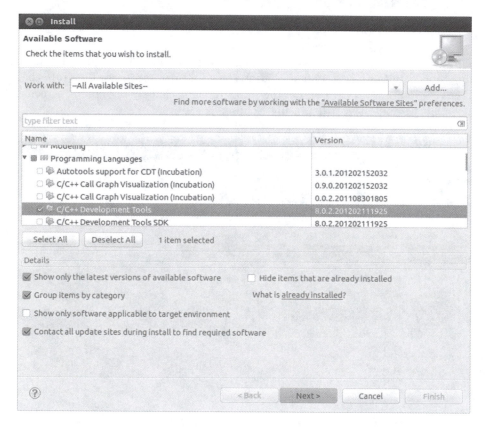

FIGURE C.2: Select C/C++ Development Tools.

C.2   Create and Build a Project

To create a new programming project, first click File on the menubar, and select New and then Project. Fig. C.3 to Fig. C.11 show the procedure of building a program in Eclipse.

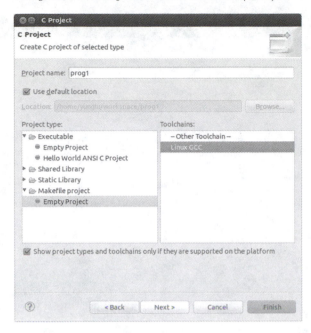

FIGURE C.3: Select Makefile Project and call the project "prog1". Click Finish.

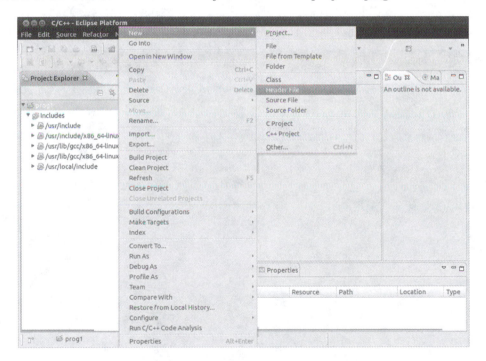

FIGURE C.4: Add a header file.

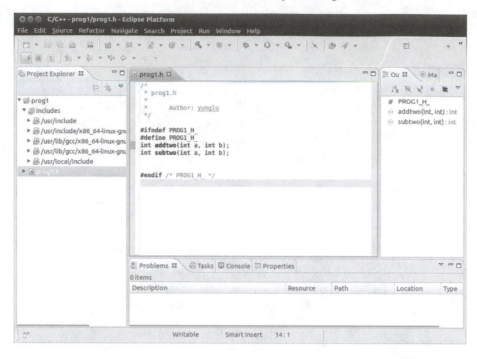

FIGURE C.5: Call the header file `prog1.h`. Eclipse automatically adds `#ifndef`, `#define`, and `#endif` to the header file. Add two function declarations to the header file.

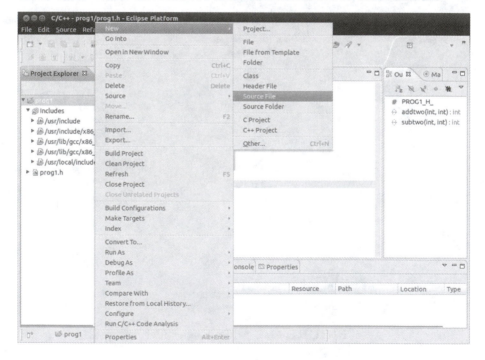

FIGURE C.6: Add a new source file.

C.3   Debugging the Program

Eclipse can simplify many steps in developing a C program. Fig. C.12 to Fig. C.17 show how to run and debug a program.

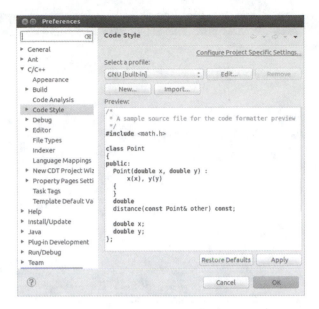

FIGURE C.7: You can customize the code formatting style by clicking Windows and selecting Preferences. Choose a style you like. You can experiment with different styles and decide which suits your preferences. This example uses the GNU style.

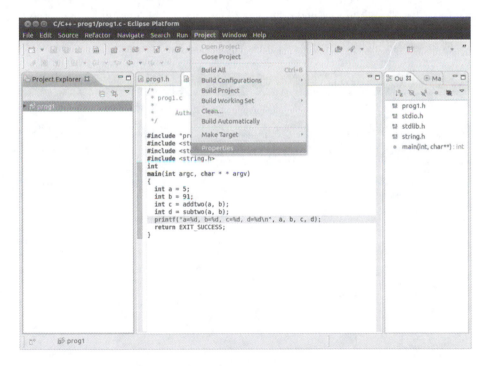

FIGURE C.8: Set the project's property. Depending on your version of Eclipse and the installed plug-ins, the build environment may already be set up correctly. Click Project (on the menubar) and select Build Project. If Eclipse says "no rule to make target all", then you need to set the build environment. Select "Generate Makefiles automatically" and click Apply.

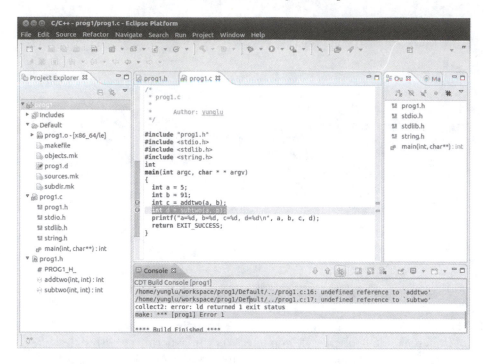

FIGURE C.9: When you click Project and select Build Project, Eclipse will say "undefined reference to addtwo" and "undefined reference to subtwo". This should be expected because these functions have not been implemented. Eclipse's error message is displayed in the Console. Eclipse also highlights the two lines that have the errors.

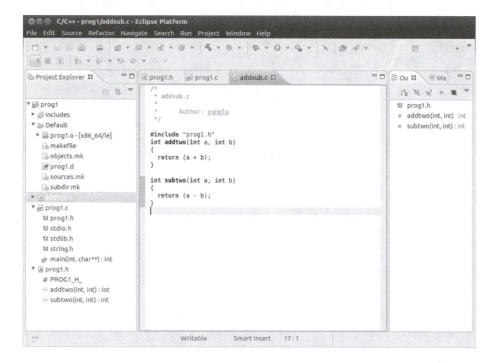

FIGURE C.10: To solve the build problem, we add another source file called `addsub.c` and in this file we define the two functions.

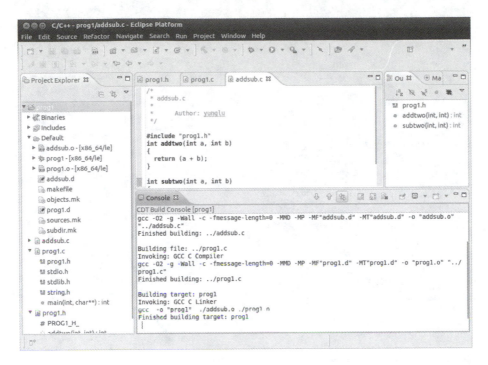

FIGURE C.11: When you build the project, Eclipse should say that the project is built successfully. A valid Makefile is automatically generated by Eclipse.

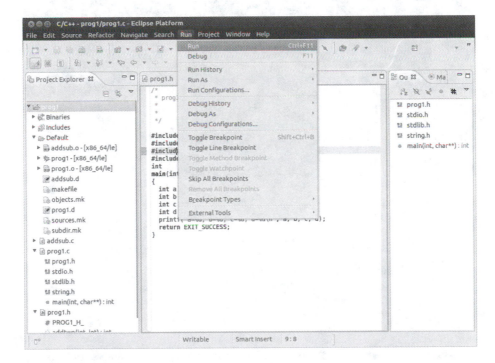

FIGURE C.12: Running: Click Run in the menubar and then select Run.

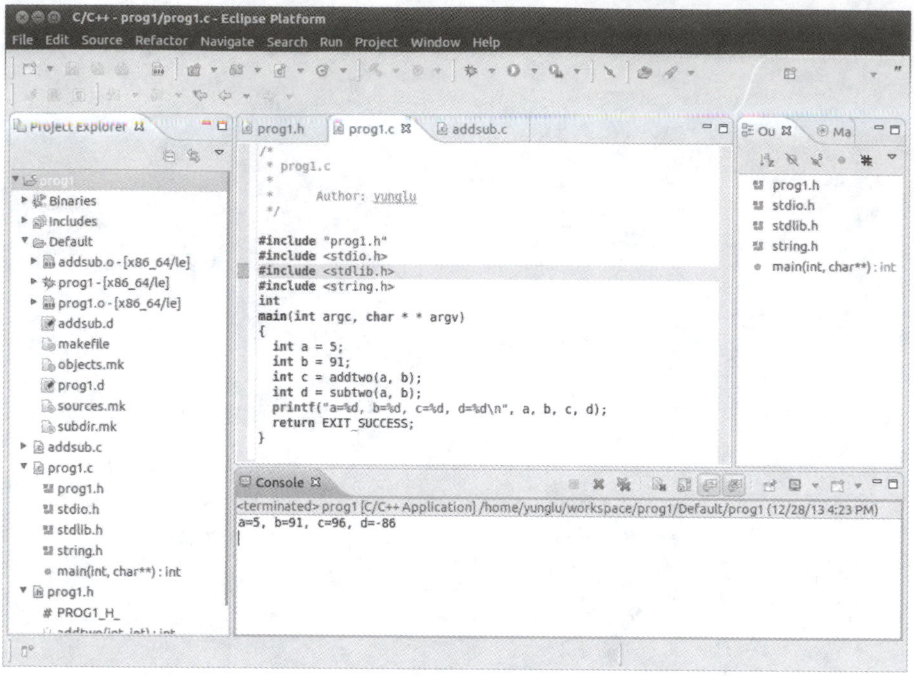

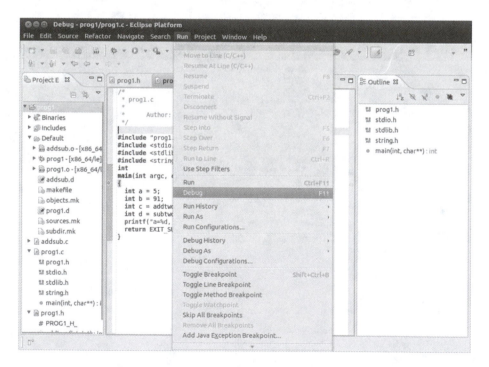

FIGURE C.13: The program's output is shown in the Console.

FIGURE C.14: Eclipse uses `gdb` to debug programs, and also provides a convenient user interface. To debug a program, click Run and select Debug.

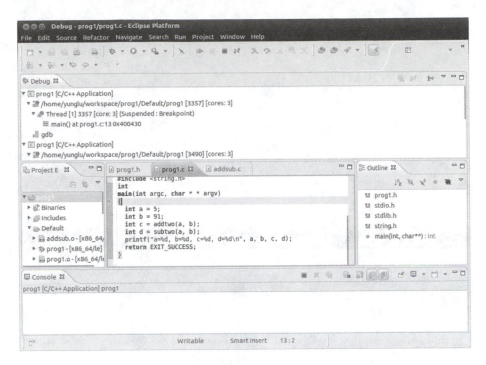

FIGURE C.15: Eclipse starts the program and stops at the first statement in `main`. This is denoted by the arrow that is shown at line 13.

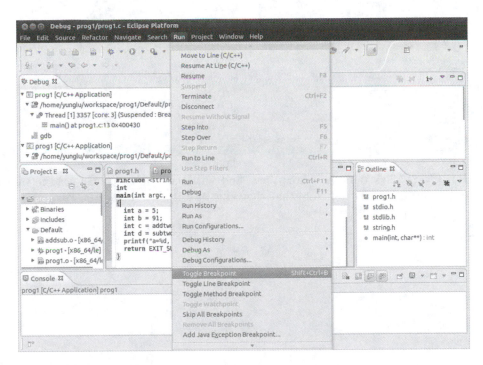

FIGURE C.16: Eclipse knows how to communicate with `gdb`, and provides a convenient method for common debugging commands such as step over, step into, and toggle breakpoint. Move the mouse cursor to line 18 in the source code, and toggle line breakpoint.

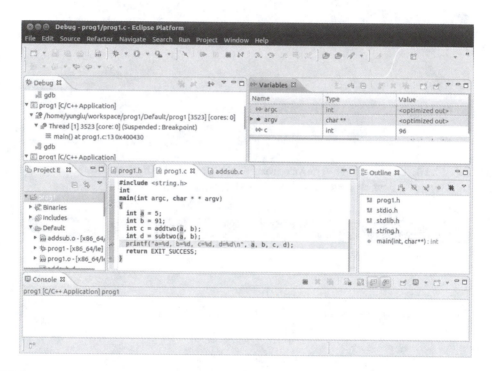

FIGURE C.17: Click Window, Show View, and Variables. Here you can see the values of variables as the code executes. Note that the value of c is 96.

Index